POLITICIAN EXTRAORDINAIRE

POLITICIAN

EXTRAORDINAIRE

The Tempestuous Life and Times

of

Martin L. Davey

———————— ❦ ————————

FRANK P. VAZZANO

THE KENT STATE UNIVERSITY PRESS · KENT, OHIO

© 2008 by The Kent State University Press, Kent, Ohio 44242
All rights reserved
Library of Congress Catalog Card Number 2007044978
ISBN 978-0-87338-920-4
Manufactured in the United States of America

Library of Congress Cataloging-in-Publication Data
Vazzano, Frank P., 1941–
    Politician extraordinaire : the tempestuous life and times of Martin L. Davey /
Frank P. Vazzano.
        p.   cm.
    Includes bibliographical references and index.
    ISBN 978-0-87338-920-4 (hardcover : alk. paper) ∞
    1. Davey, Martin L. (Martin Luther), 1884–1946. 2. Legislators—United
States—Biography. 3. United States. Congress. House—Biography. 4. Governors—
Ohio—Biography. 5. Ohio—Politics and government—1865–1950. 6. Businessmen—
Ohio—Kent—Biography. 7. Davey Tree Expert Company (Kent, Ohio) 8. Mayors—
Ohio—Kent—Biography. 9. Kent (Ohio)—Biography. I. Title.
    E748.D213V395 2008
    328.092—dc22
    [B]   2007044978

British Library Cataloging-in-Publication data are available.

12 11 10 09 08   5 4 3 2 1

To Martin L. Davey,

the most interesting man I've never met.

Contents

Preface

I FIRST ENCOUNTERED Martin Luther Davey in a graduate seminar on Ohio during the Great Depression. The former governor had already been dead for nearly a quarter-century when I chose him as the subject of my research that academic term. I'm embarrassed to say that even though I am a native Ohioan, I had never heard of him. I've racked my brain trying to recall why I selected him for my seminar paper, but no matter how hard I try, I simply cannot remember exactly how "Martin" and I first crossed paths.

Ordinarily my memory lapse would be of little consequence, but Martin Davey became a cottage industry of sorts for me. Over the years, I've written three *Ohio History* articles about his governorship, the first in 1987 (a version of which appears as chapter 12 of this book), another in 1995, and a final one in 1996. Parts of the latter two are woven into chapters 14 and 15.

After the 1996 piece, I thought I was finished with Martin Davey and had gone on to write about other things. However, a number of years ago, while on sabbatical leave, I decided to revisit him, only this time starting with his English-born father, John Davey, the founder of the modern science of tree surgery. For most biographers, the earliest period of a subject's life is the hardest to recapture because generally so little evidence remains of his "bib and porridge" years. Fortunately, there were documentary bits and pieces of John and Martin Davey's early lives in the archives of the Davey Tree Expert Company in Kent, Ohio. Moreover, Martin Davey, during his retirement in the 1940s, penned an unpublished autobiography spanning his childhood through part of his governorship. Oftentimes the autobiography is self-serving (not surprising for the genre), but it nonetheless contains priceless accounts of ordinary events that gladden a biographer's heart and enliven his writing.

I confess to being an unabashed storyteller—not in the mendacious sense, but in the sense that I believe history is essentially a story, albeit one substantiated by extensive documentation. Nothing less would satisfy the scholar in me. At the same time, I hope that my account of Martin Davey's life appeals to a wide audience, the sort that enjoys the kind of history that tells a good story. Martin Davey, after all, was a very, very interesting man, and he deserves nothing less.

Of course, researchers are invariably indebted to any number of helpful individuals, and I am no exception. Undoubtedly I have forgotten some who assisted along the way, but I shall do my best in thanking those of whom I have kept specific record.

Several years ago, Bill Birkner of the Kent, Ohio, Historical Society related some of his boyhood recollections of the Davey family and provided tips about where I might find local information on Martin Davey's early life. Bob Browne, the director of purchasing and properties for the Davey Tree Expert Company and my old high school chum, introduced me to a number of knowledgeable Davey employees who let me hunt through box after box of papers at the company's headquarters in Kent. Those records were essential as I put together the earliest chapters of Martin Davey's life.

I am also grateful to Linda Mauck, the clerk of Kent's city council, for allowing me to sift through the old ledgers and village council minutes so necessary in reconstructing Martin Davey's mayoral career as the "Boy Wonder" of Kent. I am equally indebted to Roland Baumann of the Oberlin College Archives, who gave me free access to Martin Davey materials at the Mudd Center on Oberlin's campus. I would also like to thank the staffs at the Franklin D. Roosevelt Library in Hyde Park, New York; the Ohio Historical Society in Columbus, Ohio; and the Western Reserve Historical Society in Cleveland, Ohio, for their unstinting assistance through various stages of my project.

I am indebted as well to friends and colleagues at Walsh University and elsewhere. Jonnie Guerra for years urged me to push ahead with Martin Davey, and Larry Bove has long understood the importance of scholarship and encouraged it. Richard Jusseaume, like Martin Davey, knew how to extend a kind word just when someone needed it most and expected it least. And I owe an especial thanks to my friend and colleague, Beth Secrest.

Without her computer and typing skills, this book would never have been more than 1,212 handwritten pages of illegible scrawl. To all, I am grateful.

Last, but by no means least, I would like to thank the nameless but not entirely faceless little old librarian at the Reed Memorial Library in Ravenna, Ohio, who showed me the scrapbook containing a photograph of Martin Davey's 1900 high school graduation class. Because of that photograph, I know exactly what a scared sixteen-year-old valedictorian looked like as he stood onstage in toe-pinching shoes and with knees knocking to deliver the first and most important speech of his life.

I have tried to make this book as readable, factual, and accurate as possible. Even so, since anything struck off by the hand of man is likely flawed, I apologize in advance for any errors of fact or omission and hope that my sharp-eyed readers will be kind enough to recall Horace's observation that even "mighty Homer nods."

Prologue

From the street, the three-storied, gabled white house with peeling paint at 453 West Main in Kent, Ohio, looks tired even when viewed through the scarlet maples reaching into the clear October sky. Three brick chimneys, an ornate railing, six substantial porch columns, and intricate carvings atop the gables attest that this was once a grand house, one that knew better times. The expansive grounds, with soaring pines and tulip trees, still command a regal presence, although everything is overgrown, the sad result of too many years of neglect.

Once, though, the house was one of the finest in town. Its owner, Martin Luther Davey, lived here with his wife, Berenice, and their two children, daughter Evangeline and son Martin Jr. It was always "home" to them although Martin Davey, Kent's most famous son, spent a great deal of time in Washington, D.C., and in Columbus, Ohio, as a United States congressman and two-time governor.

Rarely was the house quiet in November during the 1920s and '30s, a time when Martin Davey was winning a half dozen congressional and gubernatorial elections. Even before then, at age twenty-nine, Martin had begun to make a name for himself by winning the first of his three terms as mayor of Kent. By the time he was in his thirties, he was already an experienced politician who knew how to organize a campaign and galvanize voters better than did most men twice his age.

Before he became a "politician extraordinaire," Martin helped his father, John Davey, an immigrant from England, establish the Davey Tree Expert

Company, the first and foremost business born of the nascent science of tree surgery. For years John Davey had preached its principles in Kent, primarily to infidels who dismissed the English "prophet" as an impractical dreamer, barely able to feed his own family. Like most true believers, though, John Davey knew he was right and his critics wrong. In 1901, he published *The Tree Doctor,* a seminal work explaining the rudiments of the new science, and got his son to sell it, not in Kent where its author was a laughingstock, but in Warren, Ohio, and then Cleveland.

Every day, sixteen-year-old Martin Davey would stick four copies in his coat pockets and hit the streets. Shy at first because he was just a small-town boy of humble origin, young Davey overcame his backwardness and learned to sell not only his father's book but himself as well. The experience of greeting perfect strangers and selling them something that they had no intention of buying proved invaluable when Martin began his political career in 1913 by running for mayor.

That was only the beginning. Martin found that he needed politics. Once he overcame his shyness, he craved the limelight. Politics, of course, allowed him to bask in it. Politics also appealed to his fiery temperament; competing with another man for a single prize was the ultimate in civilized combat. Winning required strength, intelligence, ingenuity, and, in Martin's case, an acumen that his enemies called cunning. He loved the game, and when he lost a race (rarely), he could not wait to jump back in.

Hardly a day went by between his twenties and his fifties that he did not eat, drink, and breathe politics. Periodically, a defeat would send him back to Kent, where he would run the Davey Tree Expert Company without missing a beat. As soon as he could, however, it was back to the political races until two failed attempts at the governorship, in 1938 and 1940, signaled that his time had passed.

He was comparatively young when he died, only 61, but his life was fuller than most, spanning a time when America underwent perhaps its greatest transformation. Chester Alan Arthur was president when Martin Davey was born in 1884. When Davey died in 1946, Harry Truman was in the White House, and the United States had already ushered in the Nuclear Age, a stunning coda to one of the most exciting cavalcades in American history. Martin Davey lived through two world wars, the Great Depression and an industrial and technical revolution that brought the United States out of the horse-and-buggy days into a time remarkably like our own. He was born into ordinary circumstances but was not an ordinary man, and he certainly was never an ordinary politician.

Chapter One
Beginnings

STILL A MONTH SHY of his sixteenth birthday, a shaken Martin Davey retraced his steps toward center stage of the Kent Opera House to deliver the commencement address to his high school class of 1900. Only a moment earlier he had been called aside to receive a wrapped gift from his thirty classmates. His anticipation had quickly turned to mortification, however, when he opened the box and saw that it contained nothing but a handful of weeds. Forty years later, after countless successes in business and politics, he still recalled how the cruel prank "burned deep into his soul."[1]

But for the moment his humiliation had to be shunted aside and the immediate task at hand completed. He began, "Matter, Mind, and Spirit," as his proud parents, John and Bertha Davey, beamed from the audience. Years later, Martin admitted, he could recall nothing of the address apart from its title. That was understandable, though, because his father, and not he, had written every word of it. Not only was the speech his father's, but the elder Davey had drilled his son incessantly until Martin had memorized it to the point where on the Opera House stage "not even an earthquake could jar it from him."[2]

John Davey's insistence on perfection from his son was perfectly in character. His motto, applied to every job, big or small, was "Do it right or not at all." From their childhood on, the maxim had not been lost on Martin, nor on his sister Belle and brothers Wellington, James, Ira, and Paul.[3]

John Davey's nature was shaped by hard upbringing in his native England. Born in 1846 to poor farming parents in the Somersetshire countryside not far from the Welsh border, Davey, from childhood on, knew nothing but toil.

At thirteen, after the death of his mother, he was "put out to service" tending cattle and sheep for a neighboring farmer. He was well treated, having a bedroom to himself, which afforded him the privacy to kneel unashamedly in prayer morning and night. In his room he thought often, too, of his dead Episcopalian mother and her "Christian advice."

His ease ended, however, when his master hired another young man to help on the farm. The newcomer and Davey shared the same room and even the same bed. Davey described what followed as five years of hell.

He worried from the beginning that his new roommate would mock him when he recited his twice-daily prayers. His fears were well founded. No sooner had the pious Davey knelt by the bedside on the first night than the impious newcomer bolted upright and shouted, "What are you doing there, you little devil?" He then savaged the usefulness of prayer. Davey was so shaken that he stopped saying his prayers thereafter. His "sin" so troubled him that he cried even while picking apples in the orchard. He wailed, "My anchorage is gone." He hated the cowardice he demonstrated in not standing up to his taunter and began to "drift." Like so many other boys his age, he began to curse, which tortured him all the more. He could not forget his mother's constant preachment, "swear not at all." He agonized over his fall from grace, certain that all "swearers go to hell." Try though he might, the cursing habit had him, and he lamented that "daily there would be some slip of the tongue."[4]

Five years into his farm service, a middle-aged friend of his, Tom Braddock, an inveterate swearer, died suddenly of pneumonia. As Braddock breathed his last, he cried, "Hell must be my portion." When Davey learned of his friend's deathbed lamentation, he commanded himself, "John Davey, *you stop this swearing.*" From that moment he not only stopped cursing, he "set a watch against every other possible failure." John Davey was a driven man. His employer noticed the eighteen-year-old perfectionist and promoted him to chief herdsman and supervisor of all the hired hands.[5]

However, it was plants, not livestock and people, that fascinated John Davey, and at age twenty, no longer bound to position and place, he set off for Torquay in the south of England, a city known for its beautiful gardens. There he apprenticed himself to a local horticulturist and spent the next six or seven years learning everything he could about plants and landscaping.[6]

But there was more than horticulture to be learned. In nineteenth-century England, education was neither compulsory nor free, so John Davey had never gone to school, and even at twenty-one had not yet learned to read or write. A kindly man from Torquay, however, took a liking to Davey and taught him the alphabet and then encouraged him to read. With only a copy of the New Testament and a dictionary to guide him, John Davey began to teach himself to read and write. Soon he acquired a grammar book and a hymnal and from these learned how to fix words into sentences and sentences into paragraphs. There was no stopping him now. After laboring ten or twelve hours a day in Torquay's gardens, Davey read and wrote long into the night. His passion for language was limitless, leading even to the later study of Greek and Latin. Words, he said, were indispensable to thinking: "Without words one cannot think, and it is thought that moves the world."[7]

While in Torquay, Davey also developed his spirituality. Through his landlady, he met the congregation of Upton Vale [Baptist] Chapel and spent many evenings socializing and taking religion classes. He felt comfortable as a Baptist, believing that for the first time he had discovered the true "*Spirit of God*." On Sundays, he and other young men from Upton Vale traveled around Torquay seeking converts. Constant preaching and praying turned him into an excellent speaker. Later he would put the oratorical skills he honed in Torquay to good use in America.[8]

As he had impressed as a teenager tending cattle and sheep, he likewise struck those who knew him in Torquay. The rector of his church offered to use his influence to start Davey in his own business, while other friends offered to pay his tuition to Spurgeon College, one of England's best seminaries. His employer, anxious to keep so good a worker, offered him higher wages. But the promise of a lucrative business career left him cold, and the bleak prospects of salvation proffered by a career in the Calvinist theology offered by Spurgeon repelled him. Not even the temptation of higher pay working the landscapes of Torquay was enough to dissuade him from going to America.[9]

In the spring of 1873, John Davey, age twenty-seven, landed in New York and then left for Warren, Ohio, where he lived with a kind family that encouraged his passion for gardening while he worked as a janitor in a private school. He continued to study botany and bought his own greenhouse where he grew beautiful plants, particularly an amazing fuchsia that blossomed nearly from floor to ceiling.[10] The greenhouse failed, but during this early phase of his American life John Davey developed the interest that grew into the abiding passion of his life—trees. Struck by the disdain Americans had for what Davey considered one of their greatest resources and objects of beauty, the new immigrant began a lifelong study of trees and their preservation.[11]

There was, however, more to his life than trees. He joined the Disciple Church in Warren, where he met and courted twenty-year-old Bertha Reeves, the daughter of the church's pastor, Harmon Reeves. They married in 1879 and by the next year had their first child, Belle. Shortly afterward, the new parents moved to Kent, Ohio, when John Davey was hired to tend Standing Rock Cemetery, then little more than acres of tangled shrubs and neglected trees.[12]

Standing Rock became a laboratory for Davey. He now used all the years of study and hands-on experience in Torquay to the fullest. Almost miraculously, John Davey transformed what had been a public eyesore into an area of civic pride in Kent. More than a mere cemetery, Standing Rock was now a beautiful memorial park. But even more important, in converting Standing Rock Cemetery to a thing of beauty, John Davey, through trial and error and constant experimentation, saved many of the cemetery's dying maples and oaks and in the process created a new science—tree surgery.

Although Kentites were proud of their cemetery, they little appreciated the special skills that John Davey had developed and applied. Tree surgery was a science ahead of its time, something that had spectacularly transformed Standing Rock but had little, if any, marketability. Consequently, John Davey bought a greenhouse and some land, intending to augment his salary by selling produce. At the same time, he took to writing pamphlets and lecturing on politics, religion, birds, and, of course, his beloved trees. But little money came of Davey's ventures, and life for his family was hardly more than hand to mouth.[13]

John Davey, far more dreamer than realist, was fortunate that his wife Bertha was firmly rooted in practicality. While John was off saving trees, writing, lecturing, and pursuing one horticultural venture after another, it was Bertha Reeves Davey who tended to the seven Davey children when they were sick, saw to it that they kept up with their school lessons, cooked, baked, and in general kept the household together.[14]

This was the family life that Martin Luther Davey knew as a boy growing up in Kent, Ohio. Born on July 25, 1884, he was John and Bertha's third child, preceded by sister Belle, brother Wellington, and followed by Jim (named after President James A. Garfield, whom John Davey had met when Garfield was a congressman visiting Warren), Ira, Paul, and baby sister Rosella. Both Ira and Rosella died in childhood.

Kent in the 1880s was a booming village. Its population had soared more than a thousand since the 1870s and, according to the census of 1880, stood at 3,309. But in many ways it was still a backward place, far more rooted in the early nineteenth century than in the late. Its streets were unpaved and unlighted, and there was no municipal water supply. Cattle still roamed through town, destroying the old wooden sidewalks that kept Kentites from sloshing

John Davey with (left to right) Belle, Wellington, Martin, ca. 1892. Evangeline Davey Smith Collection, Martin L. Davey Papers, Kent State University Libraries, Special Collections and Archives.

through the mud in sloppy weather. The problem was so bad that the village council on July 1, 1880, passed an ordinance that fined owners of wandering cows one to five dollars. The law also covered pigs and horses and had enough bite to put an end to freely roaming livestock in the streets of Kent.

Gradually the wooden walks were ripped up in favor of stone, brick, or gravel pathways. At about the same time a dozen oil lamps were sited downtown. By 1882 the oil lamps gave way to fifty Belden Vapor gasoline lamps resting on cedar posts throughout the village. The children of Kent enjoyed following lamplighter Ovie Nichols as he made his rounds every evening until the gasoline lamps were replaced with gas lights in 1886. Electrification of town lights occurred on June 5, 1889, and, aided by the ingenuity of Thomas Edison, Kent strode into modernity.

The debate over electrification of city lighting services had stirred the citizens, many of whom thought that such modernization was too costly. But the ill will generated by the electric light issue paled in comparison to the anger fueled by the decision dictating where the village's new water supply would originate. Waterworks engineers chose Plum Creek, south of town, a source detractors claimed was so befouled with maggots and offal from a nearby slaughterhouse that its water was "not fit for hogs to drink." The Plum Creek decision so divided Kentites that even the editors of two local and rival newspapers, the *Kent Courier* and the *Kent News,* got into a public fistfight over the issue.[15]

The Plum Creek debate galvanized John Davey. A keen environmentalist even before the word became popular, he quickly threw himself against the Plum Creek promoters. He and other Kentites wanted the new waterworks located north of town, where there was abundant fresh spring water. Davey railed against the Plum Creek location, but influential Kentites, who stood to profit from the sale of adjacent land, were too powerful, and Plum Creek prevailed. Not even two lawsuits stopped the project, and construction went ahead. On May 13, 1887, the new waterworks opened its mains, and city water for the first time gushed into local homes and businesses.[16]

In fighting the Plum Creek location, John Davey made bitter enemies. Already regarded as a bit of a crank, his reputation suffered all the more. His foes sneered at him for his poverty, and the whole family became the persistent butt of cruel jokes. The family's humiliation especially stung young Martin Davey and was likely the reason his classmates treated him so contemptuously at his high school commencement.

The Davey family's poverty forced a resourcefulness upon young Martin. By the age of ten he already had his own horseradish route. His father, of course, had planted the pungent root, but it was Martin who dug it out of the frozen ground in February and March. After grating the horseradish (and frequently his knuckles), Davey canned it and then sold it for a nickel a cup. Meager though his pay was, Martin's resourcefulness kept the Davey family afloat during the cold winter and early spring months when John Davey's greenhouse business languished.

Life was hard in the Davey household but probably not too unlike that of many other nineteenth-century small-town families. John Davey buried part of his summer and fall harvest to preserve it and resurrected it during the winter. The family kept a milking cow and Bertha Davey baked delicious bread, pies, and doughnuts for the family. She knew how to stretch the meagerest of provisions. Long into his adulthood, Martin Davey remembered how his mother would buy a five-cent soup bone and, with home-grown vegetables, concoct a delicious beef stew.

Usually there was enough money to buy a small piece of meat and some flour, but there were times, especially in the winter, when the family cupboard was bare. Once, at a near desperate moment, Frank Reeves, Bertha's brother, arrived as an angel of mercy. His sister's poverty must have been evident, because within an hour or two of his visit the local grocer, laden with ham, flour, and other provisions, knocked on the Davey door. Years later Martin Davey still remembered the joy generated by Reeves's generosity. Other Reeves brothers would periodically help the Daveys by sending a few dollars out of the two or three they earned daily.

John Davey was a hard-working, honorable man, but he could not manage money. When Belle Davey, the oldest child, was chosen to deliver an address at her high school commencement in 1899, there was no money for a new dress. That bothered Martin, not yet fifteen, so he struck a bargain with his father. John Davey had grown a beautiful crop of pansies that spring, and his son agreed to sell them in return for a generous commission. Martin Davey worked hard and made not only enough money to get Belle a new dress, but also enough to buy his mother a new hat and his own first pair of long pants.[17]

Housing for the family was never grand, either. The first house John Davey provided for his family in Kent was a barnlike structure on Mantua Street near the cemetery where he worked. That was in 1881.

A few years later, in what became a familiar pattern, the family moved, this time to a two-room house that John Davey built on Grant Street near the Cuyahoga River. There he attached a greenhouse to the back of the home, and then, on some open beds on the lot, he grew vegetables and flowers to be sold. The Grant Street house, with a horse pastured out back, was where Martin Davey was born.[18]

The hard work demanded by his father failed to stifle all young Martin's youthful exuberance. One summer day, he and his older brother, Wellington, were helping themselves to a neighbor's cherries. More alert than Wellington, Martin stopped pilfering just as the neighbor's daughter spied the cherry thieves. Wellington was caught red-handed and took the scolding. Martin, far from innocent, was praised for resisting the temptation that corrupted his brother. To compound the unfairness, the victimized neighbor rewarded an undeserving Martin with a quart of cherries she had already picked. Feeling guilty because Wellington alone paid for a "crime" that both had committed, Martin shared his cherries with his brother.

Martin was not always so fortunate. There were times he paid the price for his actions. One of the Davey neighbors was an odd character named Joe Prairie. He looked and dressed more like a figure out of the early nineteenth century than the late. His hair was long, and he wore a long black coat, tie, and hat. Local gossip had it that he was a brilliant man who some time earlier had snapped. He and his wife lived in a dilapidated house on a weed-filled lot. Mrs. Prairie was as odd as her husband. Neighbors scarcely saw her. She stayed in constant seclusion behind the tightly drawn blinds of her house. The neighborhood boys enjoyed taunting her husband: "Joe, Joe broke his toe on the way to Mexico. When he came back, he broke his back, sliding on the railroad track." They knew, after this recitation, that Joe Prairie would lumber after them.

One day, while Martin Davey and some of his friends idled behind the Davey greenhouse, Joe Prairie plodded up the B&O Railroad tracks and started to cross a footbridge over the river. When he stepped onto the bridge, Davey and the other boys began their usual chant. Knowing they were quicker and more nimble than the eccentric Prairie, the taunters continued until the angry man crossed the bridge. They then ran to Davey's yard and hid in some packing boxes.

The boys, including Martin, thought they had once again gotten away with their meanness, but from a distance John Davey had witnessed it all. Prairie fumed and sputtered to the elder Davey, demanding justice. There was no need. John Davey promptly reminded his son, with a whipping, that a boy should respect his elders, odd looking and eccentric though they might be.[19]

John Davey, although not an abusive father, subscribed to the old-fashioned idea that a parent should not "spare the rod." The Davey boys knew they had gone too far when their father, jackknife in hand, headed for the nearest tree to cut a switch that would soon blister the offending party's behind. Martin Davey never faulted his father for relying on the rod to keep his children in line, and later in life said he thought an occasional firm but tempered swat or two across a child's backside was the best way to ensure good behavior. Besides, Martin and the other Davey children could count on their soft-hearted mother to intervene on their behalves, saving her children from their father's heavy hand.[20]

Hard luck generated by his lack of financial acumen continued to dog John Davey. Within a few years of moving into the two-room house on the banks of the Cuyahoga, he could no longer maintain the payments, and the family had to move again, this time closer to town, into the front half of a small house on Fairchild Avenue. This was one of the lowest points in Martin Davey's life. Even in this modest home, John Davey could barely pay the rent through grading lawns and planting flower beds. Winters were especially hard. Money was so scarce that the Davey children lacked even coats and mittens.

The family's poverty was evident to friends and neighbors. Howard Dow, who had printed some of John Davey's pamphlets, gave him a secondhand overcoat that had seen better days. The elder Davey gave it to Martin even though it was much too large for him. But Martin was elated because at least now he could better cope with winter. His classmates made fun of him every time he wore it, but, as he later noted, he "preferred not to be cold."

John Davey's finances were further straitened by the birth of yet another son, Ira, in 1892. A next-door neighbor, better off than the Daveys and disdainful of them for it, gave Bertha Davey some household goods. Hers was a case, however, of the "gift without the giver." When Mrs. Davey tried to thank her benefactor, a steadfast churchgoer, the woman snapped, "Just because a person is kind to a neighbor when she is sick, that doesn't mean she wants to make a bosom friend of her." Hurt and humiliated, Bertha Davey returned home. The following Halloween the Davey children made the insolent neighbor pay the price for her meanness by toppling some of the outbuildings in her back yard.

By the summer of 1894 John Davey was behind in the rent again. The family had to move farther west on Fairchild Avenue into still another old house badly in need of paint and repair. But it was all John Davey could afford. He was also likely drawn to the place because it sat on two acres that he quickly put to use growing vegetables and flowers for sale. Martin Davey lived here on Fairchild from age ten to fifteen. This was also the house in which the last two Davey children, Paul and Rosella, were born.[21]

Martin was put to work again, going door to door selling the produce from his father's large garden. He had a salesman's temperament, polite and smiling. And, for one still so young, he was most observant, noticing, for instance, that wherever he saw houses with neat flowers and lawns, he knew there would be friendly people and likely customers. Martin would begin his rounds early in the morning, knocking on the back doors of customers along his route. His powers of observation extended beyond flowers and lawns. Many years later he naughtily noted: "It is surprising what a little boy can see through the back door—early in the morning."[22]

Now an adolescent, Martin Davey tried the manly art of smoking. At first he sneaked corn silk from the corn patch down the hill from the family house. That experiment ended abruptly when a hawk-eyed John Davey spied smoke rising from his field, went down to investigate, and caught his son red-handed. Martin Davey did not recall the punishment he got from his father, but it ended his corn silk smoking. He did, however, take up regular cigarettes at the age of twenty. That and card playing (Pedro and Seven-Up were his favorite games) were his self-confessed vices.

Martin grew up poor but still had fun. A Fairchild Avenue neighbor, Adam Bachman, owned an old rowboat that had clearly seen better days. The wood had shrunk, leaving gaps between the boards, and it lay useless on the riverbank near the Davey house. Bachman struck a bargain with Martin and some of his friends—repair the boat (Bachman furnished the materials) and Martin and his friends could use it. The boys leaped at the chance for so rich a prize. They restored the boat and spent many a happy summer day rowing up and down the Cuyahoga, frequently jumping from the boat for a swim. Ever devilish, Martin enjoyed overturning the boat and diving under it so passersby would think its occupants had drowned.

During a typical outing on the river, the Davey boys would pause for a hearty lunch of homemade bread and butter, meat, and cookies. They had to improvise for their drinks. On one occasion, after the boys had rowed two miles upriver, they spied a herd of cows and quickly concluded that fresh milk would be perfect to wash down lunch. Just as they were milking, the owner of the herd dashed out, cursing and flailing. The would-be milk thieves retreated to their boat and slaked their thirst with water instead.

Another favorite pastime of the Davey boys was building shanties. George White, a Davey chum, made the first one, but Wellington Davey quickly established himself as the master builder. He had a knack, Martin observed, for things mechanical. His shanty was not a thing of beauty, but what it lacked in aesthetic appeal it more than compensated for in design and trappings.

Wellington's skill was not limited to shanties. Years earlier, near Standing Rock Cemetery, there had been a miniature railroad that linked an abandoned sand mill to both sides of the river. The railroad had long since fallen into disrepair, and large parts of it lay rusting in the water. Aided by a few of the neighborhood boys, Wellington salvaged some of the rails and ties and reassembled them in back of his house. He then built his own railway car out of parts resurrected from the old sand mill. He even made brakes for the contraption. The miniature railroad behind the Davey house became the hit of the neighborhood.[23]

Despite the fun and games the Davey children enjoyed, John and Bertha Davey were serious when it came to their children's education. John and Bertha Davey stressed learning for their children. Martin particularly was drawn to books. As a teenager he enjoyed the Horatio Alger tales so popular at the time and historical novels by George Alfred Henty, the author of more than seventy works about great men and deeds. Martin was enthralled by a Henty book on William the Conqueror and the Battle of Hastings. His knowledge of the event that precipitated the Norman Conquest of England allowed him to shine one day when his class discussed the battle. Martin amazed his classmates and teacher with his encyclopedic recall of virtually every detail of the struggle between Duke William and Prince Harold for mastery of England.[24]

Even in the serious atmosphere of the classroom, though, Martin could be a rascal. He disliked his eighth grade teacher; chronic indigestion made her old and cranky, and teacher and pupil just did not get along. Martin's poor grades reflected the disharmony. A number of times she made him stay after school to improve his schoolwork.

One day, a classmate, Harry, the eighth grade cutup, who could make Martin laugh at will, threw a piece of tar at the teacher while her back was turned. He missed but came perilously close to hitting her in the head. Martin burst out laughing at the very moment she turned around to try to catch the culprit. Of course, she blamed the laughing Martin, who protested his innocence but at the same time refused to rat on his friend.

The already stormy relationship between student and teacher worsened. On one occasion she ordered Martin into the hall for one of his misdeeds. Rather than remain there, he left the building and headed downtown. He returned after lunch only to be sent to the hall again. The punishment was repeated over the next two days. For three days he was exiled from the classroom, and word circulated that Martin Davey was playing hooky. Before long even his father heard the rumor and gave him an old-fashioned whipping.

But John Davey also listened to his son's side of the story and concluded that the teacher was not entirely fair with Martin. He marched down to the school, cornered Martin's nemesis and reminded her that he sent his son to school to get an education, not to be banished from the room every day. The elder Davey's firmness had a powerful effect. Martin shaped up, and the teacher moderated her behavior toward him. The truce between the two established peace the rest of the year.

Wellington Davey could have gotten his brother into serious trouble in high school the next year. Wellington, mechanically gifted but academically weak, had failed a grade, while his precocious brother Martin had been advanced a year. Consequently, they were in the ninth grade together and sat side by side in algebra class. One day, while taking a test, Wellington slipped his brother his pocket knife. Inside was a desperate note: "What is the answer to Question 5?" More loyal than honest, Martin scribbled the answer, inserted it between the knife blades, and passed it to his brother. Martin breathed a sigh of relief when his answer was correct. It would have been incriminating indeed if he and his brother had identical wrong answers to the same problem.

During high school, Martin Davey developed a keen interest in literature. Shakespeare's plays and the poetry of James Russell Lowell, especially *The Vision of Sir Launfal,* inspired him. His love affair with good literature continued even after graduation. Wherever he went he carried a book of poetry. Even while riding a streetcar he would read from a work by Henry Wadsworth Longfellow, John Greenleaf Whittier, William Cullen Bryant, Alfred Lord Tennyson, or Sir Walter Scott to pass the time. All this fed his love of language, which was heightened later at Oberlin Academy. There he delighted in the idea that some sounds—L, N, and M, for example—are liquid, while others—C and E—are "harsh and guttural." Once formally armed with a knowledge of linguistics, Martin Davey understood why he loved literature. He took his lessons to heart and used them in developing his own writing. Good language, he said, was simple and musical and ought to be used in everything spoken and written until excellence became a matter of habit.[25]

Young Davey not only honed his intellect during his formative years, he also developed a religious dimension. By age twelve, without any overt pressure or inducement from his parents, he joined the family church, the Church of Christ, Disciples. He quickly immersed himself in the congregation's activities, attending services five times every Sunday. He claimed to enjoy so strenuous a schedule on the Sabbath. For one, he had a deep spiritual longing, which church membership alone satisfied. For another, church was a haven for a young boy who, because of his father's eccentricity and notorious poverty, already felt like a social outcast in Kent.[26]

His commitment to the Disciples Church, however, did not result in blind acceptance of all its tenets. Perplexed by his church's insistence that only those baptized by immersion would gain salvation, he turned to his father for help. Why, he asked, are Congregationalists, Methodists, and other good Christians, who are merely sprinkled during baptism instead of immersed, denied heaven? John Davey, so often rigid, demanding, and even harsh in overseeing his children, demonstrated a surprising open-mindedness in answering. Deviating from his own church's teachings, he told his young son that baptism was merely symbolic. What truly determined one's eternal fate was whether baptism, of any sort, truly transformed him spiritually. John Davey's response reassured his son, who now felt relieved knowing that people gained paradise by living a moral life and not by blindly adhering to religious dogma.

Even while wrestling with theological questions that ended up strengthening his religiosity, Martin Davey was exposed to quite a different side of religion, one that came close to shaking his faith. Kentites were thrilled when they learned that the Disciples Church was bringing the film the *Passion Play* to town. It was Kent's first motion picture. The movie's promoter promised a gold watch to whoever sold the most tickets. Martin Davey wanted that watch more than anything. His entrepreneurial skills already well honed from long practice selling his father's vegetables and flowers to friends and neighbors, Martin sold tickets all over town. No one sold more. The gold watch was his. Within a few months, however, thrill gave way to deep disappointment after the thin gold wash of the watch wore through and the mechanism failed. To Martin, the promoter was despicable for taking advantage of a child. It was, he said, "the lowest form of meanness." The entire episode tested his faith.

If God ever spoke to Martin Davey during his boyhood, it was to tell him that he was never meant to be a farmer. Nobody worked harder and faster than John Davey, and he expected the same from his children. Still trying to make a living by growing vegetables, the elder Davey had bought a small farm about two miles outside Kent. Here he planted onions and celery, and, because his landscaping work dominated his time, he expected his sons to handle the celery and onion business. The work was hard; Martin hated digging the celery out of the cold, wet ground during the fall. Gloves were useless in the muddy celery field and his fingers froze. Wellington was luckier. While Martin picked in the cold and mud, his older brother trimmed the celery in a nearby outbuilding warmed by a stove.[27]

Early on, Martin recognized how utterly dependent his farming father was on economic and weather conditions. The vegetable market was frequently glutted, and more than once John Davey barely made expenses. When unfavorable market conditions failed to wreak havoc with John Davey's livelihood, bad weather often did. In April 1901, when Martin was sixteen, his father grew a bumper crop of onions. Just as the Daveys started to anticipate a nice (and rare) profit, Kent was hit by a devastating spring snowstorm. The snow began falling on Thursday night, April 18, and did not stop until the next Sunday morning. Railroad and trolley traffic ground to a halt. Snow piled ten feet high at some places on the tracks. Telephone and telegraph lines dangled from poles throughout town. For two days Kent was cut off from the outside world. By Sunday afternoon the sun broke through and undid in a few hours what the storm had taken the entire weekend to do. The trains and trolley cars started running again, and soon Kent was back in business. The same was not true of John Davey. His onion crop, once so promising, lay dead under three or four feet of snow.[28]

Daydreaming allowed Martin escape from such tribulations and the drudgery of garden toil. During brief breaks in the workday and after lunch, he would lie on his back, gaze into the summer sky, and speculate about the world beyond Kent. As the cars of the Wheeling and Lake Erie Railroad clattered past the family farm, he wondered what the people who lived in the towns and villages between Cleveland and Wheeling, West Virginia, were like. That world opened a bit to him and other Kentites in November 1895 when the town completed its first electric street car line. Inter-urban cars now left Kent every hour between 6:15 A.M. and 10:15 P.M. For a dime, Kentites could ride to Cuyahoga Falls seven or eight miles to the west, and for twenty cents they could ride all the way to Akron. Not surprisingly, the celery and onion farm grew too confining, and Martin began to think about his future and a life beyond Kent.[29]

There remained, however, pleasant local diversions sufficient to keep a young boy occupied. One summer a merry-go-round operator brought his carousel to Kent. The town children, Martin Davey among them, flocked to pay their nickels to ride the snorting and prancing wooden horses for a few moments. But while the other children just rode, young Martin, already well acquainted with entrepreneurship, talked the operator into allowing him to sell tickets to would-be riders. He could keep one nickel for every five he took in. He hustled and made a fair profit for his time and energy. But there was more than monetary reward that accompanied his deal with the merry-go-round operator. As a "partner" in the concession, Martin could ride for free, and he took great delight in jumping on and off the carousel whenever he chose. Before long he was doing it not just for the enjoyment of the ride but because he could show off before envious friends. His pleasure ended quickly, though. One day, while leaping on and off the merry-go-round before an admiring audience, a sharp voice cut through the air, "Martin!" It was his father. John Davey lectured his son about the dangers of jumping on and off the moving carousel, and that ended Martin's entry into the world of merry-go-rounds. After settling his affairs with the operator, he returned home, sadly, with his father.

John Davey trusted flesh and blood horses more than wooden ones. He kept one for years, and the Davey children had long ridden bareback on the animal, without their father's disapproval. One day, when Martin was fifteen, he rode the horse to the watering trough at the end of Fairchild Avenue. Prodded by its rider, the horse galloped back and took too sharp a turn from the street onto the Davey farm. Martin flew off. He grabbed at the horse's neck but could not hold on and fell to the ground under the animal's front hooves, which landed atop one of Martin's knees. He lay there, in excruciating pain, unable to move for several minutes. Finally, he propped himself up on his good knee and dragged himself, with the horse in tow, back to the hitching post. Afraid to tell anyone of his injuries because he feared his father's anger for riding too fast, he limped into the house and up to bed. Fortunately for Martin, his injuries were neither severe nor permanent.

That Martin would endure his pain in silence rather than incur John Davey's wrath said much about how he felt about his father. Although the elder Davey was an exemplar of toil and tenacity, his children thought him hard and driven. By his teens, Martin had had enough of his father's autocracy. At age fifteen, he defied him for the first time. The episode itself was ordinary— John Davey barked an order to his son—but the response was not. Martin snapped, "no." The elder Davey lurched toward his son as if to grab him and force him to comply. Martin stood his ground, arms folded across his chest, and looked his father in the eye, repeating, "I won't do it." All the years of hard work, all the contributions he had made to support his family over the years, fortified the young man as he stood up to the family patriarch. Rather than force a physical confrontation, John Davey simply turned, huffed off, and never mentioned the episode. From that day on, he never ordered but always asked his son to help when necessary.

The unpleasantness of this episode caused Martin to reassess himself and his relationship with his father. He was no longer a mere stripling; he was a young man who had helped support his family for years. That alone demanded that his father respect him sufficiently to ask him to help with tasks instead of ordering him about. The confrontation erased the anger and resentment growing in Martin over the years, and he could later admit that he never really knew his father. The elder Davey enjoyed his children when they were little, but as time passed, he grew "stern and distant." As Martin matured, he could finally understand how his father's ceaseless struggle to provide for his family transformed him from tender parent to distant patriarch.

Providing for a wife and seven children overwhelmed John Davey. Unable again to pay his rent, in 1899 he moved his family out of the Fairchild Avenue house to an old farmhouse two miles in the countryside. Martin remembered very little about the new Davey domicile except that it was a four-mile walk to and from school and that the winter winds knifed through the house. The Davey boys were happy when their future brother-in-law, Harmon L. Carson, moved in because they could take turns sleeping next to his big, warm body.

John Davey did not work the land on this farm. To supplement the family's income, he put his boys out to work on neighboring farms. Martin was assigned to a nearby farmer known for his diligence and neatness. His buildings, fences, and livestock were the envy of all. Hard work and thrift had gotten him where he was. He put Martin to work loading hay. Strong though he was at sixteen, Martin could not keep pace with his powerfully built boss, then in his thirties. The man worked without pause, passing hay in a continuous stream up to Martin whose back was screaming before noon. After a mere half hour for lunch, the two returned to finish a twelve-hour shift. That was enough for Martin. He did not go back a second day.[30]

In June of that year, 1900, Martin Davey graduated from high school. Apart from the humiliation at the hands of his prankster classmates, he remembered most the tight-fitting, patent leather shoes he had to squeeze into. Even though he had a hard time concentrating because of his aching feet, he nonetheless fixed on his mother and father in the audience as he delivered the commencement address. Never far from John Davey's control despite their confrontation a year earlier, Martin imagined his father challenging him: "My boy, you have to be good tonight." Notwithstanding the obvious pressure to perform, Martin regarded his high school graduation as the biggest thrill of his life. Not even his later electoral triumphs as mayor of Kent, U.S. congressman, and governor of Ohio equaled the pride he felt that commencement night. He posed proudly in the front row for the class picture, arms across his chest, a pretty classmate's hands draped over his shoulders.[31]

John Davey's fortunes improved a bit in 1900. Shortly after Martin's high

Kent High School graduating class of 1900. Martin Davey is in the front row, third from right. Evangeline Davey Smith Collection, Martin L. Davey Papers, Kent State University Libraries, Special Collections and Archives.

school graduation, the elder Davey moved his family back to town, this time to a brand-new seven-room house at 338 Woodard Avenue. Years later Martin observed that the house was cheaply built, but to his sixteen-year-old eyes it seemed like a mansion. John Davey quickly plied his horticultural skills and put in a lawn and planted flowers, shrubs, and trees. After years in ramshackle, dilapidated old houses, the Davey family could at last be proud of where they lived.

That first summer after high school, Martin helped his father in his landscaping business. He now earned a man's wages, $1.50 a day, a far cry from the small change he had toiled for as a boy selling vegetables and flowers all over town. "Big money," he called it. He was proud of how he and his father helped beautify Kent.

Martin did not stay long at his father's side during the summer of 1900. A family friend had bought the rights to sell a new aluminum comb, a "Thomas Edison invention—that would not tarnish, corrode, or rust, bend or break," according to the sales hyperbole, and wanted to crack the Cleveland market. He asked John Davey's permission to hire Martin, just a few months out of high school, to hawk the combs in Ohio's biggest city. The elder Davey agreed but only if Martin returned to help him in his landscaping business the following spring.

At age sixteen Martin Davey traveled away from home for the first time. He was accompanied by Harmon Carson, now Belle's husband, and together they went door to door in working-class neighborhoods peddling combs of various sizes and ornamentation for anywhere between ten cents and a dollar. Carson, clearly no salesman, quit after only a few days, but Martin continued. He missed home and family but enjoyed the profits from his generous one-third commission.

Martin's Cleveland experience helped shape the man to be. Particularly memorable was his encounter with a sloppy, thick-haired woman who patiently listened to his sales pitch at her door, turned on her heels into the house and returned with a twisted and bent duplicate of the very comb that the young man was pitching. Shattered because he could no longer believe his own sales line that the combs would never "bend or break," Martin quit the business and returned to Kent, unwilling to promote anything that he could not personally trust.[32]

Perhaps it was mere happenstance that forced him home, but it may have been fate as well. His father, long dismissed as eccentric by almost everyone who knew him, had a new idea. He was writing a book about tree surgery. John Davey had become an accomplished photographer and decided to combine his newest avocation with his longtime vocation in horticulture in *The Tree Doctor.* John Davey wrote it, but Martin Davey had to sell it.

Chapter Two

The Young Salesman

THE TREE DOCTOR WAS WRITTEN in 1901 but was really the culmination of more than twenty years of John Davey's research and experimentation. Davey was proud of his book, claiming in the introduction that it covered "practically all that has been written on tree culture . . . and contained the best photoengravings, the best paper, and a strong cover." He deliberately avoided scientific terms in the text so that it would be comprehensible not only to experts but also to the "merchant, farmer, mechanic, laborer, man or woman, boy or girl."[1]

It was not a big book, only 188 pages, but Davey crammed into those few pages 167 photographs of "pear blights," "peach yellows," and "leaf kills" and virtually every other known botanical affliction. Its slenderness notwithstanding, *The Tree Doctor* overflowed with details on how to save trees that had fallen victim to these ravages. The techniques were called "tree surgery" and involved the excision of rotting tissue from the trunk, sterilization and waterproofing of the remaining pith, and reinforcement of the inner tree with concrete. All this was done so that upon completion the trunk stood like a human spine, firm and strong yet flexible enough to sway without snapping.[2]

Davey's book was more than a tree primer. It trumpeted his philosophy about the necessity of man's communion with nature. For years he was an odd character in Kent, ambling about offering free tree care advice to neighbors and friends. He was the original "tree doctor" to all who knew him, and his book virtually pleaded with its readers to pay more attention to their trees and shrubs.[3] *The Tree Doctor* also allowed John Davey politely to vent his anger against the old-school "experts" whose prescription for ailing trees was hacking off diseased branches and limbs without the slightest attention to the health and appearance of the tree. "Tree Butchers," he called them, and their so-called craft was nothing more than "mutilation."[4]

Few others, however, shared Davey's zeal for *The Tree Doctor.* He persuaded a young printer in Akron, Sam Zilioux, the owner of the Commercial Printing Company, to print the book, but Davey had to put up $7,000 to cover costs. He expected to recoup his investment by selling *The Tree Doctor* for a dollar a copy. Fortunately for Davey, the kind-hearted Zilioux extended the necessary credit.[5]

John Davey never intended to hawk the book himself; he already had a seasoned salesman in the family. Martin Davey, not even a year out of high school, was the man for that job. The elder Davey was generous—Martin's commission was fifty cents per copy, half the sale amount. His first destination was Warren, Ohio (Kentites were probably too accustomed to John Davey's free advice to pay a dollar for his book), the city that had welcomed John Davey to the United States twenty-eight years earlier. Martin did his best and sold enough copies to maintain himself for a month or so in Warren, although at first *The Tree Doctor* was a hard sell. It appealed to disparate buyers. Some owned small homes but nonetheless cared deeply about the one or two trees on their lots, while others owned estates with vast numbers of valuable trees. Hiking through one Warren neighborhood after another, sixteen-year-old Martin Davey ended up selling *The Tree Doctor* to nearly one household in four.[6]

With Warren saturated, Cleveland, with its teeming population and numerous estates along Euclid Avenue and its surrounding neighborhoods, seemed like the next logical market. At seventeen, Martin Davey, with copies of *The Tree Doctor* in hand, moved on to Ohio's largest city.

Even though Cleveland was a mere forty miles from Kent, Martin had been there only infrequently. John Davey accompanied his son on this latest trip. The elder Davey, during earlier visits to Cleveland, had befriended some members of the local YMCA, and now introduced his young salesman son around. He hoped that the YMCA gentlemen would provide a social network for Martin until the young man grew accustomed to the city. Martin was grateful for his father's foresight because he missed home and family. The YMCA set liked Martin and made him feel as comfortable as any seventeen-year-old away from home could.

Cleveland was important to Martin—it helped build his confidence. Initially plagued by a sense of worthlessness stemming from his childhood of deprivation and ridicule, Martin liked it that Clevelanders knew nothing about the Daveys' notorious poverty and John Davey's reputation as the town crank. Everything was fresh in his new environment, and Martin was pleased that Clevelanders "took him at face value."

He plunged headlong into the social life of the YMCA. He joined the Tuesday Evening Club and then the Sunday Afternoon Club. The latter had a religious dimension, but it was primarily its social aspect that appealed to Martin. To sustain enthusiasm for the group, YMCA leaders divided it into two teams, the reds and the blues. Each competed to see which could attract more guests to the Sunday afternoon get-togethers. Both groups would collar men on the streets, trying to get them to attend the Sunday afternoon events. The losing side had to treat the winners to supper in the gymnasium.

Particularly influential during Martin's Cleveland stay was Augustus Nash, the YMCA's religious work director. The diminutive Nash was a friendly "bundle of energy," always with a ready smile. The deeply religious Nash took to Martin. The feeling was mutual, and before long the young Kentite and the YMCA religious work director traveled around delivering Sunday evening speeches to Cleveland church groups. Ever introspective, Martin wondered what he added to the Sunday meetings because he was just "a kid." He thought that perhaps Nash and the other adult who accompanied him were simply being kind by having him tag along.

The YMCA not only introduced Martin to public speaking, it also introduced him to physical fitness. Soon after arriving in Cleveland, Davey began spending three or four nights a week in the YMCA gymnasium. Even though he was young and lithe, he subjected himself to a new physical regimen that not even all the years spent in an active boyhood could prepare him for. His body ached from the near constant exercise, but gradually the soreness gave way to strength and endurance. He was proud of his new musculature and the way he carried himself.

He was not in Cleveland, however, to improve his physical conditioning; he was there to sell *The Tree Doctor*. Recalling how Kentites with well-tended lawns and homes were the best customers on his boyhood vegetable route, Martin began canvassing Cleveland's nicer neighborhoods. Clad in the same black suit he had worn for his high school graduation, he stuffed four books into his coat pockets and every morning started off. Outward confidence disguised his insecurity. Still bearing the scars of his impoverished upbringing, he thought potential buyers were too grand to listen to a sales pitch from a poor boy from Kent. Several times he would approach a customer's house or business and turn away before finally mustering sufficient pluck to knock on the door.

He should not have been so hesitant. He was so "persistent and polite" that he even sold a copy to a businessman who lived in an apartment and had no use whatsoever for a book on the care of trees and shrubs.[7]

From that conquest, he was on to the Lake Avenue home of Mark Hanna, the millionaire businessman, U.S. senator and Republican kingmaker of President William McKinley. Mrs. Hanna answered his knock and stood patiently in the doorway while Martin pitched *The Tree Doctor.* She asked to see a copy, browsed through a few pages and bought it. After leaving Mrs. Hanna, Martin chatted briefly with her gardener, soliciting the names of other prospects. The helpful gardener directed him to some potential customers out on Euclid Avenue, then the grand boulevard where many of Cleveland's rich and powerful lived in mansions the equal of the finest in New York or Chicago.[8]

Martin Davey, in addition to being a superb salesman, became a master practitioner of psychology, learning exactly what he had to do to sell to the masters and mistresses of Euclid Avenue. Invariably servants answered his knocks. But rather than explain the nature of his call, Martin, who already knew the name of his potential customer, would simply ask, "Would you please tell Mrs. So-and-So that Mr. Davey would like to see her?" Instead of waiting for the servant's response, he would immediately turn his back so that the butler or maid, without thinking, would interpret the request as a command.

The technique worked perfectly with one of Euclid Avenue's grandes dames. Martin was ushered into her parlor, which was decorated with paintings, tapestries, and other exquisite furnishings. Already excited by the material feast before his eyes, his heart began to pound all the faster when a rustling of silk on the staircase announced the appearance of the mistress of the mansion. She listened patiently, leafed through a few pages of *The Tree Doctor,* and then told Martin no. Shaken a bit because her politeness and apparent interest seemed to promise a sale, Martin blurted, "I sold one this afternoon to Mrs. Hanna."

"Mrs. Mark Hanna?" the grande dame asked. "Yes, I will take one," she answered immediately.

He learned quickly. Name-dropping of the prominent was a surefire way of selling.

Gradually the uprooted Kentite grew comfortable in Cleveland. He settled into a rooming house on Euclid Avenue near downtown. It was an old mansion that had seen better days and was presided over by a kindly middle-aged woman who mothered after her ambitious young roomer. One torrid day Martin was suffering from a severe heat rash. The incessant burning and itching drove him to ask his landlady for help. She mixed some cream of tartar and water and told the distressed young man to drink the concoction because it will "thin your blood and cure the heat rash." The effect, whether physical or psychological, was virtually immediate. Within a day, the suffering young man was healed.

Martin had to hustle to sell enough copies of *The Tree Doctor* to meet his expenses. Besides rent, he had to pay carfare to travel about Cleveland, and he had to buy his meals. He allotted himself 35 cents a day for food: 10 cents for breakfast, 10 cents for lunch, and 15 cents for dinner. On Sundays, he would skip breakfast, which allowed him to splurge on dinner. With a quarter to spend he could buy dessert, especially the strawberry shortcake that satisfied his prodigious sweet tooth. To help his budget, he found a place, the Belmont Restaurant on Superior Avenue, which provided unlimited rolls to anyone who spent a dime on dinner. Martin frequently bought the beef stew and enjoyed the endless supply of sweet rolls that accompanied it. He suspected that the Belmont's owner lost money every time he showed up to eat.[9]

His frugality paid off. He was able to save $20, and in the spring of 1901 he and his brother Jim, who had saved the same amount, headed for the Pan-American Exposition in Buffalo, New York.[10] Out of their $40 came boat and train fare, lodging on an uncomfortable bed for fifty cents a night and fifty cents for daily admission to the exposition itself. The Davey boys, from their lean days growing up in Kent, were already masters at stretching their dollars. Rather than buy food at inflated fair prices, they stopped at a grocery store every morning for provisions. Once inside the fairgrounds, they sought out everything that was free, paying only for things they had to.

One special attraction was a roller coaster–like ride called Loop-the-Loop. It rose steeply and then shot down until it looped a full circle before flying onto a side rail, centrifugal force driving riders hard into their seats. The daily admission ticket to the fair entitled visitors to a single Loop-the-Loop ride, but many found it too daunting. The Daveys cadged the "cowards'" tickets and treated themselves for free.

Later in the year, the depraved anarchist Leon Czolgosz fired a fatal shot into President McKinley at this very exposition. The assassination prompted some political rumination from Martin Davey. He respected the fallen president but was a William Jennings Bryan man just as his father had been. John Davey was not blindly Democratic, though. In 1912 he supported Republican

William Howard Taft. Martin, already more partisan than his father, voted for Woodrow Wilson. The political difference between father and son reflected the general division in the Davey family. For years, members were about equally split between Republicans and Democrats.[11]

While Martin tried to make a living selling *The Tree Doctor,* John Davey continued to work the celery farm in Kent and decided that Martin should set up a stall in Cleveland to market the crop. As usual, Martin, seemingly a born salesman, did a good job. The celery sold well, in no small way because Martin sent postcards to all the people who had bought *The Tree Doctor,* informing them that the Daveys were also in the celery business. Martin's latest venture on behalf of his father took him away from book selling during the fall of 1901, but when the season was over he picked up again.

Shortly, however, Martin embarked on a new venture. While selling books and celery in Cleveland, he met a man who worked for the Oliver Typewriter Company. His new acquaintance persuaded Martin to see the manager of the company about a job. Martin, who knew nothing about typewriters, nonetheless agreed to the manager's salary offer of ten dollars a week and a commission.

He learned quickly. He pored over the company's sales pamphlet and broke down its twenty-five-item sales pitch into four areas: keyboard, type bar construction, platen and carriage, and general arguments. With his newly acquired knowledge, he slung an Oliver typewriter over his back and headed to his first appointment. He came back with an order.

The new hire soon outshone his fellow salesmen. They spent too much time at their desks, he noticed. They were there in the morning when Martin reported in and were still there when he returned at the end of the day. Within three months he was outselling everyone else in the office. The manager noticed his bright new star and told him that the older office hands had predicted that the "kid [Martin] can't sell typewriters." Martin, with a determination forged on the streets of Kent selling his father's vegetables and flowers, was only too happy to prove them wrong.

He became the top Oliver salesman even though he operated at a stiff disadvantage. When he hired on at the company, he was told that the price of a typewriter was $97.50, minus a 10 percent discount. The selling price then, or so Martin believed, was $87.75. What he did not know was that the company allowed salesmen to discount the price to $60 to make a sale. Consequently, while Martin was outselling his experienced coworkers, he had to work harder than they did. He well remembered later in life how far toil and perseverance could take a young man.

He learned another lesson at Oliver Typewriter, a hard one. The company hired a new manager, a young, tall, good-looking man whose tyranny soon alienated nearly everyone who worked for him. Among the disaffected was the head of the repair department, who wasted little time persuading an impressionable Martin Davey to his point of view. Absent the discretion that might have come with a few more years, the eighteen-year-old crack salesman openly criticized the office martinet. He in turn fired Martin.

His firing, he claimed, was a "blessing in disguise." His sales record had not passed unnoticed at the Underwood Typewriter Company in Cleveland, and he was quickly hired by the rival firm. It was easier to sell Underwoods, whose single-shift keyboards were much simpler to operate than Oliver's double-shifts. Soon he was making twice as much money, $150 to $200 a month, a princely sum in turn-of-the-century America.

In the meantime, Martin moved, this time to a rooming house a little farther from the heart of town, on 18th Street off Euclid Avenue. The home belonged to a solid, hard-working German family, the Zizelmans. Mrs. Zizelman took a liking to her young lodger and enjoyed telling him how she and her husband started with nothing when they first married but gradually, through industry and persistence, had created a good life in America.

While living with the Zizelmans, Martin met a young man, Robert Bowen, a partner in a men's clothing store in Cleveland. Bowen invited Martin to visit him in his parents' home. The elder Bowens were well-mannered southerners. Mr. Bowen had failed in business and Mrs. Bowen was trying to keep the family afloat by renting their four houses, all of which were heavily mortgaged. In addition, all the Bowen children worked and contributed their wages to a common family pool.

Martin soon moved in. He enjoyed the Bowens' company, particularly that of Mr. Bowen, a gentleman of the old school. One evening, as Martin and Bowen chatted on the front porch, the older man, philosophizing over his financial reverses, passed on a bit of advice that Martin remembered many years later. "Martin," he asked, "would you like to be popular?" Martin responded, "Why certainly." Bowen continued, "If you really want to be popular, pay special attention to the wallflowers. If you pay attention to people who are very popular, they accept it as a matter of course and do not appreciate it; but if you pay attention to folks who are neglected, they will be so grateful they will sing your praises everywhere." The lesson was not lost on the younger man.

Living on his own forced other realities upon Martin Davey. He may have been making good money at Underwood, but he also realized how quickly it could slip away. He had tithed his earnings but soon recognized that while he had expenses to pay, there always seemed to be "plenty of money in the Lord's pocket." Persuaded by his friends at the YMCA that he should go to college, Martin decided that the Lord had enough, so he stopped giving his tenth to the church.

A hankering for nice clothes (maintained for the rest of his life) and the desire to go to college turned the good saver into an even better one. Thrift was easy for someone who had known Davey poverty. He prided himself that, apart from some lean times when he was in college, after the age of ten he was never broke. Discipline forced him always to keep some cash in reserve. One winter during his horseradish route days in Kent, he was down to his last nickel. Every day he would pass the bakery and virtually salivate over the tempting cream puffs displayed in the window, three for a nickel. His sweet tooth nearly won out but the nickel felt too good in his pocket. He marched down from the bakery to the grocery and stared at the oranges that tempted him almost as much as the cream puffs. Once again the nickel in his pocket prevailed over the potential treat in his belly. Hungry but solvent, he moved on.

Martin seemed embarrassed that his childhood poverty may have shaped his views of money and denied that it had. His later remarks on the subject, while praising his mother, by omission criticized his father. In his fifties he wrote that his "mother was a thrifty soul, and if she could have handled the family finances from the beginning, most of the serious difficulties would have been avoided."[12] The remark, if only inferentially, indicted John Davey for not taking better care of his family.

Martin was certain that the propensity to thrift was inborn. So, too, was the tendency toward extravagance. Neither spenders nor savers could stop themselves innately, although perhaps the spendthrifts might one day summon the discipline to curtail their prodigality. Conversely, he believed, some savers might inexplicably become spendthrifts. Between the determined savers and the wanton spenders lay the moderate spenders and savers. They spent money freely, Martin believed, but only if they had plenty of it. He placed himself in this category, and declared that he never wanted money for its own sake. It was important, he admitted, but only as an indication of achievement. He was content to save enough for "security" and, undoubtedly recalling the financial straits of his childhood, "to avoid poverty."

Being stung a few times by deadbeats in Cleveland also helped shape his financial views. One young friend borrowed twenty-five cents from Martin, promising to pay him back in a week. It never happened, and the fellow dropped out of sight for a year. By chance Martin encountered him in the Old Arcade on Euclid Avenue. Now, because he had "gotten religion," the repentant debtor offered to repay his benefactor. Martin was so pleased that his friend had changed his ways that he forgave the debt, although he wondered later if he had done the right thing by letting him off so easily.

Not all Martin's financial dealings ended so positively. A new salesman had been brought into the Oliver Typewriter office. The newcomer, needing cash, wrote a check for $10, which the office manager quickly endorsed. He then asked Martin to take the salesman to the YMCA to cash it. With Martin vouching for the man, the clerk there did so unquestioningly. The check bounced, and, although the office manager said he would force the errant salesman to make it good, he never did and Martin learned another lesson about life. The sheepish salesman afterward kept his distance from Martin.

Cleveland opened Martin's eyes in other ways. Despite his trips through the city's streets selling books and typewriters, he was still a small-town boy. Much of the world remained new to him, and he was amazed at some of the things he witnessed in Cleveland. He was particularly fascinated one evening by a "colored camp meeting" way out on East 105th and Carnegie Avenue. He and some friends decided to go just to see what it was like. They and hundreds of others squeezed into a large tent on an empty lot. The minister prayed while the black congregation rolled on the ground shrieking "Hallelujah" and "Praise de Lawd." "Deah Lawd, bless all dem what's heah tonight," the minister intoned. The choir responded, "Yes, Deah Lawd, no matter why dey comes, give dem what dey want."

The experience, so much unlike his own worship in the sedate Disciples Church back home, fascinated the twenty-year-old Davey. He began thinking about different people and the kinds of religious experiences they needed to fulfill their lives. Some, he believed, needed the emotionalism that he had witnessed at the camp meeting, while others were drawn to solemnity and ritual. Still others, he thought, needed a heavy dose of intellectualism in their faith and could get by with only a modicum of "sentiment and spirituality." All of it was necessary, he concluded, to "maintain the standards of our civilization."

The black camp meeting was not Martin's only "first" experience springing from his stay in Cleveland. While in the city, he also had his first ride in an automobile, a Cadillac. A friend of his knew the manager of the Cadillac dealership in the city, and he and Martin rented one, along with a chauffeur, to impress two young women they had asked to go for a drive. On a Saturday morning, the chauffeur, with all four smiling young people aboard,

The Davey family at home, 1903. John Davey (with beard) stands over Bertha Davey, who is seated in the rocking chair. Paul and James Davey sit on the lawn. Martin Davey, wearing a straw hat, stands on the front porch. Evangeline Davey Smith Collection, Martin L. Davey Papers, Kent State University Libraries, Special Collections and Archives.

drove off. Within an hour, however, the car broke down. Embarrassed and deflated, the two young men took their dates home on a mundane but reliable Cleveland street car.

By 1903, Martin had already spent three years in Cleveland and knew the city well. One of his favorite haunts was Euclid Beach, an amusement park on the Lake Erie shore. That summer he and a dozen friends rented a cottage within easy distance of the park and its prime attraction for ardent swains, a dance hall that drew some of the prettiest young ladies in the area.

Martin had one problem—he had never learned to dance. His church-going parents subscribed fully to their congregation's ban on smoking, card playing, and dancing, and Martin and his siblings had been raised accordingly. But now here he was, nearly twenty years old and, as he himself de-

scribed, with "good vision and warm blood." The young women of Cleveland were very attractive, and he had always liked music and had a "good
sense of rhythm." Fortunately for him, while living with the Bowens he met
a pretty neighbor who volunteered to teach him to dance. He was, he admitted, an "eager student" and soon began to twirl around with the beautiful
belles in the dance pavilion at Euclid Beach.

Certainly Martin could be expected to enjoy the passions and frivolities
of youth, but he never lost his intellectualism. He had a total of an hour's
trolley ride every day to and from work, and to while away the time he read
poetry. When accompanied by a poetry-loving friend, the two would play
a game in which each had to quote a passage from a poem, the first starting
with the letter A, the second with the letter B, and so on.[13]

Martin's mind was sharp, and selling typewriters in Cleveland, lucrative
though it might be, would never satisfy him. All along he wanted to go to
college and had already saved money toward that goal. He chose Oberlin
because of the influence of his high school principal, Frank Elliott, a proud
alumnus of the school and a role model for Martin. Elliott had filled Martin
with all the advantages of an Oberlin education, so Oberlin it was.[14]

Chapter Three

Scholar and Athlete at Oberlin

—————————— ༒ ——————————

MARTIN CONSIDERED ENROLLING in Oberlin for the fall 1903 term. He had a friendly Cleveland lawyer, Mark L. Thomsen, send a testimonial on his behalf to George M. Jones, the college secretary, in mid-March and followed that with an inquiry of his own to Jones. He had wanted to go to college for a number of years after his graduation from high school but had not crystallized his plans. Now, however, after discussing his future with Thomsen and several friends, he was certain about what he wanted to do. After two and a half years of working in Cleveland, he had only $25 in the bank but expected to save as much as $150 by the fall. He would be on his own, he told Jones, because his family could not withstand any additional financial strain, even though Oberlin tuition was only $52 a year. He expected to work during summer vacations for his tuition and wait tables to pay his rent during the school year.[1]

Jones admitted Martin to Oberlin, but by the fall of 1903 the young man had changed his mind. He wrote Jones that although he already had "a nice amount of money saved up," if he worked another year he would have almost enough to pay for his entire education. It was, he said, a "good business proposition" to stay another year in Cleveland.[2]

Jones kept track of Martin. The following spring he asked about the young man's plans for the fall of 1904. Martin was still interested in Oberlin but seemed to have lowered its priority in his life. He was late in submitting his high school records and missed the acceptance deadline. Now he would have to take entrance examinations before he could enroll. Frantic, he wrote

Jones, explaining that Oberlin's notification of the deadline had failed to reach him in time because he had moved. He pleaded, "I am not in condition to take examinations because I have been out of [high school] over four years." He assured Jones that he would forward his high school transcripts immediately and promised that he "would not be a discredit" to Oberlin if allowed to enroll.[3]

Martin had to feel relieved a few days later when Jones informed him that the admissions committee would meet on September 12 to consider late applications. If Davey's record passed muster, he would be admitted without having to take the examinations he so feared.[4]

Martin wasted no time. He had Kent High School forward his records and beat the deadline by several days. His transcript showed why he was one of the top students in his high school graduation class. His grades in English and classics were 99 and 98, respectively. During three years of history, his scores were 97, 99.5, and 98, and in geography 95. He was as good in mathematics and science—98 in algebra, 99 in plane geometry, 99.5 in solid geometry, 98.5 in physics, and 99 in botany. If he had a weakness, it was in Latin. But even here he was a solid student, earning a 93 for the year.[5]

Despite his high grades, Martin was not allowed to enter Oberlin College proper. Because his high school offered only a three-year program, he fell a year short of the Oberlin four-year requirement. He could make up the credits by attending Oberlin Academy, the preparatory school for Oberlin College. After satisfactory performance there, he could be admitted to the college.

The college's decision did not dampen Martin's enthusiasm a bit. Buoyant and exuberant, he arrived at Oberlin in the fall of 1904. He was already twenty, two years older than the typical freshman, and several years older than his peers in the academy, but undaunted he plunged ahead.

When Martin stepped on campus in September 1904, Oberlin College was already more than seventy years old. It was conceived in 1832 by the Reverend John J. Shipherd, a Presbyterian pastor from nearby Elyria, and Philo P. Stewart, a former missionary to the Cherokees of Mississippi. The two men helped clear the thick forest covering the college site some eight miles south of Elyria and thirty-three miles southwest of Cleveland. Remote and rough though the location was, it stood on level ground in the midst of a growing population of former New Englanders. The college was named after John Frederick Oberlin, an eighteenth-century Alsatian minister known for his piety and humanity. The school opened in December 1833 with forty-four students, male and female, from New Hampshire, Vermont, Massachusetts, New York, Pennsylvania, Ohio, and Michigan.[6]

Thanks to the influence of Theodore Dwight Weld, who had helped fo-
ment antislavery radicalism at Lane Seminary in Cincinnati in the 1830s, the
college quickly became a center of abolitionism and the town of Oberlin a
depot on the Underground Railroad. Weld, a fiery speaker and able organizer (he helped found the American Anti-Slavery Society in 1833), aided by
money from New York merchants Arthur and Lewis Tappan and the passionate preaching of the Reverend Charles Grandison Finney, turned Oberlin into an extension of Lane Seminary. The Lane radicals, ousted from their
campus by a conservative board of trustees, merely reorganized at Oberlin.[7]

After the Civil War, antislavery passions at Oberlin understandably cooled,
and the school in the latter part of the nineteenth century returned to its
original purpose—the education, both academic and moral, of its students.
The college had no pretensions: It was an "avowedly Christian" school, a place
where parents "desiring the completest education and the highest development in character would gladly place their children."[8] Sunday church and
daily chapel were mandatory for all students well into the twentieth century.[9]

Henry Churchill King was president of Oberlin when Martin Davey ma-
triculated in 1904. A graduate of Oberlin and Harvard, King succeeded John
Henry Barrows, who had been elected president in 1898 over the protests of
many alumni and friends of the college. Barrows had two serious flaws—he
was "urbane" and a "non-Oberlinian." His detractors were certain that he
would wreck Oberlin on the shoals of "liberal religion and eastern culture."
King, a healthy contrast, was a "religious liberal" but "reassuringly evangeli-
cal in tone and practice." Barrows's unexpected death in 1902 made many
breathe more easily and allowed the ascendancy of the safer King.[10]

Oberlin Academy was a part of Oberlin College but yet distinct from it.
It was officially one of the four departments of the school and had its own
faculty, campus buildings, and students. It began as the Preparatory Department of Oberlin Collegiate Institute but by 1892 had undergone a name
change to Oberlin Academy. The religious strictures that governed the college were equally binding on the academy.[11]

Principal of the academy was John Fisher Peck, a distinguished-looking,
mustachioed man with thinning white hair. His credentials, like his favored
garb—dark suit, crisp white collar and neatly knotted necktie—were impeccable. He was thoroughly Oberlin: AB 1875, AM 1878. He had studied
additionally at the Oberlin Theological Seminary and had taught classics at
the school since 1880.[12] When Martin Davey arrived at the academy, Peck
was in his eleventh year as principal, and it was to Peck that the young man
reported to set his schedule for the fall term.[13]

Martin was taken by Peck. The older man impressed him as "scholarly and dignified" but kind. Davey remembered him as a "great man," loved and respected by all.

Peck's scholarly nature and reserve may have impressed Martin, but he was young, and Oberlin meant more than academics—it was also a place for a good time. He threw himself into the social life of the school. Despite (or perhaps because of) strict rules against dancing, smoking, and drinking, Martin was drawn to "forbidden fruits" that made what might have been an utterly drab Oberlin experience not only bearable but fun. Since administrators viewed traditional fraternities as "works of the devil," some of the young men of Oberlin had organized their own unsanctioned society, ITK, or I Tappa Keg, whose primary purpose as a drinking club was obvious from its playful name. Martin was invited to join and did. He reveled in the secrecy of it all and enjoyed drinking beer right under the noses of the "stern and forbidding" faculty. I Tappa Keg was audacious enough even to hold a few dances, although its members were not sufficiently brazen to do so in town. The dances were all held on safer ground away from Oberlin.

Martin Davey liked defying authority when he thought it existed for its own sake, noting that nothing dire happened to the men of ITK. In fact, many of them became paragons of propriety and success. Years later, two were bank presidents, one was president of a college, another chaired the English department in a large university, while still another was the athletic director at a different university. Included in the triumphant group of former ITKers was Edward Everett Horton, a famous motion picture character actor. His success and that of the others proved to Martin that drinking a little beer in college reflected far less evil than it did the "effervescence of youth."

Smoking was equally taboo for students, and the ban was gleefully enforced by Martin's landlady. Her primary goal in life, or so it seemed, was to protect Martin and her other student roomers from sin, which, according to Davey, meant that all fun was out because "sin was almost anything you enjoyed doing." The landlady was nearly deaf and used an ear trumpet to listen, but, Martin noted, "what a nose she had!" Her olfactory sense was legendary; supposedly she could "smell smoke a mile away."

The boys enjoyed congregating in the room of one of her tenants, an old bachelor who taught in the business college. Because he was an adult, he was exempt from the landlady's ban on smoking. He puffed away freely on his pipe, and his room became a sanctuary for the boys who wanted to smoke theirs. The landlady knew something was amiss when none of her young tenants were in their rooms. Despite her advanced years, she would fly up the stairs hoping to catch a young smoker in the act. Swift though she was, she never apprehended a single miscreant because the boys always had time to duck their pipes before she reached the bachelor's room.

The strait-laced landlady became a frequent topic of conversation for the boys during their off moments. Egged on by the pipe-smoking bachelor, they began to debate if she believed in conjugal intercourse for pleasure or if she believed in it for procreation only. They were about equally divided on the question but were unanimous in one thing—they all felt sorry for her husband, a pitiful wretch who seemed little more than a mere appendage to his wife, never entering or exiting the house other than through the back door.

Interest in the landlady's sexual predilections began to assume a life of its own. The boys could not shake the topic. One day they grew weary of conjecture and decided to find out for certain. Sitting around the room, they drew numbers to see who would point-blank ask the landlady her view. Martin Davey lost, and the indelicate task was his. There was no way out of it—to back off would mean he had welshed on an agreement with his pals. But how to do it was another matter.

Martin took his meals with the landlady, so he thought that breakfast might present an excellent opportunity to ask the question. One morning, after everyone else had left the table, he verbally circled his unsuspecting prey for several moments before he finally struck: "What do you think of recreational intercourse?" Her response surprised him. She never "batted an eye" or even "blushed," Martin remembered, but answered straight out: "The ultimate goal of mankind should be to have no family relation of that kind except for the purpose of having children, but I do not believe that people are ready for that yet." Martin reported his findings that night to his comrades who had eagerly gathered in the bachelor's room to hear the result. They were surprised that their puritanical landlady shared their sexual views.[14]

The conflict between what the young men of Oberlin (and even their misperceived landlady) believed about sex and the college's official view demonstrated that Victorian morality was already being challenged while the British sovereign who lent her name to the age was barely moldering in her grave. The post-Victorian age may have begun for young Americans and sexually liberated landladies, but not for Oberlin College officials. They maintained stiff rules governing activities and behavior between the men and women of Oberlin. During the fall and winter terms, female students had to be in their residences by 7 P.M., and then in the spring (presumably because of longer daylight hours), they could remain out until 7:30. Young women were not even permitted to walk with men in the evening and, regardless of the time of year, had to be in bed, quiet and with lights out, by ten. Males would be expelled if they visited females in their rooms or had females visit them in theirs. Oberlin officials did make one concession to mercy—if students were seriously ill and confined to their rooms, they could have visitors of the opposite sex. But heaven help any young lovers who married—they immediately forfeited the "privileges of the institution," which, of course, meant expulsion.[15]

Martin Davey chafed at these restraints. Oberlin was like "living in a strait jacket," he complained. But he seemed to understand that Oberlin officials were simply conforming to the norms in the proper homes from which the sons and daughters of the college originated. Even so, he could not help but think that their "rightful liberties were being taken from them," and the denial of reasonable liberties might retard the "development of personality, initiative and poise."

But there were ways around rules, and no one is more ingenious in discovering those passages to freedom than college students, no matter their generation. An Oberlin coed could stay out until 9 P.M. every night if she were engaged and in the company of her future husband. Martin suspected that many Oberlin engagements were never intended to last longer than a school term or two.

There was yet another way around the rules for women: Extracurricular and social events in the evening provided them freedom until nine if they got permission to go. Oberlin's must have been a busy extracurricular scene, although Martin admitted that many students who announced their intentions to attend every school affair never went to any. The flouting of the rules did not bother him a bit. If anything, it demonstrated "the folly of trying to suppress . . . the spirit of youth."

Martin Davey practiced what he preached. He and a friend had arranged to escort two Oberlin women to a school function. That, of course, was not the couples' true intent. They simply wanted a chance to be together, and it mattered not at all that despite the winter season the two young men suggested a stroll in the countryside. The four set out, enjoying their walk until it began to snow. The weather worsened but, as Martin remembered, it was worth trekking through a snow storm "just to get away from that silly seven o'clock rule." But not even the exuberance and stubbornness of youth were enough to compel the four to continue. They turned around and headed back to Oberlin. However, the girls could not return to their boarding houses because they supposedly were at a school function until nine, and it was quite shy of that. Four shivering young people holed up in the outside doorway of a college hall, freezing and prattling but all the while pretending they "were having a good time."

The dreariness of a formal Oberlin affair in the early 1900s was enough to make any warm-blooded American youth choose chattering teeth and frozen toes over unbearable tedium. By custom, every year on George Washington's birthday, the college faculty held a grand reception. The male students donned their best suits and the females wore their finest dresses and, if their dates could afford them, corsages. The professors looked equally dignified as they lined up to greet each student. Both sides wore plastic smiles and "white lied" about how happy each was to be there. The strained dignity of it all made Martin hate it, but he accepted the phony cordiality and long reception line because "there was nothing else to do."

Martin's contempt for the forced formality of the stuffy faculty reception did not extend to contempt for the faculty themselves. He respected their intellectualism and dedication, but he could not help but feel sorry for them for having to endure the "strained atmosphere" that separated Oberlin from the real world. He particularly lamented that the professors tried to impress their artificiality upon young people who needed to live in a "world of human beings."

The faculty reception provided an opportunity for male and female students to gather earlier in the day to socialize. After taking a walk on a pleasant February afternoon, Martin suggested that the five or six other couples with him adjourn to his rooming house to chat. All agreed and soon were sitting around the piano in the living room. One young woman began to play a waltz. Despite Oberlin's proscription against dancing, the rugs were soon turned back and all, except the piano player and her date, began to circle the floor, some of them "affectionately" close to one another. Martin's landlady, who had been sitting nervously in the doorway watching it all, could stand no more. She leaped from her chair and ended the revelry with a yell—"No more round-dancing . . . , no more round-dancing!"

Unfortunately for the "malefactors," word of their transgression reached the dean of academy girls. The boys, lucky to be judged by a different standard, were free and clear, but the girls faced possible expulsion. The inequity of it all prompted Martin to supplicate the dean. Putting on his gravest penitential face, Martin appealed to the dean's sense of fairness, insisting that the boys had instigated the episode and should be punished equally. But, he pleaded, the entire incident was innocent, merely a "natural response of human nature to lovely music when boys and girls were together."

Martin's eloquence worked. The dean, after two or three days of consultation with faculty members, said no one would be punished except for two notorious female scofflaws who lost some privileges for a time but avoided expulsion.

Martin the persuader preferred mixed company in groups and was uncomfortable when one on one with a girl in a relationship that was unrequitedly serious. He was seeing a coed who was already thinking of marriage, something quite distant from his mind. He had already visited her parents in Cleveland, and they had openly approved of their daughter's choice, which made Martin all the more uneasy. His discomfort increased during an evening walk around the campus when the young woman could not stop her romantic gushing. He tried to change the subject: "Isn't it funny [that] they built this college on such flat ground?" he asked, hoping that the conversation might take another tack. But his ardent companion would have none of it. She sighed and answered, "Oh, Martin, that isn't what I want you to talk about!" Knowing what she wanted to discuss but feigning ignorance, he responded, "What shall I talk about?" In the universal language of young lovers, she replied, "Oh, Martin, you know!"

Martin preferred being the pursuer, not the pursued. Three years later, when he was gone from Oberlin and tending to Davey tree surgery affairs in the East, he encountered his old flame who was now attending boarding school. Martin had already married and the young woman was about to. Even though their paths had parted (certainly Martin believed for the better), she could not stop from reminding her old beau what he had missed. Her well-to-do father, she said, was building a home for her and her intended and was welcoming him into the family business. She could not resist a final jab—"Now, Martin, aren't you sorry?"

Martin was too busy with other things to become seriously involved with anyone during his Oberlin days. For one, he had to work because his savings were not enough to sustain him at school. He fell back on the familiar, selling *The Tree Doctor* in Oberlin and nearby Lorain and Elyria. But even that was insufficient. Through his Cleveland clothier friend Bob Bowen, he sold neckties and other men's clothing to his fellow students and ran a laundry route for a Cleveland cleaning company. In many ways it was like his boyhood in Kent all over again, constant hustling just to stay intact. And, also like his Kent experiences, it was never enough. He frequently borrowed small sums from friends who were only too willing to help.[16]

Summers were no different than the school year. Home for vacation that first year, Martin sold life insurance for Northwestern Mutual and did well. He believed in the product, calling it one of the "greatest institutions" of [his]

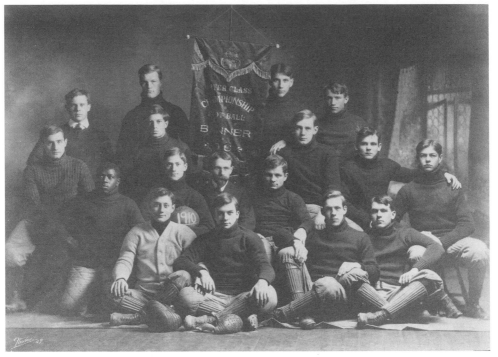

The Oberlin football team in 1906 (graduating class of 1910). Martin Davey stands out in a light sweater. Evangeline Davey Smith Collection, Martin L. Davey Papers, Kent State University Libraries, Special Collections and Archives.

time. He became one of the industry's most zealous spokesmen, later enthusiastically writing a pamphlet titled, *Why I Carry $1,000,000 Life Insurance.*[17]

He returned to Oberlin in the fall of 1905 and joined the academy football team. He knew very little about the sport but was young, healthy, and eager and was encouraged by an I Tappa Keg friend who helped coach the team. What Martin lacked in experience, he compensated for with "energy, endurance, and a willingness to obey orders." He started out as a scrub, scrimmaging against the first team offense, but soon caught the eye of coaches after hurling himself through the line time after time to break up plays. His abandon won a promotion; he moved from defensive scrub to starting left halfback in time for the opening game against Cleveland West High School. The academy won 11–0 before four hundred cheering fans, and the student newspaper noted that Davey made some "good bucks into the line."[18]

The next week the academy team traveled to Cleveland to play East High School and lost 34–0. Martin and his teammates were overmatched. The Oberlin athletes were fast, but their speed could not offset East High's twenty-pounds-per-man weight advantage. Martin and the star of the team, right halfback George Vradenburg, flew all over the field tackling East ball carriers as they broke into the Oberlin secondary. The best they could do was hold down the score so the game was a rout instead of a massacre.

The train carrying the bruised and beaten Oberlin warriors steamed into the hometown depot at 8:25 that night. A crowd had gathered and cheered each hero as he stepped from the train. No player lifted his own suitcase that October night. Appreciative fans carried first the team's luggage and then team members on their shoulders and hoisted them to a hay wagon for a triumphant return to campus.[19]

Martin's reputation was made a few weeks later in the game against Cleveland's University School. Amid cries of "Zis, boom, bah. Zis, boom, bah. Rah, Rah, Academy Rah," he took the opening kickoff and returned it fifteen yards to open the Oberlin offense. But it was on defense that he shone. Late in the game a University School runner broke free for what looked like a certain touchdown. Martin chased him down and stopped him short of the goal line with a desperate flying tackle to preserve a 0–0 tie. Many years later Martin would remember the play and nostalgically bask in a hero's glory.[20]

For the first time in his life, Martin developed more than just a nodding relationship with an African American, a scrub player on the academy team. He was not good enough to play regularly but impressed Martin with his desire and spirited practice. During one scrimmage, he tackled Martin so hard that Davey felt like he was hit with a "ton of lead" and suffered from a "charley horse" the rest of the season. He was "gonna show folks," he told Martin, who encouraged him, thinking that the young man's grit portended success one day.

Martin had no shortage of determination himself on the playing fields of Oberlin. In his freshman year of college he made the football squad and when the season ended joined the Oberlin basketball team as well. That spring he ran track, concentrating on the half-mile. He was good but in a race against a star sophomore he mistakenly thought the shot from a starter's gun signaled the end of the race. He pulled up thinking the contest was over, allowing his opponent, a half-lap behind, to overtake him. It was, he remembered, a "terrible disappointment."

Although interested in athletics, Martin knew that they were not his raison d'être at Oberlin. He appreciated Oberlin for its academics and distinguished record of public service of its graduates. He was particularly proud of the college's Conservatory of Music, already known as one of the best in the country.

His interest in the conservatory was not surprising. Even as a child he enjoyed music and wanted to take piano lessons when he was ten or twelve but never could because he had no piano and could not afford the lessons anyway. At Oberlin he attended as many musical events as possible, including a harpist's performance that dazzled him. In the middle of her playing, the auditorium lights went out, but she continued in the dark, her gifted fingers missing not a single note. It was "inspiring," Martin recalled, a moment of "high drama."

He enjoyed singing, too, although he was not very good. One day he and the leading tenor of the college glee club walked through campus and Martin started to sing away. The tenor stopped dead in his tracks and said: "You sing flat." His blunt assessment hurt Martin, who had no idea his voice so offended a trained ear. Ever afterward, he never publicly sang alone, although he would happily join in with groups where his vocal shortcomings went unnoticed.

The religious life at Oberlin impressed him least. He could live with Oberlin's compulsory church attendance rule because he had always gone anyway. Not even the professors who counted heads and reported absences upset him, but he disliked the sermons because they were not very spiritual or inspiring. To the young man they were more like "dignified lectures on religious or semi-religious subjects."

Although still young, he had already developed a keen understanding of human greatness and sensed that the professors of Oberlin were men of rare intellect and spirituality. The most distinguished of them all was Oberlin's president, Dr. Henry Churchill King. Martin never missed a chance to hear King speak and always felt "lifted up" afterward.

Martin became a campus bellwether, along with his football teammate George Vradenburg and another friend, Platt Tracy. With Vradenburg as class president, Tracy as treasurer, and Martin as entertainment committee chairman, the academy class of 1906 enjoyed a busy social season, doing everything that was "permitted under the rules."[21]

The two years at the Academy and Oberlin College proper flew by, and in the summer of 1906, Martin returned to Kent to help his father's tree surgery business. *The Tree Doctor*'s influence surprised even John Davey. He and his sons, he thought, could handle any business that the book generated. He was wrong. The book caught on, and the demand for John Davey's expertise and services spread from Ohio into Pennsylvania, New York, Washington, D.C., and even Toronto and Ottawa. In response to the demand, John Davey and his son Wellington created the Davey School of Practical Forestry to train men to perform the surgical techniques the elder Davey had perfected. Even so, there was so much business—particularly in Cleveland, Pittsburgh, and New York's Hudson Valley—that John and Wellington, aided by Jim, could not keep up with it all.[22]

Martin was sent to New York where John Davey had already made business connections through Julius French of Cleveland, the head of the Railway Steel Springs Company. The young man, who had only once before been out of northeastern Ohio, boarded a Pennsylvania Railroad train and headed east through Pennsylvania and into New Jersey, stopping on the western side of the Hudson. He ferried across to America's largest city, awestruck by its majestic skyline. Not yet twenty-two, he wondered what New York held in store for him.[23]

John Davey had not capriciously sent his son east. Through his lectures he had met J. Horace McFarland of Harrisburg, Pennsylvania, a successful printer and president of the American Civic Association. McFarland arranged a lecture tour for Davey, part of which took him to Massachusetts in 1904. Some students from the Massachusetts Agricultural College heard John Davey and hired on to work for him as his business expanded eastward. As the Davey name spread, John met W. B. Dickerman, a broker who owned an estate outside New Rochelle just north of New York City. By 1906, John Davey was performing impressive tree work for Dickerman, thereby opening the New York market and necessitating an urgent call for help to Martin.[24]

The young man so recently of Oberlin knew very little about his father's work. He had been away at school for two years, and in his absence Wellington and Jim had joined John Davey's business. Wellington, with his mechanical ability, was a great asset to his father, while Jim, a hard worker, compensated for his lack of technical skills with a sense of humor that lightened everyone's toil.

Wellington and Jim may have had a head start on Martin, but the latter wasted no time catching up on the family business. Doing so was comparatively easy. He might not have had formal training in tree surgery, but none of John Davey's sons could have grown up without absorbing everything there was to know from a man who ate, drank, and breathed trees almost all his life. Martin had also read *The Tree Doctor* several times and after three days of cramming was ready to do in New York what he had already done on the streets of Kent, Cleveland, and even Oberlin—sell.

New Yorkers were a mystery to him. He knew nothing about them and their city and felt "strange" and "untried." But he concluded that human nature was the same everywhere, and if he worked hard he would succeed.

His biggest problem was not a lack of familiarity with new people and a new environment; rather it was simply getting around in his vast new sales territory. As usual, money was short, so he walked ten, fifteen, even twenty miles a day seeking clients willing to pay for John Davey's new science, tree surgery. Even though he was young and strong, it was an ordeal; only nightfall stopped him from his rounds.

Lost time, not weariness, got him finally to rent a horse and buggy. His new transportation gave him the mobility to push farther from New York, out to Long Island's Orienta Point where several estates held the promise of rich contracts for Davey tree surgeons. One of those estates on Long Island Sound belonged to Henry M. Flagler, one of John D. Rockefeller's chief partners in the Standard Oil Company and a railroad magnate in his own right. In the 1880s and '90s Flagler extended the Florida East Coast Railway into Miami, then little more than a backwater village abutting the Everglades. He built the Royal Palm Hotel in Miami, the Royal Poinciana in nearby Palm Beach, and almost single-handedly established South Florida as a mecca for winter weary northerners and love-struck honeymooners. Now in his seventies, Flagler lived with his young wife on a sprawling estate at the end of Orienta Point.

Henry M. Flagler became Martin Davey's target. Riding out to the point, Martin introduced himself to the superintendent of grounds, hoping that he would be a conduit to Flagler. The man scarcely listened to Martin's sales pitch, determined more than anything else to keep the young salesman from Flagler.

The superintendent's curtness only strengthened Martin's resolve. After being dismissed, he loitered around talking to some other hired hands, inquiring about Flagler's habits and daily schedule. A few days later, Martin drove his carriage onto the Flagler grounds, rode directly past the superintendent's home, hitched his horse, and strode toward the front porch of the main house where the distinguished, silver-haired Flagler sat with his wife. Acting as if he did not know that the master of the estate was sitting right there, Martin tipped his hat and asked for "Mr. Flagler." The young woman answered, "What do you wish to see [him] about?" "Some of [his] trees which are in serious condition." The two on the porch tilted their heads and whispered a bit before the young woman spoke again. "I'm sorry but Mr. Flagler is a little tired this evening, but he might see you some other time." That was Martin's opening. He set an appointment for nine the following Saturday morning.

Martin arrived early on Saturday and, to avoid being too eager or con-spicuous, whiled away the time examining some of Flagler's trees. An old elm near the front porch of the main house caught his eye. It was a beautiful tree but Martin could see that it had weak branches that had already split the trunk from top to bottom, threatening the front porch.

Martin circled round and round the tree pretending to observe but re-ally killing time until his nine o'clock appointment. Nine came. No Flagler. Nine-fifteen and then nine-thirty. Still no Flagler. Martin's mind raced. Was the lord of the manor preoccupied with important guests? Had some other appointment superseded his? Or had Flagler simply forgotten about his meeting with the eager young salesman?

At 9:45 Flagler strolled out. A relieved Martin Davey handed him a letter of introduction from the New York broker Dickerman. Flagler glanced at the signature and said, "What is on your mind?"

Martin led the millionaire to his split elm but rather than dwell on its condition or what Davey tree men could do to heal it, he wangled Flagler into placing a monetary value on it. After Flagler said he would not sell it even for $5,000, Martin shifted gears and stressed how the tree with its split trunk menaced the front porch and anyone who sat there. Now, with Flagler at rapt attention, Martin explained how Davey tree experts could save the stately elm. Interested but impatient, Flagler snapped, "What next?"

For the next several minutes the subordinate became the master and the master the subordinate. Martin led Flagler to a number of trees, pointing out problems that should be addressed. The millionaire needed little per-suasion. He asked Martin what he would charge and how soon his workmen could start. The Davey crew in the East was almost out of work, but Martin did not want to let on how desperate he and they were. "I have a squad finishing today," he answered truthfully. "I can have them here Monday." He then promised to have some men over that very afternoon to secure the elm, which, he showed Flagler, was in immediate peril.[25]

Martin said good-bye but not before getting Flagler to agree to meet with him while the Davey crew worked the estate. The young man was outwardly matter-of-fact but inwardly thrilled. He had just closed the single biggest deal in the brief history of the Davey tree business, and the arrangement came at a time when precious little other work was in the offing.[26] More-over, twenty-two-year-old Martin Davey had manipulated a magnate fifty years older into parting with money for a project that he had never consid-ered before meeting an earnest young salesman from Kent.

The Flagler contract led to other jobs around New York and in the Hudson Valley. Among the new Davey clients were William Rockefeller, brother of John D., and Emil Berolzheimer, head of the Eagle Pencil Company. There was enough work to keep Davey crews busy until cold weather, which typically ended the season anyway. After a remarkable summer and with $1,500 in his pocket (his share of the profits), Martin Davey prepared to return to Oberlin.[27]

Even though he had made a lot of money, he never considered quitting college before he earned his degree. An education, particularly an Oberlin one, was crucial to him, and he returned to campus for the fall 1906 term determined to get even more out of his schooling than ever before.

Oberlin had changed him—the transformation was much more than that of boy to man. The people there had accepted him for what he was, an earnest, hard-working convivial fellow, and their kindness soothed the psychological wounds that he had suffered growing up in poverty in Kent, the son of the town eccentric. Oberlin "broadened [his] conception of life" and convinced him that the "world would give [him] a chance if he would do his part." Thanks to Oberlin, his vision and hopes were now greater than ever.[28]

Chapter 4

A Business Is Born

———————————— ✺ ————————————

JOHN DAVEY HAD kept busy while Martin was at Oberlin. His devotion to trees was boundless and his intellect perpetually restless. Within three years of the appearance of *The Tree Doctor,* he published another book, *Davey's Primer on Trees and Birds,* which tried to get people to pay more attention to their arboreal environments. Reforestation, he declared, must be the great industry of the future, and the best way of ensuring that was through the education of children. They were the world's promise, and he solemnly dedicated *Davey's Primer* to them.[1] "There is but one hope," he proclaimed. "We must educate the child. Teach the child and *one* generation will remedy our tree troubles." He deliberately wrote the *Primer* in language that children would understand and kept the price at fifty cents, half the cost of *The Tree Doctor,* to make it affordable.[2]

The new book represented John Davey at his wistful best. Certainly it contained useful information about birds and trees, but it also revealed Davey's deep philosophical and religious nature. On Christmas Day 1913, he inscribed a copy to a friend:

From every tree and plant and flower
We learn of Wisdom, skill and power.
And from the starry host above
We hear the voice that, "God is love."[3]

The book so pleased him that he sent one to King Edward VII, sovereign of his native England, and proudly saved His Majesty's reply from Buckingham Palace for all to see.[4]

John Davey had also taken to the lecture circuit, where he had become a minor celebrity. After years of ridicule, people were now listening to him. His new respectability was sweet vindication, although he never gloated, perhaps because he always knew that it was just a matter of time until the world caught up with him. It meant nothing that he and other visionaries were often called "crazy"; he drew strength from the seeming insult and considered it a compliment.[5] But gone now was the scoffing that earlier accompanied his incessant pleas to save the trees. Ridicule had given way to a growing acceptance of the idea that it was not necessarily part of nature's scheme that trees should die.

He enjoyed lecturing. It not only gave him a chance to promote his ideas about conservation and the environment but also allowed him to show off his hard-earned mastery of the English language. He spoke well; his vanity would permit nothing less. Primly clad in his customary Prince Albert coat and with his goatee and mustache full but neatly trimmed, the slender Davey would mount the speaker's dais and, in a rich baritone voice and with perfect diction, hold forth on his favorite subject, trees. Stereopticon slides illustrated his talks and helped captivate audiences in Philadelphia, New York, at Cornell University, and all along the East Coast. His celebrity was assured when he sat for eleven portraits at the New York studio of Davis & Eickemeyer, one of the premier American photographic firms.[6]

Some of his success was due, too, to good fortune. His ideas, so frequently scorned by the common people of Kent, resonated favorably with the higher classes elsewhere. First Charles C. Goodrich, the rubber entrepreneur in Akron, and then eastern businessmen J. Horace McFarland and W. B. Dickerman had taken to Davey and introduced him to their wealthy friends and associates.[7]

The effect of it all was more tree surgery business than the three Daveys, John, Wellington, and Jim, could handle and necessitated an urgent call to Martin for help in 1907. Martin had already completed most of his freshman year at Oberlin College and was home for Easter vacation when his father virtually begged him to drop out until the fall term to help the growing family business. Nothing was farther from Martin's mind. He liked Oberlin and wanted a degree, but he could not ignore his father's desperate plea for help and the offer of a full partnership in the business. As further inducement,

John Davey, ca. 1910. Evangeline Davey Smith Collection, Martin L. Davey Papers, Kent State University Libraries, Special Collections and Archives.

John Davey promised his son that he could manage the eastern trade "according to his own judgment."

The proposition proved too tempting, and Martin returned to Oberlin to gather his belongings, believing that he would return in the fall. He bade a sad farewell to friends and some members of the faculty and prepared to get on with the family business, which, he acknowledged many years later, had to take precedence in his affairs. He was already twenty-three, and it was time to get on with his life.[8]

John sent him first to Tarrytown, about ten miles north of New York City, where he established an office in an old rented house on Broadway and Main.[9] The location was a good one, leaving Martin centrally located among Davey prospects in New York, on Long Island and up the Hudson valley. The National Bank in Tarrytown extended him some early credit, and he was in business.

He was quickly jolted to reality. The $1,500 he had earned so readily the year before selling Davey services to Henry M. Flagler, William Rockefeller, Emil Berolzheimer, and other New York millionaires was misleading. The Davey Tree business, still in its infancy, was already more than $25,000 in debt. That huge obligation was of no concern to Martin when he was a mere employee selling company services, but it was a matter of serious and inescapable concern now that he was a full Davey partner.

Just as he had done with the millionaires of Orienta Point, he began to employ his proven sales techniques. One of his first contacts was with John D. Archbold, president of the Standard Oil Company. Rather than simply dash off to the Archbold estate to inquire if its owner needed any Davey Tree services, Martin reconnoitered first. He struck up friendly conversations with Archbold's gardener and other servants, inquiring about the personal habits and routines of their employer and his wife. Mrs. Archbold, he found, had free reign over the estate. Whatever she wanted done was done, and it did not take Martin Davey long to realize that the route to Mr. Archbold's checkbook ran directly through Mrs. Archbold.

Martin learned that Mrs. Archbold enjoyed sitting on her front porch daily from ten until noon, sunning herself while she read, sewed, or chatted with friends. He also learned that Mr. Archbold customarily spent Saturday mornings overseeing his estate and Saturday afternoons driving his prized team of horses. No smattering of knowledge was insignificant to the eager young salesman, now a partner in a business that needed the patronage of the John Archbolds of the world to survive.

Knowing Mrs. Archbold's morning regimen, Martin deliberately chose an especially sunny day to visit the mansion. He immediately recognized Mrs. Archbold on the porch but feigned ignorance. He approached, tipped his hat, and asked, "Is this Mrs. Archbold?" "Yes, what can I do for you?" That was all the opening Martin needed. Standing on the steps, with his hat in his hand, he one by one pointed out problems with the trees within their view and, of course, explained how Davey tree surgeons could make everything right.

Martin's easy patter relaxed Mrs. Archbold. She invited him to sit with her on the porch and conversed pleasantly for several minutes. Before her tone hinted that she had had enough talking, she promised Martin that she would discuss his proposition with her husband, and he would decide yes or no. That satisfied Martin. He left the estate, confident that he had made a sale.

He was right. Two days later, John Archbold wrote him from New York: "You may proceed with this work to the extent of $300, as a test of its efficacy."

Archbold's epistolary approval was not enough for Martin. He wanted to meet his new client and consequently deliberately started the work on a Thursday so that some of it but not all would be completed when Archbold made his usual Saturday morning rounds. He appeared around nine, providing Martin, who was supervising the crew, with an opportunity to strike up a businesslike yet friendly conversation. Archbold's warmth and courteousness impressed Martin. Despite their different stations, Archbold never assumed the role of haughty master, and Martin remembered him as "one of the biggest men of his time."[10]

Archbold's friendliness was sincere. He steered other business to the young salesman, including that of John D. Rockefeller, whose magnificent estate reposed at nearby Pocantico Hills. Martin did not deal directly with the storied founder of the Standard Oil Company himself but worked through his amiable son, John D. Rockefeller Jr., who ran the estate for his father. The dignity and gentility of the Archbolds and Rockefellers impressed Martin and convinced him that too often America's movers and shakers were maligned simply because their innovations disrupted the status quo.[11]

There were shysters among America's industrial giants, he conceded, but most could not have risen to their lofty stations if they were not essentially good. Not "perfect," he concluded, but "good." They had to have "ability, fortitude, and perseverance" and make great sacrifices for their success. And, undoubtedly projecting himself into the mix a bit, he asserted that most of them came from the "ranks of the lowly" and had to "fight their way to the top" and got there through "hard work, worry and courage."

Martin Davey needed a fair number of those attributes just to maintain the Tarrytown office. He was salesman, sales manager, bookkeeper, billing and payroll clerk, and accountant all at the same time. He also dispensed tools and other materials to the tree-working crews and trained them as well. In those early days there was no one else to fall back on. Martin had to do everything, and he had to "do it right or not at all."

His supervisory and sales responsibilities demanded mobility. To get about, he bought a used Maxwell automobile for $700. He did not have the money, so he borrowed it, feeling justified because now he could triple or quadruple his productivity. But he was not all work and no play. The second-hand Maxwell provided some opportunity for "social enjoyment" after work.

The two-cylinder car reminded him of a horse-drawn carriage. Its seat, roof, and side curtains were nearly identical to those of an old-fashioned buggy. The car had to be hand-cranked to start, and it was lighted by four oil lamps whose illumination was so feeble that night driving was more peril than pleasure. It was noisy, broke down frequently and kept Martin poor paying for repairs. But even so, there was a camaraderie among motorists during those days when horse-drawn carriages still outnumbered horseless ones many times over.

Martin and other Davey crew members rented rooms in an old boarding house known locally as the Mott House. Three stories high and with a sweeping veranda, it was grand in its day but had fallen on hard times and badly needed a coat of paint. The landlords, a decent but tight-fisted couple, prepared meals for the Davey crew and a few other boarders, primarily school teachers, businessmen, and retirees. The landlords' penury manifested itself in the meals they provided. Their menu never varied from week to week— what they served on one Monday they also served the next. Saturday was hamburger night; the only choice was with or without onions. The penny-pinchers were also contracted to pack lunches for the tree crews to take into the field, but they provided slim fare until the workers finally revolted and received the meals they paid for.

By late summer, Davey affairs were running smoothly in the East. The crews' schedules were set for weeks to come, and Martin felt comfortable enough to return to Kent for a week or so. He had more than a brief vacation in mind; a pretty young woman back home had caught his eye, and, although matrimony was not directly on his mind, it was not the farthest thing from it, either.

His romantic interest was Berenice Chrisman, the daughter of a local physician. Martin had known her since her family moved to Kent in 1898 when he was fourteen and she eleven. The two had met while ice skating on the river. Martin spied Berenice struggling with her skates and rushed over to help. Despite the differences in their ages, he could not help but notice how pretty the eleven-year-old was. Already an accomplished skater, Martin gladly offered his services as instructor. He learned where she lived, and, although she was too young to date, Martin found excuses to call on the

Chrismans whenever he could. It was no accident, too, that Berenice's house became one of the regular stops on his horseradish and vegetable route.

By the time Martin was working in Cleveland, Berenice, now a teenager, was old enough so that Martin could at least come calling on weekends and holidays. The couple, often in the company of friends, enjoyed hiring a horse and carriage for long rides in the countryside. They would stop at a hospitable-looking farmhouse and pay for feed for the horse and supper for themselves. Martin enjoyed the rides, noting that a "horse and buggy [were] better than automobiles at this stage in life." A young man could operate a car with one arm, leaving the other to slip around his sweetheart, but he could manage a carriage with no hands, letting the horse follow its instincts home, thereby freeing both arms for romancing during the ride.

Certainly Berenice was not the only girl in Martin's life. The world was full of young charmers, and he had met a fair share of them in Cleveland and Oberlin. But he could not forget his pretty girlfriend back home. She was now twenty and an honor student at Buchtel College (now Akron University), having completed her sophomore year. After a year-long courtship, she and Martin married on August 31, 1907.

Because of business demands, there was little time for a honeymoon. The newlyweds spent a day at Niagara Falls and then took a train to Albany, New York, and leisurely boated down the Hudson River the next day. From there it was a quick return to Tarrytown and back to work.

Martin and Berenice rented rooms in a home next to the Mott House and, because of convenience and not the reputation of the cuisine, boarded with Martin's old landlords. The newlyweds befriended another young married pair, the Spencers—she from Mississippi and he the son of the rector of the Tarrytown Episcopal Church. The four shared the common interests of young couples and spent many happy evenings together.

Business in the East had dropped off a bit in the two weeks Martin was gone, and the old Maxwell had broken down again. The latter problem was solved with a mechanic's repairs, but the former needed Martin's personal attention. He hustled new business and kept all his crews working until cold weather ended the season and then returned with Berenice to Kent to wait out the winter.

The seasonal nature of tree work was troublesome. No sooner had the Daveys assembled and trained competent crews than the tree-surgery season was over. Work was reasonably secure from mid-March to mid-November, but after that the men faced four months without wages. Very few could afford that, and attrition from season to season was high.

To combat the problem, Martin returned to Tarrytown in late winter, hoping to have several orders in place so that his crews could start working at the earliest possible moment. By the spring of 1908, he was joined by three other hardworking salesmen, including his brother Jim. Their efforts paid immediate dividends. That year Davey crews worked up the Hudson Valley as far north as Poughkeepsie and spilled over into western Connecticut and New Jersey.[12] The business, although still burdened by debt, began to take off.

The Davey Tree company had outgrown its founder's seat-of-the-pants operational style. It was now a business and not just one man's avocation. John Davey's dream had materialized and had to be organized and run like any other business. No one was better suited to the task than Martin L. Davey.

First, he recognized the need to formalize the scientific education of Davey field crews. They had to know botany, plant pathology, and entomology. Only then would they truly be professional tree surgeons. To this end, in 1908, Martin established the Davey Institute of Tree Surgery in Kent. The first class of twenty was admitted on December 1, 1908, and received three months of solid scientific training before advancing to fieldwork on March 1, 1909. With their new instruction, Davey tree "doctors" were not only "physicians" healing living organisms but, from their prior training, "engineers, millwrights, mechanics, and architects."[13]

Admission to the institute was not easy. By the 1920s, only two or three men out of a hundred passed the company's initial screening and training regimen. The educational facet of Davey preparation now included three years of training (four months each year) with an expanded curriculum of dendrology, soils, the feeding of trees, spraying and fruit growing, and the theory and practice of tree surgery. Students also took courses in accounting, business English, and business ethics. The institute maintained its own laboratory, library, and a faculty with college and university backgrounds.[14]

Physical training was equally important, for "tree skinning," a term coined by Jim Davey, required considerable strength and agility. The men, without climbing spurs (forbidden by John Davey because of the damage they did to trunks), frequently shinnied up trees eighty feet and higher and then, moored only by safety tethers, climbed out onto limbs, saws and other gear in hand, to do their work. The athletic program helped create a collegiate atmosphere at the institute and an esprit de corps that melded men and company into one.[15]

Integrity and customer satisfaction were the bedrocks of the company. It promised both and expected to be held to its lofty standards. Moreover, clients were not forgotten once the work was done and their bills paid. The

Davey tree surgeons in the 1920s practicing at the Davey Institute of Tree Surgery, Kent, Ohio. Evangeline Davey Smith Collection, Martin L. Davey Papers, Kent State University Libraries, Special Collections and Archives.

company invited them to have inspectors return to assess the work of Davey crews. Davey Tree was never satisfied until its customers were.[16]

To ensure the highest possible performance, workers were held to a strict code of conduct. They were expected to be punctual and neat to maintain the "dignity of the profession." The men were forbidden to smoke or drink during working hours. Violators were fired. Profanity was taboo, as was "boisterous conduct." Employees were expected to be "gentlemen at all times."[17]

Rules were even stricter for foremen. They were bound by all the strictures applied to laborers and then some. Foremen were held personally accountable for any property damage done by Davey crews. They had to fire those who violated the company bans on smoking and drinking and were responsible for the safety of their crews and the daily and weekly reports that had to be submitted to company headquarters in Kent. They were expected to turn out perfect work, please the patrons, keep the men happy, find new clients, and do all of it as "economically, promptly, and efficiently" as possible.

The company cared about the safety of its workers. The men were told "don't take chances." When any man climbed a tree, he had to secure himself with a rope before commencing work. Tree skinners were urged to take their time because haste often resulted in "bruised bodies and broken bones" and lost wages of $2 a day.[18]

By 1909, the company clearly was no longer the simple family enterprise envisioned by John Davey. It now employed dozens of workers and had spread southward into Louisiana, South Carolina, and Alabama. With southern expansion, tree work was no longer entirely seasonal. It took a while for the South to become profitable, but Davey crews could now be reasonably certain of year-long employment. Given this rapid maturation, the company incorporated on February 4, 1909, as the Davey Tree Expert Company, with capital stock of $50,000 divided into five hundred shares worth $100 each. The original shareholders were John Davey and his children, Belle, Martin, Jim, and Paul. Wellington, who had (with the family's blessing) started his own tree surgery business in Pittsburgh, Cleveland, and Michigan, was not an original shareholder, although by 1910 he became one. John Davey, never much of a money manager, signed his shares over to his more prudent wife, Bertha.[19]

The company's phenomenal development and growing sophistication were clearly evident when it began publishing a weekly in-house magazine, the *Davey Tree Surgeons' Bulletin,* in February 1910. The *Bulletin* was devoted to the "interests of Davey workers and the advanced tree surgery which they perform" and given free to all employees. Its purpose was to help workers increase their self-esteem and hence their value to the company. The Daveys earnestly believed that their success and that of their employees were inextricably intertwined. It never bothered Martin Davey when his salesmen sometimes earned more than he did. Whenever anyone pointed that out to him, he had a stock but enlightened response: "When the salesmen make money[,] the Company does too."[20]

The Daveys wanted their workers to feel that the magazine was their own. Martin, as editor, solicited literary contributions, particularly humorous anecdotes about employees' experiences on the job. "Don't be afraid," he said, "to tell a good joke on one of your [crew], nor to have one told on you." The *Bulletin* also contained informational tidbits about the horticultural world, reporting, for instance, that Michigan had just appointed a new chief forester and the state of Washington had recently purchased a million apple trees from Iowa for planting. But despite its folksiness and openness to employees, there was no question that the magazine and the company belonged to the Daveys. The April 2, 1910, issue contained a warning thinly disguised as a bit of humor:

"The man who KNOWS more than the Boss generally gets to be Boss."
"The man who THINKS he knows more than the Boss generally gets fired."[21]

As early as the fall of 1908, Martin knew that the company could no longer rely on word of mouth or John Davey's illustrated lectures to spread the news about tree surgery. To reach a broader audience, Martin ran a simple advertisement in *American Forestry,* a journal whose readers were likely to be receptive to John Davey's prescription for their ailing trees. The ad worked, reaching even George Eastman (of photographic fame) in Rochester, New York. Eastman not only ordered some work to be performed by Davey crews, he invited John Davey to his Rochester home to lecture to some wealthy friends, which in turn resulted in several new orders.[22]

The success of that first advertisement encouraged the company to publish more. By 1910 it ran others in the widely circulated monthly the *Garden Magazine.* Davey ads were no longer primitive. They were slick, half-page pieces that sensitized readers to the fact that their trees were living things utterly deserving of the finest care available, which was, of course, Davey care. One ad personified suffering trees as "our wounded friends," while another proclaimed that John Davey's scientific treatments did for trees what "dentistry [did] for teeth or what the physician [did] for ailing humanity." Still another tried to scare readers into a Davey contract: "This may be the last year *your* trees can stand neglect. It is dangerous to delay!"[23]

With Martin as general manager and the firm in the capable hands of other members of the family, John Davey, well into his sixties, withdrew from day-to-day operations. He spent his time doing the things that had long fascinated him. He revised and enlarged *The Tree Doctor,* the modest volume that in a mere eight years spawned a booming multi-state company whose future seemed limitless, and wrote *A New Era in Tree Growing,* a promotional piece directed to prospective clients of the Davey Tree Expert Company. Always a dreamer anyway, he enjoyed his new leisure and a life now vindicated by the success born of his once ridiculed passion for trees. He frequently visited Martin and Berenice, riding to their home in the morning in a cart pulled by his little pony, Nellie. He would tap on the kitchen window with his whip, a signal that he was stopping for his usual breakfast of coffee and toast. Neighborhood children knew to look for Nellie and the cart and gathered around waiting for the grandfatherly man inside to finish so he could give them a ride.

He enjoyed playing the flute and entertaining Martin and his bride with happy tales of his bell-ringing days long ago in England. Still deeply religious, he believed in and acted on the credo that he was his brother's keeper, giving to needy families the vegetables he grew in the yard of his new house on Woodard Avenue in Kent. He was more at ease with life now that the years of struggle were over. Berenice remembered him as perpetually pleasant and the first to laugh at a good joke on himself.[24]

Despite the external trappings of success, the Davey Tree Expert Company was not immune to the kinds of problems that invariably plague new businesses. For one, the company needed money to expand. Family members tried to plow as much cash as they could back into the business by taking small salaries and forgoing dividends, but that was not enough. There was no alternative but to sell stock in the company, which Martin tried to do. After a year and a half, he had raised only $15,000 of new capital. Very few Kentites and others wanted to invest their money in a venture that might well turn out to be nothing more than a fad.

Martin Davey, still in his twenties, made some understandable mistakes in the early days of the Davey Tree Expert Company. He thought, for example, that all a business had to do to double its profits was double its sales volume. His inexperience blinded him to the hard reality that doubling volume required expanding the market even farther from the company's home base. That meant additional travel and lodging expenses and the creation of satellite offices, with accompanying increases in personnel and overhead. A small business, never straying far from its local base of operations, could be run much more economically because of the eagle-eye scrutiny of its owners. But that was not the case for Davey Tree.[25]

Another problem for the company arose from its own success. Salesmen and foremen, thoroughly trained (as was the Davey custom) and firsthand-edly aware of the profits to be made in the fledgling industry, frequently quit Davey Tree to strike out on their own or to join competing firms. They, of course, took unique Davey skills with them, which in turn resulted in a number of lawsuits over patents during the company's formative years. The Daveys invariably won the suits but recovered virtually nothing for their efforts because typically their opponents had meager assets, if any at all. The best recourse, the company found, was simply to broadcast the superiority of the Davey way and expose the "butchery" of rival firms.[26]

Operation of the company fell mainly to Martin. He was not only general manager but chief financial officer, personnel director, purchasing agent, paymaster, and field director. He was also in charge of advertising. Money was always scarce, and during slow times it was difficult to meet payrolls. Many of the workers in the field, young and unmarried, willingly accepted partial pays until company coffers were refilled. Because work was still seasonal in the North, Martin always had to scramble for tools and supplies, too. Some modest bank credit helped but did not erase the young company's cash flow problems.

Publicity, beyond that generated by the usual advertising, Martin concluded, might turn the company's fortunes. There was probably no better way to gain attention than through a big contract for tree work on the grounds of the U.S. Capitol and White House in Washington, D.C. But Martin had no direct connection that might open the doors to the nation's capital. He did, however, know Judge David L. Rockwell through Kent's City Bank, and Rockwell, a Democrat, had Washington contacts that might be able to help a young man desperately trying to keep a company afloat.

Through Rockwell friends John O'Dwyer, Democratic party boss of Toledo, and Ohio congressman James M. Cox, Martin met Elliott Woods, superintendent of the Capitol grounds. The dour Woods listened to Martin's explanation of the Capitol's arboreal problems and what the Davey company proposed to do about them. Despite Martin's best salesmanship, Woods remained noncommittal, promising only to "consider the matter."

After several days, with no order from Woods on his desk, Martin stepped up the campaign. He returned to the Capitol grounds, snapped off a branch from an insect-infested maple tree, and marched directly into Woods's office and laid it on the surprised superintendent's desk. "Where did you get that?" he asked. "Right out on your Capitol grounds, Mr. Woods, and this is just one of the serious things that need your prompt attention." "Well, I guess we'll have to look into this," Woods responded. Shortly after another tour of the Capitol grounds, a work order from Woods rested in Martin Davey's hands.

The most celebrated Washington "patient" of Davey Tree was the Washington Elm, towering just east of the U.S. Senate chamber. Supposedly George Washington had sat under it while observing construction of the Capitol in 1793. The years had taken a toll on the storied tree, but a Davey crew soon had it back to the healthy state it knew when the nation's first citizen took comfort in its shade.

Although Davey's Washington work was not the panacea he had hoped for, it did lead to other jobs in the city, including one on the grounds of the White House. Private citizens noticed Davey crews working about the capital, and soon orders for residential work flowed in. The Davey Tree Expert

Company, although not out of the financial thicket yet, could boast that it was tree surgeon to the nation's capital.

Despite the Davey Tree Expert Company's financial woes, Martin felt secure enough to make two significant purchases in 1910. One was a house in Kent, about a mile west of the town square. Fred Allen, a retired druggist and Davey stockholder, owned it and offered it to Martin for $2,500. The young man balked; he hated going into debt, but the terms were easy and the instinct to own a place of his own was too strong. The second purchase was a brand new Buick. The old Maxwell had seen better days, and Martin had a fondness for sleek automobiles anyway, so the deal was made.

No Buick owner could be seen in ordinary street clothes driving such a fine touring car. Martin outfitted himself from head to toe in a "fancy duster, gauntlet gloves, a rakish automobile hat, and goggles." Even so, the dust of Kent's unpaved roads somehow found its way through his motoring garb, necessitating a bath and shampoo after every drive.[27]

Martin's new Buick helped launch his political career. Ohio governor Judson Harmon, a reform-minded Democrat, was campaigning for reelection in 1910 against the formidable Republican Warren G. Harding. The campaign trail took Harmon to Portage County, whose Democratic Party leader had earlier noticed Martin's flashy car. He asked Martin to drive Harmon to his various campaign stops in the county, and Martin, who confessed to Democratic leanings anyway, needed minimal persuading.[28]

He remembered little about the day, whizzing the governor from one speech to another over Portage County's bumpy roads, but he did recall that Harmon was tall, good-looking, and delivered a fine speech. He also remembered that the governor frequently asked him to slow down as he gunned the Buick from one corner of Portage County to the other.

Later that night, Martin had his first brush with political fame. Harmon culminated his whirlwind tour before a throng in Kent's Opera House at the corner of Columbus and Water streets, and, before beginning his formal address, thanked his young chauffeur by name. In fact, he mentioned Martin several times, and with each utterance the young man's chest swelled all the more. He never forgot how he felt that night when the governor of Ohio called him by name.

The governor's familiarity emboldened Martin sufficiently to ask if Harmon would like a little cider to cap off the evening. Yes, he said, so once again Martin and the governor sped off in the Buick, this time to Martin's home, where Harmon politely endured the sweet cider his host proffered but clearly could barely wait to leave for something a bit harder elsewhere to moisten his weary throat.

Martin's experience was an epiphany of sorts. For the first time, he noted the relationship between politics and the fortunes of private businesses like the Davey Tree Expert Company. Harmon's landslide reelection and the election of a Democrat, Ellsworth R. Bathrick, to Congress from Davey's heavily Republican district (Portage County was the heart of the old Garfield district) demonstrated that Ohioans had enough of the wooden economic policies of President William Howard Taft. The Republican Taft was taking the nation nowhere, and the Davey Tree Expert Company was along for the ride.

Of course, the hapless Taft could not be blamed entirely for the Davey Tree Expert Company's problems. The weather still greatly determined the company's fortune, good or ill. Winters were always slow, creating an inevitable cash flow problem by spring. That was troublesome for everyone associated with the company, from officers and field crews to stockholders. But the company's fate became more important than ever to Martin in 1911. On May 30, Berenice gave birth to the Daveys' first child, Evangeline, named after Henry Wadsworth Longfellow's tragic Acadian heroine in the 1847 poem.[29]

The nation's economy languished while Taft drifted through the last half of his term, alienating one faction of his party after another, until nearly all but the Old Guard defected in 1912 to their old hero, Theodore Roosevelt, fresh from his African hunts and with his eye on the presidency again. The split between party regulars and Progressives (Bull Moosers) opened the White House doors for Woodrow Wilson, the first Democratic president elected in twenty years. Wilson's "New Freedom" promised help to small entrepreneurs and others seemingly forgotten or ignored by Republicans as their party cozied up to big business in the late nineteenth and early twentieth centuries.[30]

But none of Wilson's program was in place in 1912, and the Davey Tree Expert Company was, as usual, hard-pressed for cash. Martin tried to raise money by selling more stock, but that largely failed. By June the cash flow worsened. The company met its payroll late. Desperate, Martin went to Kent's City Bank, which had already extended the company a small line of credit. This time, Martin needed $5,000. One of the bank directors, instinctively penurious and leery of a company so frequently on the brink, approved the loan but under stiff terms. The Davey Tree Expert Company had to pledge its accounts receivable monies two to one against the $5,000 and accept and pay a bank-appointed financial adviser during the life of the loan.[31]

Martin called the loan "blood money" but had no choice—he had to accept. He vowed to pay off the debt as soon as possible and within three weeks, when incoming checks swelled the company treasury, did. All this was another lesson in human nature for Martin. He saw how putative friends pressed all the harder when their desperate neighbors were backed up to the wall.[32] To survive, you had to be a fighter.

Chapter Five

"Boy Wonder" Mayor

⟨⟨⟨⟩⟩⟩

WOODROW WILSON WAS Martin Davey's choice in 1912. Martin had been a William Jennings Bryan man ever since he heard the Great Commoner speak at Oberlin Academy many years earlier. But Bryan had faded and now yielded center stage in Democratic politics to the gaunt professor from Princeton. Wilson's intellectualism and idealism appealed to Martin, as they obviously did to millions of other Americans who voted for him over the still popular and effervescent Theodore Roosevelt and the ill-starred and colorless incumbent, William Howard Taft.

On election night, Martin, with several friends, headed to Ravenna, the Portage County seat, to listen to the returns as they ticked in on the telegraph. Cheers broke out at every report that Wilson was winning. No one was more excited than Martin. Caught up in the electricity of the moment, he blurted to his companions, "I am going to run for Mayor of Kent next year." Encouraged by his exuberant friends, he decided to start his campaign that very night. This was, he said, the "beginning of my real interest and activity in politics."[1]

The Kent he wanted to lead was no particular prize. In 1912 it was scarcely more than a muddy little village; not until 1920 would it have the five thousand residents needed to make it a city. Except in the center of town, its streets were largely unpaved, electric service was virtually nonexistent, there was no natural gas system for homes and businesses and, judging by the number of outhouses still in use, the village obviously had no sanitary sewer system. Waste simply drained into vile-smelling ditches.[2]

Some public improvements had been made before Martin decided he wanted to be mayor, but if anyone ever wanted to start from scratch, Kent was the place to be. Someone older and wiser may have been put off by it all, but Martin was only twenty-eight, still young enough to think that he could move the world. He knew nothing about running a village and, apart from his Democratic instincts, had no sharply honed political philosophy. He was, however, a hard worker and an eager student of many things, including politics.

He learned a harsh lesson very quickly. His opponent in the Democratic primary election in 1913 was H. C. Eckert, a popular former mayor who thought he could simply ease his way to victory over his inexperienced opponent. A couple of weeks before the primary, Davey and Eckert crossed paths in the town square. After a perfunctory exchange, Eckert offered his rival a "sporting proposition." "Let's make this a friendly contest," he said. "Whoever is defeated will take off his coat and help the other fellow win." "That sounds good to me," Martin responded. "If you win the nomination, I'll do everything I can to help you in the fall election." Eckert promised to reciprocate, and the two went their separate ways.[3]

Martin campaigned hard during the spring and summer. He knocked on doors, stopped people in the streets, and contacted every Democrat he knew. His diligence worked. In the September primary election, he beat his more experienced and better-known opponent, 113–92.[4]

Martin's quest was only half over. He had to face another experienced and popular candidate, N. J. A. Minich, the Republican incumbent, in the general election. The race was a contest between man and boy. Minich was sixty-four and a veteran of Kent civic and political life. He had already been elected mayor twice, in 1909 and 1911, and likely assumed that a third term was his for the asking. Martin was twenty-nine and a political neophyte. His only elected office was president of the Kent Board of Trade, an organization created to promote local businesses. Even in campaigning for that minor office, Davey revealed his naïveté, voting for his opponent as a sign of good sportsmanship. Martin won the Board of Trade election by two votes and was lectured by his supporters after they learned he had foolishly voted for his rival.

He got another hard lesson when his Democratic primary opponent refused to help during the general election. Martin surmised that Eckert never expected to lose and, when he did, sought revenge against the young upstart who had bested him. Not only did Eckert refuse to help Martin against Minich, he actually sided with the Republican. So much for sporting propositions and good sportsmanship. Politics was a mean game, and Martin was learning fast.

What Martin lacked in political experience, he made up for with organizational acumen. Once he won the primary, he called a meeting of all the precinct committeemen and other Democratic candidates in Kent. Martin directed each to establish a reliable contact in every industry, lodge, church, and civic organization in Kent. Within weeks, he had nearly a hundred men representing every facet of the community ready to work for him. The hundred first met once a week and later twice to plot strategy. Leaving nothing to chance, Martin insisted on knowing the worst-case scenario—what the opposing camp was planning and saying. He intended to stay ahead of and counter Minich at every turn.

There was so much to learn and precious little time to do it. Just when he thought he knew how to meld people into an effective organization, he discovered something new about human nature. On the Saturday night before the election, Martin stood in the center of town for three hours shaking hands and soliciting votes. A friend waited alongside the entire time before finally speaking: "It must be that you don't want my vote." Dumbfounded, Martin responded, "What the heck is wrong with you? Why do you make such a remark as that?" His friend answered, "I have been standing here listening to you ask everyone else for his vote, and you haven't asked for mine." Martin admitted that it never occurred to him that he had to ask a man who had stood beside him campaigning for hours for his vote, but he overcame the shock and asked his friend, "Will you vote for me? I'd appreciate it very much." "Sure," was the ready answer. Martin turned the awkward situation to his advantage by asking his companion to promise to get fifty people to commit their votes in the coming election, and he wanted to see the names of the fifty. On election eve the man showed up with a list. Martin deduced from this episode that people wanted to be asked for their help; they did not want to be taken for granted. He never forgot this simple rule and applied it freely in every one of his political contests thereafter.[5]

Martin's mayoral campaign ended with an address in the Kent Opera House. For days Davey loyalists had swarmed through the streets of Kent, flooding the village with handbills and broadsides advertising Martin's speech. Not a seat was empty when Martin, knees knocking, took the stage for a final plea to voters. He had stood in the same spot as a sixteen-year-old to recite "Matter, Mind, and Spirit" for the graduating class of 1900. His oratory was as sharp this night as it had been thirteen years earlier, and he had no trouble winning over the citizens of Kent.

The general election in November was anticlimactic. Aided by his youth and the vigor it promised, Martin beat Minich easily and was now mayor of

Kent.[6] With a wife and daughter and an official salary of $250 a year, he kept his job at Davey Tree. At twenty-nine, he had the energy and the requisite foolhardiness to charge full ahead with both civic and personal responsibilities.

He soon earned the $250. As a private citizen he knew tangentially at best the problems, large and small, of the village. As mayor he became intimately acquainted with virtually every drunk, vagrant, and barking dog in Kent. One typical day began with the convening of the mayor's court at 9 A.M. Martin fined two malefactors $1 and court costs for public intoxication and ordered two other drunks who could not pay their $5 fines to work them off at $1 per day on the village street crew. He fined another more serious wrongdoer $10 and costs after his wife testified against him for drunkenness and firing a gun during one of their quarrels. He also sentenced the man to thirty days in the workhouse but mercifully suspended the jail time.[7]

Dealing with Kent's seamier side was not always mundane. The young mayor got a personal introduction to the village's mean face one May night in 1916. On a tough side of town, thirty-year-old Sam Sac argued with his twenty-year-old brother-in-law, Dominico Pizzuti. Both men pulled guns, but Sac was a little faster on the draw and pumped three fatal shots into the younger man. The murderer panicked and ran, cutting through the campus of Kent Normal College where he was spotted by a custodian who immediately called Martin. Still young and swift, the mayor and two police officers took chase and cornered Sac at the eastern end of town where he surrendered.[8] Clearly there was more to being mayor than sentencing drunks and controlling barking dogs.

Martin also faced problems springing from Kent's transition from nineteenth-century hamlet to twentieth-century burg. As it had done in so many other American towns and villages, the new century ushered in a myriad of technical improvements that transformed the way everyone in Kent lived. A water and light company brought indoor plumbing and incandescent lighting to village residences. However, electric and water service, remarkable if not outrightly miraculous to Kentites when introduced, began to deteriorate by 1910. Rates were too high for the meager services rendered, many claimed. Never one to think small, Mayor Davey proposed that the village should stop trying to cajole the privately owned Kent Water and Light Company into better service and lower rates. Kent, he argued, should have its own municipal water and light plant. Always thorough and meticulous, the mayor had the village engineer prepare a full-blown plan that would not only improve water and light service for Kentites but also turn the downtown business district into a "great white way."[9]

Village council endorsed the mayor's proposal, and the engineer and so-licitor prepared legislation for the new municipal water and electric com-pany. Enthusiasm soared as council and residents alike anticipated a brand-new plant that would create a water and light system the equal of any. It was exactly what Martin Davey envisioned and promised when he campaigned for the mayorship in 1913. He was now ready to deliver.[10]

Public enthusiasm for the project waned, however, after Kentites learned how expensive a new facility would be. In September 1916, council members killed the plan and reopened negotiations for a better rate structure and im-proved service from the Kent Water and Light Company. Mayor Davey, his grand plan evaporating, shrugged off his defeat and declared that he was not wedded to municipal ownership as much as he was to "any plan that brought fair results." The matter ended when council moved that the village attorney prepare a new contract with Kent Water and Light.[11]

The struggle with Kent Water and Light for better rates and service re-vealed Martin's feisty side. When the company demurred, he responded by suggesting that Kent build its own water and power plant. He similarly took on another utility when it too delivered unsatisfactory service to village resi-dents. Since 1901, the Northern Ohio Traction Company had run the trolley system in Kent and also operated a line to Ravenna a few miles to the east. Martin led a drive to get several neighboring communities—Akron, Barber-ton, Kenmore, Canton, Massillon, and Wadsworth—all serviced by North-ern Ohio Traction, to protest the company's dirty cars and shabby service.[12]

Highest on Martin's list of municipal improvements was a sewage plant. This was, of course, an unglamorous project, certainly not like the "great white way" he envisioned for Kent's business district when he pushed for a municipally owned electric plant, but clearly a necessity. Indeed, the matter was removed from Martin's hands when the State Board of Health in 1914 stepped in and ordered Kent to construct a sewage plant before January 1, 1916. Village leaders had struggled for years with plans for such a facility but nothing had been done. Now the state would tolerate no further procrasti-nation—the Board of Health threatened to fine the village a staggering $100 a day if plans were not drawn in a reasonable time.[13]

City council and Mayor Davey sprang to action. They called a special elec-tion for January 12, 1915, to pass a $90,000 bond issue to cover planning and construction costs. Every night for two weeks the young mayor hammered home to voters in churches, lodges, and movie theaters the need for the new system. No progressive community, he stressed, should tolerate the stinking, unsanitary conditions generated by raw sewage piling high in ditches and clogging even the village's storm sewers. Knowing that no one liked higher taxes, the astute mayor stressed that if the bond issue passed, large corporations, including the various railroads that operated in Kent, and the Kent Water and Light Company would have to pay half the cost of construction of a sewer system and disposal plant. And he emphasized that the village had no choice in the matter. After years of tolerating unhealthful conditions, the state of Ohio's patience was exhausted. Kent's residents would have to comply with the state's edict or else pay the fines.[14]

The mayor's hard work paid off. All his hours in churches, lodges, and theaters were worth it. The bond issue passed 576 to 16, and the contract was awarded to the W. H. Hunt Company of Akron. Work began almost immediately in 1915, and by 1916, despite the fact that escalating wages and other expenses catapulted the cost of the project to $185,000, more than twice the original estimate, Kent residents could flush away to their hearts' content.[15]

Something else was happening in Kent while Martin was mayor, something in the long term that was even more significant than the most up-to-date sewage disposal system. Martin could not lay sole claim to it, but much of its early development and later success occurred during his mayoral watch. On May 10, 1910, the Ohio State legislature authorized the creation of two normal schools in northern Ohio. One of the schools was designated for the western part of the state, the other for the eastern. The members of the Kent Board of Trade, eager to bring so significant an educational plum to Kent, created a committee to persuade the Ohio State Normal Commission that their village was perfect for the new college. Martin and other civic leaders traveled to Columbus to present Kent's case. The committee was well armed. It already had leading citizen William S. Kent's promise to donate his farm of more than fifty acres on East Main Street as a site for the college.

The committee was persuasive enough to get the commission to visit Kent in the fall. Citizens scrambled to put the best face on their village. Vacant lots were cleared, trash removed, and houses painted. Even the streets were scrubbed. Kent never looked so good. Then, on the day the State Normal Commission members arrived, it poured. The commissioners had given Kentites one hour to make their pitch. They detrained in Kent at eleven and were due in Ravenna at noon. Nothing could have been worse— both the weather and the clock conspired against the Kent forces. Someone, however, thought quickly and located boots for the visitors. Together the welcoming committee and the state commissioners slogged through the mud high atop the hill on William Kent's farm for a view of the village and the potential college site.

Despite the Kentites' best efforts to distract the commissioners into ignoring the weather, the visitors could think of nothing other than getting safely off the slippery slope and on to their appointment in Ravenna. And they would have done exactly that were it not for a ruse perpetrated by the Kentites. Reluctantly, the normal school commissioners accepted an invitation to lunch only because they were assured that it was already prepared and waiting to be served at a tavern on the way to Ravenna. That was a bold-faced lie. Lunch was waiting but not at any tavern on the road to Ravenna. It was to be served at the Twin Lakes Inn at the opposite end of town. The combination of the noon hour and a hunger intensified by the walk up William Kent's hill was enough to persuade the state commissioners to pause for what they thought would be a quick lunch. They were driven to the Twin Lakes Inn for a full meal of chicken and fish and while they ate were bombarded with pro-Kent propaganda. Before the visitors knew what had happened, the afternoon was gone and their appointment in Ravenna entirely forgotten.[16] The gloomy morning had been erased, and Martin Davey and his fellow citizens had to smile because Kent was still in the running.

A month later, the normal school commissioners returned. They had narrowed their choices to three: Kent, Wadsworth, and Warren. After a second, more pleasant trip to the proposed site of the college, they made up their minds. Kent it was. The village purchased two additional tracts of land adjacent to the Kent farm for the college, and in 1911 the state legislature appropriated $250,000 for buildings and equipment. The construction began. A faculty and administration were in place by 1912, and Kent Normal College admitted its first class, 271 strong, in September 1913.[17]

The significance of what Martin and the other zealous members of the citizens' committee had accomplished could not be overstated. Almost overnight the college began to transform the town. The quiet village was now one of Ohio's educational centers, but there was more to it than that. The college brought with it a construction boom. New houses went up all over town, new streets were built, and real-estate values soared. With justifiable pride, Martin Davey stepped back, surveyed the results of his and the others' hard work and concluded, "There was [now] a real chance for Kent to develop into a larger and better town."[18]

These were busy times for Kent. The once tiny village was ready to discard its nineteenth-century quaintness to become one of Ohio's progressive and developing communities. Martin, of course, was busy adapting to the change. He and the six village council members worked long and hard, meeting sometimes three or four nights a week just to keep pace with events.

Working in concert with the Kent Board of Trade, the mayor and council persuaded the owners of the Mason Tire & Rubber Company to build a plant in the village. Kent's citizens, agog over the prospect of landing a factory that promised to employ hundreds, capitalized most of the project themselves by buying stock in the company. In January 1916, construction began on a $50,000 plant on Lake Street in the northeast section of town. Mason Tire & Rubber moved in and flourished for years, with sales soaring from $1.2 million in 1917 to nearly $6.6 million by 1920.[19]

The company's rapid growth generated some problems. Almost as soon as the plant started up, company officials asked the village council to authorize the paving of Lake Street. That meant that the property owners in the working-class neighborhood would be hit with sizable assessments to pay for the improvement. Martin supported the company's request, rationalizing that if he had to promise to pave the road to entice a company that employed hundreds to come to Kent, it would be a small price to pay. Since the company was already in Kent, paving the street was the fair thing to do.

Lake Street residents disagreed. They stormed a council meeting to protest. Here Martin made a bad mistake. In trying to placate the angry crowd, he suggested that property owners hard-pressed to pay the street assessments should sell their homes and buy elsewhere. Martin was merely suggesting a practical solution but was misinterpreted. The angry residents believed he was essentially saying, "If you don't like it, get out." The passion of the protesters notwithstanding, Kent council authorized the Lake Street paving project, and Martin weathered the storm.[20]

The arrival of the Mason Tire & Rubber Company provided a personal headache for Martin. The company's arrogant president, D. M. Mason, thought that village traffic laws applied to everyone but him. For years he brazenly flouted Kent's fifteen-mile-per-hour speed limit in his Ford, Overland, Buick, Pierce-Arrow, and custom-built Cunningham automobiles. Once he was even arrested twice within fifteen minutes for speeding. Kent's lone traffic cop caught him at Water and Lake streets clipping along at thirty-five miles per hour. The policeman had no sooner ticketed Mason than he challenged the officer to follow him back to town. Within minutes the cop again pulled him over for speeding. It was Mason's third arrest in a month. He was already a familiar figure in Martin's mayor's court, posting his bonds and later paying $5 fines only to be on his reckless way again. Weary of Mason's contempt for the law, Martin ordered the local traffic officer to dog the scofflaw until he learned that the speed limit applied to him as it did to everybody else.[21]

Martin's success in directing a rapidly developing village proved to be a little heady. Halfway through his first term, his ambition got ahead of his readiness for bigger things. In 1914, urged on by Democratic county leader Judge David L. Rockwell, Martin decided to challenge incumbent Ellsworth R. Bathrick for the Democratic congressional nomination in the newly reapportioned Fourteenth Congressional District made up of Portage, Summit, Lorain, and Medina counties. Rockwell, whom Davey remembered as so persuasive that he could "make fifty cents look like five dollars, or five dollars look like fifty cents," despised Bathrick ever since the congressman refused to appoint some Rockwell favorites to political posts. The vindictive and manipulative Rockwell saw young Martin as the perfect foil to strike back at Bathrick.[22]

Rockwell, Davey's political mentor for several years to come, poisoned the young man's mind with exaggerated and even false tales of Bathrick's perfidy and ineptitude. According to Rockwell, the congressman had scarcely a friend left in the Fourteenth Congressional District. Martin never questioned Rockwell's charges and challenged Bathrick in the Democratic primary of 1914. The campaign was brief but brutal, with Martin unfairly accusing Bathrick of demanding abject obedience from all his constituents. One of his advertisements actually depicted the congressman clad in the flowing robes of a prince, crying out to his subjects, "Down, knaves, Democrats. Bend the knee. I am Lord Bathrick!!!"[23]

The tactics failed, and Rockwell's influence carried little beyond Portage County. Martin suffered a crushing defeat but emerged from his first big political battle a lot smarter. Rockwell's vilification of Bathrick had led Martin to believe that the congressman's enemies were legion. After the election, sadder but wiser, he correctly concluded that Rockwell had made a "dozen frogs sound like a thousand."

The young man was a good loser. He sent Bathrick a sincere note of congratulations and promised to help him in the general election. Democratic leaders in Akron took the Kentite at his word and asked him to speak on Bathrick's behalf during the campaign. Martin, who had happily returned to his mayoral duties, accepted and delivered a rousing speech in Akron for Bathrick. Although Martin at the moment had no ambitions beyond his mayorship, he had acquired some important political IOUs.

Martin's mayoral obligations kept him from devoting full attention to the affairs of the Davey Tree Expert Company, but the firm's fortunes suffered little because Jim Davey stepped into the breach. When a half-dozen salesmen quit and started their own firms, Jim moved into their vacated territories with a vengeance, outselling the defectors time and time again. Once a sales territory was safely back in the Davey fold, Jim would hire a new salesman, get him started, and then move on to the next task at hand. At the same time, Jim Davey, through the courts, relentlessly pursued the defectors for patent violations. The legal costs were heavy, but litigation was the only way to safeguard Davey patents.

Neither business concerns nor anything else mattered when Martin heard the news that stunned millions of Americans on June 28, 1914. Earlier that day, thousands of miles away in the Balkan town of Sarajevo, a nineteen-year-old Serbian ultranationalist named Gavrilo Princip fired lethal shots into Archduke Franz Ferdinand, heir to the Austrian throne, and his wife. Within days Europe was at war. The United States was out of it, but Americans were nonetheless anxious and concerned.

The political effects in America were disquieting for the Democrats. In the congressional races that year, Woodrow Wilson was given a reduced Democratic majority, and, closer to home for Martin, James M. Cox, now Ohio's Democratic governor, and the Fourteenth Congressional District's Democratic congressman, Ellsworth Bathrick, both lost. In addition, Republican Warren G. Harding was elected to the U.S. Senate in 1914 to serve the apprenticeship that preceded his move to the White House six years later.[24]

Harding's election disturbed Martin. He had nothing personal against the newspaperman from Marion. Indeed, he thought him "attractive, gracious, and kind." However, Harding won his Senate seat over state attorney general Timothy Hogan by stoking some of the most virulent anti-Catholic prejudice ever seen in Ohio. Harding should have but never decried the unwarranted intrusion of a scurrilous anti-Catholic newspaper, the *Missouri Menace,* into the Ohio campaign. In August, the *Menace* warned Ohioans that the "Nits of Columbus," shouting "the Pope is king," were ready to march 350,000 strong to ensure the Catholic Hogan's election to the U.S. Senate. In September, the *Menace's* editors played to Ohioans' basest instincts by flooding the state with thousands of copies of an article, "The Priests for Hogan." The *Menace* took credit for electing Harding in November and delighted in its own pithy description of the act, "Whew! / Hogan Hardingized." The ease with which Ohio voters succumbed to the gutter appeal of anti-Catholicism shocked Martin. He thought it "wicked and detestable," and it generated his lifelong detestation of every form of prejudice.[25]

Martin recalled Harding's victory in 1914 much more vividly than he remembered his own reelection in 1915. He was so busy promoting an array of public improvements for Kent that the need for reelection almost slipped his mind. He was burdened by the responsibilities of the office and nettled by the "innumerable petty annoyances" that inevitably accompanied the mayorship. He was also bothered by the skimpy attendance at council meetings. He did not know how to interpret that. Did it mean that people were dissatisfied with his mayoral performance and were demonstrating their displeasure via their absence, or did it mean that they were essentially satisfied with his work and were simply leaving well enough alone? He correctly concluded the latter. The election results in November bore him out. He blitzed his opponent, N. J. A. Minich again, 723–343, and swept all six Democrats into council on his coattails. His margin of victory was the largest in Kent history and provided vivid proof that the citizens of Kent stood foursquare behind their young mayor.[26]

Martin's success was easy to understand—he never took anything for granted. He repeated the organizational wizardry that got him the mayorship in 1913 and now recognized exactly what it took to succeed. He knew, for instance, that Republicans invariably voted Republican and Democrats invariably voted Democratic. Dynamite could not dislodge them from their choices. Whenever the two parties were of roughly equal strength, the key to victory lay with independent voters, and there Martin concentrated his energies.

Despite the press of his mayoral duties, Martin continued to play an active role in the Davey Tree Expert Company. The war was good for the economy; Great Britain and France could not buy enough American goods, and the success of merchants supplying the Allies trickled down even to companies like Davey Tree. The booming economy raised the price of doing business, but those costs were easily absorbed. Conditions were so good that the company even expanded its operations and declared its first dividend at the end of 1915.[27]

Business kept Martin traveling from Davey headquarters in Kent to company offices in the East. One Saturday in January 1916, as he rode the train from New York to Kent, he felt a sharp stitch in his stomach. His pulse quickened, his lower right abdomen grew tender to the touch and he began to feel nauseous. He toughed it out to Kent but drove immediately to White Hospital in Ravenna where he was diagnosed with acute appendicitis. The operating room was readied and Martin was wheeled in for surgery. The operation went smoothly and in less than a month he was on the streets of Kent again, walking briskly several blocks from his home to the offices of Davey Tree.[28]

The year 1916 proved to be a dangerous one for Martin. In August, he was best man when his brother Jim married Mary Binney, the daughter of an old-monied family from Old Greenwich, Connecticut. A few days before the wedding, the Daveys partied with the Binneys at their home on Long Island Sound. The Binneys loved the water and especially enjoyed aquaplaning behind a speedy motorboat. Martin, ever adventuresome, needed little coaxing to try the sport. He lay flat on the aquaplane and wound the two ropes connected to the speedboat tightly around both hands. The craft took off, Martin rose to his knees and then, emboldened by his preliminary success, stood upright on the aquaplane. He sailed smoothly along, the rushing sea breezes both comforting and exhilarating. Riding the wide board was easy for the young and trim Davey, but alighting from it was a different story. The boat slowed to about ten miles per hour, and Martin decided to end his ride by diving off the aquaplane. However, he forgot to free the ropes linking him to the boat. Before he knew it, he was dragged underwater for a hundred yards or more by the moving craft. The ropes bit into his flesh, but he kept his composure and ultimately freed himself, thankful for all the times as a boy he had swum underwater in the Cuyahoga. His hands were torn and bleeding where the ropes had dug in, but other than that the episode was nothing more than a close call that could have had Jim Davey desperately looking for another best man.

Martin was fortunate that all he had to show for his aquaplaning were bleeding hands and a bruised ego. His family needed him now more than ever since Berenice gave birth to a second daughter on June 15, 1916. Little Mary Berenice joined her big sister Evangeline, now five, to increase the Martin Davey family to four. Evangeline adored her little sister and treated her like a doll. She was the delight of her parents, too. Whenever Martin or Berenice came home, Mary Berenice raced to greet them even before they got through the door.[29]

All was going well for Martin in 1916. The addition of Mary Berenice only enhanced his already idyllic family life, and Kent was prospering under his guidance as mayor. Many of his municipal improvements were completed or were well under way, and no one seemed likely to unseat him if he wanted a third term.

National politics in 1916 drew more of Martin's attention than local politics did. Woodrow Wilson was popular enough so that Republicans concluded the only way to beat him was to nominate a candidate in many respects a mirror image of the president himself. They settled on fifty-four-year-old Charles Evans Hughes, an associate justice of the U.S. Supreme Court. Hughes, like Wilson, was a scholar, having taught Latin and Greek at Delaware Academy in Delhi, New York, early in his career. After earning his law degree from

Columbia, he lectured for two years at Cornell and was even elected and reelected as a reform governor of New York in 1906 and 1908, just a few years before Wilson won the New Jersey governorship as a reformer.

By 1916, there was little difference between the two men politically, despite the fact that one was a Republican and the other a Democrat. Hughes had to court the powerful progressive wing of his own party and consequently could not criticize Wilson's progressive domestic programs. His hands were tied, too, in attacking Wilson's foreign policy. Wilson campaigned hard under the slogan "He kept us out of war," and Hughes could do nothing to counter that. To campaign as the war candidate would have been political suicide.

Even with his limitations, Hughes almost won. Wilson slipped wearily into bed on election night thinking he had lost. Only after the California returns came in was it certain that a Democratic president would have two consecutive terms for the first time since Andrew Jackson. Even then, it was not determined until two days after the election that Wilson had won.[30]

Ohio went for Wilson by about one hundred thousand votes, an easy victory that aided the return of James M. Cox to the governorship and Ellsworth R. Bathrick to Congress. Martin, loyal to the party at every level, worked hard in Kent for the election of all three.[31]

Despite the best efforts of President Wilson, by 1917 the United States was drifting ever closer to war against the Central Powers. Continued German violations of American maritime rights, accentuated by several brutal submarine attacks, finally compelled Wilson to deliver a war message to a special session of Congress on April 2. Four days later, with minimal opposition, Congress approved the fateful declaration. Soon afterward, the same body passed a conscription act, and shortly thereafter, thousands of American men between the ages of twenty and thirty entered the holds of transport ships bound for the embattled ports of Europe.[32]

The war came home to Kent. Young men from the village answered their nation's call, always to a sad refrain from teary-eyed loved ones left behind. Mayor Davey invariably arranged a public farewell for Kent's young sons in a kind but often futile attempt to bolster the spirits of the draftees and their families. He even bought a large American flag and flew it proudly at each departure.[33]

Understandably, the war and the sad scenes that accompanied it dampened everyone's spirits. The conflict, though far away, dominated daily life in Kent, forcing just about everything else onto the back pages of the press. Not even the quest for a third mayoral term was enough to get Martin's competitive juices flowing again. He thought seriously about not running.

The job devoured his time and after two terms was increasingly repetitious. His $250 annual salary was hardly enough to compensate for constituents who were never satisfied no matter what he did. In March 1917, Martin shared his feelings with a Methodist church group. The mayorship, he said, is a "lonesome position because when one does what the people want, they do not compliment you. But when one does what they dislike, they will surely strike back."[34]

He did not need a third term to prove his worthiness. His record spoke for itself. Under his leadership, Kent had stepped boldly into the twentieth century with any number of public improvements that would have made even a much larger municipality proud. And he did not need politics to earn a living. The Davey Tree Expert Company was thriving, and he had never divorced himself from company business even when the mayorship demanded so much of his time. His reputation was such that no Republican wanted to run against him. He would have gladly stepped aside in 1917 were it not for the opposition of some of his fellow Democrats in Kent.

No politician is without enemies, and frequently the most passionate of those come from one's own party. Some of Martin's jealous partisans abandoned him and sided with the Republicans to nominate an independent candidate for mayor in 1917. That was all the challenge Martin needed. He organized better and worked harder than he ever had to win in November. He swamped his opponent, Ira R. Marsh, 861–350. One Kent precinct voted a six to one majority for the mayor, and he swept five Democratic councilmen into office with him.[35] The sixth councilman was an independent. The landslide was a smashing triumph for Martin and sent a clear message to his foes, Democratic and Republican alike, that he was no one to trifle with.

Martin already had a gift indispensable to the successful politician. He had the "common touch," a way of instinctively doing the right thing even when the rules dictated otherwise. That gift was never in clearer evidence than during the fall and winter of 1916–17. The cold came early that year. By October it was already freezing, and as fall advanced into winter it grew colder still. Many Kentites, caught off guard by the premature onset of winter, were without coal, and, because the severe weather and the war effort created shortages everywhere, they could not get any even in the heart of the heating season.

The growing number of Kentites shivering in their unheated homes stirred Martin to action. He noticed two carloads of coal just sitting on an Erie Railroad siding in the village. For days no one came to move the cars. Finally, ignoring the illegality of the act, Martin seized the coal and got a local bank to take orders for it from the needy. Local teamsters then delivered it to grateful Kentites. Martin did not charge enough for the coal, so when the Erie Railroad sued him he had to make up the difference out of his own pocket, which he gladly did.[36]

Martin's enemies accused him of grandstanding, taking advantage of the plight of freezing Kentites to appear as the village savior. That may have been partially true, but Martin, sensitive since boyhood to the down and out, also felt that he had to do something to help people in need. If his enemies thought they now had an edge because the mayor was technically a "thief," they were sadly mistaken. Martin may have appropriated the coal, but to Kent's grateful citizens he was far more hero than crook. Martin knew it, too. In his final speech during the mayoral campaign of 1917, he raised the coal issue himself, asking the throng jammed into the Kent Opera House, "Which would you rather have me do, let you people freeze or seize the coal?" The crowd roared back, "Take the coal!" Martin's easy reelection and the public's concomitant repudiation of his foes were sweet revenge for the criticism he suffered.

Martin settled in comfortably for his third term. By now the job, although occasionally nettlesome, was easy. He knew what had to be done to keep Kent moving, and he did it. Davey Tree was doing well and so was Martin's young family. Evangeline was six, Mary Berenice was going on two, and Berenice was pregnant again.

Martin L. Davey Jr. was born on February 7, 1918, one of the coldest days of one of the coldest Ohio winters on record. Many nights the thermometer bottomed out at twenty or twenty-five below zero, and February 7 was one of those nights. The water pipes in the Davey home on West Main Street had frozen solid the night the baby was born. An anxious Martin Davey, bundled from head to toe, drove several times on the ice-rutted road to town to get buckets of water to aid in the frigid but uneventful delivery.

Martin's political ambitions were growing as fast as his family. Congressman Bathrick had died in December 1917, and the thirty-three-year-old mayor of Kent was interested in the job. Shortly after the Christmas and New Year holidays, Martin sounded out the Democratic power broker of Portage County, Judge Rockwell. Rockwell remembered and appreciated Martin's attempt to unseat Bathrick in 1914 and encouraged the mayor enough to lead him to believe that his chances for Bathrick's seat now were as good as anyone's. His primary opposition would likely come from Democrat William T. Sawyer, the popular former mayor of Akron. Sawyer, however, was in Florida and therefore physically removed from Ohio politics. Martin hoped Sawyer enjoyed the Sunshine State so much that he would prolong his stay. Every day that Sawyer basked in the warm sun was another day that Martin had unchallenged access to the Democratic politicos crucial to his success. Many of them remembered the good sportsmanship Martin had shown by supporting Bathrick after the congressman had trounced him in 1914. By the time Sawyer decided to run, Martin had already lined up enough support to emerge as Bathrick's likely successor.

Since Bathrick died near the end of his term, Governor Cox, whose call it was, decided that the election in 1918 would be for both the late congressman's unexpired term and the coming full term. That simplified the elective process but complicated the lives of the aspirants to Bathrick's seat. Each candidate had to run for two nominations and then two elections simultaneously.[37]

Sawyer returned from Florida in time for the race, but he was not Martin's only opponent. Judge Rockwell's enemies put up a candidate they knew he would find objectionable, Portage County probate judge Edward F. Robison. Rockwell and Robison had once been friends but were now estranged after a falling out years earlier. Martin had been dragged into that quarrel by his political mentor, Rockwell, and had actively campaigned against Robison when the judge sought a third term in 1916.[38] Resurrecting this ghost from an old political squabble would allow Rockwell's enemies to strike at both him and his young protégé, Martin Davey. Robison and Davey, the anti-Rockwell forces hoped, would negate each other in Portage County, thereby giving Sawyer the nomination.

Martin knew he was in for the fight of his political life and worked hard to win. He started early and organized well, holding meetings, public and private, and using extensive newspaper advertising and mass mailings. Everything worked; Martin won the Democratic nomination for both the short and full terms. He now had the formidable task of defeating the Republican nominee, Charles Dick of Akron, in a district that had a Republican majority of eighteen to twenty thousand.

For the first time, Martin had to appeal to unfamiliar voters in a much larger arena, Portage, Summit, Medina, and Lorain counties. He wondered if they were like the ones he knew in Kent. The best way of finding out was to take to the road, particularly in Republican country where his struggle in November would be the hardest. One visit took him to overwhelmingly anti-Democratic Lorain County. During the trip he got a flat tire on a country road. He pulled to the side in front of an old farmhouse, retrieved a jack from the back of the car, and tried to raise the frame. The jack was too short to allow Martin to pull off the old tire and slip on the spare. He sent his traveling companion to the farmhouse to borrow a board to prop up the jack.

The companion returned with the lumber and its owner, an old, bewhiskered farmer. Martin's friend introduced him as "Mayor Davey of Kent, our next congressman." Unimpressed, the old man stroked his beard and responded, "Well, I guess we gotta have congressmen." Martin tried to break the ice. "Are there any Democrats up this way?" "I hope not," growled the farmer. Martin changed the tire and moved on, knowing that even if he won Lorain County, the vote would not be unanimous.

During the fall he crisscrossed the Fourteenth Congressional District, shaking hands of friends and strangers. From county fair to town square he learned a thousand names and remembered most. He saw early on the significance of recognizing a face, recalling a name. Politics was largely a concession to human vanity. Everyone Martin met wanted to believe that he was special above all others. Martin grudgingly acknowledged, "Human vanity is one of the hardest things to deal with . . . in politics."[39]

As a newcomer to state politics, Martin made an obligatory courtesy call on Governor Cox. At age forty-eight, Cox was serving his second term in Columbus and was running for a third. His first term had been one of the most remarkable in Ohio's history. Capitalizing on the nation's progressive surge in the early twentieth century, Cox had swept into office as a reformer and rammed through the state legislature a spate of bills reorganizing Ohio's judicial system, safeguarding initiative and referendum, centralizing the state's tax collection system, and ensuring workmen's compensation, mothers' pensions, and the welfare of Ohio's children. He was renominated in 1914 but lost narrowly to Republican Frank B. Willis as Ohioans temporarily wearied of the whirlwind pace of the Progressives. He had run against Willis again in 1916 and won.[40] Now comfortable in the governor's chair, he wanted a third term in 1918, thinking that his Ohio successes might translate into something even bigger in 1920 when his party met to select a candidate for president.

In September, shortly before the all-out campaigning began, Martin, accompanied by Judge Rockwell, met Cox in his suite at the Deshler Hotel in Columbus. After dinner, the three men sat back, lighted cigars, and began to talk politics. Martin and Rockwell reported that Ohio wheat farmers were angry that congressional Democrats had fixed the price of wheat but, as a concession to the powerful southern wing of their party, had left cotton to seek its own market level in the war-heated economy. Acutely aware that all politics are local, Martin and Rockwell warned that those wheat farmers might wreak their vengeance against any and all Democrats, including Cox, in the November elections. That bad news, the two Portage Countians related, might be partially offset by a Republican tendency to cross party lines in 1918 to support Democratic candidates as a sign of wartime unity with the president. But that was only a possibility, and the governor seemed far more interested in the bad news he was hearing. He shifted in his chair, his tone urgent, his irritation evident. "What do you think my majority will be in Akron and Summit County?" he asked. Rockwell answered honestly, "Well, Governor, I am not very sure. I think you will carry Summit County, but I do not know by how much." Cox disliked Rockwell's candor. He snapped, "My friends in Akron tell me that I will carry the county by ten thousand, and everything seems to indicate that." Sensing Cox's growing agitation, Rockwell replied that he hoped the governor was right, but the Kentite's tone hinted otherwise. Turning to Martin, Cox said, "I think Dave is a joy-killer. Isn't there anything good in your section of the state?" Tactfully but truthfully, Martin answered, "Yes, Governor, there are many good things, but the good will take care of itself. . . . I think you are going to win all right, but these unfavorable signs worry me a little."

The evening dragged after the frank assessments by Cox's visitors. Clearly, the governor wanted to hear good news only, while Martin and Judge Rockwell offered forthrightness instead. The conversation continued into the evening, but Martin sensed that the governor had already distanced himself from the two men who told him things he preferred not to hear. Martin admired Cox for his accomplishments but after their meeting thought him cold and insincere.

Martin had another important political stop to make prior to the election. Shortly after conferring with Cox, he went to Washington to talk with leaders of the Democratic National Committee. Martin immediately sensed the somber wartime mood in the nation's capital. The conflict had affected everyone, particularly the sensitive philosopher inhabiting the White House. Wilson, like Lincoln a half century earlier, was a poet-warrior who loathed the role thrust upon him and longed for the day when he could cast it aside. Martin was struck by how the great man's name was whispered, not spoken, all over Washington. One party official captured much of the public's mood when he told Martin, "[The president] has only to speak, and [the people] will follow him." Before leaving Washington, Martin conferred briefly with Joseph Tumulty, Wilson's secretary, who assured his visitor that Democrats had nothing to fear in the coming elections.

Tumulty spoke confidently, but Martin could not act accordingly. His opponent in the Fourteenth Congressional District, Charles Dick, had every advantage. He had been a congressman, U.S. senator, and chairman of the Republican National Committee. At fifty-eight, he was a seasoned veteran; at thirty-four and at this political level, Martin was raw and untested. Martin concluded that he had to make the maturer, more experienced Dick appear the fool so that voters would not equate age with wisdom. Accordingly, Martin exhumed a speech that Dick had made when he ran for Congress in 1898 during the Spanish-American War. The speech exhorted Americans to vote for a Republican Congress to help President William McKinley conclude a peace with Spain. Cleverly but meanly, Martin substituted Democrat for Republican, Wilson for McKinley and Germany for Spain throughout Dick's address, and then delivered it verbatim.

Dick took the bait. Failing to recognize his own words of twenty years earlier, he lambasted Martin for blatant partisanship at a time when Democrats and Republicans had supposedly shunted aside their differences to present a united front against the Central Powers. The pro-Davey *Akron Times* then published Dick's 1898 speech word for word alongside Martin's version. Dick was humiliated while Martin's stock soared. The young fox had outsmarted the old dog, and voters of the Fourteenth Congressional District now saw the Kentite in a new light.[41]

Dick tried to recover by emphasizing his experience and his opponent's lack of it in national politics. Martin Davey, he insisted, was a mere tyro and, if elected, would be relegated to the back benches of the Capitol where he could do little to advance Ohio's interests once the fast-concluding European war was over. As a former congressman, Dick would either be restored to his original committees or assigned to new ones of equal importance. Congress's hoary tradition of seniority would work to Ohio's advantage with a Dick victory.[42]

Martin tried to negate Dick's obvious edge by appealing to the passions of angry voters hell-bent on punishing Kaiser Wilhelm II and Germany for the great evils they had perpetrated. Martin ran newspaper advertisements proclaiming that there could be no peace until the kaiser, crown prince, generals Paul von Hindenburg and Erich Ludendorff, and other German leaders were arrested, tried as criminals, and punished. Anything less, he argued, would be "a hollow mockery—a betrayal of the heroes who have fallen in the cause of world freedom. Unconditional surrender [was] the price of peace."[43]

Dick, in marked contrast to the bellicose Davey, "hoped" that the war would end in 1918. Rather than total triumph and a harsh victor's peace, Dick believed that Americans wanted a "conclusive and enduring" resolution.[44]

His moderation made him appear soft and less decisive than his younger opponent, who demanded that "Kaiser Bill" either swing from the gallows or face a firing squad.

Martin tried to transform his youthfulness, a disadvantage in a contest with a man of near-perfect political age, into an asset. His newspaper advertisements trumpeted the fact that he was "young—just 34, virile, rich and 100% American." The ads were a colossal blunder. They not only made Martin look silly and juvenile, they exposed him to a whole new Republican counterattack. The *Akron Beacon Journal* asked editorially, if Martin Davey were so "young, virile and 100% American," why was he not on the battlefield killing Germans? Men older than he were currently at the front doing exactly that. Even the fifty-eight-year-old Dick, who had served in the Spanish-American War, volunteered his services when the United States declared war in 1917.[45]

Martin tried to recover by proclaiming that his brother Paul was already on active duty in France while Dick's three sons in the military were tucked safely away stateside. However, Paul Davey's front-line peril failed to deflect criticism of his "young, virile and 100% American" brother for avoiding military service during the war. The conscription law of 1917 required young men between twenty and thirty to declare for the draft. A second measure, enacted in 1918, however, was broader, requiring eighteen- to forty-five-year-olds to register.[46] A man could avoid the draft if he worked in a war industry or had dependents. All he had to do was claim exemption. The draft form also contained a box that could be checked if the registrant waived exemption. Millions of men claimed exemption without sullying their reputations, but if one were a "young, virile, 100% American" with congressional aspirations, doing so would be politically disastrous. Consequently, when Martin reached the waiver checkoff, he simply left it blank, neither claiming nor rejecting exemption. The *Beacon Journal* investigated and learned that although Martin himself never claimed exemption, Berenice had filed a separate affidavit of dependency for her husband. As a result, Martin was now classified 4-A and ineligible for the draft because he was a family man. The *Beacon Journal,* eager to advance Dick's candidacy by undermining Davey's, reminded its readers how the Kentite who demanded the head of the kaiser was himself content to "fire verbal shots" at him from the comfort and safety of the family living room.[47] As election day neared, Dick forces intensified the attack, running an ad based on Woodrow Wilson's campaign slogan during the 1916 presidential race:

1916—WILSON Kept Us Out of War
1918—DAVEY Kept Himself Out of War.

Martin scrambled to neutralize the damage from this latest turn. Three days before the election, he denied emphatically that Berenice had filed the dependency claim and swore that no one else had intervened on his behalf. At the bottom of his newspaper rejoinder, in big bold letters, ran the words, "Remember, A Vote for Davey is a Vote of Confidence in President Wilson and his Conduct of the War." In an attempt to link himself all the more closely with Wilson, Martin, along with several other Democratic candidates, ran his picture prominently in the *Beacon Journal* under the banner, "The Ticket That Supports The President."[48]

Martin was desperate; the *Beacon Journal* attacks on his patriotism were potentially devastating. He was running against a man who epitomized the true-blue American. Not only had Dick served in the Spanish-American War twenty years earlier, his office was a virtual shrine to American heroes. Pictures of Abraham Lincoln, Ulysses S. Grant, and the martyred William McKinley hung from every wall.[49] He was still an important man with friends in high places and certainly not an opponent to be taken lightly.

Governor Cox butted into the Fourteenth Congressional District contest. Two things troubled him. First, President Wilson had complicated every Democratic candidate's life on October 24 by asking American voters to return a Democratic Congress to Washington. Only then, the president contended, would the Central Powers recognize that they were dealing with an American people solidly behind their leader.[50] Wilson's plea violated the unspoken wartime truce between Republicans and Democrats. During the war, Republicans acceded to the time-honored tradition that foreign peril meant that partisan politics was temporarily adjourned. Republican anger over Wilson's perfidy could generate a dangerous backlash against the Democratic Cox. The same was true of the Davey draft exemption. Cox had warned Martin during his and Rockwell's meeting at the Deshler Hotel that the Kentite had better waive exemption when he registered for the draft. "Write it out in red ink and shoot it through," he had ordered. Now, with just days to go before the election, the fallout from Martin's disobedience threatened Cox's chances, and he did not like it one bit.[51]

Dick let the rift in Ohio Democratic ranks play out without personal comment. Instead, he took on the president and his call for a Democratic Congress, hoping that Wilson's treachery would galvanize Fourteenth Congressional

District Republicans. "The president," he proclaimed, "in his greed for power has made support of [his] administration the supreme test of loyalty—not
loyalty to the country or to the government, but loyalty to [his] administration. The declaration of that most autocratic of monarchs, Louis XIV of
France, 'I am the state,' is scarcely more arrogant."[52]

Unfortunately for Dick, he better captured the national mood than that
of voters in Ohio's Fourteenth Congressional District. Across the country,
voters, blaming Wilson for everything from deflated wheat prices to inflated
cotton prices and from prohibition to a rising tide of socialism, struck out
against his party. The Republicans captured both houses of Congress. Instead
of heading to Versailles as the anointed spokesman of a united people, he
was a leader repudiated, a fact not lost on veteran politicos like Britain's David Lloyd George and France's Georges Clemenceau. But none of that mattered for Charles Dick. He lost to Martin Davey by 1,500 votes. Particularly
disheartening was the fact that he failed to carry his own Summit County.
He also ran counter to Ohio's trend. Voters statewide had turned a thirteen
to nine Democratic edge in Ohio's congressional delegation into a fourteen
to eight Republican majority. Governor Cox escaped Republican wrath and
won, but only by eleven thousand votes, a margin considerably short of a
third-term mandate.[53]

Martin, too, defied the state's Republican swing. He had worried that President Wilson's call for a Democratic Congress would backfire in the Fourteenth Congressional District and give his opponent the victory. Wilson's
declaration, Martin lamented, was one of the "greatest political mistakes ever
made." Perhaps it was mere luck that Wilson's blunder did not cost Martin
Davey the election. More likely, however, Martin's victory resulted from his
hard work and skillful organization. He had to be helped, too, by the fact
that Charles Dick was known for not paying his bills. He was a wealthy man,
drawing in one year, for example, $96,000 in dividends from the Goodyear
Tire and Rubber Company, but was notorious for "stiffing" his creditors back
home. Considering his reputation, it surprised no one that he lost his hometown and county to Martin.

Given the national mood, Martin breathed easily only after the returns
were finally in. He was, of course, elated over the result but wondered if he
would be equal to his new job. His father seemed almost disappointed that
his son had won. The Sunday after the election, when Martin, Berenice,
and the children visited the elder Davey and his wife, seventy-two-year-old
John Davey, his expression grave, greeted his son with, "You know I never
wanted you in politics, but now that you have been elected to Congress I

want you above everything else to do your duty." Martin Davey, thirty-four and a U.S. congressman-elect, might just as well have been a six-year-old boy being ordered, "do it right or not at all."

Any disappointment that Martin may have felt over his father's unease gave way, however, in the next few days. On November 11 came the news that America and the world had been praying for. The generals had signed an armistice in a French railroad car in the woods of Compiègne. After four years of incalculable death and destruction, the Great War was over. Joy and relief were palpable everywhere. In Kent, people surged into the town square where Martin delivered a speech, not a single word of which he would later remember. All he recalled was the relief "written on the faces of [his] people."[54]

He had one official task left. On November 23, 1918, he walked into the Kent Village Hall for the last time as mayor and addressed the councilmen with whom he had toiled so diligently for the past five years. "Gentlemen," he began, "I respectfully submit my resignation as mayor of the village of Kent, effective immediately. This action causes me great personal regret and brings to a close a period of service for my hometown which has been arduous and yet satisfactory in a personal way and which leaves me happy recollections of the devotion and cooperation of all those with whom I have been associated in municipal work."[55]

With that it was done. He said good-bye to friends and family and within a few days he left his tiny village for Washington and a new life. Kent would always be home, but he could never really go home again.

Chapter Six

Off to Congress

MARTIN WAS STRUCK by how deeply the Great War had affected the nation's capital. Washington was a jumble of temporary buildings thrown up hurriedly to accommodate the proliferation of bureaus and workers spawned by the exigencies of war. The physical ugliness of the "tempos," as the structures were called, had transmogrified the great Mall between the White House and the Washington Monument from a span of marble and grass into an eyesore of lumber and glass. Not even Union Station, within walking distance of the White House, was immune to the blight. The magnificent railroad depot, just completed in 1908, was still encased in an iron web of scaffolding erected by laborers constructing war workers' dormitories in the Station Plaza.[1]

The wrought iron gates of the White House, locked tight for security reasons during the war, remained shut even afterward, a cold reminder to Washingtonians that their city was not the same and probably never would be, either. That reality had been brought home earlier when Washington—unlike New York, which had held a huge ticker tape parade—scarcely celebrated the armistice.[2] The capital's sobriety reflected the temper of its chief resident, Woodrow Wilson. The president, serious and driven in ordinary times, was a man possessed as he readied for Versailles and the making of a formal peace.

Three weeks to the day after the signing of the armistice, Martin L. Davey, still youthful at thirty-four, entered the Capitol to be sworn in as the representative of Ohio's Fourteenth Congressional District. Two other freshmen, Florian Lampert and Adolphus P. Nelson, both of Wisconsin, joined him in taking the oath of office on that December day. Although he never regretted

Martin Davey early in his congressional career, ca. 1920s. Ohio Historical Society.

his decision to run for Congress, Martin could not help but ponder his new responsibilities. Thoughts of his brother Paul, still in Europe, occupied his mind, too, as he swore his oath.[3]

Champ Clark of Missouri, who had nearly beaten Wilson for the Democratic presidential nomination in 1912, was Speaker and presided over the House during the waning days of the Sixty-fifth Congress. However, the Democrats had lost their majority in the November elections, and although they technically still controlled Congress until March 4, there were signs that the Republicans were already in charge.[4]

Woodrow Wilson was the first to feel the Republican sting now that the Democrats' days were numbered. On Martin Davey's second day in Congress, the president appeared before a joint session in the House chamber to announce that he would go to Versailles to work personally in forging a formal treaty ending the war. Wilson's decision shattered precedent. No American president had ever taken a personal hand in promulgating a formal peace. Such work had always been left to the diplomats. But Wilson did not view himself as merely the chief magistrate of the nation. Rather (living out his scholarly interests in the British parliamentary system of government), he saw himself as a prime minister, the bearer of both executive and legislative power. As such, he was, in his own mind, ideally suited to negotiate the peace with David Lloyd George, prime minister of Great Britain, and Georges Clemenceau, the premier of France, and others. Although his intentions were extraordinary, he told his audience that the peace conference was of "transcendent importance" and demanded his presence.[5]

In the House chamber, Republicans sat in stony silence, their disapproval palpable. They still seethed over the president's abrupt termination of the wartime truce between the parties prior to the congressional elections of 1918 and were not going to suffer gladly the arrogance of a man who presumed to be the savior of Versailles. The president had long since exhausted whatever reservoir of goodwill had existed when both sides fought the common enemy in Europe. Congressional Republicans would no longer serve Wilson's ego, and their truculence mounted amid rumors that the Senate would introduce a resolution removing Wilson (because of his absence from the nation) and elevating Vice President Thomas Marshall to the presidency.[6]

Martin carefully noted all this and quickly concluded that if not even the brilliant and dignified Wilson could unite Americans, there was no way that he himself could become a "statesman overnight." Although he would support his fellow Democrats in dealing with the nation's postwar problems, he would be better off concentrating on the needs of his constituents in the Fourteenth Congressional District.[7]

There was no shortage of work for the new congressman. Hundreds of telegrams flooded his office, most of them from worried parents and wives asking Martin to find out if their sons and husbands overseas were safe. He kept a direct cable line to General John J. Pershing's headquarters in France, inquiring about servicemen from the Fourteenth Congressional District. Pershing answered every request, whether the news was good or bad. It saddened Martin to report the worst, but despite the grief of heartbroken parents and wives, the knowledge that some sons and husbands would never return at least provided a sense of closure so that life could go on.

Martin's commitment to his task transcended the simple discharge of professional duty. What he was doing for the fretful relatives of missing servicemen came home personally to the entire Davey family. Paul Davey, Martin's younger brother serving with the U.S. Army Engineers, was missing in France. Martin finally located him in a military hospital overseas. On

Christmas Day 1918, the younger Davey contracted pneumonia and after a week of misery was admitted to an American Expeditionary Force hospital. Two weeks of medical care had worked wonders, and although Paul Davey would not be able to accompany his division to the United States, he would return as soon as he recovered.[8]

"Commercialized politics," as he called it, forced Martin to return home in January. Judge David Rockwell, so instrumental in Martin's political success, wanted to see his protégé about a pressing matter. Dutifully, Martin marched to Rockwell's Kent home. About midnight, after hours of conversation, Rockwell got to the point of his meeting with Martin. He wanted to be paid for the work he had done in getting Martin elected in 1918.

The younger man was shocked. He had reimbursed Rockwell for his expenses during the campaign and had never sensed that his mentor expected more. Moreover, Rockwell was already wealthy through his family and from a lucrative job with the Geiger-Jones Company, a Canton, Ohio, brokerage firm.

Martin explained that he had spent all his available funds and could not pay Rockwell for his past service. Undeterred by Martin's claim of penury, Rockwell suggested Davey Tree Expert Company stock as alternative compensation. Martin agreed and for $3,000 worth of company shares discharged his obligation to Rockwell. The relationship between the two men was never the same afterward, especially when Martin repurchased the stock from Rockwell seven or eight years later for $65,000.

The next day, a Sunday, Martin entrained for Washington. Berenice, Evangeline, Mary Berenice, and baby Martin bade him good-bye at the station. It was the last time his family would be whole.

On the following Friday, a worried Berenice called Martin in Washington to say that two-year-old Mary Berenice, known to the family as Happy, was seriously ill. She had taken sick the previous Tuesday with what was suspected as tonsillitis, a common affliction among the Davey children. By Friday, however, the family doctor altered his diagnosis in favor of diphtheria, for which he administered a vaccine.[9]

Martin quickly caught the first train for Kent, arriving at noon on Saturday. In the meantime, without confirming his diagnosis of diphtheria, the doctor administered another shot even as little Happy's condition worsened. She was still conscious when her father stepped into her room. She smiled weakly and spoke but faded into unconsciousness shortly after the physician administered yet another injection.[10]

The worried family brought in another doctor and then a third, a specialist from Cleveland, but nothing mattered. Happy worsened, lingering for six days before dying early in the morning on Friday, January 31, 1919. Her death was a "stunning blow" to the family. Martin called it the "most acute and lasting sorrow" that he had ever experienced. Understandably, he second-guessed the original tending physician. Should he have been more careful in diagnosing diphtheria? Should he have administered so many shots for the affliction without being absolutely sure of his diagnosis?[11] And certainly what underlay all Martin's questions was a parent's torment: How much of this was my fault? Should I have stopped the doctor from administering shots that likely did more harm than good? Should I have called the specialist sooner? If I had done these things, would little Happy have overcome her illness? Martin's once idyllic world was no more. In his hour of deepest grief he was certain that the "sun would never shine again."[12]

The family ultimately recovered, although the "sting" of Happy's death was always there. Berenice still had two young children to raise and Martin had important business to tend to in Washington. President Wilson had returned from Versailles in March to tend the home fires and to begin to sell the peace negotiations to Congress and the American people. By now, however, the Republicans had assumed control of both houses and were in no mood to make a Democratic president, especially one who had played dirty politics during the off-year elections in 1918, look good by rubber-stamping what he was doing at Versailles. Tired of high wartime taxes, years of Democratic domination, and the president himself, Republicans were bent on making Wilson's life miserable. They opposed virtually everything he wanted, especially his beloved League of Nations, which he was so ardently fashioning in his negotiations with European leaders. Republicans were also readying for the presidential campaign of 1920, so there was no reason why they should accede to anything Wilson wanted. Doing so would only make it seem as if the Democrats were leading America down the right path, and that would be utterly foolhardy in the coming campaign.

Martin observed the partisan bickering and noted that it was "good politics but bad statesmanship." Much of the congressional debate was pure bluster, highly dramatized for the public but really insubstantial. Once the curtain was drawn, bitter partisanship more often than not evaporated and public combatants on either side of the aisle left chambers arm in arm. John Nance Garner of Texas, later Franklin D. Roosevelt's vice president, and Nicholas Longworth of Ohio, Theodore Roosevelt's Republican son-in-law, appeared to despise one another on the House floor but frequently left the chamber together. They were the best of friends and, once away from the Capitol, frequently socialized. Martin noticed that members of the opposition were often closer to one another than they were to many of their fellow partisans.

Martin also sensed, even with the constant bickering, that a certain decorum pervaded the House. The chamber was both the most "exacting" as well as "tolerant" body that Martin ever knew. Members, despite their capacity for hearty debate, had no time or tolerance for "demagoguery, loose talk, or inaccurate information." Martin also found, to his relief, that senior members were kind to freshmen and did their best to help them succeed, even if they differed philosophically and politically from the newcomers.[13]

Understandably awed by the history of the chamber and the grandiloquence of its current occupants, Martin hung back, more observer than participant. It took him seven months to speak his first words on the House floor. Even then he delivered a rambling, silly, and essentially innocuous three-minute speech against daylight saving time, which had been enacted during the war to give farmers an extra hour of daylight to produce foodstuffs for American servicemen overseas. He could hardly wait to leave the "well" at the front of the chamber and during the entire three minutes was in a daze, as if someone had "hit him over the head with a gavel." He would have "given his right arm if the floor opened up and swallowed him." When it was over, he breathed a deep sigh of relief and somehow found the way back to his seat.[14]

His awkwardness notwithstanding, Martin worked hard to learn the ins and outs of being a good congressman. He sought the advice of senior members, thereby establishing himself as an eager and respectful tyro. He memorized the names not only of his colleagues but also of every doorkeeper, page, and attendant in the House. He also wanted his colleagues to know who he was. Accordingly, he made it a point to greet each by name. Although his seniors did not know him, by the second or third time Martin said hello they would ask their aides who the friendly young man was. "That's Davey, a new member from Ohio," would be the inevitable response. Within a few months, Martin knew everybody and, more importantly, everybody knew him.[15]

Everybody would have known him, anyway, after his response to an outbreak of violence in Centralia, Washington, on November 11, 1919. Members of the radical labor organization known popularly as the "Wobblies" (Industrial Workers of the World) fired on former soldiers who were marching in an armistice parade in Centralia. The volley from the Wobblies killed four and seriously wounded two others. Several other soldiers were injured in the lethal spray coming from the upper windows of the IWW hall.

It was the wrong thing to do. The marching veterans, armed and still comparatively fresh from their wartime service, regrouped, stormed the union headquarters and marched several Wobblies off to the city jail. Fortunately for the Wobblies, the soldiers kept the furious Centralia crowd at bay, or else the unionists would have never made it to the town lockup. At 7:30 that evening, however, the city's lights "mysteriously" flickered and went out. In the darkness, a mob burst into the jailhouse and dragged away Britt Smith, secretary of the local IWW chapter. He was shoved into a car surrounded by six other automobiles full of men, taken to a bridge on the outskirts of town, and lynched. Later that night, his body was found dangling about ten feet above the water.[16]

The Centralia Wobblies could not have chosen a worse time to fire their shots. Many Americans had already had enough of labor unrest and violence in 1919. In January, dock workers in New York City went on strike and were joined two weeks later by city workers. In early February, shipbuilders in Seattle, Washington, walked off their jobs and called for a general strike to cripple the American economy. In March, transportation workers in New Jersey struck, followed in July by New York City cigar makers, and by construction workers in Chicago. On August 1, 1919, seventy thousand striking railroaders shut down a good share of the nation's rail industry.[17] Union radicals, Bolshevik-influenced many believed, were blamed for it all.

The public's passion against unionists and other radicals intensified on April 30, 1919, when New York City postal workers found sixteen bombs about to be sent through the city mail. On June 2, a bomb intended for U.S. attorney general A. Mitchell Palmer ripped apart his Washington home and shattered the windows of his nearby neighbor, Franklin D. Roosevelt, assistant secretary of the navy. Almost simultaneously, bombs exploded at the home of the mayor of Cleveland and the homes of judges in New York City and Roxbury, Massachusetts.[18]

The *New York Times* and other newspapers blamed the Bolsheviks and the IWW for all the violence. Responding to the cries of angry Americans, Congress ordered Attorney General Palmer to crack down on the radicals. Palmer charged Assistant Attorney General Francis P. Garvan with the task. Garvan, with Palmer's approval, created a General Intelligence Division led by twenty-four-year-old J. Edgar Hoover, recently named a special assistant to the attorney general. Hoover's zeal for his job was boundless. If Palmer wanted to crack down on Bolshevik radicalism in America, Hoover was the man to do it.[19]

In the days after the Centralia "massacre," Americans grew angrier and more paranoid about the "Red Scare." An anarchist stool pigeon, trying to save his own skin, confessed to Philadelphia police that his cohorts were about to spread their terror through the mail. Bombs hidden under yards of bright ribbon and festive holly were to be sent as "Christmas presents" to a slew of federal, state and local officials who were cracking down on radicals across the nation. At the same time, police in Cleveland raided a Bolshevik nest, arrested seventy, and confiscated Communist literature and flags, and Attorney General Palmer was threatening to send the incendiary Emma Goldman back to Russia.[20]

The news from Centralia shocked Martin. He was already tired of "pandering" to foreigners who refused to "assimilate the ideas of America," but what had happened in the state of Washington was too much to bear. Within days of the Armistice Day shootings, Martin was in Hoover's office in the Department of Justice. He wanted to know more about the "Communist agitators" and their "sinister purpose," and no one could better supply that information than the Red-hating special assistant to the attorney general. Hoover and other Justice Department attorneys played to Martin's worst fears about the Bolshevik menace. In Washington's poisonous anti-Red atmosphere, Martin needed minimal persuasion. The lawyers under Hoover's command helped the young congressman draft a bill calling for up to a $10,000 fine and a twenty-year jail term for anyone convicted of trying to undo the U.S. government by force.[21]

Martin introduced the measure on November 17, 1919, a mere six days after the Centralia shootings. Its first provision, establishing a fine and imprisonment for those who would try to topple the government through violence, was controversial enough, but Martin had added a second provision that demanded as much as a $10,000 fine and ten years' imprisonment for anyone "making, displaying, writing, printing or circulating any sign, word, speech, picture, design, argument or teaching which advocates or justifies . . . sedition." Moreover, under Martin's measure, anyone belonging to any organization advocating sedition would be subject to the same penalties.[22]

Not everyone saw things as Martin and J. Edgar Hoover did. M. Claude Kelly, a Pennsylvania Republican, scored the Davey bill on the House floor. If enacted into law, he cried, it would "Prussianize" America. To underscore the difference between the American and Prussian way, Kelly described the cat-o'-nine-tails he saw in 1919 when visiting Maragne Chateau, the German general staff's headquarters on the Franco-German border. The weapon, a vicious-looking whip of nine leather thongs with a sharp piece of steel embedded in the end of each, was used by Prussian officers to beat raw the backs of common soldiers who periodically needed a dose of proper Teutonic medicine. To Kelly, Davey's sedition bill and a similar measure then under consideration by the Senate were nothing more than a Prussian cat-o'-nine-tails that would force Americans to fear the "punishing power of [their] rulers."[23]

Martin could barely wait to respond. Clearly taken in by Palmer and Hoover's Red Scare, he answered back: "It is a fine thing to wave the American flag," but, "unfortunately we face a real fact in the existence of a group of men [Communists] whose sworn objective is the destruction of the American government." If the Reds, aided by unfettered speech and print, succeeded in subverting the American government, he added, "where would free speech be then?" Urged on by applause from supporters, he reminded his colleagues that one of the first things Lenin did when he toppled the czar in 1917 was kill free speech. Martin's sedition bill, aimed only at the obvious enemies of the United States, would preserve the sacred American right to free expression.[24]

Despite the nation's Red paranoia, Martin's measure never generated enough popular or congressional support to become law. That was true even though he personally pumped thousands of dollars into a nationwide campaign for the bill. He was as thorough in this campaign as he had been in every other, sending copies of the bill and arguments for it to every major newspaper in the United States and to thousands of business, patriotic, and fraternal organizations. His efforts did compel many like-minded Americans to flood their congressmen and senators with letters supporting the bill, but all was for naught.

Too many radicals and near radicals, he complained, deliberately misrepresented his bill, turning it into something "vicious" when that was not its intent at all. Particularly nettlesome was the relentless criticism of the *Akron Beacon Journal* and its editor, Charles Landon Knight. Martin was convinced that Knight's *Beacon Journal* deliberately misrepresented his position to portray him as an "enemy of liberty" when nothing could be farther from the truth. Knight, with political ambitions of his own in the Fourteenth Congressional District, was, to Martin, "unscrupulous and vindictive," a man who demanded "slavish devotion" from everyone and punished anyone who acted otherwise.[25]

Knight's sting was no more venomous, though, than that of the Republicans in the House and Senate who had legitimate differences with the president over the Treaty of Versailles and also relished the prospect of making him pay for his "treachery" during the wartime elections of 1918 and for not sending a prominent Republican to the negotiations. Chief among the president's foes were Republican senators William Borah of Idaho and Hiram Johnson of California. The two headed a group of about fifteen "Irreconcilables" who refused to accept any treaty that might bind the United States to defend the colonial and general interests of such decadent powers as Great Britain and France. Johnson summarized the group's feelings when he proclaimed, "I am opposed to American boys policing Europe and quelling riots in every new nation's backyard."[26]

Equally opposed to the Treaty of Versailles and especially to the League of Nations to be born of it was another group of Senate Republicans soon known as the "Reservationists" for their tactic of amending the treaty until it met their approval. The imperious Henry Cabot Lodge of Massachusetts, who in 1915 confessed to his fellow patrician Theodore Roosevelt that he "never expected to hate anyone in politics with the hatred [he felt] towards [Woodrow] Wilson," led the Reservationists.[27] Lodge particularly despised the president for sacrificing American interests on the altar of British and French amity at Versailles, although he was less rabid about it than Borah.

Wilson could not ignore his senatorial opponents. The treaty, with its provision for his beloved League of Nations, had to pass the Senate by a two-thirds majority or else die. Moreover, Lodge chaired the powerful Senate Foreign Relations Committee, which had preliminary purview over debate. The Senate was already under Republican control forty-nine to forty-seven, but Lodge did not even need his partisan majority to kill the treaty. All he required was thirty-three votes, and he soon had those. Emboldened by the support of his colleagues, he had challenged the president by circulating an anti-League round robin declaration among his fellow senators and senators-elect on March 3, 1919. Thirty-seven of them had signed it, so victory was already his.[28] The stubborn Wilson would not have his way on this one.

Although this struggle was playing out in the Senate, Martin Davey keenly observed it all from the House side. He knew the treaty had flaws, but the Senate Republicans were not so interested in mending it as they were in wreaking their vengeance against the president by savaging his version of it. The Republicans were clever, Martin noted. They stirred Italian-Americans against the treaty by emphasizing Italy's failure to gain Fiume, an Adriatic seaport Italians had long coveted and thought was theirs because they had been on the right side during the Great War. Wilson's senatorial enemies had fanned similar flames of resentment among Irish-Americans by reminding them that the peace hammered out at Versailles left a strong British presence in Ireland. And, of course, Wilson had on his own won the undying enmity of many German-Americans who would forever associate him with the harsh victor's peace forced on their fatherland. The Republicans, Martin believed, had also deliberately fired the passions of thousands of other disgruntled hyphenated Americans by funneling incendiary articles into various ethnic newspapers.

Martin noticed, too, how the Borah- and Lodge-led Republicans constantly harped on Article X of the League of Nations covenant, the provision that according to critics would have had American soldiers scurrying from one European hot spot to another to preserve peace. Martin felt that this Republican charge was exaggerated, but even if it were not, it might have been necessary and wise to use American power to ensure a stabler world. During the Second World War, Martin wrote that the bitter partisans of the 1920s bore at least some responsibility for the second global conflagration in less than a generation.[29] The United States rejected the Treaty of Versailles and consequently never joined the League of Nations. The poisonous atmosphere in which the League struggle was fought destroyed more than the president's dream of a world in mutual accord; it destroyed his health as well. As stubborn as Lodge was determined, Wilson decided to take the League issue to the nation in a western tour in the late summer and early fall of 1919. Already frail and shaking visibly, the president delivered thirty-seven speeches in twenty-two days. After an address in Pueblo, Colorado, on September 25, the president boarded his train en route to five more destinations in the West. At two in the morning, his doctor, Cary R. Grayson, and personal secretary, Joe Tumulty, found him nauseated and drooling in his private compartment. Reluctantly, he canceled his remaining speeches, returned to Washington and on October 2 suffered a major stroke that debilitated him mentally and physically for the rest of his term.[30]

Wilson's breakdown was not surprising. A delicate man, both physically and temperamentally, he cracked, not only because of the assault on his League of Nations but also because his Republican enemies scourged his entire conduct of the war. They blamed him for the high taxes Americans endured during the conflict and scrutinized his every wartime decision in hopes of finding some scandal that would discredit his administration. Will Hays, the Republican national chairman, looking ahead to the 1920 elections, continually inflamed Americans against their president for transgressions largely imagined. Martin grudgingly gave Hays his due. Although the Republican leader was "unscrupulous," he cleverly conducted his smear campaign knowing that people generally "voted their major prejudices." That Hays's charges against the Democrats were more rhetoric than substance was obvious, Martin noted, when the Republicans, triumphant in 1920, curiously stopped looking for evidence of Democratic wrongdoing during the war.[31]

Throughout his first two terms (one short, one long), Martin supported his party's wartime and postwar programs. Like so many freshman representatives, he trod carefully at first (except for his sedition bill), not stepping on toes or stealing into the limelight. He took care of his constituents in Akron by raising the limit on a spending bill for a public building in the city, supported a nationwide salary increase for postal workers who were struggling to get by after the war on salaries of $1,200 a year and, reflecting his long-standing ties to the principles of his father and the Davey Tree Expert Company, argued passionately for a $225,000 increase in the budget of the Bureau of Entomology. All of these were essentially mundane.[32]

If Martin distinguished himself, it was as a Red baiter. When his fellow representatives investigated the 1920 railroad strike that ground much of the nation's transport to a halt, he jumped gleefully into the discussion. He had no quarrel with the rank-and-file railroaders striking for better wages, but he believed those innocents were led by IWW radicals who had but a single purpose, the destruction of the U.S. government. What made the IWW all the more nefarious and dangerous, according to Martin, were its direct links to Russian Bolshevism. A union friend of his had warned him that "the Red radicals" had infiltrated the friend's local in Akron and were simply awaiting a signal from Moscow to unleash the *Internationale* against the United States.[33]

Martin, like so many of his colleagues on the House floor and fellow citizens nationwide, remained captive to the Red Scare as 1920 wound to a close. Two weeks before Christmas, he urged the passage of legislation that would limit the flow of aliens to the United States and make citizenship more difficult for those already in the country. He felt a little guilty for doing so because his own father had immigrated to the United States some fifty years earlier. But these times were different, he said. "America needs to be protected now against too great an influx of those who do not and cannot appreciate our country and her institutions and whom we cannot assimilate by any process."[34]

His position, if not defensible, was understandable. The United States' entry into the Great War ended a long period of American somnolence where Europe was concerned. Prior to 1917, the United States had primarily bumped heads with European nations only when they intruded into the affairs of states in the Western Hemisphere. Even then the confrontations essentially involved jostling and blustering and never resulted in an actual clash of arms on American or European soil. But the Great War had changed all that. Europe was no longer some far-off place; thousands of Americans had died there fighting for people who neither spoke English nor shared American culture.

Now so many of these "strangers" sought sanctuary in the United States and, even worse to many Americans, wanted to become full fledged citizens.

The idea of a European "contamination" was exacerbated by the Lenin-led triumph of the Bolsheviks in Russia in 1917. Ever since Chicago's Haymarket Square Riot of 1886, many Americans were certain that foreign-born anarchists were determined to destroy the American way of life. Lenin's dark tyranny revived that old fear and gave it a new and very real face. If America kept open her doors, how long would it be before the European hordes, Bolsheviks among them, would inundate the nation and destroy everything it represented?

America's answer was to turn inward in the 1920s. The defeat of the Treaty of Versailles and the League of Nations was more than a rebuking of Woodrow Wilson; it reflected the popular will. Clearly, Americans had their fill of European entanglements. The Republicans already sensed that, and the Democrats, as the presidential election of 1920 neared, were going to learn the same lesson.

Ohio's James Cox strode off with the grand prize at the Democratic national convention in San Francisco. As a kindness to the enfeebled Wilson, still the nominal head of his party, the delegates at San Francisco chose the administration's assistant secretary of the navy, thirty-eight-year-old Franklin D. Roosevelt, as Cox's vice presidential running mate. Roosevelt was the sole personal link between postwar Democrats and the past and represented New York State with all its electoral votes. Cox would run against the Republican nominee, Senator Warren G. Harding, in a contest that pitted one Ohioan against another.

Euphoric over his nomination, Cox felt honor bound to pay his obeisance to the specter living out his final shadowy days as president of the United States. Shortly after the convention, he and Roosevelt called at the White House where Wilson, in a wheelchair, was taking in some fresh air. The president's appearance was shocking. Not only was he wan and thin, his aides had draped a shawl over his shoulder in a weak attempt to hide his useless left arm. Cox could not stop the tears from welling up as he approached the man who only a few years earlier had been the savior of democracy.

"Thank you for coming," the president uttered barely loud enough to hear. So pathetic was Wilson that Cox blurted out words that he thought would comfort the stricken man. "Mr. President, we are going to be a million percent with you and your administration, and that means the League of Nations." From his wheelchair the president looked up at Cox and summoned the strength to mutter, "I am very grateful. I am very grateful."[35]

In the few seconds that it took him to promise Wilson that he would support the League of Nations to the end, Cox sealed the fate of the 1920 Democratic ticket. Martin thought the commitment was foolish, a bad decision born out of Cox's emotion upon seeing the broken-down president. It never should have happened in the first place, he concluded, because Cox's visit with Wilson was nothing more than vain grandstanding. The Republicans could scarcely have asked for more—Cox had not only pledged the national ticket to a lost cause in 1920, he had also likely delivered up a number of other Democrats in the process.[36]

Martin surmised that he might well be one of those. The Fourteenth Congressional District was already overwhelmingly Republican, and any Democrat who hoped to carry it could ill afford anything other than a flawless strategy and campaign. The national ticket's commitment to the League of Nations left Martin (and for that matter every other Democratic candidate) with two platforms to defend—his own and James Cox's. Troubled but undaunted, Martin decided to seek reelection in 1920.

His Republican opponent was Charles Landon Knight, the editor and publisher of the *Akron Beacon Journal,* the major newspaper in the Fourteenth Congressional District. Knight was a newcomer to politics—he had never run for office before. A Georgia native born two years after the Civil War ended, he graduated from Columbia University and had spent his entire adult life in the newspaper business, first as a reporter and ultimately as an editor and publisher. His closest connection to political office came when Governor Cox appointed him to the northern Ohio Board of Appeals for industrial exemption, which required him to determine who was and who was not to be spared from the military draft during World War I. During the war, Knight also served as food administrator of Akron's Summit County, again through appointment by Cox.[37]

Knight's nomination for Congress had been engineered by one of Akron's wiliest politicos, C. Nelson Sparks. Sparks had started out as a Democrat but switched to the Republican side after he was denied a state appointment to the Summit County Liquor License Board in 1918. Incensed by his party's ingratitude after his years of loyal service, Sparks adroitly managed Akron's Republican affairs for years. He operated best from behind the scenes. As Martin colorfully noted, Sparks "made the bullets, and . . . other people shot them."[38]

The Fourteenth Congressional District race was fought against the backdrop of national politics. Both sides brought in their big guns. On October 23, thousands swarmed inside and outside Akron's Armory to hear Senator

Borah excoriate the League of Nations and the Democratic Party that created and supported it. Five days later, the Republican presidential nominee himself braved a driving rain to hammer home the same theme to another Akron crowd. Sitting on the platform next to Harding was Charles Landon Knight.[39]

Not to be outdone by the Republicans, Akron Democrats had arranged for Cox to speak at the city's massive Goodyear Hall. Ten thousand of the Democratic faithful ignored the season's first biting cold on October 29 to hear their man denounce Harding as an incompetent who was nothing more than the pliant pawn of Republican Party bosses and a willing tool of big business. Harding's opposition to the League of Nations, Cox explained, was easy to understand—the Republican nominee was a reactionary rooted in the past, while Americans who supported the world organization were progressives with an intelligent eye to the future. Martin Davey, who personally supported the League of Nations but thought it foolish to inject it into the campaign, did not stand alongside Cox in Akron. Instead, on the same night, he addressed a smaller Akron crowd in the Goodyear gymnasium where he mentioned not a word about Cox's beloved League.[40]

Martin needed a different issue to beat Knight, whose powers of persuasion were enhanced exponentially because of his editorial control over the *Akron Beacon Journal.* Never at a loss for cleverness, the Kentite hit upon the idea of using Knight's own words as a weapon. During the war, Knight had editorially flayed the Wilson administration for its wastefulness and toleration of "grafters," politicians and businessmen who had capitalized on the war to line their own pockets. With the proper twist and turn, Knight's own words, Martin thought, might undo his bid for office. Such an attack would have greater validity if it came from a source other than the Davey camp. With Martin's approval and financial support, a group of former servicemen, Democrats and Republicans alike, formed the Ex-Service Men's Davey-for-Congress Club, which soon took on the more manageable name, the Loyalty League. The Loyalty League compiled a number of Knight's wartime editorials and published them under the provocative title, *Light on Knight.* The thirty-page booklet scored Knight as unpatriotic and pro-German for criticizing the administration during the war.[41]

Light on Knight caught the eye of F. W. Galbraith Jr., national commander of the American Legion, and J. R. McQuigg, commander of the Summit County Legion. Investigators from the state Legion pored over Knight's wartime editorials and speeches and concluded that there was some substance to the charges in *Light on Knight.* Little more than a week before the election, McQuigg, acting under Galbraith's authorization, wired the Summit County Council of the American Legion, telling its members that if it were indeed true that Knight intended never to "vote a dollar" to sustain the Bureau of War Risk Insurance (the agency created to aid disabled veterans) and would refuse to vote any funds to rebuild the U.S. army and navy, then "every loyal citizen in the district should unite in defeating him at the polls."[42] Lest anyone think that the Legion attack was purely partisan, both Galbraith and McQuigg were Republicans of long standing.

The Legion telegram stung and surprised Knight. He reacted quickly to control whatever harm had already been done. First he issued a statement to the press claiming that he was not surprised by McQuigg's telegram because McQuigg was blindly pro-military. Knight forces then quickly marshaled the support of several hundred local legionnaires and former servicemen to send an angry telegram to Legion headquarters in Columbus. Knight took the offensive in Barberton a few days later, by proclaiming that his only sin was exposing the wartime waste that was endemic in the Wilson administration. His remarks were greeted with thunderous applause.[43]

Martin's attack on Knight's patriotism exposed the Kentite's own vulnerabilities. Through his editorials and speeches, Knight informed his readers and listeners that the man who criticized his loyalty was himself nothing more than a draft dodger. Knight was only too happy to resurrect Davey's 4-A status and remind voters that it was Berenice Davey who signed her husband's dependency affidavit. Martin had his nerve questioning another man's patriotism when at the moment of hard truth he had hidden behind a woman's skirts. His own words that he was "rich, virile, and 100% American" suddenly had a new meaning, and Knight supporters only too gladly suggested to Fourteenth Congressional District voters that their man's opponent never made it into the trenches "because the trenches never reached Kent."[44]

Clearly the campaign had become a bitter personal struggle between two men who loathed one another. Genuine issues were swept aside as both Knight and Davey were caught up in a contest of insults. Here Martin was at a distinct disadvantage because he had declared a war of words with a man who purchased his ink by the barrelful. Assured of the most favorable coverage in his own newspaper, Knight took after Martin, proclaiming, in a mean reference to Davey's background in tree surgery, that Fourteenth Congressional District voters should send the "Kent prodigy back to filling woodpecker holes with cement." Knight's campaign surrogates were nearly as clever (and mean), with one claiming that the Fourteenth Congressional District campaign was "between brains and brass. The brains [came] from Akron and the brass from Kent." Knight kept up the personal attacks by sneering at Martin's claim of personal service to seven thousand of his constituents. He dismissed the Kentite as a mere "errand boy."[45]

Charles Knight may have had the power of the mighty *Akron Beacon Journal* behind him, but Martin Davey, weaned on hard toil and steeled by the poverty of his early boyhood, was no stranger to combat. He had an ally in Democratic councilman Gus Kasch of Akron. Kasch had long despised Knight and was only too willing to strike out against him in any way he could. The Akron councilman had learned some damaging things about Knight's past. In 1899, Knight managed the *Miners' Journal,* a daily newspaper published in Pottsville, Pennsylvania, a small town about sixty-five miles northwest of Philadelphia. He had been hired primarily to revivify the struggling daily and to that end persuaded two men, Charles G. O'Bleness and Cleland Schwarr, to invest $3,000 and $1,000, respectively, in the paper. The enthusiasm of the two waned, and after about three months they persuaded a constable to arrest Knight for embezzlement and fraud. The charges, borne more out of the disillusionment of O'Bleness and Schwarr with the newspaper business than out of any criminal deceit, were dropped after Knight returned their original investment.[46]

The episode had lain dormant for more than twenty years until Kasch, eager to level any blow against his sworn enemy, unearthed the story and published it as an advertisement in the *Akron Herald* on October 8, 1920. There it lay, apparently dead, just one more salvo in the mudslinging of the Fourteenth Congressional District race. Near the end of October, however, with the Democratic candidate's chances dimming, along came Kasch to poke the corpse. It stirred. In a letter to the editor of the *Akron Sunday Times* and then in an advertisement in the same paper on election eve, Kasch resurrected the charges, forcing a desperate Knight to proclaim his eleventh-hour innocence on the front page of his own newspaper.[47]

It was now up to the voters, and they chose Knight but not by much. Out of nearly 120,000 votes cast, the Akronite won by 5,800. The victory was not so much Knight's as it was the Republican Party's. Harding won easily over Cox, Republicans swept to overwhelming control of Congress, and Ohioans elected a Republican governor, Harry L. Davis, and a Republican state legislature. Martin must have felt at least minor satisfaction knowing that Knight ran 25,000 votes behind Harding, meaning that many Fourteenth Congressional District Republicans had crossed over to vote Democratic. The satisfaction was compounded by Martin's victory over Knight in Summit County and in the Republican's hometown of Akron. Martin could not, however, be smug about his small triumph because Knight nearly returned the favor in Portage County, losing on Davey's home soil by a mere thirteen votes, 6,701–6,714.[48]

When it was over, Martin retreated gracefully: "The majority have spoken and I accept the verdict cheerfully. I shall lay down the duties of the office with no excuse or apology and retire with a measure of relief. I congratulate the winner and wish for him a successful and useful period of service."[49]

The victor seemed wearier and angrier than the loser: "I have no sense of undue elation over my election," Knight told the public. And, unable to forget and forgive the hard hitting during the campaign, he could not help but lecture his foes: "For those persons who did not hesitate to use any means, however foul, to defeat me I have no feeling except of sorrow and pity. Perhaps the day may come when even they may see that good morals no less than good politics will no longer endorse or sustain such methods."[50]

Martin's postelection reflections were less somber. He had lost, but much of the blame could be justifiably laid at the feet of the leader of the Democratic ticket, James M. Cox. The presidential candidate had misjudged the American public on everything from the League of Nations to women's suffrage. It was easy to see that he had erred when he injected the League, essentially a dead issue, into the presidential campaign. But he had also worked hard for female balloting, especially in Tennessee where the issue hung in delicate balance. Tennessee ratified the nineteenth amendment, as ultimately did the rest of the nation. Cox believed that the new voters would cast Democratic ballots. He was badly mistaken.

Martin was less enthusiastic than Cox about female suffrage, commenting that it seemed to him that in 1920 women were suddenly "plunged into politics, almost without training and experience." He, accurately as it turned out, was less inclined to think that women would vote the Democratic ticket than was Cox. Martin believed in harsher political rules than did idealists like Cox. After his 1920 defeat, he philosophized that "most people do not vote for favors that already have been received, but rather for those they hope to obtain in the future." That certainly held true for men and now was apparently true for women as well. The nineteenth amendment had come with a Democrat in the White House. It was now time for women to see what a Republican president could do for them.

Although he had labored valiantly for victory, Martin had prepared himself for defeat. Consequently, the loss, though hard to take, was nonetheless not shattering. He had worked hard on Capitol Hill but knew better than to make politics the be-all and end-all of his life. If it were, defeat would be so anguishing as to make recovery virtually impossible.[51]

With four months left in his term, he had little to do other than loll around Washington. On his last day in the House, he delivered a passionate but meaningless speech on the significance of trees, largely as a paean to his father.[52] After that, it was a quick overnight train ride home to Berenice, Evangeline, and Martin Jr. Washington belonged to the Republicans now. He was out of it, and anyway the Shadow of Blooming Grove was about to descend upon the nation's capital.

Chapter Seven

Out of Office

IT WAS NOT A BAD TIME for a Democrat to be out of Washington. Republicans would soon have to hang their heads for all the trouble the charming, silver-haired Harding was about to deal them. Teapot Dome and Elk Hills and the names Albert Fall and Harry Sinclair would conjure up memories of public thievery unheard of since the days of Ulysses S. Grant a half-century earlier. Harding may have had no *direct* hand in the scandals that tarnished his name, but he knew what his thieving friends were doing during his watch and failed to act. The only thing that kept the president from public dishonor was his death before the scandals broke wide open in 1923.

All that was bad enough, but there were more skeletons in the president's closet. Whispers about his extramarital affairs, including a lengthy one with a woman thirty years his junior, followed him from Marion, Ohio, to Washington, D.C. To those who did not know the real Harding, no one looked more but acted less presidential. Privately, Washingtonians had their misgivings but maintained their silence. Only Alice Roosevelt Longworth, Theodore Roosevelt's sharp-tongued daughter, was unafraid to speak the truth— "Harding was not a bad man," she said. "He was just a slob."[1]

Martin missed the action of the Capitol, but only briefly. For the first time in eight years he was free of the constant pressures of public affairs. It felt good to be home where he could devote his full time and energy to the Davey Tree Expert Company, although he had never really been totally away from it when he was in Washington. Kent was only an overnight train run from the nation's capital, and Martin, when in Congress, typically had spent two or three days a week back home. His secretary had kept him current on congressional affairs, and whenever important votes or debates were scheduled he would catch a quick train back to Washington.[2]

Kent had changed dramatically in the few years Martin had been away. Its population jumped from under 4,500 in 1910 to over 7,000 by 1920, and it was now officially a city. The burst necessitated construction of a new high school on ten acres purchased in part from John Davey. A new hotel went up on Main Street, and in 1921 the town council launched an ambitious paving program that turned dusty roads into elegant streets. Kentites also realized that their old volunteer fire department was no longer sufficient and voted a $60,000 bond issue to create a full-time firefighting force. The city went all out and spent the first monies, a princely $10,500, for a brand-new LaFrance fire truck.[3]

The Davey Tree Expert Company had experienced a similar exuberance. By the war's last year, the Kent-based firm had established offices on 5th Avenue in New York City and in the McCormick Building in Chicago. It had also branched out all over New England and elsewhere on the East Coast and in the Midwest as far as St. Louis and Kansas City. The company even had a posh Canadian address, 22 Victoria Square, Montreal.[4] John Davey, so often maligned and ridiculed, had to enjoy it all from his Woodard Avenue home. Once the town joke, he was now one of Kent's leading citizens.

The elder Davey had long been removed from the daily operations of his company. While Martin was off in Washington, Paul Davey had taken over, and Davey Tree prospered under his guidance. His initial successes led to a contract with Kent's public utility company, Northern Ohio Power and Light, to clear trees for its power lines. Utility companies at the time were notorious for lopping off branch after branch until a tree stood virtually leafless with sawed-off limbs as an ugly testament to the linesmen's butchery. Both Martin and John believed Paul had erred by agreeing to do the clearing work for Northern Ohio Power and Light, and they let him know it. Paul persuaded them, however, that he could do the job right and in a way that would not compromise the Davey company's reputation. He succeeded and was soon offered similar work in Ravenna, Medina, and Toledo. Before long the Davey Tree Expert Company got a contract to clear utility lines for Boston Edison in Massachusetts. As the company's reputation spread, it was given jobs in other states, and utility line clearing became one of its mainstays, allowing the employment of more men year round.[5]

Still under Paul's lead, the company moved into large-volume spraying to control insects and fungal diseases. Spraying large trees was difficult and demanded massive manpower. All that changed, however, when an ingenious employee built a new spraying rig, and the company bought a huge power sprayer appropriately dubbed "Friend." Its three-hundred-gallon tank mounted on the front of a one-ton truck could spray twenty gallons of pesticide and fungicide per minute under such force that Davey men could reach the tops of even the tallest trees. Their first few jobs were in Greenwich, Connecticut, but from there Davey crews moved on to Boston, Philadelphia, back to Connecticut and then into New York and New Jersey. In the first five weeks of the spring and summer of 1921, the Davey Tree Expert Company earned $5,000 merely by spraying trees.[6]

While Paul was advancing the company's technology, Martin directed sales. It was a good combination, one that allowed the mechanically oriented Paul to prove his skills and the people-oriented Martin to do what he did best, sell. Relieved of any technical responsibilities, Martin had time to cultivate personal relationships that served him well in the years ahead. Especially important to Martin was Charles Sharp of Ravenna, a friend since 1918. While Martin was in Congress, Sharp tended to every detail in the Fourteenth Congressional District. With a remarkable memory, Sharp recalled virtually verbatim everything Martin's constituents said. His reports kept Martin close to the pulse of his district. Sharp's only fault was a lack of confidence, a shortcoming that turned him into little more than a yes-man for Martin. But that flaw could be easily overlooked given Sharp's skill at tending the home fires of the Fourteenth.

Unlike Sharp, but equally significant to Martin, was L. L. Poe, editor of the *Akron Sunday Times*. Where Sharp never differed with his boss, Poe had a fierce independence that sometimes bothered Martin. He was not stubborn, Martin concluded, but simply had strong convictions. Poe had a rare ability—he could cast his personal likes and dislikes aside and render judgments based solely on the hard facts of any given situation. He was brilliant, Martin recalled, and, despite the lack of a solid formal education, was one of the best-read men around. If he had a fault, it was a bluntness that sometimes alienated even his friends.

More important than Martin's friendships with Sharp and Poe was his relationship with Myrna Young (later Myrna Smith). Young graduated as Kent High School's valedictorian in 1919 when she was only sixteen and soon after took a secretarial job at the Davey Tree Expert Company. Her diligence and intelligence caught Martin's attention. He drafted her to work in his congressional race against Charles Knight in 1920, and she served in every one of his subsequent campaigns. When he captured the Ohio governorship in 1934

Davey Tree Expert Company office staff, 1922–23. Myrna Young Smith stands in the front row, tenth from left. Evangeline Davey Smith Collection, Martin L. Davey Papers, Kent State University Libraries, Special Collections and Archives.

and 1936, he took her along as his personal secretary. She shone in Columbus just as she had in Kent, and no one ever served Martin more loyally.

By 1921 the American economy was sputtering. Davey Tree continued to attract clients, but profits plummeted. Although Martin did not blame Harding directly for the nation's difficulties, he could not help but fault voters who blindly believed that prosperity went hand in hand with a Republican president. That was certainly not true, and by the time Harding swore the presidential oath on March 4, 1921, the country was in a full-blown recession.

Martin's involvement in politics, which certainly had its upside, had a downside as well. The sluggish economy forced Davey Tree to rely on a line of credit from a local bank. Ordinarily loans were extended perfunctorily, especially when companies had solid credit histories, which was certainly the case for the Davey Tree Expert Company in 1922. However, when Martin appeared at the bank office to formalize the loan, he was told that no money would be forthcoming. Stunned by the unexpected reversal, Martin asked why. The conservative banker who turned down Martin told him that it was rumored he was going to run for governor, and it was the bank's policy not to mix business with politics.

Once again, Martin, who had no intentions of running for governor, was reminded how fragile banking relationships could be. Fortunately, he could meet the company's cash shortage by borrowing against the life insurance policies he and other family members had bought years before. Even though the Davey Tree Expert Company had been on solid ground for more than a dozen years, it was still prisoner to rising and falling economic tides.

Undaunted by temporary setbacks, Martin sought to increase Davey Tree's volume through even broader advertising. Each new advertisement stressed the perfection of Davey techniques and services. Testimonials from the prominent Americans who had used Davey services dotted every ad. In many cases, the ads were works of art, gorgeous reproductions of fine paintings intended to entice tree lovers everywhere to hire Davey Tree.

At the same time, the company expanded its experimental and research operations. Using the experience gained from treating thousands of trees over the years, Davey chemists concocted a superior tree food, combining organic and chemical compounds. The company also expanded its educational programs for crewmen. By 1922, workers were required to spend a good portion of three years sharpening their laboratory and field skills before dealing directly with clients. Davey workers became renowned for their skill and professionalism.

The company prospered, and Martin was certainly busy enough ensuring that the success continued. However, something was wanting in his life—he missed politics. By the spring of 1922 he thought about running for Congress again. Ever the organizer, he wrote prominent Fourteenth Congressional District Democrats to sound out their sentiments about another Davey candidacy. All who answered urged him to run and promised their support. He easily won the Democratic primary over Akron judge A. F. O'Neil, and by the fall of 1922 was ready to take on the Republicans again.[7]

Charles Landon Knight, who had beaten Martin in 1920, had had enough of Congress after one term and sought the Republican nomination for governor instead. Martin's opponent, consequently, was Frank E. Whittemore, an eight-year member of the Ohio State legislature with no experience in national office. Whittemore was promoted as a keen student of banking, agriculture, commerce, and the tariff, and as a friend of farmers, merchants, working men, consumers, and women and children. Also, Republicans proclaimed, it would be wise for Fourteenth Congressional District voters to send a Republican to a Congress they were certain to control.[8]

Shortly after his primary victory, Martin went to Washington to confer with Ohio's Democratic senator, Atlee Pomerene, who had already served two terms in the Senate and wanted a third in 1922. A tall, dour man invariably clad in black, Pomerene was a bit of a party maverick, particularly in his strident antilabor views borne out of what he believed was Communist agitation in the railroad strikes of the early twenties.

Fearful that Pomerene's fierce antiunionism might generate widespread working-class disaffection for other Democratic candidates in 1922, Martin politely urged the senator to forgo his usual attacks on labor. Pomerene's opponent, Simeon Fess, Martin suggested, was so notoriously antilabor that working men would readily overlook Pomerene's own antiunionism and vote Democratic. However, if Pomerene antagonized labor in the campaign, unionists across the state might well vote Republican just to spite him. Pomerene seemed to resent the presumptuousness of the younger man, and simply harrumphed, "Well, they better not start any fight with me."[9]

Pomerene ignored Martin's suggestion and in his first speech of the 1922 campaign needlessly attacked labor. As Martin had feared, union forces united behind Fess and sent Pomerene down to defeat by nearly fifty thousand votes.[10] Pomerene's stubbornness sealed his fate. Martin had proven wiser than the man several years older and more experienced.

Martin was equally interested in the Democratic nominee for governor in 1922, Alvin Victor Donahey. State auditor for eight years, Donahey had run for governor in 1920 but lost to Harry Davis despite running a quarter million votes ahead of presidential nominee James M. Cox in the Democratic electoral fiasco that year. Now he was back and, despite the tepid support of party leaders, was the darling of the rank and file, who readily identified with his rough-and-tumble style. While more urbane party chiefs like David L. Rockwell cringed at Donahey's butchering of the King's English, ordinary Ohioans appreciated a man who said "ain't" and could chew and spit with the best of them.[11]

Even more intriguing to Martin, for personal reasons, was what the Republicans were doing in the 1922 race for the governorship. His old foe, Charles Landon Knight, sought the nomination, but, as Martin gleefully noted, the *Beacon Journal* publisher's reputation and influence were limited to the Fourteenth Congressional District. He lost to Carmi Thompson of Cleveland, a man with impeccable credentials in state and national government. Thompson had been Speaker of the Ohio House of Representatives, secretary of the state of Ohio and served as assistant secretary of the interior and treasurer of the United States under Republican presidents.[12]

The Donahey-Thompson and Pomerene-Fess contests could affect Martin's own chances in 1922. A Republican sweep might carry over into Martin's

Fourteenth Congressional District race against Whittemore. To minimize that possibility, Martin worked hard to ensure that as many Democrats as possible were registered to vote. Demonstrating his already sharp organizational skills, Martin concentrated on the biggest city in the district, Akron. The city's high industrial wages had lured many southerners (most of them Democrats) northward. It was imperative that they be registered to vote, so Martin hired seventy-five women to visit house to house in Akron to find any unregistered Democrats. Martin's female force discovered twenty-five thousand of them. Within a week, each had a letter from Martin urging the recipient to register. All those potentially lost votes impressed still another lesson on Martin, a lesson that served him well throughout his political career—"Garner your own."[13]

In the fall campaign, Martin stressed the importance of returning an experienced hand to Congress. "A new man in Congress," he proclaimed, "[was] just like a freshman in college. He has to serve long enough to get into the sophomore class." He reminded Fourteenth Congressional District voters that, according to the House's seniority rule, veteran members of Congress laid claim to memberships on the prime committees, while former congressmen like Martin had second choice. New members, and Whittemore would be one of those, were assigned the leavings. In the last ten years, the Fourteenth Congressional District had elected a new representative every time, thereby diminishing its influence in the highest circles of government. Citizens of the Fourteenth, Martin asserted, deserved better.[14]

Martin also reminded voters of his personal service to constituents during his first two terms. The "Human Touch," he called it in his campaign ads. "[I] never forgot the folks back home," he claimed. "No letter ever went unanswered; no request for service was ever ignored." And, he stressed, those letters went out the very day they were received, and if a writer had a particularly pressing problem, Martin sent a telegram so that the worried constituent would not even have to wait the few days it took mail to reach Ohio from Washington. His track record in solving problems was remarkable; his motto was, "It can be done."[15]

Martin's opponent was a colorless man disinclined to brawl publicly. He certainly was no Charles Landon Knight. And with no real issues in the Fourteenth Congressional District dividing the two candidates, Martin was essentially contesting an election with a phantom. Consequently both candidates were reduced to attacking (in Martin's case) and defending (in Whittemore's case) the Republican Congress sitting in Washington. As they so typically had for decades, congressional Republicans responded to the downturn in the nation's economy by enacting a high protective tariff in 1921. The 1921 measure was an "emergency" tariff, one intended to prop up American industry and commerce while Congress worked out a permanent levy, the Fordney-McCumber Bill. The emergency tariff, Martin charged, had failed miserably. Wheat prices, for example, had plummeted from $1.82 per bushel before the tariff to $1 a bushel a year after. With that kind of Republican-inspired protection, American wheat producers would soon be bankrupt. The Fordney-McCumber tariff, Martin warned, would be even worse. Sugar and wool prices would soar, unconscionably raising the cost of living for millions of Americans. The day before the election, Cordell Hull, the chairman of the Democratic National Committee, fortified Martin's claims about the evils of the Republican-sponsored Fordney-McCumber tariff. It would, he predicted, force Americans to pay an additional $4 billion in taxes, most of which would be funneled into the pockets of the nation's plutocrats. Less than $300 million would end up in the U.S. Treasury.[16]

Whittemore was forced to respond. Speaking in Akron, the Republican candidate proclaimed that the Fordney-McCumber Bill was the "greatest tariff measure ever introduced" because it protected everyone from manufacturers to consumers. Moreover, without the protection of Fordney-McCumber, the sugar beet industry in the United States would wither and die, and wool prices, so vital to the clothing industry, would skyrocket.[17]

He tried his best, but his defense of the 1922 tariff recalled the inanity of William Howard Taft's fulsome panegyric to the Payne-Aldrich tariff in antiprotectionist Winona, Minnesota, in 1909. But in an election without genuine issues, Whittemore could do little other than defend what his opponent attacked. Indeed, the contest for the Fourteenth Congressional District seat was as mild as any Martin ever waged. The campaign expenses each man incurred testified to that. With only a week left before the election, Whittemore had spent $415 and Martin $77.[18]

As election day on the seventh neared, Democrats were buoyant. Hard economic times and the pervasive sense that the tired Republican administration in Washington was standing still portended a swing to the Democrats. Cornelius (Con) Mulcahy, the Summit County party chairman, forecast that Martin would carry the county by at least five thousand votes, and the *Akron Press* reported that the Democrats expected to capture fifteen of Ohio's twenty-two congressional districts, including the Fourteenth.[19] It was a good time to be a Democrat in Ohio.

On election Tuesday, the weather was good and the turnout heavy. Nature claimed full credit for the first, and the mechanization of America was partially responsible for the second. The *Akron Beacon Journal* reported that even farmers now had cars and could drive to the polls just as easily as city folks did. There were long lines already by 6:30 in the morning when the polls opened, and a steady stream kept up the whole day.[20]

When it was over, Martin had won the district by two thousand votes, and Ohio mirrored the national trend by sending a slew of other Democrats to Congress. The Republicans kept control of the House and Senate, but only by the slimmest of margins. Donahey had won. That was good. Pomerene had lost. That was bad, but not terribly so because he had been his own worst enemy. Martin had taken three out of the four counties in the district, Summit, Portage and, surprisingly, typically Republican Lorain, and he had run neck and neck with Whittemore in Medina.[21]

Afterward, Martin publicly congratulated his opponent for waging such a clean contest. But that was typical of Whittemore. In all his campaigns he kept a dignified distance above the fray. He had proven that politics did not have to be personal. Martin responded in kind, and in fact acted so gentlemanly that even Charles Landon Knight's *Akron Beacon Journal* called him a "man of pleasing personality."[22]

The *Beacon Journal's* kind description did not necessarily mean that Knight had softened on Davey. In fact the opposite was true; Knight never forgave an old enemy. But the 1922 Fourteenth Congressional District race had created a new foe for Knight, his own Republican Party. Knight wanted the Republican nomination for the district to go to D. C. Rybolt, the mayor of Akron. Against Knight's wishes, Whittemore was chosen instead, which automatically catapulted him to the top of Knight's enemies list. Knight seethed over the choice, his anger compounded by his loss to Carmi Thompson in the Republican gubernatorial primary. But he could not come out openly against his fellow Republican. Instead he merely withheld his support from Whittemore, a selfish act that helped Martin.[23]

But none of that mattered now. Martin Davey was returning to Congress. He had been out and did not like it. He was going back. He liked that.

Chapter Eight

Back to Washington

ON MARCH 4, 1923, Martin Davey raised his right hand to be sworn to his third term as a member of the House of Representatives. As a congressional veteran, he was appointed to the Committee on Foreign Affairs, ordinarily a choice assignment. But circumstances had changed. The war had ended nearly five years earlier, and the United States was pulling back from the rest of the world. Most Americans had stomached enough foreign entanglements to last a lifetime and demonstrated that by repudiating Woodrow Wilson's League of Nations and its champion, James M. Cox, in the presidential election of 1920. Americans preferred Warren G. Harding's "normalcy," and normalcy meant an America essentially isolated from the rest of the world. Consequently, Martin's seat on the House Committee on Foreign Affairs did not carry the lofty cachet that it typically would have.

Even in those ordinary times, the nation would have been distracted by extraordinary events. On August 2, 1923, after a trip to Alaska and California, the fifty-seven-year-old president of the United States died suddenly in San Francisco. Washington insiders had heard rumors that Harding suffered from heart problems, but most Americans believed that their beloved Warren was in the prime of his life. Clear across the country, in the sleeping village of Plymouth, Vermont, John Coolidge climbed the stairs to the second story of his house, calling his son Calvin. The younger Coolidge, visiting during a summer respite from his vice presidential duties, recognized the quavering voice; he had heard it before—at the announcement of family deaths. His direst fears were confirmed when his father addressed him as "Mr. President."[1]

A stunned Coolidge knelt momentarily in prayer, asking for the strength to shoulder his new and unexpected burdens. He and his wife quickly dressed and moved into the family sitting room, still and dark save for the light emanating from a kerosene lamp in the corner. There, the two were joined by their chauffeur, a stenographer, and a friend from nearby Island Pond, Vermont, Senator Porter H. Dole. All stood quietly while Justice of the Peace John Coolidge intoned the presidential oath to his son. With his hand still resting on his dead mother's Bible, Calvin Coolidge became the thirtieth president of the United States.[2]

In San Francisco, the undertakers were completing their grim work. The dead president's face was rouged and primped, his body dressed in a slick cutaway, and then nestled into a brown, silk-lined coffin in preparation for a long train ride to Washington. This was the fourth time in six decades that Americans had to endure the sight of a funeral train bearing the remains of a fallen president. The frequency of the occurrence failed to diminish the nation's sorrow. As they had for Abraham Lincoln in 1865, James A. Garfield in 1881, and William McKinley in 1901, saddened throngs assembled all along the rail route. In Stockton, California, theaters and restaurants closed as the cars passed through. Thousands turned out alongside the tracks in sparsely populated Nevada, Utah, and Colorado, and forty thousand braved a drenching rain to pay their respects in Omaha, Nebraska at 2 A.M. Three hundred thousand mourners massed in Chicago, and similar crowds stood in silent respect as the late president's train rolled into his native Ohio.[3]

Not until well after ten at night did the engineer pull into Washington's Union Station. Under the unflinching eyes of an honor guard of soldiers, sailors, and marines, the fallen chief's flag-draped coffin was hoisted onto an artillery caisson hitched to a six-horse team for a final journey to the White House. Harding's body reposed in the East Room for the night, tended by family and friends, and at ten in the morning was moved to the Capitol Rotunda, where the powerful and the ordinary alike paid their last respects. By five in the afternoon, Washington formalities were over, and the closed coffin was placed again aboard the train for the ride back to Ohio, where the president's body would be laid to final rest in Marion.[4]

Although Congress was not in session when Harding died, Martin was in Washington at the time, and he and a number of other capital dignitaries rode the funeral train to Marion. They were joined later by President Coolidge, who arrived in his own presidential special. Harding's coffin was brought to his house on East Center Street, where the public was allowed to file past for one last look at Marion's most famous son. All afternoon and evening mourners streamed in. Finally at two in the morning, the president's widow bade farewell to the last of them. By 9 A.M., the lines outside the East Center Street home had materialized again, and for the next five hours the saddened and the curious filed past the open coffin.[5]

At two in the afternoon, a gray hearse pulled up to the house, and the presidential coffin was readied for its trip to Marion's cemetery. Amid the booming of cannons and the final farewells of President Coolidge, Chief Justice William Howard Taft, and family friends Thomas Edison, Henry Ford, and Harvey Firestone, Harding was laid to rest in an iron-gated, ivy-covered stone vault. A bugler sounded taps for the dead commander-in-chief, riflemen jolted everyone to attention with a twenty-one-gun salute, and then it was over.[6]

Martin had been part of Coolidge's official party and consequently was invited to ride the presidential train back to Washington. He was not going that far—only to Akron—but the distance from Marion was sufficient to give him time for a lengthy conversation with the new president. About an hour outside of Akron, Martin walked to Coolidge's private car to pay his respects. The president sat alone except for his wife, a female relative of Mrs. Coolidge, and the president's male secretary. Coolidge, notoriously laconic in public, was surprisingly voluble in private. Obviously aware of Martin's business background, the president spoke at length about the care of trees and how he had practiced a bit of amateurish but nonetheless successful tree surgery himself back home in Vermont. The easy conversation with the president forced Martin to reevaluate the Vermonter's reputation for silence. A casual remark the president had once made to a reporter suddenly made sense: "what I didn't say never hurt me." Public remarks were one thing; personal conversations yet another.[7]

Despite Coolidge's friendliness on the train, Martin never thought of him as anything more than a "do-nothing" president with a "one-string fiddle." That one string was the economy, but even here, Martin believed, the president talked a better game than he played. Although Coolidge harped constantly about thrift in government, he never practiced it. Martin recalled that federal expenditures rose by a half-billion dollars annually during the Republican's five years in office. If he ever truly practiced thrift, it was only with his own money.[8]

Coolidge did practice economy in some areas of government, Martin learned in 1924, but only at the expense of those who deserved the government's generosity. Some congressmen, many of them Democrats, tried to follow the lead of Canada, Great Britain, Italy, and New Zealand, which had rewarded their ex-servicemen with cash bonuses in appreciation for their efforts during the Great War. The United States, richer than any of the others, had done nothing of the kind. The government's shunning of its valiant sons was, to many, a national shame. The Democrats, with some Republican support, proposed payment of a $60 bonus to four million former servicemen.[9] Tighter-fisted Republicans tried to substitute a graduated insurance plan for the cash payment, which rankled Martin and other representatives who believed that a $60 bonus was the least a grateful government could give to those who had so selflessly defended their country.

Martin's side won the battle but not the war. The bonus bill passed and was now the president's to decide. He vetoed it, and although the measure had easily cleared both houses, there were not enough votes to override, so the veto stood.[10]

The president's position contradicted long-standing Republican policy toward veterans. From the Civil War onward, ex-servicemen had no better friend than the Republican Party. It had time and time again dipped into the national treasury to provide pensions, particularly for Union Army veterans. Indeed, the Republicans had traditionally been so generous to veterans of the Grand Army of the Republic that their largesse had provided Democratic candidates with abundant political fodder during the heated campaigns of the late nineteenth century.[11]

But that kind of generosity no longer made sense in the economic atmosphere of the 1920s. The twenties were a time when laissez-faire ruled. It was now every man for himself. One's destiny was up to the individual, unless the individual was an industrialist who might profit from a high protective tariff or some other generous probusiness program. And nobody was better suited to the times than Calvin Coolidge, who truly believed that the business of the country was business.

The president was allowed his biases because most Americans were faring well at mid-decade. The national debt between 1919 and 1926 decreased by more than $7 billion, and the treasury was full enough in 1925 so that Secretary Andrew Mellon recommended a $300 million tax cut for Americans. In addition, the nation was sufficiently flush to cut two million Americans from the tax rolls entirely. All in all, it was hard not to like the Republicans.

There was, however, a large pocket of discontent in the country. While nearly everyone else prospered during the twenties, many farmers languished. As the prices of machinery and other manufactured goods increased, allowing wages and investment incomes to rise, farm prices declined. The deflation of the agricultural market meant that farmers, faced with higher costs for

manufactured goods during the 1920s, were actually earning less than they
had a decade earlier.[12]

Martin was appalled that the Republicans, with Coolidge in the lead, could
be so probusiness and yet so blind to the plight of American farmers. Farming, Martin ardently believed, was crucial to the nation's material health, and
yet the Republicans ignored this crucial facet of the economy.[13] Something
had to be done and soon, or else it would be too late for thousands and perhaps even millions of farmers who would be forced over the brink.

While farmers faced hard times, manufacturing, thanks to Republican-
inspired tariff protection, prospered. The unfairness of the situation was suc-
cinctly summarized by George N. Peek, president of the Moline Plow Company, who ominously quipped, "You can't sell a plow to a busted farmer."[14] If
manufacturers were so well protected by the U.S. government, why should
farmers not be too?

Farmers were victims of their own success. Because of constant improvements in fertilizers and technology (nearly every farmer had a tractor by
the twenties), American farms produced large surpluses of everything from
corn and wheat to cotton and tobacco. The domestic market simply could
not consume all that was grown.

Farm protectionists began to formulate plans to lay a government-subsi-
dized floor under farm prices. One of the most promising schemes was based
on a concept known as parity. Under parity, the value of commodities would
be set by comparing farm prices during ten prewar years with the average
price of all American goods for the same period. Once a price for agricultural
produce was established on that basis, the government would buy farm surpluses to sell on the world market. Farmers would be charged a nominal fee
on their production, and anything above that fee on the world and domestic
markets would be returned to farmers as profit.[15]

By 1924, backed by a powerful farm lobby, Oregon senator Charles Mc-
Nary and Iowa representative Gilbert Haugen began marshaling support
for the plan in Congress. President Coolidge was not pleased. In Chicago
on December 7, 1925, he explained to delegates at the annual convention of
the American Farm Bureau Corporation, "Agriculture [had to] rest 'on an
independent business basis.'" If farmers hoped to improve their lot, they
would have to do so through such strategies as cooperative marketing. Hard
times and self-control, he lectured his audience, "create[d] character."[16]

The speech was Coolidge at his laissez-faire best. To no one's surprise,
when the McNary-Haugen Bill reached the president's desk in 1927, he vetoed it on the grounds that it was preferential legislation utterly antitheti-

cal to the principles of laissez-faire. American farmers could justifiably resent the president because on the same day that he vetoed the farm bill, he
signed a measure raising the tariff on foreign pig iron 50 percent, which
was perfectly consistent with his belief that an impost protecting American
manufacturers was "a great benefit to agriculture as a whole." The profarm
bloc in Congress closed ranks and repassed the McNary-Haugen Bill the
next year, only to have Coolidge veto it again.[17]

Martin could only shake his head in disbelief at how callously the president ignored the needs of farmers. Coolidge was undoubtedly sincere of mo-
tive but terribly shortsighted. His blatant disregard of the farmers' plight in
the 1920s, Martin believed, was largely responsible for the hard times of the
depression-ridden 1930s.[18] None of that mattered now, though. The 1920s
were a good time to be alive. Radio consoles stood majestically in many living rooms in America, thousands of families already had one of Henry Ford's
$500 Model Ts in the driveway, or hoped to one day, and sports heroes Babe
Ruth, Jack Dempsey, and Red Grange, and slick-haired, mustachioed movie
actors and eyelash-batting actresses daily diverted the attentions of Americans. A devastating stock market crash and a devastated economy were the
last things on anybody's mind.

The 1920s were good for Martin and the family business, too. By 1924
Davey Tree was making $1 million a year. But not all went well for the Daveys.
In little over a year, tragedy struck twice. Shortly after three in the morning on
November 8, 1923, a jangling telephone woke Martin from a sound sleep at his
Kent home. At the other end of the line, a distraught Bertha Davey implored
her son to rush over because she had discovered her husband, still and cold,
on the floor alongside their bed. She feared the worst.

Martin hung up and phoned the Davey family doctor and, after hurried
calls to brother Paul and brother-in-law Harmon Carson, raced to his parents' home. It was too late. As the frantic family hovered about, the doctor
pronounced John Davey dead. Although he was seventy-seven and had been
sleeping in a chair for years because of the constant pulmonary congestion
generated by his weakening heart, John Davey's death was unexpected. A few
days earlier he had complained that he was not feeling well but had quickly
improved, and no one thought for a moment that "the good night's rest" he
was looking forward to the evening before would be his last.[19]

Three days later, on Armistice Day, a grieving Bertha Davey laid her husband to rest in Standing Rock, the cemetery so lovingly fashioned and tended
by her husband when they both were young. Martin was heartbroken. It was,
he remembered, "nothing but a period of utter sorrow."[20]

Thirteen months later, Martin, Belle, Wellington, Jim, and Paul stood on the same cold ground to bury their mother. On December 10, 1924, sixty-five-year-old Bertha Davey suffered a stroke. She lingered unconscious for a few hours before dying. Her funeral was not as grand as John Davey's the year before.[21] After all, she was overshadowed by her nationally prominent husband. Few knew that it was she who held the family together while the impecunious John Davey wandered about Kent dreaming up the science of tree surgery.

The deaths of both parents in so brief a span hurt. Not even the sympathy of friends attenuated the pain. Martin reflected on how much his parents meant to him. Now that he was an adult he could appreciate all that his mother and father had done for him.[22] It was a dark time in his life, but he also recognized that death was in the natural scheme of things, and it was time to move on. After all, he had had both parents until he was nearly forty, and Berenice and thirteen-year-old Evangeline and six-year-old Martin Jr. needed him and restored joy to his life.

Politics, too, provided an outlet. The summer before his father died, Martin drove to Washington's Shoreham Hotel to meet William G. McAdoo, who in 1923 was already preparing for a run at the Democratic presidential nomination the next year. McAdoo, a native Georgian and former secretary of the treasury under Woodrow Wilson, was a Democratic bellwether, although he had his fair share of enemies within the party. Martin did not like him. He was too ingratiating and never looked Martin in the eye. He seemed insincere and consequently untrustworthy, neither of which Martin conveyed to the erstwhile presidential candidate nor to his chief spokesman and promoter, Daniel C. Roper, who had invited Martin and other Democratic congressmen to the Shoreham to meet his man.

Roper's invitation to Martin was more than a courtesy. He was looking for a campaign manager for McAdoo and solicited Martin for suggestions. Whoever it was would have to know politics from bottom to top, from precinct committeemen all the way through county, state, and national organizations. Also, the campaign manager would preferably be a northerner to counterbalance McAdoo's roots in Georgia and Tennessee. But political know-how was not enough. The man entrusted with the job would have to have enough rich friends so that the candidate's war chest never emptied.

As Martin and Roper huddled outside the door of McAdoo's personal quarters in the Shoreham, one man's name kept popping into the Ohioan's mind—Judge David L. Rockwell, his old mentor from Kent. He offered Rockwell's name and qualifications. Roper seemed interested but beyond that made no commitment. Martin returned to Ohio shortly afterward and stopped at Judge Rockwell's to inform him of his conversation at the Shoreham. Rockwell was pleased that his fellow Kentite had apparently forgiven him for demanding payment for helping him in his congressional campaign in 1918, and Martin was simply happy to "do a favor for an old friend."

The truce between the two did not last long. In the fall of 1923, Senator Thomas J. Walsh of Montana opened hearings on the Teapot Dome and Elk Hills oil scandals. Among the names that continually arose during the hearings was that of Edward L. Doheny, a California businessman who had leased highly profitable government oil lands in Elk Hills from Harding's secretary of the interior, Albert Fall. It was no coincidence that shortly afterward Doheny "loaned" Fall $100,000. The loan was an outright bribe and resulted in Fall's conviction and incarceration in 1931. Doheny was charged with bribery but acquitted in 1930, although being found "not guilty" was not the same as being declared innocent.

The whole episode was a sordid mess, and no one associated with it could be free of taint, including a native Georgian with presidential aspirations in 1924. William Gibbs McAdoo, "Chief" to his friends, had been one of Doheny's lawyers before the scandal broke. As soon as the Senate spotlight shone on Doheny, McAdoo withdrew his services from the California oil magnate. Although it was the circumspect thing to do, McAdoo's resignation conjured up an image of the proverbial rat deserting a sinking ship. Martin thought his action "cowardly."

McAdoo's judicious escape made others leery of him, although he remained one of the front-runners for the 1924 Democratic nomination. Martin sensed, however, that McAdoo's cause was lost even before it began. Consequently, when Rockwell insisted early in 1924 that Martin assume control of the Ohio-for-McAdoo movement, he declined. He intended to run for reelection in 1924 and expected Ohio to support the favorite son candidacy of James M. Cox at the presidential nominating convention in New York that summer. To declare for McAdoo, thereby alienating the Ohioans for Cox, might well be disastrous in the Fourteenth Congressional District race, he explained to Rockwell.

The judge would have none of it. His request became a demand and was soon backed by threats of reprisals if Martin held fast to his refusal. Martin stood his ground, and Rockwell, unaccustomed to "no," fumed. The threatening escalated, but Martin left without giving the furious judge what he wanted.[23]

Not wanting to cut his ties completely to Rockwell, Martin later met with McAdoo supporters in Cleveland but was unimpressed. Outside of Judge Rockwell, no one there, he concluded, had any genuine political savvy, and that meant any Ohio-for-McAdoo movement would likely fail. At the meeting, Rockwell continued to pressure Martin, but his response remained the same: no. Rockwell raged and threatened Martin anew, but Martin stood firm, insisting that any Ohioans who stood for McAdoo at the convention would offend Cox and kill any chance for an Ohio man to win the vice presidential nomination. Martin left Cleveland unchanged, and so did Judge Rockwell. The Republicans met first to choose their candidate. On June 12, to no one's surprise, Calvin Coolidge was overwhelmingly nominated on the first ballot in Cleveland, Ohio. Of the 1,109 convention votes, Coolidge received 1,065. Robert M. LaFollette and Hiram Johnson, two maverick Republicans whose political fortunes had long since waned, got the rest of the meager scattering. LaFollette's star, so bright when he led the Progressive wing of the party a decade and more earlier, was now so clearly descendent that mere mention of his name brought hisses and, even worse, laughter from the Cleveland conventioneers.[24]

Coolidge was eating lunch at the White House when Isaac Hoover, his chief usher, brought him the news. He nodded and went back to his lunch. Reporters immediately flocked to the White House, thinking that so singular an honor as a presidential nomination might crack the president's stony facade. They were wrong. "Silent Cal" had nothing to say.[25]

Two weeks later, the Democrats, optimistic about their chances because of Teapot Dome and Elk Hills and anticipating voter backlash against the president for his veto of the Veterans' Bonus Bill and antipathy toward the plight of farmers, met in New York City's Madison Square Garden. Martin, like most of his fellow partisans, believed that 1924 was the Democrats' year. Never before was the White House in such easy grasp. No one liked Coolidge except dyed-in-the-wool Republicans and big business.[26]

The two leading candidates for the Democratic nomination were McAdoo and New York governor Al Smith. McAdoo wore the mantle of prince-in-waiting. Not only had he distinguished himself in Woodrow Wilson's cabinet (he had helped launch the Federal Reserve banking system and had raised $18 billion in Liberty Bonds to finance the war), but he also married the president's daughter, Eleanor. He had spent the last several years as a distinguished lawyer in New York City with all the right ties to money and power. Smith, in stark contrast, owed his success to hard work, an engaging personality and Tammany Hall connections that would have turned old Boss Tweed green with envy. It was a long way from Lower Manhattan's Fulton Fish Market where Smith had toiled as a young man to the governor's mansion in Albany, but he had gotten there with comparative ease.

The strength of each handicapped both. After fifteen ballots on the convention's first day of voting, the Democrats were not even close to choosing a candidate. They adjourned at midnight with McAdoo leading Smith, 479–305½. John W. Davis of West Virginia was a distant third with 61. All were far short of the two-thirds vote of 732 needed for the nomination. Rockwell was doing his best for McAdoo, but it was not nearly enough. He remained outwardly confident, though. His man, he said, "will be nominated, if not tomorrow, [the next day.]" Rockwell could not have been more wrong. The Democrats' quadrennial affair would drag on longer than any of them could have ever imagined. Even on that first day of balloting, tempers were flaring on the steamy convention floor. Joseph Shannon of Kansas City drew back his right arm and let fly with a punch that landed flush on the jaw of a fellow delegate, Charles Hay from St. Louis.[27] Why not? Tempers were short, and the combatants were, after all, standing on the floor of flamboyant boxing promoter Tex Rickard's shrine to pugilism, Madison Square Garden. It might not have been Dempsey-Firpo, but it stirred the blood nonetheless.

From the onset, it was clear that McAdoo would never yield to Smith, nor Smith to McAdoo. Ohio, as Martin had predicted, stood by its native son, James M. Cox. But even with a scattering of support from other states, the nominee of 1920 lagged at the back of the pack with sixty votes.[28]

By the second day of voting and the thirtieth ballot, the Democrats were no closer to choosing a candidate. McAdoo's total dropped to 415½, Smith's rose, to 323½, and so did John W. Davis's, to 126½. Cox faltered slightly with 57. If nothing else, the diminution of McAdoo's numbers indicated that the Democrats were farther away than ever from choosing a standard bearer. Word circulated that perhaps as many as 100 delegates were disgusted enough to give up their pricey New York hotel rooms and head for home. After the fifty-third unsuccessful ballot, delegates from North Carolina announced that they were ready to "drop the whole matter." At the news, spectators in the galleries burst into applause.[29]

None of it mattered, though. After fifteen more ballots, the sixty-eighth time in four days that the Democrats had tried to name a candidate, Arizona cast a vote for Will Rogers. It was the most popular move of the day, and a Massachusetts delegate suggested that the cowboy humorist be invited to address the 1,098 weary, temper-frayed souls on the convention floor. Chairman Thomas J. Walsh, hoping to prevent the convention from becoming even more farcical, hammered down his gavel and ruled the proposal out of order.[30]

If anyone suffered most through it all, it was the pre-convention frontrunner, McAdoo. Clearly, his own party did not want him. Once during the balloting his vote reached 505, still far short of the 732 necessary for the nomination. Shortly afterward he slid back to 427. He had to wince inside his Madison Square Hotel suite when the *New York Times* began to refer to the proceedings as the "Decline and Fall of William G. McAdoo." Over at McAdoo headquarters in the Hotel Vanderbilt, reporters asked Judge Rockwell what changes he had in mind for his candidate. "None," he snapped.[31]

Things were no better for the second strongest candidate, either. Al Smith's vote had increased slightly, but he continually languished a hundred votes or so behind McAdoo. The *Times* noted that although the New York governor's support was slowly increasing, the "grade [for him seems] pretty steep," it appears very "doubtful that [he] can make it." The two front-runners were simply "wearing each other out."[32] It was clear that Smith's candidacy, like McAdoo's, was going nowhere.

McAdoo moved first. On July 9, during the second week of the nominating marathon, he wired Chairman Walsh, "I am unwilling to contribute to the continuation of a hopeless deadlock. Therefore, [I am leaving] my friends and supporters free to take such action as their judgment may best serve the interests of the party."[33] Smith, knowing that McAdoo supporters would ensure that he never got the party's nomination in 1924, followed suit. The withdrawal of the two leaders opened the door to John W. Davis of West Virginia, a Democrat who never had the broad appeal of the front-runners but who had for ballot after ballot hung tenaciously in third place.

Davis, long active in Democratic politics, had been a congressman, an advisor to President Wilson, solicitor general of the United States, and, from 1918 to 1921, ambassador to Great Britain. He had returned to the United States from Europe to take a job with a New York law firm that numbered among its clients the Standard Oil Company, J. P. Morgan and Company, and the American Telephone and Telegraph Company. At the moment of his nomination on the 103rd ballot, he was enjoying a cigar in the 68th Street home of Frank L. Polk, one of his friends and law partners. He was not even listening to the radio; it was his wife who heard the news first. She ran to the stairs and screamed to her husband: "You've won—you're nominated!" Davis dropped his cigar, raced up the steps, and hugged his wife.

Newspaper reporters, cameramen, and security-conscious police units quickly swarmed the 68th Street house.[34] The atmosphere was euphoric as Davis accepted the hearty congratulations of friends and well-wishers.

Despite their jubilation, the Democrats had written themselves a prescription for defeat. Their long, divisive convention showed the nation that they had settled for a nominee, not declared one. Disappointment and anger reigned in the McAdoo camp. The sullen loser sent a terse telegram to the victor: "Please accept my congratulations on your nomination. W. G. McAdoo." There was no promise of support, no hint that the former secretary of the treasury would lick his wounds and help the party to victory in November. Al Smith was more gracious in his wire to Davis: "Sincere congratulations and best wishes for success and my promise of hearty support." He told reporters that Davis would wage a "great campaign" and that he would do anything the nominee requested and looked forward to stumping in New York State and throughout the country.[35]

Martin watched the New York proceedings keenly from his convention seat. He liked Davis and thought he would make a far better president than Coolidge. But, he concluded sadly, the West Virginian "never had a chance." The lengthy and bitter infighting at the convention had been broadcast nationwide over the radio, and Americans everywhere heard the Democrats at their foolish worst. Martin was disgusted. The Democrats' performance in New York, he thought, was the stupidest thing any political party had done "since America became a nation."[36]

Understandably, Martin worried that the failure of the Democrats' national ticket might jeopardize his own reelection in 1924. In addition to concerns about a negative coattail effect, he was troubled by the growing influence of the Ku Klux Klan in Ohio politics. By the 1920s the Klan was not merely a southern aberration. It had advanced rapidly northward, fueled by a growing suspicion of and antipathy toward anybody and anything "foreign," including native-born Catholics and blacks. More and more Americans were attracted by the Klan's iron stand for "100 percent Americanism."[37]

Scoundrels and thugs were not the only Americans drawn to the "Invisible Empire." The Klan numbered among its ranks, doctors, lawyers, businessmen, politicians, and even Protestant clergymen who appreciated the Klan's supposed rigid moral code and lionization of Christian religion. Moreover, moonlit meetings, bonfires, and the fraternal bond generated by membership in something secret made the Klan all the more attractive to men whose lives were otherwise humdrum and mundane.

It was like being in a private and exclusive club to many. Klansmen even had their own cryptic language called "Klonversation."

"Ayak" (Are you a Klansman?)
"Akia." (A Klansman I am.)
"Cyknar." (Call your Klan number and Realm.)
"No. 1, Atga." (Number 1 Klan of Atlanta, Georgia.)
"Kigy." (Klansman, I greet you.)
"Sanbog." (Strangers are near. Be on guard.)[38]

Ohioans were not immune to the allure and mystique of the Invisible Empire. In 1920, the first klavern sprang up in Cincinnati, and within months there were eight others scattered around surrounding Hamilton County. Soon Dayton was infected with Klan mania. Emboldened by their success in southwestern Ohio, Klansmen audaciously set up headquarters in the state capital, Columbus. From the heart of the state, the knights branched out to Cleveland where they encountered a passionate anti-Klan mayor who ordered police to crack down on the organization's activities everywhere in the city.[39]

Ohio politicians had plenty to worry about where the Ku Klux Klan was concerned. Their state was second only to Indiana in Klan membership. At the peak of their popularity in the 1920s, the Knights of the Invisible Empire numbered about 4 million nationwide, 500,000 of them in Indiana and 450,000 in adjoining Ohio. The two northern states' enthusiasm for the Klan far exceeded the secret society's popularity in southern states like Alabama, Arkansas, Florida, Georgia, Louisiana, Mississippi, and Tennessee (the birthplace of the Klan) whose individual membership rolls numbered between 50,000 and 200,000.[40]

Particularly troubling to Martin was the Ku Klux Klan's popularity in Akron, the largest city by far in his Fourteenth Congressional District. Thousands of Akronites belonged either to the Klan itself or to its copycat auxiliaries, the Royal Riders of the Red Robe, the Junior Klan (for children), and Women of the Ku Klux Klan. The groups met openly in nearby Tallmadge, Perkins Woods, and even in the city's Masonic Hall. Klan fever was so pervasive in the area that the Akron branch actually recommended that the city's Summit County be changed to "Ku Klux Kounty." It was no secret that several local politicians, including the school board president, and even the county sheriff were members.[41]

Anyone running for political office in Ohio during the 1920s had to walk a tight line where the Klan was concerned. Some candidates, although personally repulsed by what it stood for, recognized that winning might well depend on the support of Klan members. Consequently, conscience-bound politicians of both parties found themselves decrying the Klan but not passionately so. Another strategy had candidates joining the Klan, hiding the fact that they were members, and then accusing their opponents of being "Kluxers." Martin believed that Summit County Republicans were master practitioners of this below-the-belt tactic.

The architect of the underhanded Republican strategy, Martin thought, was Maurice Maschke, a Harvard-educated party boss from Cleveland. Maschke was a Jew, but that did not stop him from cozying up to Klansmen if he sniffed some political advantage. What Maschke did was unethical, but Martin had to concede his "cunning and resourcefulness." Grudgingly, he acknowledged that "Ohio [had never] seen an abler politician" and lamented in general that during the 1920s Republican managers "outsmarted and outmaneuvered Democratic leaders year after year."

Martin had been invited to join the Klan but refused because of its racist, nativist philosophy. To avoid any risk of personal taint, he would drive miles away to avoid even being in the vicinity of any Klan activity. He regretted that many of his fellow Democrats had been taken in by Klan propaganda to the point where they were blind to its darker side.

Despite his antipathy to everything the Ku Klux Klan represented, Martin was reluctant to denounce it because doing so might jeopardize his chances for reelection in 1924. His refusal to rebuke the Klan incensed Con Mulcahy, the Summit County Democratic Party boss. Mulcahy, an Irish-Catholic, despised everything the Klan stood for, particularly its vicious anti-Catholicism. Mulcahy's passion was understandable. Klansmen, either out of meanness or stupidity, gladly spread the rumor that Catholics were stockpiling arms and ammunition in church basements, anticipating that one day the pope would order the overthrow of the U.S. government. So grotesque a lie was, of course, intended to heighten long-standing Protestant suspicions that American Catholics were more loyal to Rome than they were to their own country.

Mulcahy had cornered Martin after the Democratic convention in New York and tried to pressure him into publicly condemning the Klan. Martin refused, although he assured the party boss that he disliked the organization as much as anyone did. That failed to mollify Mulcahy, and he continued to push Martin. Finally Martin said, "Con, there are thousands of Democrats who belong to that outfit, and if we let them alone, I think most of them will vote their own ticket. But if I or any other Democratic candidate slaps the whole group in the face, there isn't a chance to get one of these Democratic votes. It just doesn't make sense to me." He tried to assure Mulcahy that the Klan, if left alone, would self-destruct. Mulcahy was not persuaded. He stormed off, warning Martin, "Well, you can look out for yourself."

Martin could not understand his friend's passion. Mulcahy was a man of integrity, but, Martin concluded, he was "not smart in politics." His hard-headedness blinded him to political realities that were already a common-place to Martin. Mulcahy, Martin believed, would rather see the "entire Republican ticket elected, with everyone on it a 'Kluxer,' than have a single Klansman on the Democratic ticket." Martin was more practical, more will-ing to compromise principle for the sake of victory, rationalizing his expedi-ency with the belief that it was a politician's "first duty to serve his party."[42]

The high point of Ku Klux Klan influence in American politics was in 1924. Martin's Republican opponent in the Fourteenth Congressional Dis-trict race that year was Arthur W. Doyle, a young Summit County pros-ecuting attorney. Martin knew Doyle was a Klansman, but never made the accusation during the fall campaign. Doing so would be foolhardy because candidates from both parties were either Klansmen or sympathized with them. If a Democrat condemned a Republican for his Klan ties, he might just as well be condemning one of his own partisans. It was a classic case of the pot calling the kettle black. Mulcahy was right in principle, but Martin was right in reality. The Klan issue in the 1920s could not be ignored, but it was like a sleeping dog, and anyone who climbed the fence to poke it with a stick was just looking for trouble.

The Ohio Ku Klux Klan did not share Martin's reticence. It endorsed Re-publican Calvin Coolidge for president and Democrat Vic Donahey for gov-ernor. The choices were born more out of necessity than enthusiasm. William G. McAdoo, the Klan favorite in 1924, had been rejected by his party, so the Democrats were out. The Republicans at their convention, after seven hours of hot debate, refused to adopt an anti-Klan plank, so, although Coolidge was no friend of the Invisible Empire, he was not its sworn enemy, either. Dona-hey was acceptable to the Klan more because of his gubernatorial opponent, Harry L. Davis, than for any favoritism he had shown the organization. Davis had been a three-term mayor of Cleveland between 1915 and 1921 and zeal-ously shared that northern Ohio city's animus toward the Klan.[43] There was no way that Klansmen wanted him in the governor's mansion.

Neither Martin nor any other serious candidate, for that matter, wanted the endorsement of the Ku Klux Klan, but Davey was pleased to see that the Akron branch of the Invisible Empire split into Doyle and anti-Doyle factions. The leader of the anti-Doyle faction appreciated the fact that Catholics of the Fourteenth Congressional District refused to endorse Martin. By omission, then, that made Martin attractive to thousands of anti-Catholic Klansmen. Shortly before the Fourteenth Congressional District election in November, the head of the Akron Klan apprised his cohorts of Martin's desirability in anticipation that they would know how to vote.[44]

Poor Doyle did not have a chance. He mounted a feeble attack against Martin for trying to pass himself off as nonpartisan in this election, and for mailing seventy thousand letters to that effect to district voters. Nothing, of course, was farther from the truth. Martin was a Democrat through and through, Doyle proclaimed. He consistently voted against Republican president Coolidge's initiatives and was claiming nonpartisanship only to distance himself from the doomed candidacy of the Democratic presidential nominee, John W. Davis.[45]

The *Akron Beacon Journal* reminded its readers how Davey in 1918 proclaimed his youth and patriotism in the campaign against Charles Dick but at the same time dodged military service during the Great War. Doyle, in contrast, the *Beacon Journal* alerted its subscribers, volunteered to fight and served as an artilleryman on the front lines in France while his opponent remained safe at home four thousand miles away. The *Beacon Journal* urged voters to drum the "errand boy" Davey out of office and replace him with a congressman who would support the policies of President Coolidge. Davey, nothing but a "naysayer" during the preceding two years, would not be missed.[46]

Martin scarcely responded, ran on his record of personal service to his constituents and won by a 2,500-vote margin. Most of his edge came in Summit County, although he also took his home county, Portage, but only by a few hundred votes. Doyle won two out of the four counties in the Fourteenth Congressional District, traditionally Republican Lorain and Medina. His margins there, however, failed to offset Martin's totals in Summit and Portage. The *Beacon Journal,* in a lame, sour grapes editorial, claimed that Davey won only because he received a late endorsement from the Lorain County Ku Klux Klan.[47]

Popular Vic Donahey won the Ohio governorship over his Republican opponent Harry L. Davis, but almost everywhere else it was a Republican sweep. Coolidge drubbed John W. Davis in Ohio and across the nation, nearly doubling his opponent's popular vote totals, 15.7 million to 8.4 million. The electoral vote was even more lopsided, 382–136. Bob LaFollette, now nothing more than a protest candidate trying to resurrect the moribund Progressive Party, was a third man in the race but garnered fewer than five million votes nationwide and carried only his native Wisconsin with its thirteen electoral votes. The Republicans also kept their majorities in both houses of Congress.[48]

During the campaign, John W. Davis had tried to force the Republicans to pay for their Teapot Dome and Elk Hills sins, but the 1924 Republicans refused the guilt. Harding was dead, Albert Fall, Harry Sinclair, and the other evildoers were under intensive investigation, and not even a drop of oil bubbled up through the lawn at 1600 Pennsylvania Avenue. The president was clean. He knew it, and the American people believed it. But, more important than anything else, times were good under the Republicans and there was no reason to change a thing. Even the Davey Tree Expert Company became a million-dollar business in 1924.[49]

Advertising, Martin was convinced, was largely responsible for the company's success. When he went into business with his father in 1906, almost no one had ever even heard of tree surgery, let alone paid for it. Davey crews, of course, had to do good work at a fair price once contracts were signed, but it was advertising in newspapers and magazines that "unlocked the doors for [Davey] representatives in tens of thousands of American homes."

As the company's fame grew, hundreds of requests poured in asking the Daveys to treat historically significant trees for free. Acceding to all these was impossible. The company did, however, honor some of the requests. One of them took a Davey crew to Fredericksburg, Virginia, where George Washington had planted thirteen horse chestnut trees in honor of the original states. Only one was left now, a decaying giant in dire need of lifesaving surgery. Davey men removed the rot, disinfected and waterproofed the trunk, filled it with concrete and braced damaged limbs. After feeding the tree with the company's patented formula, the crew let nature do the rest. Martin returned two or three years later and was pleased to see that new bark covered old wounds (some from Civil War bullets), and that new leaves and growth were evident all over the horse chestnut. The tree, one of the few living things linking George Washington to Americans of the 1920s, he happily observed, was now "the picture of health."[50]

Martin acknowledged that he was better known as a tree man than as a congressman. Whereas few knew him outside the Fourteenth Congressional District and beyond the corridors of the Capitol, the Davey name in tree surgery was recognized nationwide. By 1926, twenty years had passed since Martin was summoned out of Oberlin by his father to help run the fledgling family business and twenty-five since John Davey had started it all by publishing *The Tree Doctor*. To commemorate the silver anniversary of the book that started the Davey Tree Expert Company, Martin threw a grand party in March for Davey employees and hundreds of invited guests. Three thousand people jammed into the Akron Armory on a Saturday night to be entertained by one of America's greatest showmen, Will Rogers. For an hour and a half, America's master of satire and homespun wit worked the armory audience. Flashbulbs popped by the thousands, movie cameras whirred on, and scores of newspaper reporters scribbled as fast as they could to capture the magic. When it was over, three thousand pairs of hands registered thundering approval.[51] Rogers was well worth his $1,500 fee for the evening; not a guest left feeling cheated out of laughter. For one night at least, the entertainment spotlight shone not on New York or Hollywood but on the armory of an industrial city in northeastern Ohio, thanks to Martin L. Davey.

Martin knew the value of publicity and saw to it that his company was no stranger to Hollywood cameras. In 1925, newsreel crews from Pathe, International, and Fox shot footage of Davey treemen working in New York City's Central Park. The film was shown in movie houses across the nation.[52]

The country's sesquicentennial gave Martin yet another opportunity to promote Davey Tree. An international exposition was planned for Philadelphia, the birthplace of the nation. After bitter infighting among the city's politicos, $5 million in seed money and hundreds of acres on Philadelphia's South Side were set aside for a world-class exposition reminiscent of the Centennial Exhibition fifty years earlier. It was to be a fete celebrating America's success, at one and the same time honoring the past and trumpeting the present. There were to be a Forum of the Founders, a colonial village, and an eighty-foot-tall Liberty Bell, all tokens of the old linked to symbols of the new, a radio station, a modern bank, and restaurants.[53]

Secretary of State Frank B. Kellogg and Secretary of Commerce Herbert Hoover officially opened the exposition amid much fanfare on May 31, 1926. Two days later, King Gustavus Adolphus of Sweden, commemorating the contributions of his seventeenth-century countrymen to colonial Philadelphia and the Delaware Valley, opened a Swedish exhibit. Dignitaries from other foreign countries followed suit over the next several weeks, their massive international pavilion drawing visitors from far and wide. On the Fourth of July, President Coolidge appeared and gave the keynote speech. Two months after that, Jack Dempsey lost his heavyweight championship to Gene Tunney before thousands of frenzied fight fans in massive Municipal Stadium built on exposition grounds.[54]

Before the show shut down in November, nearly 6.5 million Americans had jammed through exposition turnstiles. Attendance would have been even higher had it not rained (sometimes torrentially) 107 out of 184 days of the exposition.[55] Critics complained that attendance fell far short of the crowds drawn to the Centennial Exhibition in 1876, but nothing else except the Chicago World's Fair of 1893 came close to equaling the draw.

Driven both by patriotism and the desire for a stupendous public relations coup, Martin offered Davey Tree services for an exciting sesquicentennial project. He suggested that his company plant thirteen trees, one for each original state, in Philadelphia's Independence Square as part of the sesquicentennial ceremonies. The idea was certainly appealing enough, but Martin intended more. He told exposition officials that his company would carefully bag native soil from each of the original thirteen states and use it to fill the holes dug for the trees. The National Sesquicentennial Committee was taken by the novel idea and approved it for the fall of 1926.

But Martin had more in mind than a mere tree-planting ceremony. He invited the governors of the thirteen original states, the national commander of the American Legion, representatives of the Daughters of the American Revolution, the Colonial Dames, and the Sons of the American Revolution, and leaders of several Civil War organizations to participate. All told, two or three hundred dignitaries assembled for lunch in Philadelphia's Bellevue-Stratford Hotel and then departed for a massive parade that wound its way through the heart of the city to Independence Square where, with thousands watching, the thirteen trees were lowered into place and backfilled with their native soil by officials from each state. Martin and the Davey Tree Expert Company, of course, enjoyed the limelight for the day, but the promotional genius from Kent did not do all this for the sake of publicity alone. Years after the sesquicentennial hoopla had passed, Davey crews, without charge, still tended to the trees to ensure their survival.

During preparations for the sesquicentennial, Martin met two of the most fascinating men in early twentieth-century political life, Gifford Pinchot and Al Smith. Pinchot, former chief forester of the United States, had made his reputation in 1910 by taking on William Howard Taft's secretary of the interior, Richard Ballinger, in one of the most celebrated conservation free-for-alls of the Progressive era. A Theodore Roosevelt favorite, Pinchot overstepped his bounds with President Taft when he accused Ballinger of corruption in opening Alaskan coal fields to private enterprise. Ballinger was exonerated and Pinchot, for all his pains, was fired.

Roosevelt, the conservation-minded former president, entered the fray in 1910 when he returned from an African hunt. He spurned Taft's invitation to the White House and openly sided with the fired Pinchot. The president and former president, once close friends, became both personal and political foes, with Roosevelt actually undermining Taft's bid for reelection by siphoning away Republican support from the incumbent in the abortive Bull Moose movement of 1912.

Pinchot, who had started it all by challenging Ballinger, by the early 1920s had found a new political life. He was governor of Pennsylvania at the time of the sesquicentennial, and Martin dealt with him extensively in planning the tree-planting ceremony. Because they were both in the tree-preserving business, one as a businessman and the other as a public servant, the two men were naturally drawn to each other. Pinchot was tall and lean with graying hair and an easy smile. Martin noticed that he imitated the mannerisms of his mentor, Theodore Roosevelt, especially his speech. Whenever something struck Pinchot's fancy, he would respond with an unmistakably Rooseveltian, "bully!"

Martin admired Pinchot. He was a conscientious public servant and certainly a man of principle and conviction. No one was more the friend of conservation, yet something bothered Martin. Pinchot, his honor and dedication as a public servant notwithstanding, appeared too much the dreamer, a man better suited to the pursuit of conservation than politics.[56]

Al Smith left Martin with a completely different impression. Smith seemingly was born to politics, although his coarseness could put a man off. In firming up plans for the Philadelphia tree-planting ceremony, Martin traveled to Albany to visit Smith. After identifying himself, he was invited into the mansion where he saw the governor engaging in one of his favorite pastimes, defying the Volstead Act. Smith and several visiting pals, liquor glasses in hand, welcomed Martin, their cordiality even warmer once they learned that he was a Democrat.

Martin explained the purpose of his visit—he wanted Smith to participate in the tree-planting ceremony in Philadelphia. He would have been better off had he stopped there, but he tried to sell Smith on the idea. "Governor," he said, "your friends are talking much about you for the Democratic nomination for president in 1928. I would like to see you nominated and elected. This is a wonderful opportunity for you to appear under [the] finest auspices."

Smith, whose personality was forged on the mean streets of New York's Lower East Side, knew when he was being hustled and resented it. His demeanor shifted. "When is this affair going to be held?" he demanded. Martin told him but did not have the sense to stop his patronizing. He continued to irritate Smith: "Governor, this whole proceeding will be staged [in] the finest possible patriotic surroundings. It is a rare opportunity for you to appear before the American people on the highest plane and under the finest circumstances," to which Smith, his patience utterly exhausted, growled, "Oh, I don't give a good G-d d—about it."

Martin left the governor's mansion "mystified" by Smith's brusqueness, knowing that New York would be represented by someone else during the sesquicentennial celebration. The unpleasantness with Smith, however, did not sour Martin on the New Yorker as a presidential candidate. Smith, he believed, had a "genius for government," was a "real progressive with his feet on the ground," and was "moored firmly to the established principles of American life."[57]

Few men would have remained as steadfast in their praise of someone so rude. But Martin was, above all, a loyal Democrat. The poverty of his boyhood more than anything else bound him psychologically to the philosophy of the founder of the party, Thomas Jefferson. To Martin, no one ever better championed the masses than the Virginian who stood firm against the monarchist Alexander Hamilton in the early days of the Republic. Hamilton, notorious for catering to the financial and commercial classes, cared little about the common run of folk; to Jefferson, ordinary Americans were the ones who mattered most. Martin was a Democrat because of Jefferson. The Virginian, he unabashedly proclaimed to two thousand Democrats at a state rally in the summer of 1926, was a gift from God.[58]

It was easy enough, given Martin's privation growing up in Kent, to understand why he so readily identified with the party of Jefferson. Moreover, Martin made a congressional career out of tending to the interests and needs of the ordinary citizens who comprised most of his Fourteenth Congressional District constituency. Yet there were times when he talked like a Democrat and acted like a Republican.[59]

Martin's "apostasy" was most evident in the winter of 1925–26. Appalled by the massive growth of the federal bureaucracy in the 1920s, Martin introduced a government reorganization bill on December 10, 1925. His measure would allow the president, working with a special advisory board, to fire a hundred thousand or more "unnecessary" and "useless" federal workers at a savings to taxpayers of at least $500 million a year. No private company, Martin contended, could survive thirty days doing business as the federal government did. His fellow Democrats cringed when Martin buttressed his case by citing an argument advanced fifteen years earlier by millionaire Republican senator Nelson Aldrich who claimed that he could easily save taxpayers $300 million annually merely by running the government more efficiently. The profligacy that provoked Aldrich in 1910 was all the more astounding in 1925. Federal civilian payrolls had soared from $786 million a year when Aldrich made his claim to about $2.7 billion annually by 1925. More than twenty thousand employees had been added to an already bloated federal bureaucracy in just the few months after Coolidge swore his presidential oath on March 4, 1925.[60]

Martin was not merely trying to outpreach the Republicans on fiscal restraint. He had done his homework by studying several government departments and concluded that many of them were top-heavy with superfluous personnel. The United States Postal Service alone, Martin contended, had forty thousand drones who never sorted mail, never walked a postal route, or did anything else in the public interest. What peeved Martin all the more was the fact that the post office was one of the more efficient government departments.

It would have been sufficient had Martin simply introduced his bill, argued for it and let the House debate its merits or lack thereof and then vote accordingly. But Martin did not operate that way. The fight for the bill was just another campaign for him, and he approached it with all the firepower he typically used in his political races. At his own expense, he sent copies of his bill, along with explanatory letters, to hundreds of business and civic leaders across the nation to solicit their support. He also similarly bombarded newspaper editors everywhere, hoping that they would endorse the measure. He urged private citizens to write their congressmen and senators in support of his measure.[61]

Martin thought he had a sure winner in the reorganization bill. It seemed in perfect harmony with the business-oriented administration in Washington and should have struck a responsive chord with taxpayers who invariably thought that government was too fat. The congressman from Kent could not have been more wrong. Coolidge was not interested in it, most of Martin's colleagues in the House were unimpressed, and, although editors from the *New York Commercial* to the *Tacoma (Washington) Ledger* and dozens in between took up Martin's cause, the public was equally uninterested.[62]

The Washington bureaucracy struck back. Donald Ramsey, writing in the weekly journal *Labor,* claimed that Martin was now the laughingstock of the capital. How could anyone take seriously an attack on working people, Ramsey gibed unfairly, when it came from a dilettante who "inherited his business and the greater part of his personal fortune from his father"? Moreover, Ramsey continued, much of Martin's "evidence" was of the anecdotal sort offered by his brother Paul, who, when working for the government in

Washington during the war, was told by dawdling coworkers to slow down because he was making them look bad.[63]

Ramsey jabbed all the harder, making the attack even more personal. Martin, he said, was nothing more than a "slacker" himself. He drew $10,000 a year in congressional salary but hardly earned it. Ramsey, too, had done his homework. He checked House roll calls on thirty-two "important issues" during the current session and reported to his readers that Martin had missed twenty of them. The *Labor* writer did not stop there. He reviewed records of the previous session of Congress and found that Martin had missed 145 out of 309 roll calls, almost half. But that was not all—Ramsey examined all seven years of Martin's record in the House and revealed that the Kent congressman had been absent for 527 out of 1,035 roll calls. He concluded his *Labor* piece with, "[I]t would be pretty hard to beat that record for 'time wasting and buck passing.'"[64]

There was no escaping the truth. Although Martin was not the only congressman with such a spotty record, perhaps there had been too many overnight train rides home to tend to the family business and to see Berenice, Evangeline, and Martin Jr. What had seemed like innocent and understandable diversions from his public responsibilities were now returning to haunt him. He had, without thinking about it when he offered his reorganization bill, been living in a glass house of his own making, and now Donald Ramsey was passing out stones to anyone who wanted to take a shot.

Some did. One anonymous critic wrote Martin: "It takes a thief to catch a thief . . . , and it takes a loafer to catch a loafer. And you, in my estimation, are more than a loafer, you are a white-livered, spineless skunk." The letter writer added that she was a hard-working, ill-paid government employee who toiled daily from 9 A.M. to 4:30 P.M. with only a half hour for lunch and a "few measly half Saturday afternoons [off] during the summer." She despised congressmen—they were nothing more than that "crooked bunch upon the hill." The writer's wrath extended beyond Martin and Congress. All men, she wrote, were crooks and there was "nothing too mean to be said about the sex, and the more discomfort I am able to put them to the happier I am."[65]

Not every writer was so venomous. Martin received several letters that fortified his claims of bureaucratic inefficiency and waste. But the attacks hurt, and it was to those that Martin had to respond, if only to save face and salvage his wounded reputation before his peers in the House.

A representative could defend himself against reputation-destroying criticism by asking the Speaker to allow him to "rise to a question of personal privilege." If the request were granted, all other House business would be suspended and the representative given an uninterrupted hour on the floor to parry the criticism and restore his wounded reputation. Doing so was especially important to Martin because he had been humiliated by Ramsey's attack and those of other critics and because he also wanted to set the record straight about his "inherited wealth."

Nicholas Longworth, Theodore Roosevelt's son-in-law, was Speaker of the House and, although a Republican, gladly accommodated his fellow Ohioan. Longworth assured Martin that his request for a question of personal privilege would be honored. On February 22, 1926, as criticism of his bill poured in, Martin rose in the House chamber to be recognized by the Speaker.

Formally, Longworth inquired: "For what purpose does the gentleman from Ohio rise?" Martin, equally formally, responded: "Mr. Speaker, I rise to a question of personal privilege." After being told to proceed, Martin began recounting the attacks he had suffered in the two months since he had introduced his reorganization bill. Clearly, he had been hurt by the revelation of his spotty attendance and tried to defend his record by claiming that his absences were insignificant, generally occurring only when a fellow congressman made a "political speech of no consequence to Congress or to the country." Taking the offensive, he added, "[Any] member of Congress who answers all roll calls faithfully will have little time left to get important things done in his district." No constituents, Martin emphasized, received better service than his own. By his own count, during a congressional career going back to 1918, he had personally tended to the requests of twenty-five thousand constituents in his district, ranging from a high school student asking for information for a writing assignment to corporation presidents seeking business advice. Moreover, his congressional salary was not enough to cover all expenses related to his service, and he had to make up the difference, usually $500 or $600 a month, out of his own pocket.[66]

Martin also disabused his colleagues of any notion that he had inherited his wealth. All the memories of the early years of struggle welled up in him and finally erupted. "I had no inherited wealth," he proclaimed. "I did receive from my good old father a great idea, the basic principles of a great and useful science, and a fine philosophy of work and service." The Davey Tree Expert Company, he explained, started out humbly, and if he was now well off, it was only through twenty years of toil and sacrifice.[67]

Most of Martin's fellow congressmen listened attentively if not sympathetically. They had either suffered similarly at the displeasure of the press or at least could imagine that one day they might. Only Fiorello LaGuardia, serving a fourteen-year apprenticeship as a congressman before becoming New

York City's celebrity mayor and already well known for his feistiness, showed Martin no mercy. Crying "point of order," he challenged Martin's "personal privilege," claiming that his colleague was entitled to defend himself against slander but not to spend time explaining why he missed so many roll calls.

LaGuardia had a knack for needling people, and Martin L. Davey was now among his victims. With an irritation born out of his vulnerability, Martin snapped: "I have not talked quite as much in the House as [you have.]" The short-fused LaGuardia spat back: "[At least I have] attended all the sessions."[68]

The New Yorker may have been callous and even rude in disregarding House protocol, but he knew that Martin was weaseling around the facts. The Ohioan had introduced a controversial bill declaring that a fair portion of the federal workforce was lazy and superfluous. He failed to see that his own performance and commitment were questionable. Defending his record by saying that the congressional sessions he missed were "meaningless" insulted the efforts of his colleagues and demeaned the House in general. LaGuardia, the self-anointed defender of the lower chamber, was not going to let him get away with it.

Martin finished his speech, sensing that his exculpation was less than complete, but he accepted that fact and that his bill was doomed. He hated LaGuardia, but what was done could not be undone. Martin simply dismissed his New York antagonist as a "repulsive demagogue" with "more nerve than a Missouri mule." He may have been "smart and industrious," but he never did anything unless it proved personally advantageous. He was nothing more than an opportunist extraordinaire, and Martin had no trouble recognizing him for what he was because he knew the type intimately, perhaps too intimately.[69]

Defeat was no stranger to Martin. His sedition bill in 1919 died quickly and mercifully, and he lost the 1920 Fourteenth Congressional District race against Charles Knight. He took this most recent setback, like the others, in stride. More than two decades later, his judgment was at least somewhat vindicated when Congress authorized an executive department reorganization plan. President Harry Truman charged Herbert Hoover with the job, and by 1949 the former president's task force recommended hundreds of eliminations and consolidations. Ironically, the man in charge of it all in the 1940s, Herbert Hoover, was the very same person Martin believed Coolidge would turn to in the 1920s to do the job.[70]

The angry response of federal bureaucrats to Martin's reorganization bill made him rethink his position on civil service. Certainly the old spoils system that allowed politicians to raise armies of loyal but essentially useless bureaucratic hacks carried immense potential for abuse at the taxpayers' expense. Civil service, which took much appointive power out of the politicians' hands, bore its own potential for misuse. Once protected by civil service, government workers without a conscience could laze on the job without fear of being fired. Unfortunately, Martin concluded, civil service bred "idleness and inefficiency." That was true not only at the federal level but in state and local circles as well. If Martin had his way, it would be harder to get a civil service job and easier to be fired from one.[71]

Martin's humiliation over the defeat of his reorganization bill and the revelation of his shaky attendance record in Congress had Fourteenth Congressional District Republicans drooling over their prospects in 1926. Martin, of course, was expected to run for the fifth time and had all the advantages of a long-time incumbent, including face and name familiarity and a congressional track record of personal service to his constituents that not even his worst detractors could erase. However, if Republicans chose the right candidate, Martin could be beaten.

The Republicans believed they found their man—Arthur W. Sweeny, a successful Akron businessman and state senator. He was offered to Fourteenth Congressional District voters as a Coolidge Republican, a safe, sure bet to second the policies of the man in the White House who was leading America through some of its greatest prosperity ever. Sweeny was so attractive an alternative to a shopworn Martin Davey that his supporters early on shifted the Fourteenth Congressional District seat from the Democratic to the Republican column.[72]

The prediction was premature. Martin was by now a seasoned campaigner with remarkable organizational skills. He had already rendered enough services and done enough favors to count on hundreds of volunteers to get out the vote. In addition, Martin sent 125,000 letters to potential voters, single-handedly breaking the Kent post office's record for one day's mailing. Postage alone was $2,500, and the total cost (out of Martin's pocket) of the letters was $7,500.[73]

The Fourteenth Congressional District had never witnessed such a campaign blitz. E. L. Marting, the Summit County Republican campaign chair, was stunned. He had never seen anything like it, but other than futilely protesting that Martin had violated the Ohio Corrupt Practices Act, which limited a candidate's spending to $2,000 per campaign, he was powerless to act. Ross F. Walker, the Democratic campaign manager, dismissed the accusation as nothing more than a "smokescreen" and, in a classic example

of "you're another," demanded an investigation of Sweeny's campaign funding.[74] Neither charge went anywhere.

Not even Sweeny's attempt to hang an "absent and not voting" label on
Martin worked. Nor did his attempt to hoist Martin on his lame excuse—
"It so happened that I have a business to look after"—do the Kentite any
harm.[75]

The Republican also made tactical mistakes. For one, he alienated the "dry
vote" by declaring to beer-loving German-Americans that he supported the
repeal of prohibition. Martin, throughout his career, had been smart enough
to tiptoe around the liquor issue in every campaign. In heavily ethnic Lorain,
the largest city in Lorain County, Sweeny published an ad in a Hungarian-
language newspaper proclaiming that he opposed the laws that Congress
had passed in the 1920s, which limited the numbers of southern and eastern
European immigrants allowed into the United States. Martin had no reser-
vations about publicizing Sweeny's remarks for the edification of what he
called "older type American citizens."[76] Appealing to ethnic prejudices may
have been low-blow ethics, but it was good old-fashioned politics.

The election results proved that. Martin swept all four counties in the district, Portage, Summit, Lorain, and Medina, and he nearly doubled Sweeny's
vote count, 50,445 to 26,997. The victory was all the more remarkable because
the Fourteenth Congressional District in the 1920s was generally Republican
by eighteen or twenty thousand. Martin's bête noir, the *Akron Beacon Journal,* editorialized that the Republicans lost only because their primary election campaigns of the summer were exhausting ordeals that left their party
angry and divided by the time of the general election in November. That
observation, however, was more sour grapes than it was sober analysis. The
Akron newspaper came closer to the truth when it noted, almost in passing,
that Sweeny had lost to a "practical and ambitious politician."[77]

Martin returned to Washington in the winter of 1926–27 as a five-term
congressman.[78] It was no record for longevity, but his tenure was lengthy
enough to demonstrate considerable drawing and staying power. His success
was all the more telling because it came in a decidedly Republican strong-
hold, the old "Garfield district," as some Republicans old enough to remember the former congressman and martyred president still called it.

Although the challenge of a campaign and the thrill of victory still excited him, legislative work in Washington had become mundane. Never in the
first rank of representatives, Martin remained content rendering personal
services to his constituents. He spoke for and against pending legislation
during his fifth term but initiated none of it. He was troubled by the con-

Martin Davey in the family garden in Kent, 1927. *Left to right:* Martin Jr., Martin, Evangeline, and Berenice Davey. Evangeline Davey Smith Collection, Martin L. Davey Papers, Kent State University Libraries, Special Collections and Archives.

tinuing economic plight of farmers during the late 1920s and argued for a revived McNary-Haugen farm bill that passed Congress a second time only to be vetoed again by Coolidge in 1928. He also supported a congressional proposal for a national arboretum in Washington, D.C.[79] But other than that, he sat back while the majority party Republicans enjoyed their time in the legislative sun.

Ominous economic statistics worried him. Farmers were suffering most, but a number of industrial indicators hinted that manufacturing was headed for a downturn, too. The Department of Labor revealed that employment in late 1926 was only 91 percent of what it was in 1923. Sixty-five or seventy thousand people were out of work in Cleveland, a hundred thousand in Detroit.

Americans were running up billions of dollars in installment debt, and much of that was for luxury items like automobiles. How far could the economy go before it reached a saturation point and came to a screeching halt? Martin also fretted over America's sybaritic bent in the 1920s. Nothing more vividly represented that frightening turn than Americans' love affair with jazz. That unique, indigenous art form, so closely linked to New Orleans's seamy back alleys, was nothing more than a fatal siren song for unwitting Americans headed toward a moral abyss. To Martin, jazz was an expression of "recklessness and irresponsibility." It was the "excrescence of American life" and increasingly threatening to the well-being of society because its devotees, although a minority, were growing bolder.[80]

He stood for other things—traditional things that were and always should be the bedrock of an American value system. Home, family life, and a healthy spirituality were what the nation should idealize.

The rapid economic and social changes of the 1920s were forcing Martin to reexamine his role in the scheme of things. Had he done all he could in Washington? The answer to that was probably yes. For some time he had wondered if he might prefer administrative tasks in Columbus over legislative duties in Washington. Periodically his name would arise whenever Ohio Democrats discussed possible gubernatorial candidates. Although never openly encouraging the talk, he never discouraged it either. Maybe it was time to test new waters.

Chapter Nine

Governor?

A WIDESPREAD PHONINESS that permeated Washington society began to grate on Martin even years before he decided he had endured enough of the capital scene. As a member of the House Foreign Affairs Committee after his 1922 election, Martin periodically felt obligated to participate in the diplomatic corps' social life and one evening attended a dinner party hosted by Henry White, a career envoy under several Republican administrations. White was a gracious host, but Martin was put off by the pretensions of the other guests, particularly their contrived British accents. Especially annoying was White's sister-in-law, Martin's dinner partner for the evening. Peeved by her artificiality and feeling puckish, Martin began to banter with her. Disarmed by the congressman's apparent levity, the pompous grande dame dropped her guard and unwittingly slipped into her natural "American." The moment other table guests drew her attention, back came her affected "British." Martin remembered nothing of the specific conversation but laughed all the way back to his hotel as he mused over the pomposity of Washington's elite. He was still small-town Ohio, and back home nobody put on airs like that.

Washington folks, Martin also noticed, took themselves too seriously. Particularly affected by a sense of his own importance was Stephen G. Porter, chairman of the House Foreign Affairs Committee. Gracious but stiffly formal, Congressman Porter had no sense of humor whatsoever, a fact that Martin learned by accident.

One day, the Ohio congressman entered the House dining room and saw the chairman talking to a colleague at a table. Martin, not yet familiar with

Porter's starchy reserve, approached the pair and decided to introduce himself with a bit of fun. "Mr. Chairman," he said, "I have been appointed a member of your committee, and of course I would like to become an expert on foreign affairs as quickly as possible. Do you happen to know of a correspondence course I could take that would make me an expert in a few weeks?"

Martin thought that Porter would immediately catch the humor of his query. After all, who could become an expert on foreign affairs after a correspondence course of a few weeks? Martin's jocular attempt to break the ice with his new boss crashed with a thud. Porter never smiled, paused for a moment, and then responded with a deadly serious, "No, I am afraid I do not know of any correspondence course that you could take. There may be some books on the subject that you ought to read, and I will have my secretary look them up." The Foreign Affairs Committee chairman, Martin thought, would have been a perfect guest at Ambassador White's stuffy dinner party.

There were, however, people in Washington he liked. Cordell Hull, then a congressman from Tennessee, struck Martin as a true gentleman with the nation's best interests at heart. He was gracious and mild-mannered, bright and well studied on every issue before the House and country. Franklin D. Roosevelt in 1933 recognized Hull's talents, naming him secretary of state. The Tennessean went on to serve longer in that post than anyone before or since, with a Nobel Peace Prize in 1945 as an appropriate capstone to a long life of distinguished public service.

John Nance Garner, later Roosevelt's vice president for two terms in the thirties, equally impressed Martin. Unlike the suave and urbane Hull, Garner was a rough-and-tumble politician from Texas who could give as well as he could take in debates with his House colleagues. His gravelly exterior, however, never hid his intellect. He was a quick thinker and always on top of the issues of the day. Like Hull, he too seemed to understand better than most the nation's problems and could put partisanship aside when necessary to do what was best for all Americans.

Martin disliked Garner's fellow Texan, Tom Blanton. He respected him for his industriousness and mastery of parliamentary procedure, but the Texan was too combative. Where Hull and Garner, even in the midst of hot debate, retained their poise and good manners, Blanton enjoyed skewering his opponents with one of the sharpest tongues in the House. He was too much like the acerbic Fiorello LaGuardia without the New Yorker's redemptive panache.

After five terms in the House, Martin was growing weary of Washington. Everyone in his capital circle ate, drank, and breathed politics and lived in a world where misbegotten rumor stood on equal footing with the truth. "No one could remain normal" in such an environment, he concluded. A man needed contact with the America beyond the capital, someplace where politics was not the be-all and end-all. Some men, he noted, had been in Washington so long that they no longer fit anywhere else. The "procession at home [had] gone way beyond them, and [now] they find themselves walking alone."[1]

Martin did not want that to happen to him and by 1928 was certain that his current term would be his last. However, there was still important business to tend to for his constituents in the Fourteenth Congressional District. During the Great War, the European powers, with Germany in the lead, used dirigibles, massive airships, for reconnaissance and occasional tactical bombing. By the 1920s, the American military, aided by supportive congressmen, intended to bolster the nation's defenses with additional airships of its own. In 1926, the Navy Department signed an $8 million contract for two dirigibles to be constructed by the Akron-based Goodyear-Zeppelin Company. By 1928, however, Goodyear raised its original bid to $9 million—$5 million for the first ship and $4 million for the second. In addition, the Goodyear-Zeppelin Company now wanted $2.5 million to build a huge hangar to accommodate the helium-filled behemoths. Given the massiveness of the proposed hangar (Niagara Falls could fit inside), the cost did not seem exorbitant, but the changes in the contract opened the door to an eleventh-hour bid by a rival firm.[2]

In March 1928, under pressure from Burton L. French, the Republican chairman of the subcommittee on naval appropriations, Secretary of the Navy Curtis D. Wilbur reopened the bidding, and a New Jersey company, Brown-Boveri Shipbuilding, undercut the Goodyear-Zeppelin figure by $1 million, although it had to finagle the company's use of the government's airship hangar at Lakehurst, New Jersey, to do so.[3] The last-minute wheeling and dealing was more than the usual cutthroat competition between two firms vying for government dollars; it became, as some Ohioans thought, a contest between East Coast fat cats and hungry midwestern entrepreneurs who wanted to share in the government's largesse. It was Camden, New Jersey (close enough to New York to be Goliath), against David-like Akron, Ohio, the Rubber Capital, and the heart of Martin L. Davey's Fourteenth Congressional District.

Martin needed help to keep airship production in Akron. He was a Democrat in a Republican-controlled Congress, but the dirigible contract cut across party lines. Ohio Republicans wanted the government, as much as Martin did, to honor the contract with Goodyear-Zeppelin. Crowing rights, of course, would belong to Democrats and Republicans alike come election time. Martin, as the lead man of the Fourteenth Congressional District, could count on the aid of his fellow partisans in the House but worried that Republicans might not support a Democratic initiative, particularly those Republicans at some remove from northeastern Ohio.

First, Martin persuaded the Goodyear Company to hire a lawyer, Bascom Slemp, formerly a Republican congressman from Virginia, to lobby Republican votes for an amendment to the appropriation bill that would seal the deal for Goodyear. Martin had an ally in Pennsylvania's Thomas Butler, chairman of the Naval Affairs Committee and a staunch supporter of military preparedness, and in Georgia's Carl Vinson, the naval committee's ranking Democrat. Still, he needed an Ohio Republican to front the bill. Martin approached James T. Begg of Sandusky, a medium-sized town on Lake Erie and the geographical portal to the western part of the state. Sandusky was far enough away from Akron so that Begg worried little about what happened in the Rubber City. There was, however, a mitigating factor. Begg wanted the Ohio governorship and would need statewide recognition and votes to win the job.[4] If a gubernatorial nomination eventuated, Akron's voters were as important as Sandusky's, and even more so because there were a lot more of them.

Begg led the floor debate, and Martin followed, harassed by a familiar foe, Fiorello LaGuardia. The New Yorker was at most only mildly concerned about the fortunes of an airship company based in Camden, New Jersey, but he disliked Martin and enjoyed peppering the Ohioan with hypothetical and impertinent questions about possibly having two companies share the navy contract.[5] Martin kept his cool, let his allies argue for him, and, aided by the navy's preference for Goodyear anyway, steered the measure through the House. The Senate followed suit, and on October 6, 1928, the Goodyear-Zeppelin Company had the contract. Construction of the first airship, the *Akron,* began on November 7, 1929, and was completed on August 8, 1931. Given the immensity of the airship, the twenty-month project was no boondoggle. The *Akron* would be 785 feet long, weigh 215 tons, and could hold 270 passengers. Perhaps most remarkable, the craft bore its own individual hangar that could carry five small airplanes aloft.[6]

Although no one questioned Martin's sincerity in the fight for a contract for Akron, there was no doubt that his effort showed that he was not only looking out for Ohio's interests but also his own. Simply put, it was always helpful to bring federal dollars to Ohioans, especially for a man who was thinking about running for governor in 1928.

A full month before the House debate on the dirigible contract in March, Martin had prepared a press release broadly outlining his program were he to seek the governorship. He would cut the cost of government, he said, and would insist on honest law enforcement and a comprehensive program of conservation of Ohio's natural resources, an area in which he believed the state was woefully lacking. The "plain people," he emphasized, would be his primary concern, and he promised to maintain a "wholesome contact" with them. Proud of his service to his constituents during his congressional career, he urged Ohioans to check his record over his last several years in the House.[7]

By April, Martin had assembled a publicity team that blanketed the state with a mailing of pro-Davey letters. He now knew exactly what to do in letter-writing campaigns. He got a doctor in Kent to write every other doctor in Ohio; a dentist to write every other dentist; a pharmacist to write every other pharmacist. Letters from ministers to ministers were even broken down by denomination. The same was true for car dealers—a Buick dealer wrote other Buick dealers, and so on down the entire American automotive line. If no suitable group representative could be found in Kent, Davey forces sought appropriate sponsors in Akron. A spate of letters went out to Kiwanians, Eagles, Veterans of Foreign Wars, Knights of Columbus, Grangers, school superintendents, Kent Normal College (changed from Kent Normal School in 1929) and Oberlin College alumni, and virtually anyone else who might cast a ballot in Ohio.[8]

Not even Martin could recall how many hundreds of thousands of letters he mailed. But that was not all. He later sent a personal follow-up letter to everyone who had received one initially.[9] The time, energy, and expense were telling, but Martin knew how much potential voters enjoyed a candidate's attention.

His team also sought support individually, creating in Kent a "Hometown Davey for Governor" club to which even local Republicans were warmly invited. Davey campaigners did the same at the state level. They contacted labor and business heads across Ohio and sought the support of Democratic leaders in every county and town.[10] If Davey workers missed anyone, it had to be because that person was either wearing diapers, in an asylum, or reposing for eternity in an Ohio cemetery.

Aided by old friends and confidants Charles Sharp and L. L. Poe and by Myrna Smith, his trusted secretary from the Davey Tree Expert Company, Martin took on an ambitious public speaking tour. No invitation was rejected, and indeed any request from the Rotary, Chamber of Commerce, or a women's group resulted in the Davey organization seeking three or four other speaking engagements in the same locale. A typical day saw Martin addressing an audience at a high school in the morning, delivering a luncheon talk to another gathering at noon, holding a late afternoon session with yet another audience before finishing his day with an evening address to still another group. Indefatigable, Martin also never rejected an opportunity to meet with high school students. Those teenagers, of course, could not vote, but, Martin astutely noted, they went home after school to talk with parents who did.[11]

In the Democratic primary election on August 14, 1928, Martin outdistanced his two closest opponents, former lieutenant governor Earl D. Bloom of Bowling Green and Cleveland councilman Peter Witt, by better than a two-to-one margin. The size of the victory demonstrated Martin's strength statewide. He won eighty-two of Ohio's eighty-eight counties, demonstrating that his popularity cut across the state's geographical and rural-urban lines, with the exception of Witt's hometown of Cleveland.[12] His opponent in the fall would be Cincinnati businessman Myers Y. Cooper, who had come from behind in the Republican primary to defeat James T. Begg, Martin's congressional ally in the dirigible contract fight earlier in the year.

Prior to his primary election victory, Martin was confident that 1928 might be a banner year for the Democrats, not only in Ohio but nationwide as well. In a "Dear Friend" letter to the Ohio party faithful, he declared that voters had had enough of the tired and (hearkening back to the Harding presidency) scandal-tainted Republicans and would welcome a return to Democratic-led government at all levels. Ever the organizer, Martin had a specific plan for the general election. There were about nine thousand precincts in the state, and if party workers attracted a mere twelve additional voters per precinct on election day, there would be an additional hundred thousand ballots cast for Democratic candidates. Every precinct committeeman and woman would have to be carefully chosen, with special emphasis on his or her dynamism and capacity for hard work. They should solicit all Democrats, independents, and even maverick Republicans who might shift allegiances on election day. Crucial, too, Martin concluded, were the thousands of young people who turned twenty-one, voting age, in any given election year. Newcomers like these, and absentee voters as well, too often slipped through the cracks, their valuable ballots never cast because no candidate had gone after them.[13]

Martin was further heartened by the reconciliation of an old-friend-turned-foe, David L. Rockwell. By April 1928, the bad blood generated by Rockwell's unexpected dunning of Martin for his expenses in the congressional campaign of 1918 and their differences over McAdoo's bid for the

Democratic presidential nomination in 1924 had largely dissipated. Rockwell, still important in Portage County politics as the Democratic Party chair, committed the local organization to Davey's gubernatorial bid. The decision was welcome news to Martin, especially since the committee's decision was unanimous, meaning that Rockwell, too, supported it.[14]

Martin's campaign in the fall was played out against the backdrop of a presidential election, one made all the more fascinating because of the incumbent's almost angry refusal to seek reelection. Calvin Coolidge, a curiosity among politicians because he despised the celebrity and forced sociability of political life, simply refused to run. His terse declination revealed his contempt for politics. Rather than call a Washington press conference to announce so significant a decision, the president, vacationing in Rapid City, South Dakota, on August 2, 1927, summoned reporters to a mathematics classroom at the local high school, told them, "the line forms on the left," and then handed each a one-sentence note: "I do not choose to run for president in 1928." The stunned newsmen asked if the president had any explanation and were met with a response, brief even for Silent Cal, "None."[15]

No one ever thought that Coolidge loved being president—it was a responsibility thrust upon him after Harding's unexpected death in 1923—but even so the announcement shocked almost everybody. There were signs here and there, however, that the Vermonter had had more than enough of the White House. Mrs. Coolidge had earlier sewn a quilt with a simple "Calvin Coolidge, 1923–1929" prominently displayed, broadly hinting that she and her husband had already decided what to do about a second full term. Moreover, the president's chronic indigestion, constant sleepiness, and the painful loss of his fourteen-year-old son through blood poisoning had turned the White House and the presidency into a psychological prison.[16] The office never meant that much to him. It was easy to walk away from it.

Coolidge's refusal to seek renomination left Republicans in only a minor quandary when they assembled in June 1928 in Kansas City, Missouri, to choose a presidential candidate. The probusiness policies of Harding and especially Coolidge had so far provided a perfect blueprint for continued prosperity, and nothing loomed immediately on the horizon to threaten that. All the Republicans had to do was choose a candidate who essentially promised more of the same. Despite the minor concern that Herbert Hoover was not sufficiently beholden to party managers, no one seemed better suited to carry on in the fine Republican tradition of peace and prosperity.

In many ways, Hoover represented the quintessential American success story. Born in West Branch, Iowa, in 1874, he was orphaned at age ten and shuffled off to various relatives in Iowa and Oregon. By 1895, he had put himself through Stanford University and within a few years had made a small fortune as a mining engineer. During the Great War, he distinguished himself as the head of the Belgian Relief Committee and continued his humanitarian service, at Woodrow Wilson's invitation, as the food administrator for a war-torn Europe. In 1921, President Harding named him secretary of commerce, a position to which he was reappointed by Calvin Coolidge. Untouched by the scandals of the Harding administration and known for his efficiency while heading the Commerce Department, Hoover emerged as the most attractive Republican candidate for president in 1928. His first-ballot triumph in Kansas City was in fact more of a ratification than a nomination.[17]

The Democrats, meeting in Houston, Texas, had a similarly easy time choosing a candidate. Unwilling to savage themselves as they had in 1924, on the first ballot they nominated Alfred E. Smith, whose popularity had only grown since the Democratic convention debacle four years earlier. Smith, born in 1873 to Irish-Catholic immigrants on New York's Lower East Side, was, like Hoover, a living, breathing Horatio Alger success story. After his father died when Smith was only twelve, he went to work at the famed Fulton Fish Market and later at a pump house in New York. As a young man, he frequented Lower Manhattan's saloons and met Tammany Hall pols who introduced the amiable Smith to New York political life. After several years as a proven Tammany loyalist, Smith was elected a New York State assemblyman. He quickly honed his leadership skills and won the statehouse speakership in 1913. In 1915, he was elected sheriff of New York County and two years later became president of New York City's board of aldermen and was now clearly a force in the Empire State. In 1918, he won the first of four gubernatorial terms, three of them consecutively, 1922, 1924, and 1926.

Unable to escape his working-class origins (he still said "woik" instead of "work," "he don't," and "ain't"), Smith's natural friendliness and sincere commitment to reform nonetheless catapulted him to the top of the Democratic presidential heap in 1928.[18] His Roman Catholicism, Democratic kingmakers knew, was a serious handicap in predominantly Protestant America, but if the party were ever to offer such a candidate, 1928 was the year. Although the Democrats' enthusiasm for Smith was genuine and they convinced themselves that their man could win, in their hearts they knew that no Democrat could counter the prosperity that Americans associated with the presence of a Republican in the White House. Despite all the Democratic hoopla, Smith was just a sacrificial lamb.

Hoover acknowledged that in many respects little separated the two candidates on issues. Both supported general reform of the judicial and prison systems, child welfare, housing, national conservation, etc.[19] Given the Republican's service during the Wilson administration and his apparent political neutrality, some Democrats thought Hoover an intriguing possibility as their party's presidential candidate earlier in the 1920s. The Iowan's rise from rags to riches and his humanitarianism during the Great War only added to his attractiveness as a "man of the people."

Despite their similarities, the Republican knew that he and Smith were more unlike than they were alike. Their humble beginnings notwithstanding, the two candidates had evolved into different social and intellectual beings. Hoover and his wife, Lou, oozed patrician urbanity, while Smith and his wife, Katie, could never shuck the habits, attitudes, and behaviors born of their working-class origins. Even the name "Katie" evoked images of a barmaid in one of Lower Manhattan's Irish saloons.

Adding to the social disparity between the two men were their opposing stances on prohibition. Hoover stood foursquare behind the constitutional ban on alcohol, while Smith openly disapproved of it. The Republican's support of temperance elevated him to the moral high ground in the struggle against the damnation and ruination inevitably accompanying the allures of "demon rum." To Protestant fundamentalists and other self-anointed arbiters of the nation's morality, the upright Hoover was their man. Smith, conversely, represented the coarseness and vice of the weak-willed masses who were unable to resist the seductive and destructive power of alcohol. In the minds of many, Hoover would be a deserving steward of the White House, while Smith should don an apron, roll up his shirtsleeves, and do what his basic nature dictated, sling drinks in one of New York's numerous speakeasies.

The liquor debate, as passion-provoking as it was, paled, however, next to the religious issue in 1928. Hoover was a Quaker. That made him at worst "quaint" to millions of American Protestants, but at least he was still one of them. Smith, on the other hand, was a Roman Catholic and consequently repugnant to many because he was certain to bow to Rome even in political matters. Hoover never personally exploited the religious issue in his presidential campaign, but he did not have to—there were fire-breathing Protestants who were happy to do it for him. Evangelist Billy Sunday, still belching hellfire and brimstone from the pulpit at sixty-five, excoriated Smith as a "force from hell" and denounced the Democratic candidate's male followers as "bootleggers, crooks, and pimps." Any woman supporting Smith was surely a whore.[20]

Virulent anti-Catholicism was nothing new in American politics. The Know-Nothing Party had administered voters a heavy dose of it in the mid-nineteenth century, and the Ku Klux Klan derived much of its agenda by appealing to the scarcely concealed Protestant fear that every American Catholic was merely biding time until the pope took over the government of the United States. Even so, no one had seen anything quite like it before Smith ran for president in 1928. All Protestant denominations were to some degree infected by the bigotry, but Baptists were the worst. One Baptist newspaper in Arkansas described the Catholic Church as a "brutal, hell-born power," and another in Texas predicted that Smith's election would result in open persecution of Protestants as Rome stamped its "cruel, blood-stained heel upon all who refuse her authority." The Arkansas paper knew just how to stir its already frightened and angry readership when it declared that a Catholic president would invalidate Protestant marriages and in the process turn all offspring of such unions into bastards.[21]

All this was sheer nonsense, but the truth mattered not at all in the pell-mell of presidential politics in 1928. Even the staid *New York Times* fueled the fire by quoting from the *Fellowship Forum,* a fundamentalist rag that published what its editors "knew" to be an oath sworn by all members of the Knights of Columbus: "I will spare neither sex, age nor condition, and I swear that I will hang, waste, boil, flay, strangle and burn alive these infamous heretics [Protestants]; rip up the stomachs and wombs of their women and crush infants' heads against the wall, in order to annihilate forever their execrable race. That when the same cannot be done openly, I will secretly use the poison cup, the strangulation cord, the steel poniard, or the leaden bullet." Unfortunately, other publications ran the *Times* copy, giving the original piece an authoritativeness it would never have enjoyed under normal circumstances.[22]

More levelheaded Republicans tried to take the higher road, but their purpose was much the same as that of the fearmongers who knew they had a hot issue in Smith's Catholicism. Charles C. Marshall, a New York attorney knowledgeable in canon law, used the pages of the sophisticated *Atlantic Monthly* to query Smith about how he would resist the power of Rome if elected. Marshall contended that although the Roman Catholic Church's motives were beyond reproof, there were significant differences between what its adherents and non-Catholics accepted as articles of faith. Crucial to Marshall was Pope Leo XIII's 1885 encyclical, *The Christian Constitution of States,* which declared that God Himself established ecclesiastical and civil powers over mankind. The two powers may coexist and operate freely in any number of human endeavors, but when they collided, to Roman Catholics at least, the civil must yield to the ecclesiastical, a point earlier elaborated by Pope Pius IX in his *Syllabus of Errors* in 1864. Given all this, Marshall asked politely in the *Atlantic Monthly* piece how Smith would reconcile conflicting views of church and state in ordinary matters such as marriage, foreign relations, and domestic policy. Although reluctant to draw attention to his religion, Smith replied in a follow-up article in the same journal that he would have no problem making secular decisions in a secular state. A president, loyal in his faith to Rome, could still be, in Smith's own words, a "Catholic and a Patriot."[23]

Moderate voices tried to raise the debate above raw religious prejudice by claiming that Smith's faith alone should not bar him from the presidency, but his wet stance on prohibition and his association with political undesirables (Tammany Hall) ought to. The editor of Boston's *Christian Leader* claimed that the pope knew better than to interfere in American civil life. Catholics were loyal citizens and Smith deserved a "square deal." Despite the moderation of some voices, though, Smith's candidacy struck a raw nerve, best demonstrated by a Catholic journal's angry response to Protestant America's constant challenge of Smith's loyalty. In three words, the Jesuit editor of *America* gave it right back to Smith's anti-Catholic critics: "Are Protestants Americans?"[24]

Smith also had to defend himself against frequent charges of public drunkenness. A woman in West Virginia claimed that she had a letter from a Syracuse, New York, woman attesting that Smith was so drunk while addressing a crowd at the New York State Fair that it took two men to keep him from toppling into the grandstand. Photographs and movies of Smith shot during the speech proved the accuser false and so, too, did her failure to produce the alleged letter. But none of that mattered to Smith haters. The mere fact that the candidate understandably always had two bodyguards at his side was translated into "the man was so drunk that it took two people to hold him up."[25]

Zealous partisans on the other side could play dirty politics, too, although their attempts to smear Hoover were so transparent that they did not even constitute good old-fashioned mudslinging. One story had Hoover, while living in London after the Great War, cheating a "Chinaman" out of his property. The charge was utterly false, publicly repudiated by the supposed victim himself. Another "saboteur" hoped to capitalize on America's scarcely latent racism by snapping a photo of a "No White Help Wanted" sign at the Hoover ranch in Bakersfield, California. The photograph, intended to rouse white labor against Hoover, was distributed nationwide but was traced to Kern County labor leaders operating under the clandestine auspices of the local Democratic county committee. Another Democratic smear charged that Hoover, again while living in England, was a naturalized British subject and had actually voted twice in English elections. The truth was that Hoover, as a temporary resident of the United Kingdom, was required to pay taxes and, because of the electoral law in force at the time, was automatically placed on the roll of eligible voters. The American embassy in London verified that Hoover was not a British subject and had never voted in any British election.[26] None of these attempts to hurt Hoover in 1928 even remotely bore the same weight as the calumnies against Smith, but they were evidence that neither the Republicans nor the Democrats had a monopoly on fair play in 1928.

Ohio's 1928 gubernatorial campaign, although certainly smaller than the national contest, was just as mean. Martin denounced the religious bias that Smith had to endure, but he, too, absorbed and leveled personal attacks that had nothing to do with issues or political philosophies. Indeed, issues were conspicuously absent during Martin's contest with his Republican opponent, Cincinnati businessman Myers Y. Cooper.

Martin could be combative, and by 1928 he had waged enough political battles to generate a slew of enemies. Prominent among them was Cleveland Republican Maurice Maschke, with whom Martin had clashed during his 1924 congressional campaign. Maschke was everything that Martin was not. While Martin was small-town Kent and an Oberlin College dropout, Maschke grew to young manhood in an eastern world of comfort and ease, graduating from New Hampshire's prestigious Phillips Exeter Academy and later from Harvard University, class of 1890. He was admitted to the Ohio Bar in 1891.

Not particularly ambitious as a young man in Cleveland, Maschke drifted into Republican politics by campaigning for the reelection of Mayor Robert E. McKisson in 1897. Maschke gradually took on more party responsibilities, and over the next thirty years became the Republican power broker of Cuyahoga County. Democrats were his sworn enemies, but even his own partisans feared his wrath. If Maschke anointed a candidate for office in Ohio's largest county, invariably that candidate received the party's nomination. Maschke's control of Cleveland politics was so complete that one Republican congressional aspirant who was denied the kingmaker's blessing denounced him as a "dictator" for unfairly manipulating the nomination of a rival.[27]

Maschke enjoyed skewering his enemies and took special delight in going after Martin. In an address to Cleveland's Western Reserve Republican Club during the 1928 gubernatorial campaign, Maschke ridiculed Martin's

congressional record. The Kentite's attempt to cut a bloated federal workforce was a farce, Maschke told his audience. Any man who missed half of
his congressional roll calls had no business calling anyone else a slacker.
The Clevelander similarly slammed Martin's failed 1919 sedition bill as anti-
American and claimed that its author was the active tool of the Ku Klux
Klan in the matter.[28] That, of course, was not true, but the truth mattered
little to Maschke in such a bitter campaign.

Maschke had even more to say about Martin's supposed Klan connections. The Republican charged that Martin had used Indiana's grand dragon,
D. C. Stephenson, currently imprisoned in his home state for murdering a
girl, to harass Charles L. Knight everywhere the Akronite spoke during the
1920 congressional campaign. The accusation was unprovable, likely bogus,
and foul enough to provoke an immediate and angry denial from Martin,
who struck back by denouncing Maschke as "the vulture of gang politics"
and a racist who never allowed a "Catholic, Negro, or foreign-born" citizen
to appear on a Cuyahoga County Republican ticket.[29]

The name-calling worsened when Charles L. Knight, still publisher of the
Akron Beacon Journal, entered the fray. Speaking before a crowd in Cooper's
hometown of Cincinnati, Martin's foe of 1920 not only kept alive the putative Davey link to the imprisoned D. C. Stephenson, he also exhumed the
Kentite's 4-A draft status, an embarrassing remnant of Martin's 1918 congressional campaign against Charles Dick. Still a keen wordsmith, Knight scored
Davey as a man "willing to die by proxy," while true patriots actually did so
on the battlefields of Europe. Knight added insult to injury by reminding his
Cincinnati audience that Martin had hidden behind his wife's skirts to avoid
conscription. It was, after all, Berenice who checked the exemption request
that kept Martin safe at home in 1918.[30]

Martin could hit as hard as his Republican foes. Before a delirious crowd
in Akron, he not only assailed Maschke, he quickly linked his Republican
opponent Cooper to the Cleveland party boss. Cooper, he claimed, had
"sold out" to Maschke in return for Cuyahoga County's votes, the prepon-
derance of which had earlier gone to Cooper's primary election opponent,
James T. Begg.[31] Given Maschke's iron control of Cuyahoga County Republican politics, Cooper naturally wanted the local boss's support, but that
proved nothing of a Cooper "sellout" to the Clevelander. In Martin's politicking, however, that mattered not at all. Nobody enjoyed a bitter political
fight more than the would-be governor from Kent.

Cooper, less fiery than Davey, nonetheless struck back, albeit not terribly
fiercely. Davey, he charged, was just mudslinging when he tried to link the

Republican candidate with Maschke and Cuyahoga County politics. The real issue, Cooper maintained, was a continuation of Republican-generated prosperity under Calvin Coolidge.[32] By inference Cooper wanted Ohioans to think that a Republican in the governor's mansion in Columbus would do for Ohio what Coolidge had done for the nation.

In truth, the 1928 gubernatorial campaign was more a contest between Martin Davey and Maurice Maschke than one between Davey and Cooper. The race, as Martin described it, was a contest to determine who was to run Ohio government—the duly elected agent of the people or a behind-the-scenes power broker from Cleveland. Martin resorted to any means to ensure that it would be he and not Maschke who ran Ohio. Consequently, no accusation was too small. Late in the campaign, Martin accused Maschke's law firm of receiving $7,600 to regain eight barrels of whisky seized from a client. The implication of course was clear—Maschke was at least tacitly involved in a criminal act because prohibition was in force, and the Clevelander should have nothing to do with a client's attempt to regain eight barrels of illicit liquor. What Martin failed to disclose was the fact that the case dated back to 1919, well before prohibition went into effect. John H. Orgill, Maschke's law partner, pointed that out to the *Cleveland Plain Dealer*, relegating in the process Davey's accusation to "yesterday's news." Martin's hometown newspaper, however, continued coverage of the candidate's attacks on Maschke as election Tuesday neared.[33]

The campaign, its meanness notwithstanding, became almost cartoonish on preelection Sunday. While Maschke and other Cleveland-area Republicans met that afternoon in the city's Mayfield Theater, an ammonia-laced bomb exploded, forcing the party boss and his teary-eyed cohorts to throw open windows and turn on every available fan. No finger of guilt could be pointed at Martin or his supporters, but, curiously, Republicans had been warned not to meet in staunchly Democratic Mayfield. The police were summoned and found a suspicious-smelling bottle but could not trace it and the noxious prank to anyone.[34]

Things grew only worse from there. On election day, a fuming Maschke charged into Cleveland's Board of Election offices at city hall and demanded that police be dispatched to four precincts in the nineteenth ward because "hired gunmen" were "stealing the election for the Democrats." A reporter sent to the scene found "hard-looking" men on street corners and teenage boys congregating in nineteenth-ward doorways. Even more sinister, the *Cleveland Plain Dealer* reported, were a number of men in Precinct F loitering with their hands deep in their pockets, watching everyone who approached the polls. To Maschke, the loiterers were gunmen (their hands in their pockets were incontrovertible proof of that) ready to invade election booths to threaten any voter even thinking about voting Republican. None of that turned out to be true, but the truth fared poorly against the Mayfield Theater stink bomb on Sunday and a more serious neighborhood explosion on election morning that shattered windows in a half dozen businesses and summoned a swarm of police to investigate.[35]

Against the "Keystone Kop" scenario in Cleveland, Republicans swept to easy victories nationally and in Ohio. Never before had so many American voters flocked to the polls—more than twenty-one million voted for Hoover. Smith lagged more than six million votes behind. The electoral vote was even more lopsided, 444–87.[36] Americans had spoken loudly and clearly. The first eight years of the Roaring Twenties were inextricably linked to Republican presidents and policies, and no Democrat with the heavy Catholic and "wet" baggage of an Al Smith could hope to counter that. Although Smith had to feel disappointed, fate treated him kindly, for in less than a year the Great Depression began, and it was Hoover, not he, who bore the brunt of it.

Martin lost the governorship to Myers Cooper by nearly a quarter million votes but still ran 514,000 ahead of the national ticket. He was not surprised by his opponent's victory. Too many signs pointed to the Republican ascendant. Besides the prosperity associated with Republicanism and the burden of Smith's weighty baggage, Martin believed that the Democratic candidate made several tactical errors during the campaign, errors that hurt the party in Ohio, too. For one, Martin concluded, Smith had erred in attacking the Ku Klux Klan when, because of his Catholicism, he was certain of winning the anti-Klan vote without agitating the Klan and its sympathetic fence-sitters. For another, Smith had foolishly attacked the "Drys" during the campaign. Everyone knew Smith was a "Wet" on prohibition, and all he did was drive a passionate dry vote to the polls on election Tuesday. In attacking the Klan and the Prohibitionists, the Democratic candidate had needlessly stirred two bees' nests and come out of it with all stings and no honey. Smith would have been far wiser had he attacked Hoover and the Republicans for their antipathy toward farmers and labor and for their "slavish devotion to the interests of big business."[37]

Martin saw the handwriting on the wall. Despite it all, though, he campaigned on, promoting Smith and Ohio Democrats statewide. But a week before the election, he confessed his private concerns to Burr Gongwer, Cuyahoga County's Democratic chief. Weary of Gongwer's urgings to attack the Ku Klux Klan and the "Drys," Martin flat-out told the Clevelander that the race was already over. "I'm licked," he said, and so was the whole Demo-cratic ticket in Ohio. Gongwer protested, but Martin turned for confirma-tion to David L. Rockwell, who was also in the room, and Rockwell nodded yes, "It is a pity, but it is true."[38]

The defeatism of the two Kentites irritated Gongwer, but they were right and he was wrong, completely wrong. Not even Gongwer's Cuyahoga County went Democratic in 1928. Indeed, only two of Ohio's eighty-eight counties, tiny Mercer and Putnam, did. Even with Martin's loss, encour-aging signs abounded. He ran ahead of the national ticket in every Ohio county and won 1,106,739 votes, more than any other Democratic guber-natorial candidate ever in Ohio. Hoover beat Smith by nearly 77,000 votes in Martin's Fourteenth Congressional District, while the Kentite trailed Cooper there by only 4,336. Had Hoover's Ohio margin been only 500,000 or so instead of 700,000, there might have been a Democrat instead of a Republican in the governor's mansion in 1929.[39]

The positives notwithstanding, the losing campaign had enervated Mar-tin. Despite postelection encouragement from supporters who saw him as the potential savior of a fractured party, Martin had had enough. Certainly he was disheartened by his loss to Cooper, but there was considerable truth in his complaint that the gubernatorial campaign, conducted while tending to his congressional and private business affairs, was simply too strenuous. He was "literally worn out," and even skipped his election night party at the Kent country club. He was consoled, though, that ten-year-old Martin Jr. looked forward to having his father home for a change.[40]

Still, Martin burned no political bridges. His staff scoured the state for the names of any Ohio Democrats who may have been overlooked in 1928. In addition, he mailed two hundred thousand letters thanking supporters, spending more than $4,000 of his own money on postage in the process. He congratulated the few Ohio Democrats who won in 1928 and consoled those who lost. He also responded coyly but encouragingly to a fellow Democrat, who thought that, because of the Smith candidacy, 1928 was simply a bad time for Martin to run. The defeated gubernatorial candidate was already thinking of the next campaign tack—the avoidance of no-win issues such as prohibition and a return to the common-man principles upon which Thomas Jefferson based the original Democratic Party.[41]

More politics lay ahead, but for now the business of the Davey Tree Ex-pert Company dominated Martin's life. On December 3, 1928, 450 students, an increase of one hundred over the previous year, were to begin classes at the Davey Institute of Tree Surgery. Since its creation in 1914, the institute had trained more than a thousand tree surgeons, who had in turn made the Davey name synonymous with tree work nationwide.[42]

Aware that the firm could not expand by word of mouth alone, Martin bought an hour of weekly radio time beginning in January 1930 and ending in 1932. Between five and six every Sunday evening, from the Fifth Avenue studio of the Skinner Organ Company in New York, he spoke for ten minutes about various facets of the Davey Tree business, and the rest of the time listeners were treated to a variety of old sing-along favorites played by an organist or a string quartet. The program always began with an instrumental version of *Just a Song at Twilight* as soothing background for a recitation of Joyce Kilmer's classic poem "Trees." The program was immediately successful; the fan mail and personal responses from clients attested to that.[43]

Business for the Davey Tree Expert Company was good in 1929; the firm did better than $3 million worth and continued to do well even after the stock market collapse in October. Early 1930 was profitable, too, but by the spring, just when the tree business should have taken off, the inevitable effects of the economic downturn hit Davey Tree. Business declined through the summer and by September was 18 percent off the previous year's. Martin tried to stanch the losses, cutting expenses by $275,000, but that was only the beginning. Business languished for the next three years, and Martin almost grew accustomed to monthly financial bloodletting to save the company.[44]

Although Martin's goal was to preserve the family business, his instinct for politics ran strong. Urged on by supporters, he thought about running for governor in 1930. He accepted speaking engagements throughout Ohio, but his heart was not wholly in the political game. One sleepless night, riding the train from New York to Columbus, he simply told himself, "h——, I will not run." Comforted by his decision, he finally settled into sweet, refreshing slumber.[45] Politics in Ohio could go on without Martin L. Davey. It would be good for a change just to watch the parade.

Chapter Ten

The Great Depression Hits Home

———————————— 🐿 ————————————

RADIO WAS TAILOR-MADE for Martin Davey. Years of stump speaking had sharpened his oratory, and his ego was such that center stage, even in a closed New York studio, suited him perfectly. The diversion from politics was pleasurable, too. The Davey Tree broadcasts provided an opportunity to return to his roots, to resurrect memories of a hardscrabble but pleasant youth. He reminisced about his father, dead now for seven years, and especially enjoyed relating how the British-born John Davey shed tears of joy when he became a citizen and swore allegiance to the United States.[1]

The financial success of the Davey Tree Expert Company for a generation now also allowed Martin an opportunity to say in his own way, "I told you so." John Davey's critics in the early days sneered at him and treated him as the oddball of Kent because of his unabashed love affair with trees, but he was by the 1930s regarded far and wide as an entrepreneurial visionary.[2] Now, Martin could all but forget the mockery and condescension he endured as a young boy growing up as the son of the "village fool." Even old-monied Harvey Firestone Jr., son of the founder of one of America's great rubber companies, sought his help. Interested in conducting a radio program similar to Davey Tree's, the younger Firestone came to Martin's New York studio to watch him perform. Martin was nervous under the rubber magnate's scrutiny, but despite his jitters impressed Firestone enough so that he asked Davey to write his broadcasts for him. Martin agreed and was paid a princely sum of $3,000 for three months of ghosted addresses for the tire king.[3]

Unfortunately, Martin's personal good fortune was not shared by his own company. There were signs that business was weakening everywhere, including the Davey Institute of Tree Surgery on North Mantua Street in Kent. The school opened, but enrollment for the fall class of 1929 was 275, down 175 from just the year before. Given the declining economy of 1929, opening the institute was somewhat surprising. Earlier in the year, word circulated that it might not open at all that fall.[4]

The full force of the Great Depression, of course, still lay ahead. Although the stock market was obviously queasy, and Black Tuesday was only a month away, most Americans, including Martin L. Davey, had no idea of what they were about to face. For Martin, possessed of the businessman's requisite optimism, 1929 seemed like a good year to move into the Kent newspaper business. He had mulled over the idea for several months, thinking that his hometown, now a city of eight thousand, deserved a top-notch daily, one that he could create by merging the city's current two, the *Courier* and the *Tribune*.[5] The deal was struck in September; Martin was now a newspaperman running the *Kent Courier-Tribune*, and all seemed well—for a while, that is. Advertising revenues rolled in over the Christmas and New Year holidays but ebbed soon after. Then the paper's typesetters unionized and demanded higher wages, which Martin could not pay.[6]

Labor problems aside, Martin also learned how fickle and demanding a small-town readership could be, even over something so seemingly unimportant as a minor detail in an obituary. The decedent's death was dutifully noted in the *Courier-Tribune*, so Martin was surprised when he received a letter of rebuke from the dead man's niece no less. Her complaint: she did not want the newspaper to print the name of the funeral director in charge of the obsequies! Within six months Martin gladly sold his newspaper to Emmit C. Dix, a true newspaperman from nearby Wooster, Ohio.[7] Martin's dalliance with the paper was one of his few missteps in life so far, but he knew it early on and got out of it with no harm done.

Martin was proving himself as good a businessman as he was a politician. Both endeavors required keen instincts—knowing what to do and when to do it. During the darkening 1930s, when most Americans were in survival mode, Martin founded the Davey Investment Company. Assisted by his brother Paul and a few close associates, Martin began acquiring real estate throughout Kent. With Martin as president and treasurer, the new firm soon owned an apartment building, several houses, city blocks of businesses, and two large parcels for future development.[8]

Paul Davey was instrumental in still more Davey business diversification. Always mechanically inclined, Martin's younger brother constantly thought about further mechanizing the Davey Tree Expert Company. His desire to replace muscle power with machine power in the field led him to experiment with air compressors. The brothers quickly saw additional applications for the compressors and envisioned manufacturing their own. Capitalized with $100,000 of family money, business number three, the Davey Air Compressor Company, was born. When the Daveys decided to incorporate the Canadian branch of their tree company in November 1930, Martin found himself the president of four different firms, and he was not finished yet.[9] Before the year was out, through a combination of financial and personal events, he got into the banking business, too.

By 1930, Martin was Kent's leading citizen. Hand in hand with his stature went civic obligation. Accordingly, in January 1930, Martin "permitted" his election as a director of the Kent City Bank, largely an honorific title. Martin knew little about the inside of the banking business, although he had been borrowing from banks for years.

Martin's position with the City Bank allowed him a close look at David L. Rockwell's financial affairs, and they were a mess. Judge Rockwell had used his weight as the bank's largest stockholder to run up risky loans that ate up much of the small bank's capital. To casual observers, Rockwell appeared to be one of the richest men in town. His real-estate holdings alone were visible proof of that, except that they were encumbered by not only a first mortgage of $100,000 but also a second for the same amount.

That was not the end of it, either. Rockwell owed $80,000 to the Guardian Trust Company of Cleveland. When he defaulted on the loan, the Cleveland bank foreclosed on Rockwell's 435 shares of Kent City Bank stock. However, given the Kent bank's near insolvency, Guardian Trust essentially owned $80,000 of worthless paper.

Now desperate, the political boss once so powerful and arrogant that he could ruthlessly dun a young Martin Davey for campaign expenses in 1918 and try to bully him into supporting William McAdoo's nomination in 1924, slinked into Martin's Kent office, a beaten man. Using every weapon in his persuasive arsenal, Rockwell begged Martin to lend him $10,000 to stave off his creditors. Martin listened attentively and, given Rockwell's meanness toward the young congressman in 1918, enjoyed saying no. Campaign expenses from 1928 had left Martin's coffers pretty bare anyway, so there was no money for a Rockwell loan.

Ordinarily, that should have ended it, but Rockwell was not through. "You're my last hope," he bemoaned. "If you cannot let me have the money, I will have to commit suicide." Rockwell was pathetic, and Martin suspected that he was watching a performance worthy of the Shakespearian stage. However, overborne by Rockwell's pathos and suicide threat, Martin relented. He went to the City Bank, borrowed the $10,000 and gave it to Rockwell against the judge's worthless IOU. Martin learned later that Rockwell used none of the $10,000 to discharge his obligations and never did discover how the unrepentant prodigal spent the money.[10]

Legally, the Guardian Trust Company could not own stock in another bank and had to divest itself of the Kent City Bank stock that Rockwell used as collateral when he borrowed from the Cleveland institution. Eager to strike any deal they could, Guardian Trust directors agreed to sell Martin the $80,000 Kent bank stock for $50,000.[11] Knowing a bad deal when he saw one, Martin demurred. Even at a $30,000 "discount," $50,000 of bad paper was exactly that—$50,000 worth of bad paper. However, Martin was sharp. All the years of selling Davey Tree services across the United States as a young man had honed his business senses, so he saw how the Guardian Trust deal could be made good. For that to happen, he had to indemnify the stock of the Kent City Bank and, coincidentally, strip Rockwell of much of his fortune. Despite the two men's political reconciliation in 1928, doing the latter hardly broke Martin's heart.

In November 1930, Martin, Rockwell, and representatives from area banks doing business with the latter met in Martin's Main Street home. There, Martin agreed to pay $15,000 in interest charges that Rockwell had run up and in return accept the judge's unsecured note as payment. Martin's "charity" gave him the upper hand with Rockwell from that point on. The judge was given six months to clean up his self-generated financial mess. If he did not, the Kent City Bank would sell his stock in his own Rockwell Company, whose primary assets were vast real-estate holdings.

Rockwell fumed for the next six months but did nothing to extricate himself from his financial morass. Accustomed to giving orders, he was now reduced to taking them, which he refused to do. Consequently, as prescribed at the meeting in Martin's home, the City Bank bought Rockwell's real estate at the bargain price of $200,000 and sold it to the Davey Investment Company for $250,000. The $50,000 profit strengthened the local bank, allowed Martin to take the Guardian Trust Company's offer of $50,000 for Rockwell's now solid City Bank stock and added valuable real estate to the already impressive holdings of the Davey Investment Company.[12] It was heady stuff for a one-time poor boy from Kent. John Davey would be proud. Martin had more than heeded his father's constant advice, "Do it right or not at all." By the summer of 1931, a mere six months after all the wheeling and dealing began, he had not only done it right, he had done it all.

Martin may have maneuvered brilliantly through the shoals of the banking business in early 1931, but no one could be prescient enough to know what was yet to come, not only for financial institutions but for the nation's entire economy. When Herbert Hoover accepted his party's nomination in the summer of 1928, he proclaimed that never before had any people been "nearer to the final triumph over poverty." Eight months later, as he swore the presidential oath, nothing had changed. The "Great Engineer" was as buoyant and optimistic as anyone could be, and for good reason. The American economy of the 1920s, despite some ups and downs, was like a battleship plowing through heavy seas with everything following in its powerful wake.

If there ever was a collective American hubris, it was now. After the Great War, the United States was the world's leading nation in almost every measurable way. The once-mighty European powers, and many of the lesser ones too, owed the United States money, and as a result, New York—not London or Paris or Brussels—was the financial capital of the world. The New York Stock Exchange responded accordingly. It drew eager speculators from all strata of American life. The great brokerage houses were big players, and even mom-and-pop investors believed they were going to become rich overnight. Wild speculation and rampant margin buying drove the stock market higher and higher during the summer and early fall of 1929. On Wall Street, the bull was ascendant; nobody seemed to remember seeing a bear other than in a zoo.

Then it began. In October there were days when there was more selling than buying, and by late in the month stockholders spied their first bear, and it was no cuddly cub. It was *Ursus horribilis,* full grown and hungry. Selling accelerated, not enough to cause a panic but enough to prompt the grandees of Wall Street to assure Americans that, despite some setbacks here and there, all was well. From New York on October 22, Charles E. Mitchell, chairman of the National City Bank, the world's largest bank, added his assurances and said Americans should ignore the temporary market slump.[13]

Mitchell was more fool than prophet. For no particular reason, the very next day, Wednesday, October 23, investors dumped millions of stock shares on the New York Exchange. When accounts were tabulated that evening, the market had lost $4 billion in a single day.[14]

The selling frenzy continued on Thursday, October 24. Worried financiers called a hurried meeting at the House of Morgan to devise a plan to right the foundering ship. Although the House's founder, John Pierpont Morgan, lay moldering in his grave for the past sixteen years, it seemed altogether fitting to meet in his Temple of Mammon across the street from the New York Exchange. Almost single-handedly Morgan had bailed the country out of serious monetary trouble during Grover Cleveland's second term. Perhaps similar magic could be worked again through a House of Morgan consortium that would pool money and allow the financial titans to prop up the market through stock purchases that would reinstill investors' confidence.[15]

Unfortunately, it was too late for that. This was not 1895, and America's problems were beyond the curative powers of even the most powerful movers and shakers. If October 24, 1929, was "Black Thursday," October 29 had to be "Even Blacker Tuesday." Frightened investors dumped sixteen million shares of stock on a market already saturated with unwanted paper. By the end of the month, the market was down $16 billion, and continued panic selling over the next two weeks left stock values 40 percent lower than they had been when the madness began.[16]

No one should have been terribly surprised by what happened. All the signs were there; too much money reposed in the hands of too few—after all, how many Cadillacs and mink coats could America's millionaires buy in any given year? For months consumer goods were piling up in warehouses across the country. Also, although comparatively few Americans played the stock market, those who did were shooting craps and expected to roll nothing but winning sevens or elevens. It was all illusory, and when the party was over there stood F. Scott Fitzgerald's urbane Jay Gatsby finally unmasked as the vulgar James Gatz. Soon, millions of Americans were going to live in their personal versions of Fitzgerald's dismal valley of ashes, and Gatsby's posh Long Island lifestyle would no longer be part of even the wildest American dream.

Martin's primary asset, the Davey Tree Expert Company, lost money during the first few years of the Great Depression but by 1934 turned a modest profit of $3,700. There was no occasion to celebrate, but any profit was better than a loss. The company's relatively good fortune stemmed from its adaptability. If tree surgery was slow, then the company tried harder to win power line clearing bids and succeeded in doing so. What innovation did not do during the dark days of the early depression, inspired dedication on the part of Davey employees did do. When howling daytime winds kept crews from a massive spraying job on a four-hundred-acre dairy farm, the men started the work at 3:30 A.M., when the air was calm.[17] Determination was one way to weather the storm, figuratively and literally.

Martin knew that if America was going to see better days, there would have to be wholesale change in Washington, D.C. A continuation of the Hoover administration was a blueprint for disaster. The Republicans renominated Hoover, but what else could they do, repudiate him and admit they had erred in 1928? Since they were doomed anyway, why not let the captain of the sinking ship go down with it in 1932 and hope for better things in 1936?

By the summer of 1932, the Democrats were salivating over their prospects. If they could not win after the abysmal Republican record since 1929, they ought to disband the party. Hoover, widely excoriated for ignoring the plight of millions of beleaguered Americans, was already the pathetic butt of mean jokes, the cleverest of which jibed that if he were reelected, Mahatma Gandhi, known for wearing only a loincloth, would make the best-dressed list.[18] Already the opposition was taking the president lightly. Any Democrat lucky enough to get his party's nomination would essentially be running against a political corpse.

Talk about possible candidates abounded in Democratic circles during the early summer. Some liked Texas son John Nance Garner; others believed Al Smith deserved a second chance (Smith himself thought so), while still others slipped back to the Wilson administration to advance the case for Newton D. Baker, then secretary of war and now a successful businessman in Cleveland. But more and more, one heard the name of the two-time governor of New York who had worked wonders in Albany after being elected in 1928.

The possibility that Franklin D. Roosevelt might be president of the United States scared some people, including many of his own partisans. His record in New York was too liberal, and he was maverick enough to make some Democrats think he might be uncontrollable as president.

Martin was one of those less than sanguine about a Roosevelt candidacy. Early in the campaign season, he was a Newton Baker man but switched to Al Smith after Wilson's former secretary of war did little to promote his candidacy going into the convention in June. Martin was a delegate at Chicago and witnessed the rising Roosevelt tide and fourth-ballot nomination of the New Yorker, but even after the rest of the Ohio delegation jumped on the Roosevelt bandwagon, Martin stubbornly voted for Al Smith. The Kentite, who would years later bump heads with the president, believed that Roosevelt remembered his convention vote for Smith and always held it against him.[19]

The Democrats were absolutely right about 1932 being their year. Roosevelt won easily with nearly 23 million popular and 472 electoral votes to Hoover's fewer than 16 million and 59. Socialist Norman Thomas and Communist William Z. Foster scuffled over a remaining million protest votes. The incumbent never stood a chance. He looked tired and old on the hustings, and when he warned that a Roosevelt victory would allow "grass [to] grow in the streets of a hundred cities and a thousand towns; [and] weeds [to overtake] the fields of millions of farms," voters thought, hell, doesn't the president see that that's already happened?[20]

Despite America's obvious affection for Roosevelt, Martin remained skeptical. He later thought the new president was overly enamored of untested schemes and moved "too fast" in implementing them, never pausing to consider that the country might suffer as a result of his impetuous decisions.[21] Martin failed to concede that the 1930s were desperate times and demanded extreme measures. He also misunderstood the president's tactical philosophy—if something was not working, then try something else, and if that too failed, move on to the next plan.

An entirely truthful Martin would have had to admit that his view of Roosevelt was colored by the president's refusal to give him a cabinet post. Usually such aspirants, no matter how ambitious, are restrained enough to let others advance their cause. Not Martin. Despite the absence of any experience that would qualify him for the job, he asked the president-elect to appoint him secretary of agriculture, a position given instead to former Republican Henry Wallace of Iowa. Martin also had the temerity to ask Ohio Democrats at all levels to inundate the president with pro-Davey testimonials, which they did. Thousands of letters poured in to Roosevelt, but all to no avail.[22] Henry Wallace it was.

No president other than Abraham Lincoln assumed office with more immediate and grave problems facing him than did Franklin D. Roosevelt. Particularly troubling was the precarious state of most of America's banks. Americans refused to deposit their money in unsound banks, and the moment they sniffed one, they would rush off to withdraw their savings, no matter how meager. Bank runs depleted deposits, and depleted deposits prevented banks from lending money for houses, cars, and business ventures in general. Straitened banks and a bottomed-out stock market were devastating enough to bring the American economy virtually to a screeching halt by the time Roosevelt swore the oath of office on March 4, 1933.

Of all the crises he faced, Roosevelt felt that the banking problem was the most serious and had to be solved first. In the waning hours of Hoover's term, with banks in twenty-one states already closed and others teetering on the brink, the exiting president sought the cooperation of his successor.

On March 3, Roosevelt visited Hoover in the White House. The call was partly obligatory, a traditional courtesy extended from the old president to the new. However, once the social niceties were attended to, Hoover asked the president-elect to agree that the federal government would not close the banks and that the current crisis could be handled through a presidential proclamation tightening foreign exchange transactions and individual withdrawals. That, Hoover believed, should be as far as government ought to go in dealing with the crisis. Closing the banks, Hoover contended, would force the president to use emergency financial powers granted Woodrow Wilson in 1917 under the Trading with the Enemy Act, a measure generated by the exigencies of war. Hoover feared that Congress would repudiate such an action because the banking crisis, serious though it was, still was not war. The Republican wanted Roosevelt's concurrence before he moved ahead in dealing with the bank issue on his final day in office.[23]

Roosevelt was astute enough to recognize that Hoover was not interested in any suggestions that he might offer. What the president wanted was his successor's acquiescence. Roosevelt was too clever to shackle himself to any plan that bore the lame duck president's personal stamp. He wanted to be his own man, free to act as he saw fit. He justified his refusal to intervene on March 3 because on that day he was merely a "private citizen, wholly without authority, expressed or implied," and participating "in the daily relations between the Executive and Congress would have been, not only improper, but wholly useless."[24] What that really meant was that Hoover would be left dangling on his last day in office, and Roosevelt could then become the savior of the American banking system.

In the wee hours of March 4, as Hoover slept away his final night in the White House and Roosevelt slumbered through the last one before he moved in, the frantic governors of Illinois and New York closed their states' banks. State after state followed suit. When Franklin D. Roosevelt swore his presidential oath that afternoon, the nation had free-fallen into financial collapse.[25] No nineteenth-century panic or twentieth-century depression could match what had just happened in early 1933.

In his inaugural address, Roosevelt, sensing the country's mood, denounced the nation's bankers as "money changers [who] have fled from their high seats in the temple of our civilization."[26] The biblical reference was intentional; Roosevelt had declared holy war on the greedy bankers who had gotten America into this financial mess. The days of a money monopoly in the hands of America's shylocks were over. They had misused and abused the trust of the American people, and a messiah was now at hand to make things right.

A lesser man might have been daunted by the challenge. However, the new president never intended to go it alone. By 1932 he had already tapped into Columbia University's talent pool and brought Raymond Moley, Rexford Tugwell, and Adolph Berle on board as advisers. Along with a few others, the Columbia cadre came to be known as the "Brain Trust," and Roosevelt was content to let the geniuses loose not only to solve the banking crisis but to shape the New Deal itself. The Columbia professors, and Roosevelt too, were committed to something revolutionary for the United States—bringing the full weight of the federal government to bear on a nation in the throes of economic despair. Hoover, who had rejected his predecessor's laissez-faire philosophy, recognized how desperately the nation needed all the resources of the national government to right itself. To the mild surprise of his critics, he had supported the Reconstruction Finance Corporation, which pumped $1.5 billion of federal money into key industries such as banking and railroads. However, by the time the president turned to large-scale intervention in the private sector, the economy was too far gone. For many Americans, his shift to the left had come too late, and they told him so at the polls in 1932.

The new president had barely finished his "so help me God" in front of the Capitol when the Senate assembled, confirmed all of Roosevelt's cabinet appointments in a matter of minutes, and left the president, now fully armed, to deal with the banking emergency as he saw fit. Although the Senate's action was unprecedented, it was obvious that something had to be done and done quickly. This was not the time for tedious debate by the legislative branch; it was time to throw caution to the winds and let the newly anointed chief executive do whatever had to be done. In a Sunday cabinet meeting, Roosevelt, backed by his attorney general, Homer S. Cummings, decided to use the Trading with the Enemy Act to declare a national bank holiday from Monday, March 6 through Thursday, March 9. The president also ordered Congress to meet in an extraordinary session that same Thursday to consider a bill spelling out the specifics.[27]

Within hours of convening on March 9, Congress passed the Emergency Banking Act, authorizing the closing of weak banks and the reopening of strong ones. The strong banks were promised an ample money supply from the Federal Reserve and loans from Hoover's Reconstruction Finance Corporation to ensure their viability. Weaker banks were allowed to die, their licenses denied by federal inspectors. The Emergency Banking Act also took

America off the gold standard (done officially on April 19, 1933), thereby ending the massive drain of coins and bullion from the U.S. Treasury. The act was drawn up so quickly that only the Senate had copies. It quickly passed the bill. Members of the House followed, with a rolled-up newspaper standing in proxy for the actual measure. The Emergency Banking Act, despite its draconian tone, closed only 5 percent of the nation's supposedly safe banks, although many remained under federal supervision. However, more than two thousand weak ones closed permanently through the government's banking triage.[28]

On March 12, Roosevelt settled into a comfortable chair, a microphone on his desk, to deliver his initial fireside chat to millions of Americans listening to the man they hoped would save them all. In a calming but distinctly patrician voice, the thirty-second president of the United States told his eager listeners that the crisis was over and assured them that "it [was] safer to keep your money in a reopened bank than under the mattress." Such was the president's power in those early days that on his promise alone Americans' faith in the banking system was restored. Sound banks reopened their doors on March 13; confident depositors renewed their accounts, and at least one crisis was over.[29]

Ohio had shared in the nation's banking misery. Between 1926 and 1929, forty-five Ohio banks went under, a worrisome but not necessarily alarming occurrence. But the failures continued—twenty-five in 1930 and 125 in 1931. The next year was not so bad; only twenty-six banks shut their doors in 1932. However, all this was but a harbinger of worse to come. Ohio's banking bottom fell out in 1933.[30]

In a way Martin had seen it coming when he fretted over distressing American economic trends in the mid-1920s. But no man was seer enough to predict the totality of the bank failures and the disaster that followed. Had he known what was truly coming, he never would have become a director of the Kent City Bank in 1930. Despite Judge Rockwell's shaky loans, the local financial institution weathered the first three years of the Great Depression. On March 30, 1932, the small-town bank still had assets of nearly $1.5 million. But by 1933, bank runs elsewhere scared Kentites into withdrawing their savings. It started as a trickle, but soon became a torrent, and the Kent City Bank welcomed Roosevelt's mandated holiday in March. However, after the federal moratorium, the Kent City Bank was not allowed to reopen. Too many of its outside deposits were in larger banks in Akron and Cleveland that were also shut down, so the Kent City Bank had to close its doors.[31]

The nation's financial crisis hit the Davey Tree Expert Company, too. Business had declined so precipitously by 1931 that the firm could not repay its loans, primarily $98,000 to the First Central Trust Company of Akron and $103,000 to the Guardian Trust Company of Cleveland. Some money in the form of checks continued to flow into Davey Tree, but deposits were delayed until recipient banks made sure those checks cleared. In those trying times, such a policy was understandable, but the resultant cash trickle, combined with the company's declining revenues overall, hurt badly.

The company's problems had a bright side—one that lifted Martin even during this grim period. Its financial problems prevented Davey Tree from paying its employees, a message that Martin conveyed via a personal letter to each of them. Martin encouraged his workers to stand by the company until it regained its feet. It had always been good and would be good again, he promised. Hoping for the best, Martin was nonetheless stunned by the response. Every employee but one accepted Martin's word. Many said that they could survive for several weeks buying groceries and other necessities on credit, and the rest assured Martin that if he could send them "five or six dollars a week" they could "get along" and help the company ride out the storm. Martin was deeply moved that adversity, instead of destroying company morale, strengthened it.[32]

Martin scrambled to do whatever he could to save Davey Tree. He borrowed heavily against an $800,000 company insurance policy and later cashed in half of the policy's face value. That lowered the remaining premium and helped the company's cash flow a bit. Martin was also able to get a few banks to extend a line of credit, but all of these were stopgap measures. By early 1934, he had to borrow family funds just to keep the company afloat. Even Berenice had to empty out her personal savings account.

Martin had a certain flair about him, a quality that separated him from most men. He seemed to sense just when to do the unexpected. He had done the same when he was mayor of Kent and confiscated coal that was sitting in two idle Erie Railroad cars and then meted it out to shivering Kentites during the brutal winter of 1916–17. Although he had technically stolen the coal, he was a hero to his fellow townsmen and easily won another mayoral term the following November.

Similarly, in January 1934, Martin did something that demonstrated that he was indeed an unusual man, someone who knew just how to grace people with a kind touch when they needed it most and expected it least. He called what began as a typical meeting of all the Davey Tree Expert Company's eastern sales representatives. After a banquet on the second day of the conference, he rose to speak to his men, most of whom had not sold enough to equal their weekly draws and collectively owed the company more than $100,000, with very little hope of ever paying it back. Martin sensed the pervasive discouragement among his salesmen and knew that they were all good employees up against a formidable foe, the Great Depression. In a move that even he described as "bold," Martin told them their debt to the company was forgiven, they owed nothing. They could start fresh in 1934.

His audience sat there, stupefied, not moving, not clapping, not cheering. Martin was perplexed, thinking that somehow he had said or done the wrong thing. It was only afterward as the group adjourned to the hotel for an evening session that the men rushed up to Martin and gushed their thanks. They had not done so earlier because they had been shocked into silence by Martin's gesture. Now that his generosity had sunken in, they realized what had actually happened.

Once again, Martin had demonstrated his keen understanding of human nature. He could always size up people—from the time he was a small boy selling flowers and horseradish to his neighbors, he knew who would be a good customer and who would not. The same was true when as a teenager he sold his father's tree primer and later typewriters on the streets of Cleveland. Years later at the business conference, he could detect the despair among his employees. Certainly, generosity inspired him to waive their debts, but he also recognized that a troubled salesman was likely an ineffective salesman. He could have held the men to their obligations but did not. He preferred to let them start fresh and with enthusiasm.[33] All he and the company would have to do was wait out the bad times. Nineteen-thirty-four would be a better year—he was certain of that.

Chapter Eleven

Governor!

──────────── ⟨🐾⟩ ────────────

CONSTANTLY IN THE public eye, Martin by the 1930s began to loom larger than life to ordinary Ohioans. No matter how hectic a campaign might be, no matter how repetitious a memorized stump speech might be, no matter how tired he was, Martin tried to appear indefatigable, resilient, and enthusiastic. He bounded up to a podium, arms skyward in triumphant acknowledgement of the crowd, a smile always on his face. He was a celebrity and in public he was always on.

Martin had wearied of all this forced enthusiasm while campaigning against Myers Cooper in 1928. Running for governor was draining and, as he admitted, he had too many irons in the fire to concentrate on winning. He was bone tired afterward and glad that it was over. Certainly he preferred victory over defeat, but the gubernatorial race in 1928 in that respect was a pretty close call. For his psychological and physical health, it was probably better that he lost.

Martin's supporters, though, had no sense of how their man really felt. Less than a year after his loss to Cooper, speculation arose that he would run for the governorship in 1930. By September 1929, Cleveland Democratic leaders, always a potent force in Ohio politics, were bandying his name about, claiming that he was entitled to a second chance.[1]

Martin had thought about running in 1930, but merely contemplating a campaign two years after the first was enough to dissuade him. Just the thought of another gubernatorial race kept him awake nights. If even thinking about running was that troublesome, he knew enough to stand aside. After all, he was only forty-six and just entering the prime of his political life. Ohio's center stage could be temporarily surrendered to someone else, and if the political gods ordained it, there would still be opportunities for Martin L. Davey.[2]

There was no shortage of men who wanted the job anyway, one of them Marietta's George White. Born in Elmira, New York, in 1872, White and his family in 1873 moved to Titusville, Pennsylvania, where White's father worked as a watchmaker and jeweler. After graduation from high school, the younger White went to Princeton University, taking a class under Woodrow Wilson. In 1895, the new Princeton graduate shunned traditional Ivy League vocations in commerce and law and instead roughed it in a lumber camp and as an oilfield roustabout in Pennsylvania. He taught school briefly, but that was too mundane, and when gold was discovered in the Klondike, White joined thirty thousand other hearty souls in the rush north in 1898. Digging for riches in Canada and Alaska provided White with a wealth of stories afterward, but he found far more glitter than gold and lamented later that all he got for his trouble was enough money "to buy a silk hat and a suit of clothes to get married in."

He returned to Titusville, married Charlotte McKelvy in 1900 (she died in 1929), and by 1902 moved to Marietta, which he considered home for the rest of his life. White was an oilman in Ohio, West Virginia, and for a while in Oklahoma. He continued to dabble in oil throughout his life, but black gold was never his passion; politics was. In 1905, White won a seat in the Ohio House of Representatives as a Democratic "Dry," and by 1906 sought election to the U.S. House of Representatives from Ohio's Fifteenth Congressional District. He lost, as he did again in 1908, but won in 1910, 1912, and 1916 (after a defeat in 1914). A loss in the congressional race of 1918 prevented him from serving in Washington with first-term congressman Martin L. Davey. By 1920, he was a political "name," working for the presidential nomination of James M. Cox and ultimately becoming the Ohioan's campaign manager and then chairman of the Democratic National Committee. In 1921, after conducting Cox's losing bid for the presidency, White gave way under pressure to Cordell Hull and returned to his oil interests, although by now they were merely a diversion. Politics was in his blood, and by 1930 he wanted to be governor of Ohio.[3]

Concerned that his ambition might thwart Martin's and split the party, White requested a meeting with his potential rival. The two met in Judge Rockwell's home in Ravenna, just a few miles away from Martin's in Kent. Although White was literally and politically on Martin's turf, the Kentite could not have been more gracious as he stepped aside for his fellow Democrat. Essentially, what White sought was Martin's blessing, and he got it.

Martin, however, had private misgivings about White. He thought him dull and lifeless and found it disconcerting in the fall when a Democratic crowd in Zanesville cheered more loudly for Martin, the party's loser in 1928, than it did for White, the party's hopeful in 1930. On another occasion, again in Judge Rockwell's home, White dozed off—as his own campaign biography, *The Story of a Man,* was being read aloud to company. Rockwell and Martin glanced at each other and smiled, knowing that they and other Democrats had their work cut out for them in the fall.

If nothing else, Martin was a loyal partisan and worked assiduously for White's election. He gave White the extensive mailing lists he and his Kent campaign forces had so painstakingly amassed over the years. Nothing in Ohio could match them; they were like gold to anyone running for office. Two weeks before the November election, two hundred thousand "personal" letters from George White (actually written by Martin) went out to the party faithful. White paid the postage and related expenses, but Davey Tree Expert Company trucks hauled the letters from Kent to Marietta so they could bear the candidate's hometown postmark. Martin also used Davey Tree facilities to address three hundred thousand copies of *The Story of a Man* and trucked those to Marietta as well, all free of charge, and then donated $1,500 of his own money to White's campaign.[4]

By 1930, many Ohioans were beginning to feel the effects of the great crash of '29 and blamed the Republicans for it. Their disillusionment with the Republican Party peaked in 1932 and 1936, but only a fool failed to sense that 1930, too, would be a Democratic year. Myers Cooper, running for re-election, kept the race relatively close but did not have a chance against the rising Democratic tide. White polled more than a million votes, defeating Cooper by 109,000.[5]

Martin had, of course, been generous to the candidate with both time and money and understandably believed he was partly responsible for White's victory. Consequently, he had no compunctions about calling in his political markers. Three weeks after the election, Martin met with White and made several cabinet "recommendations," two of which the governor-elect accepted. The appointees were Martin's old friends and allies: Theodore Tangeman of Wapakoneta and John McSweeney of Canton. Tangeman became director of commerce and McSweeney, director of welfare. Years later, Martin believed that Tangeman had served well in his post, but the

Kentite was disappointed with McSweeney, thinking him prone to the contradictory shortcomings of timidity and stubbornness.

White agreed that both of Martin's choices were good men and was comfortable appointing them to his cabinet. Martin should have been satisfied with that. There was, however, something disconcerting to White in their postelection tête-à-tête. In addition to his cabinet suggestions, Martin told the governor-elect, "There are a number of my best personal friends who did great work for you in the campaign whom I would like to have you take care of."[6]

The remark, on its surface, was not a demand, and perhaps no one would have noticed if White winced at the mere prospect of providing state jobs for Martin's legion of friends. White recognized that he was now confronted with the good and evil dichotomy of patronage. The knights-errant of politics could "tsk, tsk" all they wanted, but most experienced pols recognized that patronage was the lifeblood of their profession. It represented organization, and organization won elections. What else was politics about? A man could not "serve the people" until he had gained office.

White understood all this, but Martin's bluntness troubled him. The Kentite, who prided himself on representing the old Garfield congressional district, should have been mindful of his illustrious predecessor's view of the evils of patronage. One morning the nineteenth-century congressman, and later president of the United States, was shocked to find seventy-five office seekers in his parlor before he had even come down for breakfast. Disgusted with their endless pleas for appointment, Garfield likened them to "vultures" eyeing a "wounded bison."[7]

Had Martin known Garfield's views, he still would not have been dissuaded. Whatever it was—his childhood of deprivation and scorn, his toil in taking the Davey Tree Expert Company from nothing to the top of the tree world, or the cold lessons of politics dating back to the treachery of his first mayoral opponent in 1913—Martin was by 1930 a hardened man. He had helped White and now had come to claim his fee.

Six weeks into White's term, Martin called on the new governor again and presented him with a list of three or four dozen Davey loyalists from 1928 who needed jobs. Martin recalled that White promised to "take care" of them as soon as he could. Taking White at his word, Martin wrote his friends that he had seen to matters with White, and they should hear from the governor about their new jobs.

Weeks passed and the hopefuls heard nothing from White. They began to hound Martin, who was beginning to feel embarrassed that he did not have as much pull with the governor as he had intimated to his friends.

Martin telephoned White and even saw him a number of times, but White always put him off with, "wait until the new legislature adjourns." However, that date passed without any action from the governor. In the interim, Martin's friends kept pestering him about White's promises. Finally, in July 1931, Martin wrote White and asked for jobs for only three people instead of the original forty or fifty and added that this last request was a "test" of his and White's "friendship." The governor never responded.[8]

Not surprisingly, the relationship between Martin and White deteriorated. Because he had been so helpful during White's campaign in 1930, Martin believed that the governor owed him more than he delivered. But by now, Martin, a seasoned politico, should have realized that the governor was undoubtedly bombarded with similar requests from every Democrat in Ohio who believed he had helped White win in 1930. However, Martin was easily offended and held grudges, but never could understand why his opponents sometimes did too. He knew how to make steadfast friends, but his temper frequently created steadfast enemies as well.

In 1932, with the Democrats surging everywhere, White did not need Martin's help or much of anyone else's to win a second term. By now Ohio and the nation were dotted with "Hoovervilles," cardboard and tin can shanty towns, where the destitute lived out their shattered lives. Countless others slept on park benches, protected against the cold only by newspaper coverlets quickly dubbed "Hoover blankets." And, as if he had to do anything more to prove his heartlessness, President Hoover ordered General Douglas MacArthur to march hundreds of bayonet-pointing troops into Anacostia Flats in Washington, D.C., to disperse harmless war veterans who had encamped there to pressure Congress into early payment of a bonus they had been promised. Given the Republican Party's track record, White's two-hundred-thousand majority over David Ingalls of Cleveland in 1932 was no more surprising than the sun's daily ascent in the East.

White spent his entire second term trying to cope with all the problems stemming from the Great Depression. There was never enough money for anything. One million Ohioans depended on the state for relief, but where were the monies to come from? The state could not expect to increase taxes on a populace already hard-pressed just to survive. Schools also suffered. To cut costs, the academic year was shortened to eight and even seven months. Teachers' salaries were reduced, sometimes by 40 percent, and frequently many teachers were not paid at all. To show that everyone was in the mess together, state and county officials took pay cuts. Farmers, too, were desperate after suffering 40 percent declines in their incomes in the early thirties.[9]

All these were Governor White's problems, not Martin's. He had enough of his own. By September 1933, with business in the doldrums at Davey Tree, Martin had to fire several excellent workers because the company was losing $3,000 every month. Compounding Martin's difficulties was the fact that Roosevelt's Public Works Administration, created by the National Industrial Recovery Act of 1933, was siphoning away many of what remained of his company's well-trained tree surgeons. Government pay was $1.20 per hour; the Davey Tree Expert Company's was seventy cents. The math was simple; the defections were no surprise.[10]

Alarmed, Martin telephoned F. A. Bartlett, head of the Davey Tree Expert Company's biggest rival, to see if he was suffering similarly. He was, so the two men decided to travel to Washington to explain their plight to the president himself. Although the visit was presumptuous, Martin believed that he could use his old Washington ties to gain an audience with Roosevelt.

He pulled what strings he could to see the president's secretary, Marvin McIntyre, who at first told Martin and Bartlett that meeting the president was impossible. Martin refused to take no for an answer and finally persuaded McIntyre to allow the two men one minute with his boss. McIntyre insisted, "one minute at one o'clock on Friday." It was only Monday, but so desperate were the two tree men, they waited the four days and arrived at the White House at 12:30 for their one o'clock appointment. For more than an hour they watched cabinet members and senators enter and exit the president's office. Martin and Bartlett fretted as their appointment time came and went. Certainly, they thought, the president would soon break for lunch and not see them at all. At 1:45 McIntyre finally ushered the two anxious men into Roosevelt's office, reminding them that they had only one minute.

Fortunately for the two, the president gave them more than a minute, but not much more. Martin and Bartlett explained that they would be forced to close their doors if the federal government continued to lure their skilled workmen by paying them nearly double what private tree companies could. Roosevelt listened sympathetically and told McIntyre, "Marvin . . . call Harry Hopkins, and arrange an appointment with him for these gentlemen and tell him to find a solution."[11] With that, Martin and Bartlett were ushered out of the great man's presence.

That same afternoon the two met Hopkins, Roosevelt's minister of relief. Martin recalled that Hopkins had a "wild look," especially in the eyes, and was "not unfriendly" but not exactly cordial, either. As a professional social worker, he seemed to Martin the businessman quite comfortable "spending the money that someone else has made." Despite Martin's misgivings, though, Hopkins listened attentively and agreed to lower the government's hourly rate for tree surgeons to eighty cents. At least now, private firms such as Martin's and Bartlett's could compete for skilled labor.[12]

Even though Martin benefited from the federal government's intervention in the wage matter, he disliked the New Deal's intrinsic socialism. He may have been a Jeffersonian Democrat politically, but as a businessman he spouted Republican laissez-faire rhetoric almost as easily as Coolidge or Hoover did. It would have been better, he thought, to funnel federal monies to individual businesses rather than to government agencies prone to a boondoggling that would never be tolerated in the private sector. Colored by his probusiness leaning (and later his anti-Roosevelt bias), he claimed that public money turned over but once while private sector money did so eight times.[13] He conveniently forgot that relief recipients bought milk, paid rent, got haircuts, and thereby turned over their "government" money time and time again.

Steering the Davey Tree Expert Company through the early depression was so trying that Martin's antipathy to Roosevelt's New Deal was understandable. Every day brought new challenges, and, resourceful though he was, Martin had to scramble constantly just to keep from closing Davey Tree for good. It was not until 1934 that some light appeared at the end of the long, dark tunnel, and that allowed Martin to start thinking about the Ohio governorship again.

It all began one day early in the fall of 1933 when a Cleveland lawyer, Francis W. Poulson, drove to Kent to see Martin. Poulson had been the losing Democratic candidate for attorney general of Ohio in 1928 and had impressed Martin during that campaign, but he and the Kentite had had no real contact with one another for five years. Naturally, Martin was curious about the Clevelander's request for a meeting. The two men settled into chairs at Martin's summer home in Twin Lakes, a few miles north of Kent, and Poulson began to talk. He wanted Martin to run for governor in 1934 and pledged his support. Although Poulson's suggestion had come from nowhere, Martin was taken by the Clevelander's enthusiasm and assurances of loyalty through thick and thin.[14]

Martin made no promises that day but took a genuine liking to Poulson, who, out of the blue, had driven forty miles from Cleveland to swear fealty to a man whose odds of winning, first his party's gubernatorial nomination and then the governorship itself, were remote at best. It had, after all, been five years since Martin had even run for political office, and that was a losing campaign. The relationship between the two men was curious. Martin was

wealthy, but had come up the hard way and, even though he spent money easily, did so wisely. Cautious and wary, Martin always seemed to have a backup
plan to avoid financial disaster. Poulson could not have been more different.
Martin in the 1940s recalled that Poulson claimed he had been worth, on
paper at least, a half-million dollars while living in Florida. After some bad
real-estate investments, he was down to his last $500. He and his wife debated
whether they should leave the Sunshine State with the $500 intact as seed
money for a new start in Cleveland or spend it on one final fling under tropi-
cal skies. They chose the latter and returned to Ohio dead broke.

Martin shook his head in disbelief over that story, but still found it hard
to dislike Poulson, who in many respects was like a fun-loving kid. He had a
beautiful voice and would spontaneously fire up crowds by leading them in
song. His zest for life was matched by a prodigious appetite. On the campaign
trail, he would invariably order a thick steak while Martin, worried about
stretching their meager funds, settled for a ham sandwich and cup of coffee.[15]

Poulson's support for the governorship, although welcome, was not necessary for Martin. The decision was his and his alone. In the late winter of 1933,
with word circulating that George White wanted a seat in the U.S. Senate, Martin announced that he would seek the Democratic nomination for governor.

The field was crowded. Dayton's William Pickrel, the party's candidate
for lieutenant governor in 1928, had resurrected his career and early on appeared to be the favorite. Charles Sawyer, a young, polished lawyer from
Cincinnati and currently lieutenant governor, had widespread support,
especially in populous Hamilton County. A third candidate, Clevelander
Charles Hubbell, was never a serious challenger and got most of his press by
promising to walk 113 miles from Marion to Cleveland but fell eleven miles
short and rode the rest of the way in a coal truck.[16]

Recognizing that Pickrel was at the onset his most formidable adversary,
Martin went after the Daytonian first. Hoping to sabotage the front-runner,
Martin, at every opportunity, proclaimed that Pickrel was "slipping." That
was untrue, but Martin knew that voters invariably shied away from potential losers, and if he could get people to think that Pickrel's candidacy was
doomed, it would turn out to be exactly that.[17] With one leading rival out
of the way (whether by fair means or foul) Martin could concentrate on the
suave, boyish-looking Sawyer.

At a rally in Akron on July 16, Martin denounced Sawyer as the lackey
of Cincinnati political boss Billy Leonard and the candidate of the unpopular White administration. Though neither charge was provable, Martin intended from the start to undermine his Cincinnati opponent. Although the

charges were unfair, anything in a campaign brawl was acceptable to Martin. But the Kentite did not stop there. While firing up the Akron crowd, he ripped Sawyer as a man without a platform and as a creature of wealth who could never identify with Ohio's ordinary folk. The latter remark referred to Sawyer's marriage into the millionaire Procter side of the Cincinnati-based Procter and Gamble soap company. Without thinking of the consequences, Martin had fired a mean shot at Sawyer and hit his rival's innocent family. Martin obviously did not think that he had violated any "Marquis of Queensberry" campaign rules. After all, he had suffered similarly when the *Akron Beacon Journal* flailed him for hiding behind Berenice's skirt to avoid the draft in 1918. Also, Martin, who never forgot any affront, remembered that Sawyer had dragged his feet before finally endorsing Martin's bid for a cabinet post under Roosevelt in 1932.[18]

Sawyer was too much a gentleman to respond in kind, but others, incensed by Martin's tactic, were not. Two days later, Democratic congressman Martin L. Sweeney of Cleveland lashed out at him for "a most unfair and unjustified personal attack" against Sawyer and openly supported the Cincinnatian over the Kentite for the nomination. Sweeney's allegiance to Sawyer threatened to undermine Davey support in populous Cuyahoga County, a problem that worsened when Newton D. Baker, chairman of the county's general committee, also came out for Sawyer.[19]

Sawyer now occupied the high moral ground. With Pickrel fading and Martin depicted as "Peck's Bad Boy," the Cincinnatian should have been able to surge ahead of his rivals. Unfortunately, though, the Princeton-educated Sawyer stumbled. When asked about his platform, he responded: "Platforms are a lot of nonsense [and are] always made up of a lot of generalities." Already excavating his own grave, he dug even more deeply: "I do not believe a candidate should go about the state announcing platforms and making a lot of personal pledges and commitments."[20]

Not since General Winfield Scott Hancock stunned his Democratic supporters and elated his Republican opponents by sloughing off the tariff as a "local issue" in the presidential campaign of 1880 had any candidate said anything more naive. Martin pounced on his adversary by citing his eighteen-point platform that covered everything from old-age pension reform to the elimination of waste and inefficiency in state government. The *Cleveland Plain Dealer,* which had endorsed Sawyer, rapped Davey's platform for its generality, but its editors had to feel embarrassed that the man they had recommended to voters lacked the common sense to elaborate a platform before trying to become governor. Sawyer attempted to minimize his blunder by saying that Ohio Democrats should concentrate on "picking a candidate who can win," but even the most simple-minded voters recognized that his response was lame.[21]

While Sawyer was busy shooting and reshooting himself in the foot, William Pickrel gained a second wind. At a rally in Cleveland, he denounced Sawyer as a candidate without a platform and Davey as a man with one "designed to cure everything from dandruff to fallen arches." He had also unsettled Martin by resurrecting rumors about the Kentite's purported Ku Klux Klan sympathies in the 1920s.[22]

Martin cried foul, but the malodor of his supposed Klan links lingered. Within days of Pickrel's accusation, reports of a photostated copy of an April 16, 1934, letter (on Davey Tree Expert Company stationery) from Martin to Ohio's grand dragon, James A. Colescott, requesting a meeting splashed across the front pages of Ohio newspapers. Martin denied any connection to Colescott, but voters needed more than the candidate's personal refutation of the charge.

Martin responded. He produced a receipt from New York City's Biltmore Hotel for April 16 and 17, 1934, showing that he had occupied room 1130 there on the date in question, April 16, and consequently could not have written to Colescott then. The letter was a damnable forgery, and he quickly blamed Pickrel, Sawyer, and even Governor White for it. One of their minions, he claimed, had stolen Davey Company stationery, typed the letter, and forged Martin's signature before photostating it for dissemination to the press. Colescott's only role in all this, Martin protested, was to extort money from him, which the Ohio grand dragon vehemently denied.[23]

Martin weathered this storm, although it drove him to distraction. He had never really cozied up to the Klan even during its Ohio heyday in the 1920s. At the same time, neither had he ever openly attacked the organization when he was running for Congress. However, that strategy was merely circumspect. Nearly a half million Ohioans belonged to the Klan and countless more sympathized with it in the twenties. Why alienate so many potential voters by attacking the hooded knights when one could simply ignore them? Astute politicians all along had done exactly that. Even the Republicans refused to adopt an anti-Klan plank in their national platform of 1924. Only hotheads like Con Mulcahy wanted to wage unremitting war against the Klan no matter the consequences. There may have been some minor Klan skeletons in Martin's closet, but they hardly proved that he was a sympathizer.[24] Most politicians in the 1920s likely had similar "mementos" that they hoped would never see the light of day.

All the Klan and other furor aside, the Democratic gubernatorial primary election would be decided by organization, and no one was better at that than Martin L. Davey. He still had the only "good and complete" mailing lists of Ohio Democrats, which Davey workers had kept current over the years. Every judge, election clerk, county, city, and state official, and Democratic precinct committeeman was on Martin's list. So, too, were "influential Democratic women" and any Democrat who had been active in campaigns even years ago. These people were bombarded with pro-Davey literature and urged to get out the vote.

But there was more to Martin's strategy than simply inspiring voters. He broke down the state into clusters of counties, singled out one county within each cluster and held meetings there for Democrats from the surrounding counties. He then repeated the process until he covered the state eight or ten times during the primary campaign. Before each meeting, Martin curried the favor of county leaders by treating them to an early dinner, invariably in a church where the food was good and cheap—and where Martin and his entourage could charm the women who prepared the meal. With his driver, Jimmy Gibson, Martin sped from one corner of Ohio to another in his sleek Cadillac, systematically reaching voters as few other Ohio gubernatorial candidates ever had before.[25]

On election day, August 14, a smiling Martin Davey, accompanied by an equally beaming Berenice and twenty-three-year-old Evangeline, posed for photographers after voting in Fred Haymaker's Ford dealership in Kent. Sixteen-year-old Martin Jr., too young to vote, remained at home. Amid heavy balloting, Martin garnered 215,000 votes, Sawyer 195,000, and Pickrel more than 180,000. Charles Hubbell, never a serious contender, lagged far behind with 17,500 and a pair of badly blistered feet as sole reward for all his trouble.[26]

Pleased and relieved, Martin hoped for party unity after the general election and promised that there would be no "reprisals" against any of his Democratic foes. A gracious William Pickrel telephoned his congratulations and promised to support Martin in the fall, but no similar message came from Sawyer. The disappointed runner-up waited a full day after the election before wiring the winner: "It looks like you win. Congratulations."[27] It was not gracious, but given Martin's personal attack on Sawyer and his family, it was understandable—and portentous.

Unlike the Democrats, who had nitpicked themselves to distraction, the Republicans easily chose their gubernatorial candidate for 1934, Clarence J. Brown, Ohio's secretary of state and a former lieutenant governor. Brown, a bear of a man at 240 pounds, was "old school," so formal that he wore a long-tailed coat while presiding over the Ohio Senate, the last lieutenant governor to do so.[28] From little Blanchester, near Cincinnati, Brown was in the publishing business and widely respected in Republican circles for nearly twenty years.

With an unpopular governor in Columbus, Brown had an easy time ignoring his Republican opponents in the primary campaign by emphasizing everything the Democrats had done wrong during the last four years. George White was a sitting duck for Brown. The Republican scored White's regime for failing to fund the state's schools, allowing lobbyists to dominate Ohio's public utilities and permitting the "Tammanyizing" of state government. He promised a return to "common sense, common decency, and common honesty" if elected, and his fellow Republicans loved what they heard. With over 340,000 votes in the primary election, he nearly doubled the total of his closest opponent, Daniel E. Morgan of Cleveland.[29]

On September 28, 1934, Brown opened the general election campaign in Columbus with a continuation of his "Tammanyization" theme, only this time the charge was directed against Martin Davey instead of George White. There was one other change—a clever substitution of words—no longer were the Democrats "Tammanyizing" Ohio, they were "Daveyizing" the state in anticipation of providing jobs for "a horde of political drones." Although the campaign heated up later, Brown's opening salvo was fairly tame and not enough to prompt Martin into a vicious counterattack. Much of the dirty work would be left to Republican surrogates anyway, and Brown never won Martin's undying enmity. In fact, the Kentite later called Brown "friendly" and not particularly formidable.[30]

Even though Martin liked his opponent, he did not take him lightly. He knew that candidates never erred by overestimating their opponents, but there were many who rued underestimating them. To ensure that he would not succumb to the latter, Martin mended as many Democratic fences as he could, particularly with George White, who had run a disappointing third in the 1934 U.S. senatorial primary. He also engineered the election of Francis Poulson as state committee chairman to ensure loyalty in that important post. After smoothing all the ruffled feathers Martin could, only Charles Sawyer continued to sulk.[31]

Once again, in the fall campaign, no one could out-organize Martin L. Davey. From mid-September to election eve, Martin's message was delivered statewide over the radio. And, as in past campaigns, Martin bombarded Ohio Democrats with "personal" letters. His campaign brochures, cards, and lapel buttons were given out by the millions. All told, his general election expenses were more than $250,000, with radio time accounting for about $50,000 or $60,000 of that.

He tolerated lazy and inefficient workers who promised to help him win but really wanted just to hang around a campaign or milk a job from their modest efforts. They could not be ignored, Martin concluded, because they still represented votes and for that reason alone had value. Others meant well but could never perform effectively even if their lives depended on it. Martin also deplored meetings, which he believed had to be held only because so many people thought a campaign could not be run without them. Martin preferred strategy sessions with a handful of confidants (particularly Poulson) in a car while racing from one campaign stop to the next.

Most of the actual work in winning an election, Martin believed, occurred in the precincts. A few votes either way in Ohio's nearly nine thousand precincts very often meant victory or defeat for a candidate. Consequently, he long thought that the most important workers in any election were dedicated precinct captains who could mobilize voters.[32]

As he had in the primary election, Martin blitzed the state with personal appearances. He wanted to cover each of Ohio's eighty-eight counties but could do so only through the most careful planning. Martin broke down Ohio into several regions and each week sped through the counties there. The pace was grueling, with nothing more than a brief ride between speaking engagements as respite. A typical schedule had him in Clermont County at noon; Brown County at two; Adams County at four; Scioto County at seven and Lawrence County at nine. He tried to keep Sunday as a day of rest, but this was usually the best time to hit Ohio's largest cities. Mondays were reserved for his radio broadcasts, which were delivered in the evening after hours of preparation during the day.[33]

Essentially, campaigning, except for an occasional free Sunday, was a seven-day-a-week job, and each of those days was sixteen hours long. When Martin was not speaking to a group, he was closeted with advisors, planning the next address or strategy. He frequently ate on the run; sandwiches and hot coffee in the car kept him going. This was his life, day after day and week after week from September until election day in November. The pace was exhausting, the physical and nervous strain obvious.[34]

No detail was insignificant. When a black man from Akron wrote offering to help solicit African American support in the November election, Martin, through Myrna Smith, responded quickly. The correspondent's bona fides were checked out, and when they cleared, the Akronite was instructed to contact Francis Poulson at Democratic state headquarters in Columbus. Martin recognized that, because of Franklin D. Roosevelt's broad appeal, blacks were beginning to abandon the party of their great patron, Abraham Lincoln, and vote Democratic for the first time in their lives. Hence, a promise of aid from an obscure black man in Akron was not to be ignored. Martin was anxious to get the support of "colored people" whenever and wherever he could.[35]

Martin's sensitivity to the black vote was undoubtedly linked to charges of Ku Klux Klan sympathy that dogged him even during the general election campaign. No matter how much he denied the accusation, somewhere, someone would resurrect the issue. One longtime Democrat, torn between party loyalty and her conscience, wrote Martin that she could not vote for a "Clansman" [sic] and wanted his pledge that he was not. Martin assured her that his so-called association with the Klan was a mendacious remnant of the mean-spirited primary campaign in which his opponents resorted to the vilest means to defeat him.[36]

The James Colescott letter, a hot issue earlier, continued to plague Martin. A Jewish Democrat in Cleveland had seen the photostated letter linking Martin to Ohio's grand dragon and wanted to know if the Kentite truly had such ties. Martin, anxious to dispel any association with the Klan, responded, "I never had any connection with it whatsoever." Again, he blamed the scurrilous charge on primary election opponents bent on destroying his candidacy.[37]

Any link between Martin and the Ku Klux Klan would, of course, drive Catholics by the thousands into the Republican embrace. That would be welcome enough for Republicans, but they had a double-edged religious strategy in mind. On October 15, with the election only three weeks off, Clarence Brown issued a press release that immediately colored the rest of the campaign: "I am unalterably opposed to the spending of public money or the extending of financial aid from public funds for the support of private or parochial schools," he declared.[38] If Martin opposed Brown and supported the public funding of parochial schools, Protestants would be up in arms and vote overwhelmingly Republican. Bereft of Catholic and Jewish support because of the Klan accusations and deprived of Protestant backing if he took the "wrong" side on the school issue, Martin would have to rely on the atheist-agnostic bloc for any votes in November. Brown's strategy was bold but was borne out of desperation. Franklin D. Roosevelt's popularity was such that 1934, like 1932, was destined to be a Democratic year. If Ohio Republicans expected to get their man into the governor's mansion with anything other than a visitor's pass, they had to try anything. The school issue, reeking of anti-Catholicism, might resurrect the Protestant prejudices that had destroyed Al Smith in 1928.

The topic dominated the front and inside pages of the press for days, with the notoriously anti-Davey *Akron Beacon Journal* goading Martin through headings such as "Davey School Aid Reply Demanded" and "Church Storm Hits Davey; Accused of Double Cross." The attacks bore the unmistakable stamp of a *Beacon Journal* Knight, but not Martin's old enemy, Charles Landon Knight. This time it was his editor son, John Knight, who carried on his father's feud.[39]

Martin was too smart to take the bait. He had already lined up Catholic support in the Cincinnati and Cleveland dioceses and was in the process of doing the same in Columbus. There was nothing to be gained by opposing Brown on the parochial school issue. Martin likely had a good portion of the Catholic vote already, and by remaining silent he minimized the risk of alienating Protestants. His strategy was far wiser than Brown's. In fact, Brown's was a gamble, and a bad one at that. One Democratic precinct leader, after querying several of her coworkers, summarized it best—most people did not care about Martin's religious views.[40]

Martin was happy to let Brown thrash about on the parochial school issue. The Republican was desperately trying to keep his head above water in an election that seemed to be going Martin's way. For the Kentite, silence was the best response while waiting for Brown to go down for the third time. Martin's assessment of his Republican foe was correct; he was not really a formidable adversary.

That did not mean Martin had an easy campaign. If Brown was not a potent enemy, there were other Republicans who were, particularly Paul Herbert, the party's candidate for lieutenant governor. Speaking to a crowd on October 11, Herbert accused Martin of manipulating a series of loans through the Kent City Bank and banks in Cleveland and Akron. A loan of more than $89,000 from Martin's hometown bank, according to Herbert, violated an Ohio law forbidding the lending of more than "twenty percent of [a bank's] capital and surplus to any one individual or company." Martin, Herbert charged, had circumvented the law by dividing the loan three ways— $36,000 to himself, $36,000 to the Davey Investment Company, and almost $17,000 to the Davey Compressor Company. He had also "stiffed" the now closed First Central Trust Company of Akron for $126,000 and Cleveland's Guardian Trust Company for nearly $169,000. Especially galling, Herbert proclaimed to his Akron audience, was the fact that while Martin had skated off with all this "free money" from these closed banks, thousands of their faithful depositors had no hope of ever recovering theirs. Herbert closed his attack by asking, should a man who had walked away from his obligations to

three banks be elected to an office that allowed him to appoint a state superintendent of banks who would supervise the collection of debts?[41] Herbert's
message was clear: Putting Martin Davey in the governor's mansion was tantamount to letting the fox guard the henhouse.

Martin, who had let the inept Brown jab away harmlessly at him during the campaign, now sprang to action. Herbert had attacked his personal
integrity, and he would not allow that. Con Mulcahy had raised questions
about Martin's bank dealings during the primary campaign when Mulcahy
supported William Pickrel over Davey, but Herbert had elevated the issue
to a whole new level. The day after the Republican's Akron speech, Martin
threatened to sue him for libel.[42]

Herbert's accusations, Martin retorted, were a pack of lies. His Kent City
Bank loans were perfectly legitimate; Martin had not used his position as
director to manipulate anything in his favor. He and his companies were
still solvent, and he intended to repay all of his obligations once the depression eased. "I never, in my life, defaulted [on] a note," he shot back. Herbert
was nothing more than a "petty politician" and a "character assassin."[43]

Herbert was unruffled by Martin's threat of a lawsuit. "I am perfectly
willing to defend any libel charges he may bring," he defiantly told an audience in Payne, Ohio, and a week later intensified his attack by claiming that
Martin and his family had borrowed more from the Kent City Bank than
he first claimed. The Daveys had looted the bank for $159,000 at a time
when the bank had only $125,000 in capital. Martin's brother Paul had bor-
rowed $13,000 and another brother, Jim, now living in Connecticut, had
come all the way to Kent to borrow $25,000 from the local bank, which,
Herbert charged, was under Martin's "control." The Republican welcomed
the chance to air Martin's banking affairs in court.[44]

Martin's promised lawsuit was a knee-jerk reaction to charges that wounded him deeply. It was one thing to assail him politically, but it was something
else to attack his integrity. However, he was a realist. It was impossible, during the heat of a campaign, to wage war on two fronts—on the hustings and
in court. Suing Herbert was impractical. There had to be a better way of
dealing with this ruthless foe.

By now few men were better at politicking than Martin L. Davey, and no
one could more cleverly turn a liability into an asset. Herbert had accused
him of several banking improprieties, all of which centered around Martin's
huge debts. Rather than ignore Herbert's accusations, he brought them up
to his audiences, always in the context of his personal indebtedness. At every
meeting he asked, "How many of you folks are in debt? Please raise your

hands." Typically, hands shot up all over the room. "Well, I guess we are all in the same boat. If it is a crime to be in debt after this Hoover depression, you folks are just as guilty as I am." Martin had adroitly sidestepped Herbert's charges. His clever glissade negated the Republican's attack and allowed countless debt-ridden Ohioans to identify with a millionaire who, temporarily at least, shared their plight. Martin could sense that his listeners sympathized with him. His confession that he was deeply in debt gave his speeches a "human touch" and "drew [him] closer to every audience." He was "glad that the opposition had given [him] so good a weapon."[45]

The Republicans could be expected to harass Martin at every possible turn, but one of his most pressing problems during the campaign of 1934 was generated by members of his own party in Mahoning County. By the early fall, quarrels between rival Democratic factions in Youngstown threatened to split the party and allow Brown to take the county. The concern was real; even when most of Ohio voted for Roosevelt in 1932, Mahoning County went to Hoover by six thousand votes. Martin could not allow that to happen to him in 1934.

Martin was understandably worried about the division among Democrats in one of Ohio's most populous counties. The dispute began with bitter infighting between Mahoning County Democratic Central and Executive Committee Chairman Alvin W. Craver and rival Democrats who viewed Craver as an iron-fisted master of patronage. Many Youngstown Democrats complained that he had been forced down their throats by Mahoning County party boss John J. Farrell and refused to cooperate with him.[46]

Concerned that the turmoil in Mahoning County boded ill for his election, Martin asked a longtime Youngstown friend, B. Frank Thomas, to meet him at Cleveland's Statler Hotel on Friday, September 21. After discussing the bickering, Martin handed Thomas a letter designating him as Mahoning County's authorized campaign manager and official Davey spokesman.[47] Thomas returned to Youngstown and disseminated the letter among Democrats to explain why he had taken over Martin's campaign in Mahoning County.

Craver, a three-time mayor of Youngstown, knew something was in the offing even before Martin summoned Thomas to the Statler Hotel. Two days earlier he had written Francis Poulson at Democratic headquarters in Columbus asking if the rumors about a Mahoning County shakeup were true. He sent a copy of the letter to Martin as well. Martin confirmed the changes in a phone call to Craver three days later. Angry that he had been bypassed and, in his eyes, "discredited," Craver demanded a copy of the Davey letter naming Thomas as official campaign manager in Mahoning County. Martin did not respond directly to Craver, but in the interests of conciliating Craver's supporters said that his decision should not reflect poorly on their man. He had acted only because there was "so much turmoil in [Mahoning] County that there appeared to be no other alternative."[48]

The Mahoning County storm ultimately blew over, and Martin carried it on election day by eight thousand votes. Craver, too embarrassed and angry to advance his cause, used his wife to claim he was responsible for Martin's victory. Oozing sweetness in a letter to Martin's assistant, Myrna Smith, Mrs. Craver congratulated Martin for his victory and reminded Smith that had Mr. Craver kept control of Mahoning County affairs, the margin would have been even greater. In her last paragraph, Mrs. Craver complained that her poor husband was now "worn to pieces" by Democrats seeking jobs and asked Smith to send him a list of patronage openings. Martin would be assured of a strong machine in Mahoning County, Mrs. Craver informed Smith, if all patronage went through the "proper channel," meaning Mr. Craver.[49] Despite his embarrassing demotion, Craver still thought he should control Mahoning County patronage.

Everything looked favorable for Martin as the campaign ground to its final days. Even then he took nothing for granted and devised one last stratagem to ensure victory. He would link himself as much as he could to the popular Roosevelt administration, which he had often privately criticized. His opponent provided him with the opportunity to do exactly that. The blundering Brown late in the campaign argued that if elected, he could coax more money out of Washington, D.C., than a Democratic governor could. On its face alone, it was a fatuous remark. Martin ridiculed Brown's contention and offered that a Democratic administration would clearly get more out of Washington than a Republican one ever could.[50]

Astute Republicans knew that Roosevelt's New Deal had resonated with the vast majority of Americans, and the president's popularity certainly trickled down to Democratic politicians everywhere. Even so resolute a conservative as Robert A. Taft, practicing law at the time in Cincinnati, tried to get Republican senatorial candidate Simeon D. Fess to curtail his attacks on Roosevelt's New Deal relief program because doing so was bad politics. Fess rejected his fellow partisan's advice and lost his U.S. Senate seat to former governor Vic Donahey by more than 437,000 votes in 1934.[51]

Martin knew a good thing when he saw it, and for Democratic politicians everywhere there was nothing better than a New Deal association during the heady early thirties. With only two days left before the election, Martin stood on the same Cleveland stage with U.S. senator James F. Byrnes and smiled when the South Carolinian told the audience, "You will render a service to President Roosevelt by electing Davey your governor." Things looked good so far; Martin actually boasted that he would win by 250,000 votes, but that was pure bluster.[52] Election day would tell for sure.

Showers swept across much of Ohio on Tuesday, November 6, but they failed to dampen the enthusiasm of the state's voters as they turned out in record numbers. Nearly three million of them cast ballots throughout the day. Martin voted early, again at Fred Haymaker's auto dealership, returned home for a while, and then spent the evening at his brother Paul's. He passed the time with friends, playing bridge, but his mind was elsewhere. Every time the phone rang through the late night and early morning hours, he leaped out of his chair, knowing that at the other end someone would be reporting voting tabulations from some crucial precinct.[53] For the most part, what he heard was good, allowing him at last to return home and fall wearily into bed.

The final count gave him a sixty-five-thousand-vote edge over Clarence Brown, not overwhelming but solid enough. Ohioans had also elected a Democratic state senate and had reduced the Republican majority in the house to one. Ohio's results were mirrored nationwide—the Democrats won a two-thirds majority in the U.S. Senate (no party had ever done that) and added to their majority in the House of Representatives. It was a Democratic year; the Republicans were reeling and had to reassess their basic philosophy of government. The *Canton Repository*'s headline two days after the election summarized it well: "LIBERALIZED G.O.P. LIKELY AFTER STAGGERING DEFEAT."[54] Led by a polio-stricken president, America was moving to the left and leaving the Republicans farther and farther behind.

Martin was too tired to exult. Counting the primary, he had either been preparing or running for election for eight or nine months. He, of course, was happy with the result but knew difficulties lay ahead. He claimed that he was more pleased by the hard work and organizing efforts that got him the win than he was by the victory itself, but that was a remark for posterity's sake, the kind of postelection prattle that voters expected to hear. Victory was sweet because no one more so than Martin loved (figuratively) to hold his opponent's head in his hands. Certainly the Kent Democrat smiled from ear to ear at the news that his nemesis, Paul Herbert, lost the lieutenant governorship to Democrat Harold G. Mosier by sixty-five thousand votes.[55]

Shortly after the election, Martin interviewed prospective appointees for key posts in the new administration, and in early December left for a much-needed vacation in Florida. Poulson and his wife joined Martin, Berenice and

Evangeline for a leisurely drive to Miami. On the way, the two men visited party leaders in Washington and then spent time in Colonial Williamsburg, then undergoing massive renovation through the generosity of John D. Rockefeller Jr. From there it was on to the Miami Biltmore in Coral Gables, where Martin Jr. joined the rest of the family after school let out for Christmas.[56]

Florida was only a temporary haven for Martin. When he departed Ohio, he left Myrna Smith, his personal secretary, and Daniel W. Duffy, his executive secretary, to deal with affairs until he returned in early January. They were competent and trustworthy, and no one better than Smith knew Martin's mind, but there were already rumblings back home about the changes the new administration would bring. The *Ravenna Evening Record* in Martin's Portage County and the *Canton Repository* in neighboring Stark County predicted that he would "clean house" in Columbus. Most ominous, though, was a bitter postelection shot from the *Akron Beacon Journal* that denounced Martin as everything from a college dropout (thereby undeserving of the governorship) to a "Master of Propaganda."[57]

By January 1935, Martin L. Davey, now fifty, his once dark hair rapidly graying, had left a slew of foes in his political wake and had not dealt gently with any of them. In campaign after campaign he had given no quarter and could expect none, even now as he headed to Columbus to become governor of Ohio.

Chapter Twelve

Battling the Roosevelt Bureaucracy

———————— ☙ ————————

MARTIN RETURNED to Ohio from Florida in early January. Seemingly endless discussions about appointments in the new administration and the constant presence of reporters, including two who had followed him south, left him as weary as he had been after the November election. The Florida sun provided a welcome respite from northern snow and ice, but it allowed no escape from the problems Martin knew he would face when he returned to Ohio.

His inauguration was scheduled for Tuesday, January 15 at the Capitol Building in Columbus. George White had already vacated the governor's mansion the Friday before, so Martin and Berenice drove to Columbus early to reconnoiter their new home. The city itself was already quite familiar to Martin. He had become well acquainted with it while a congressman and during his gubernatorial campaigns in 1928 and 1934.

Inauguration day was frigid; a glass enclosure partially protected Martin from the chill as he placed his left hand on an old family Bible and raised his right to swear the oath of office administered by Ohio chief justice Carl V. Weygandt. In front of his proud family and before thousands of onlookers outside in the January cold, Martin L. Davey became the fifty-third governor of Ohio.[1]

In deference to the shivering crowd, he delivered his inaugural address as quickly as possible and then both smiled and suffered through the obligatory hour-long parade. His back ached and his feet hurt by the time it was over, but his "punishment" was incomplete. Martin then had to greet hundreds of well-wishers in the Capitol Rotunda. By the time he finished shaking hands, both right and left were a mass of blisters. Martin had to wear gloves at the inaugural ball that evening just to protect himself against a new wave of "friends" who simply had to shake the governor's hand.[2]

The inauguration with its attendant gaiety should have been one of the happier times in Martin's life, but even as he, Berenice, and the children descended on Columbus, they detected an air of hostility. Columbus newspapers were already complaining about the $8,000 in public money appropriated for inauguration costs.[3] At a time when so many Ohioans were without jobs and the bare necessities of life, it seemed decadent to hold a "coronation" when a simple swearing-in ceremony would have sent the message that everybody, including the new governor, shared in the state's belt-tightening.

The icy reception from the press was the wrong way to get started, Martin knew, but the inauguration appropriation was not his doing—the state legislature had set aside that money while he was in Florida. Already he believed he was being judged unfairly. By the time his term was over, more than just the Columbus papers would be criticizing his every move; nearly every newspaper in the state would, and most of them became increasingly hostile as Martin brought a new and flamboyant style to the governorship.

He did not move into the governor's office; he swept into it. Within ten days of taking over, he fired the longtime warden of the Ohio penitentiary, Preston E. Thomas, after an investigation revealed that he allowed outside mobsters easy access to their incarcerated brethren and violated numerous other prison rules as well. Thomas's firing was justified, but Martin was not satisfied with a simple discharge. He also fired the warden's wife and daughter, both of whom worked at the penitentiary, and had the National Guard evict all of them from their state-owned home and pile their furnishings on the street.[4] Martin's critics were not surprised when an old friend from Kent, James C. Woodward, replaced Thomas.

There were other firings in the state bureaucracy as well, all of them causing alarm in at least some circles, but the furor might have abated had Martin otherwise restrained himself. However, he generated more trouble by spending $1,000 to replace worn carpeting in his office. When the state legislature refused to vote funds for it, Martin solicited private contributions to pay the bill and joked about it. In early February, after the legislature denied an appropriation for a new limousine for the governor, Martin bought a $4,900 Lincoln with National Guard monies, sweeping aside criticism by declaring he was entitled to do so because he was the state's commander in chief.[5]

Reviewing the Inauguration Day parade, January 15, 1935, are (left to right): Mrs. Frank Poulson, Evangeline Davey, Frank Poulson, Martin Davey, and National Guard Adjutant General Emil Marx. Evangeline Davey Smith Collection, Martin L. Davey Papers, Kent State University Libraries, Special Collections and Archives.

Martin's dramatic flair may have captivated many Ohioans, but it failed to impress hardened politicos in Washington who were more interested in making the New Deal work than they were in the theatrics of a flashy new governor. Consequently, only a few weeks after his inauguration, a confident and pugnacious Martin L. Davey became embroiled in a bitter patronage dispute with the New Deal's equally combative chief relief administrator, Harry Hopkins. By 1935, despite encouraging signs that the worst of the depression had passed, 1.2 million of Ohio's 6.6 million citizens remained on relief rolls.[6] With so many dependent on funds from the Federal Emergency Relief Administration (FERA), the threat of losing federal subsidies because of the Columbus-Washington feud stirred the public and New Dealers alike.

FERA director Hopkins, appointed by Roosevelt in 1933, determined the disbursement of national relief monies, and Ohio depended heavily on its $8 million monthly allotment. In return for FERA assistance, Ohio had to accept federal supervision, although in the spirit of cooperation Hopkins worked through an Ohio State Relief Commission.[7] In addition, the FERA director had the final say in key personnel assignments throughout the relief system. Armed with these extensive powers, Hopkins fought to keep politics out of relief by maintaining a nonpartisan organization.

The front-page headlines of the March 17, 1935, *Cleveland Plain Dealer,* "Roosevelt Hits Davey With U.S. Probe," signaled the onset of still another Hopkins struggle with Democratic politicians who saw political patronage as a welcome adjunct to New Deal reform. Ohio had already been under federal scrutiny after Cuyahoga County Relief Administration chairman Marc Grossman, Cleveland businessman Dudley Blossom, and FERA Midwest liaison Charles C. Stillman reported to Hopkins that Martin intended to turn Ohio's relief administration into a political machine. A series of gubernatorial removals and appointments, although not unusual during a change of administrations, heightened tensions on both sides.

Shortly after his inauguration, Martin fired acting state relief director Frank Henderson and replaced him with William A. Walls, former school superintendent in Kent, Martin's hometown. Hopkins disapproved but accepted the decision to placate the new Ohio administration.[8] Relations between state and federal relief bureaucracies began to strain, however, when Ohio Republican legislators generated a civil service dispute with the governor by refusing to support a renewal of the State Relief Commission. Martin, contending that the Republicans' desire for civil service classification of relief workers would create a permanent bureaucracy, allowed the state organization to expire. When the State Relief Commission disbanded on March 1, Hopkins ordered Martin to administer relief in Ohio as the agent of the federal government, retaining, however, his position as general overseer. Even before assuming his new responsibilities, the governor had begun to replace some county relief heads with his own appointees.[9]

One of Martin's administrative changes in Cuyahoga County's relief organization generated an uproar. When the governor fired Mary Irene Atkinson, who had authorized all Cuyahoga County Relief Administration (CCRA) personnel assignments before final approval by the now defunct State Relief Commission, angry critics charged that he intended to dispense Cuyahoga County relief jobs to his loyal supporters. Atkinson's firing only started Martin's attacks on the CCRA. Apparently convinced by what he had seen of Cleveland relief during his 1934 campaign, the governor assailed the "inefficiency" and "waste" of the Cuyahoga County bureaucracy and threatened to cut its staff by a third.[10]

Martin's criticism of the CCRA and his general disillusionment with the FERA in Ohio provoked an angry response from CCRA chairman Marc Grossman. Defending his organization, Grossman countercharged that the

CCRA was understaffed, underpaid, and overworked. To prove his point, Grossman cited figures from the latest FERA monthly report, which showed that Cleveland (the heart of Cuyahoga County) ranked third out of the nine largest cities in the country in per-family relief costs. Operating expenses for Cleveland relief consumed only 7 percent of the budget, far better than the national average of 10 percent. Hopkins concurred, describing Cleveland relief administration as "one of the best in the country." Davey, he said, "didn't know what he's talking about."[11]

Martin's foes were not as worried about his charges of malfeasance as much as they feared his intention of turning Ohio's relief organization into a political machine. That apprehension and the bombast it engendered temporarily blunted the governor's attack. Martin recanted his proposed CCRA staff reductions and complained that his statements had been distorted by an unfriendly press. He now maintained that he merely wanted to cut the administrative costs of relief to make the program as efficient and humane as possible. By March 5, however, many began to wonder what the governor actually did have in mind. In a letter to Hopkins, Martin again denounced Ohio's relief setup and demanded that the federal government assume all responsibilities for relief in the state. The CCRA typified the kind of responsibilities he no longer wanted.[12]

Within minutes of receiving the letter, Hopkins called a press conference. Waving Martin's letter wildly in the air, a fuming Hopkins flayed the Ohio governor for demanding a federal takeover of Ohio relief only after finding that tending to the poor offered no political reward. According to Hopkins, Martin cared nothing about Ohio's needy once he had their votes. Ohio, the FERA director insisted, remained responsible for its $2 million share of the monthly relief bill no matter what the governor wanted.[13]

Martin again wavered. He said he was not opposed to the "fine, responsible people administering relief" but to the "theorists" in Washington who now found government sanction for their experiments with human misery. This accounted, Martin argued, for the endless reports and red tape that prevented relief workers from actually handling cases. The governor steadfastly maintained he had no desire to create a political machine through patronage and his only prerequisites for appointments would be "character and ability."[14]

Angered by Hopkins's assault, Martin defended his position in a statewide radio broadcast on March 9.[15] Comfortable behind the microphone, the governor explained that under the existing federal-state arrangement he was powerless to act in any relief matters and that FERA head Harry Hopkins should therefore accept all responsibility for Ohio's relief problems. In his message, Martin accused county relief heads of using their authority to arrange dates with female employees, and added that "chiseling," his pet term, was endemic under the existing relief setup. Denying that he wanted to create a Davey organization through political patronage, the governor cited sample statistics from Logan and Miami counties showing that Republican relief workers there far outnumbered Democrats. To fortify his charges of inefficiency in Ohio relief, Martin read a telegram from the president of the Ohio Townships Trustees and Clerks, an organization of five thousand elected local officials, which said that Ohio's relief administration indeed was ineffective and wasteful.[16]

Martin's battle against relief corruption began to assume the moral fervor of a crusade. In another angry letter to Hopkins, he said he had no intention of asking the state legislature for the funds to provide Ohio's share of relief costs for the rest of 1935. To do so, he felt, would force Ohio taxpayers to aid and perpetuate fraud in the state. In Washington, Hopkins acknowledged that he had received about fifty telegrams defending Martin but announced that, aside from discontinuing federal financial assistance, he was taking no action in Ohio. The FERA director had a month earlier sought a precedent for withholding federal monies from a state and apparently found it in a government memorandum titled, "Analysis of Types of Federal-State Relationships in Relation to a Program of Economic Security."[17] He knew he was on sound legal footing when he took on the feisty Ohio governor.

State Auditor Joseph Tracy helped avert an immediate crisis by diverting $1 million of state sales tax proceeds to state relief. Hopkins then approved a $4 million grant for Ohio's relief recipients. However, the near crisis had prompted several Ohio legislators, including some Democrats, to consider going over the governor's head with a direct appeal to Hopkins.[18] The transfer of funds, a temporary measure at best, and hints of a compromise between the governor and the FERA administrator dissuaded them.

Martin's interest in reform, although expedient, seemed genuine. He prepared a message to the state legislature proposing a relief investigation into ten or twelve representative counties, including Cuyahoga, and carried his appeal to the state in a second radio broadcast on March 12. Again, the governor cited examples of dishonesty on the part of relief employees and emphasized that $5 million could be saved for the rest of 1935 if relief administration were carried out in businesslike fashion.[19]

The governor's stubborn stand against an equally unyielding Hopkins demonstrated the futility of compromise. While two hundred representatives of Cleveland civic, labor, religious, and welfare organizations bom-

barded Martin with telegrams protesting his stance on relief, Marc Grossman went to Washington, at Hopkins' invitation, to confer with the FERA
director and the president himself.[20]

Hopkins had earlier informed Roosevelt of the trouble brewing in Ohio
and eagerly awaited a confrontation with Martin. During a rare pause from
his whirlwind schedule, Hopkins noted in his diary, "the evidence is complete in Ohio—the political boys went too far this trip and I shall take great
delight in giving them the works." Roosevelt shared Hopkins's enthusiasm
for the Ohio struggle, which prompted Hopkins to remark, "the president
doesn't take a week to decide things like this. . . . His action will throw into
the ash can a Democratic governor and his political machine. In fact I think
the boss liked the idea of their being Democratic."[21]

The president had asked Hopkins on March 16 to draft a letter instruct-
ing the FERA director to take over relief in Ohio. That same day Hopkins
received his own letter bearing a presidential signature: "I have examined
the evidence concerning corrupt political interference with relief in the state
of Ohio. Such interference cannot be tolerated for a moment. I wish you to
pursue these investigations diligently and let the chips fall where they may.
This administration will not permit the relief population of Ohio to become
innocent victims of either corruption or political chicanery. You are authorized and directed forthwith to assume entire control of the administration
of Federal relief in the state of Ohio."[22]

That the dispute had escalated by mid-March was obvious when Hopkins,
with Grossman at his side, declared to the press he had "incontrovertible"
evidence proving that the Davey organization had virtually extorted funds to
defray the governor's campaign and inauguration expenses. Hopkins further
claimed that he had the signed confessions of the men who had solicited the
contributions and the names of those who paid. The "shakedown," according
to Hopkins, had pumped $8,000 into Davey coffers. Hopkins quickly linked
his latest revelation to Martin's earlier problems with relief when he added,
"the people of Ohio want to take care of the unemployed, only the governor
doesn't want to." Although the federal government had previously intervened
in relief matters in other states, Hopkins said that only Ohio had provoked
a special presidential order (Hopkins's own letter, of course) to that effect.
Hopkins told Martin that he was forwarding the evidence to Ohio attorney
general John W. Bricker and placed Charles C. Stillman, the FERA Midwest
liaison, in complete charge of relief administration in the state.[23]

The accusations from Washington fired passions in Ohio. The *Cleveland
Plain Dealer* reported that several faculty members of Western Reserve

University would join any "oust Davey" movement. Among Ohio legislators, sentiment ran from Republican state senator Robert Pollock's cry for
the governor's impeachment to Democratic state representative Tom Gallagher's denunciation of Hopkins's charges as "baloney." Grossman, after flying back to Cleveland, sniggered over the telephone to Hopkins, "the whole
city is yelling for [Davey's] impeachment."[24]

Seemingly unconcerned about the coming investigation and eager to continue his feud in the press, Martin accused Hopkins of simply trying to divert
attention from the real issue—the inefficiency of federal relief in Ohio. The
governor denied any knowledge of campaign fund shakedowns and claimed
that he knew as much about fund-raising as Roosevelt did of James Farley's
zealous solicitations during the 1932 Democratic presidential campaign.[25]

Francis Poulson, Democratic state executive committee chairman, verified Martin's ignorance of party financial affairs. Momentarily sharing the
spotlight with the governor, Poulson admitted to the press that there was
a $14,000 deficit after the 1934 campaign, and contributions to offset it had
been solicited. However, he saw no reason for concern because political parties had always asked for money. In a blanket defense of the entire Democratic slate in 1934, Poulson added that neither the governor nor congressional and judicial candidates knew anything about party finances during the
campaign. He concluded confidently, "I accept full responsibility and have
no apologies to offer."[26]

If anyone seemed unsure, it was Hopkins. After sending a fiery letter to
Martin and charging Stillman with the responsibilities of Ohio relief, he
admitted he had no idea how long federal control would last. He conceded
the possibility of dual federal-state management but hoped the Ohio legislature would provide funds for the state's relief share. Curiously, though,
perhaps as a concession to his friend Grossman, Hopkins emphasized that
there would be no changes in the CCRA, although Stillman was supposedly
empowered to work out his own relief setup throughout the state.[27]

On March 18, Martin addressed a joint session of the state legislature
and, amid occasional outbursts of applause, scored Hopkins and relief administration in Ohio. His arguments were familiar, denouncing inefficiency
and waste, but he added a new twist to the dispute. The governor told the
joint session that he had sworn out a warrant for Hopkins's arrest, charging
him with criminal libel, and he dared the FERA director to come to Ohio to
stand trial.[28]

Hopkins's challenge had been accepted. State Democrats quickly rallied
around their leader. The Ohio Senate, under Democratic control, passed a

resolution calling for a legislative investigating committee to inquire into federal relief corruption. Martin got another vote of confidence on March 20, when Ohio House and Senate Democrats, meeting in caucus, unanimously adopted a pro-Davey resolution condemning Hopkins and calling for a public redress from Roosevelt.[29]

Meanwhile, Stillman informed Hopkins that Martin intended to move into Ohio relief headquarters in Columbus to confiscate public records of relief transactions. Hopkins sprang to action. Within minutes he got the Department of Justice in Washington to authorize the use of U.S. marshals in Columbus and assured Stillman that help was on the way. "If the governor throws you out," he said, "just laugh at him."[30]

As Hopkins had promised, that very day two U.S. marshals moved into Ohio relief headquarters to safeguard federal property, and, by the next, three FERA agents from Washington arrived to take charge of the disbursement of all federal funds. On March 20, Stillman reported to his boss in Washington, "things are breaking beautifully here," and then began his "housecleaning" with a series of firings. Among the first to go was George Eppley, assistant to William Walls, Martin's appointee as state relief director. Six additional relief department employees were dismissed, and others, fearful that they might be implicated in some wrongdoing, also offered their resignations.[31]

Stillman's investigation ultimately reached the Ohio Surplus and Commodities Division. Several employees were fired after Stillman found that two men had been paid a total of $1,100 over a seven-month period for guarding seventy-five tons of hay valued at $1,350. By March 27, nine days after the relief investigation began, Stillman had fired seventy-three relief workers, including his own daughter. His contention that he could save $10,000 each month in Columbus relief administration alone and his admission of irregularities throughout the state elated Martin. The federal inquiry had found a great deal of inefficiency and waste just as he had claimed.[32]

On another front, the Ohio House defeated a resolution authorizing an investigation of the "shakedown" charges by Attorney General John Bricker's office. But the inquiry generated by Hopkins's accusations continued through the legislative investigating committee. At one of its hearings, Poulson revealed that John McCombe of Ravenna, chief fund-raiser of the party's executive committee, had collected $20,000 since the November election. Poulson was in Florida with Martin when the money was raised, and when he returned McCombe gave him a safety deposit box filled with a "considerable amount" of cash and checks. The money and checks were deposited in the executive committee's account and used when needed. Never, Poulson said, were state contracts awarded to businesses in return for their contributions, although he confessed that when prices and quality were the same, the administration's "friends" would be remembered.[33]

Hopkins, in the meantime, revealed that his incontrovertible proof of a shakedown consisted of affidavits signed by three men associated either directly or indirectly with the Ohio Surplus Commodities Division—William R. McNamara, Tom E. Jones, and Kenneth P. Aller. McNamara, superintendent of the Surplus Commodities Division, swore in his affidavit that McCombe had asked him to help collect $10,000 to offset the deficit from Martin's gubernatorial campaign. McNamara assigned the job to two of his assistants, Jones and John A. Lee. Promised that fruitful fund-raising would secure their jobs, Jones and Lee began to solicit contributions from firms doing business with the state. Initial collections of $4,250 by Jones and $900 by Lee were turned over to McNamara and then to McCombe.[34]

Jones, in his affidavit, named individuals he had solicited for contributions, adding that he had been told to accept cash only. He understood that McNamara's anticipated appointment to the directorship or assistant directorship of the Emergency Relief Administration of Ohio depended on successful fund-raising. Aller's affidavit merely confirmed Jones's solicitation of $250 from Aller's trucking firm, which hauled meat and animal carcasses under state contract.[35]

These affidavits constituted the heart of Hopkins's charges against Martin. Although the Davey organization's fund-raising techniques were questionable, they were likely common practice in other states and at the national level as well. Even the anti-Davey *Plain Dealer* called the McNamara, Jones, and Aller affidavits "one-day sensations." After the initial furor arising from the public announcement of the federal investigation into Ohio relief, most observers concluded that the charges were not so serious as they originally appeared. Furthermore, criminality would be difficult to prove, thereby dashing any prospect of prosecuting anyone. By the end of March 1935, tensions eased and, although the legislative investigating committee continued its inquiry for some months, the general legal consensus was that the Davey organization's actions were reprehensible but not indictable.[36]

With the federal investigation already relegated to the back pages of the press, Hopkins's decision to visit Cleveland on May 24 was almost anticlimactic. Knowing the FERA director had agreed to address the Citizens League, Ohioans wondered if Cleveland police would serve Martin's libel warrant. On the fourteenth, during lunch at the White House, Roosevelt kidded Hopkins, asking him if he wanted a presidential pardon. While Hopkins and Roosevelt bantered, back in Ohio Martin remained grim, refusing to comment on the matter.[37]

The suspense ended on May 22 when Martin withdrew the charges against Hopkins. In Washington, the FERA director, smirking over his foe's retreat, announced, "the action speaks for itself." The comment from Columbus was, of course, different. Explaining that he dropped the charges in the interests of party solidarity, the governor contended that he had been completely vindicated because the Stillman investigation verified his claims of inefficiency and waste in Ohio relief.[38]

The dispute, a bitterly contested personal quarrel as well as a public issue, consequently came to an apt conclusion, with both protagonists claiming victory. Hopkins, however, had the last word. Amid speculation that his Cleveland visit would initiate a healing of the federal-state breach, Hopkins insisted that there had been and would be no compromise with the governor. Addressing the Citizens League, Hopkins repeated his position, insisting that Ohio would have to maintain its share of the relief burden. To queries about his clash with Martin, he snapped that he disliked the governor and was utterly contemptuous of the threatened libel action.[39]

The stormy events of mid-March were succeeded by relative calm. Hopkins eyed bigger game later in the spring when a new presidential bill calling for a $4 billion work relief appropriation created the Works Progress Administration. Both he and Harold Ickes, Roosevelt's secretary of the interior, wanted to administer the program, and their ensuing struggle sounded another dissonant note in the New Deal's familial harmony. The "great resigner," Hopkins called Ickes. "He threatens to quit anytime things don't go his way. He bores me." Perhaps Hopkins had been too quick to condemn Martin's petulance in the Ohio dispute, for he suffered from a similar baseness in his sometimes petty rivalry with Ickes.[40]

Yet such a turnabout was not inconsistent with the character and personality of Harry Hopkins. The chain-smoking, coffee-drinking FERA director combined the seemingly incongruous views of both cynic and idealist. Sardonic and quick to cut, Hopkins nevertheless possessed a genuine sympathy for America's impoverished. His background in New York social work had shown him firsthand the despair and destitution of the unemployed. He brought understanding and empathy to a position that could have easily turned into another soft bureaucratic post miles away from the reality of the depression's cold and hunger.[41] His quick temper and frequent fusillades against the New Deal's detractors made interesting press, but, despite personal shortcomings, his concern for beleaguered Americans and his disdain for pompous, condescending politicians were always evident.

If nothing else, Hopkins fought to maintain an unquestioned probity in the New Deal. The obligations and duties of his office were sacrosanct, and he sincerely believed he could handle patronage-hungry politicians and, either through persuasion or coercion, ensure integrity in a public dole. Martin had not been the only politician to feel his wrath. Hopkins's threats to withhold federal funds from other errant states had forced legislatures in Illinois and Kentucky to raise larger shares of their own relief monies, and his unwavering insistence on honesty in relief administration had triggered clashes with such notables as Louisiana's Huey Long and North Dakota's William Langer even before his dispute with Martin Davey.[42]

Nationally, it was politically expedient for the Democrats to prove that they were spending taxpayer money discriminately. Despite initial successes, the decision was still out on the New Deal, and 1936 was an election year. A measure of party dissension could be tolerated as long as a majority at the polls approved the national administration. Martin, not highly regarded by New Deal leadership, was expendable.[43]

Yet outwardly the break between Washington and Columbus appeared to be healing. The Ohio legislature had passed the Carey Act, which provided additional county relief funds through a 1 percent tax on utilities. This bill, combined with other stopgap measures, helped meet the demands of Ohio's needy. Although the return to local relief responsibility was no panacea, by November 1935, the federal government started dismantling its administrative machinery in Ohio and began to confine its activities to indirect assistance through WPA and other work-relief programs.[44]

The struggle over the administration of Ohio relief was really a contest between competing ideologies. Martin was a spoilsman, and spoilsmen were the very bane of the nonpartisan relief program that Hopkins intended to run. To Martin, Hopkins was a distant Washington bureaucrat living in a world of theory because he could afford to. He never had to scavenge for every available dollar to keep his job. He served at the president's pleasure and dined at the public trough, oblivious to what it was like for someone like Martin who needed an army of loyal supporters and a constant flow of money to win office. Many of the party loyalists understandably expected reward, frequently in the form of a job. That did not bother Martin because he believed that the faithful were the "nucleus around which ... party activity [was] built." No one should have been surprised that Martin assumed office with the intention of dispensing patronage as he saw fit. In his inaugural address, he had warned that he would demonstrate "reasonable" partisanship in such matters.[45] His critics could debate the meaning of "reasonable" all they wanted, but it was Martin, sitting in the governor's chair, who defined it.

The Hopkins episode set the tone for the rest of Martin's term and the next one, too. His Fourteenth Congressional District constituents already knew him as a wily fighter, unafraid of any opponent. Now everyone in the state recognized him for what he was, a battle-hardened pol, and not to be entirely trusted because of it. He had forged a reputation for slickness and would have to live with it. Fortunately for him, the everyday tasks of the governorship demanded his constant attention. He could put the Hopkins affair behind him because he had to move on to other matters.

Chapter Thirteen

Running the State

———————— ⟨🦅⟩ ————————

IN THE 1930s, Columbus already had 250,000 residents, which qualified it as a good-sized municipality. However, in many respects it was still homogeneous, small-town America, with the vast majority of its citizens native-born.[1] Settlers had first established themselves on the west bank of the Scioto River in 1797, and by 1816 their frontier outpost was chosen as the state capital. Yet Columbus remained a country burg until it became a full-fledged city in 1834. Even then it was largely a crossroad destination for freight wagons and stagecoaches heading east, west, north, and south through the geographical heart of the state. However, that changed. Early in the nineteenth century, local entrepreneurs began building buggies and wagons there, and when the railroad came in, Columbus became a budding manufacturing center.[2]

In 1913, a devastating flood destroyed much of the original downtown, forcing residents to build anew along the Scioto River. Up went a civic center, an annex to the State Capitol Building, and other government offices as well as hotels, restaurants, and shops. A few years later, on the banks of Columbus's other river, the Olentangy, Ohio State University football fans by the thousands filed into a brand-new horseshoe-shaped stadium to cheer on their beloved Buckeyes.[3]

Martin L. Davey was ready for Columbus in 1935, but the city was not quite ready for him. He was a small-town boy but had put that behind him. He was now polished, glib, experienced in Washington politics, and rich. Columbus was slower paced, reflecting its pioneer roots and rural surroundings in the center of the state. Life was faster in Cleveland, Akron, Youngstown, and other cities in Ohio's heavily industrialized northeastern quadrant. Even Toledo to the northwest and Cincinnati in the southwest seemed less somnolent. The essential business of Columbus was government, and, apart from a vigorous governor now and then, the conservative, rural-dominated state legislature was the moving force in Ohio politics. Martin could be as fiscally conservative as any of the state legislators, but his style was more flamboyant and energetic. The day after his election, the *Columbus Citizen* aptly described him as a man who "generates ideas as fast as he can talk, which is pretty fast."[4]

One of the new governor's first tasks was choosing a cabinet. To reunite the party, he appointed six supporters of his 1934 primary election opponents, Charles Sawyer and William Pickrel. The remaining four were Martin's own selections, including Ohio's first woman cabinet member, Margaret Allman, the director of public welfare. He made several additional appointments in other state agencies, among them Robert Bowen (superintendent of insurance), whom Martin had befriended during his typewriter-selling days in Cleveland.[5]

Within two weeks of Martin's inauguration, an old friend and foe, Con Mulcahy, the Summit County Democratic Party boss, visited the governor in Columbus. The two had settled their differences after the 1934 gubernatorial primary, and the Akronite had helped Martin during the general election. Mulcahy now came to collect. Never satisfied with half a loaf, he demanded total control over Summit County patronage. Stunned by Mulcahy's audacity, Martin refused, explaining that he had a lot of Summit County debts of his own to repay. But Mulcahy refused to take no for an answer, and, several hours later, when Martin refused to yield, he stormed out of the governor's office, the breach between the two politicos now complete and irreparable.

Martin was not about to surrender one of his greatest ancillary gubernatorial powers to anyone. He knew how important it was to have an army of loyalists at the ready before, in between, and during elections. They were crucial to any candidate's success. More nobly, he also believed that winners owed the faithful, although he knew he could never find enough jobs to satisfy all who came clamoring for them. Unfortunately, too many of those ignored would turn on the man they helped elect.

Nobility, however, was not Martin's guiding force in patronage. He simply wanted to control it. Contending that he intended to save money by eliminating thousands of unnecessary jobs, in January 1935 Martin asked the state legislature to suspend the civil service rules that protected state workers. Fearing that the new governor's motives were driven less by a desire for economy and more by a drive for power, the legislature refused, and Martin temporarily dropped his plan.[6]

The legislators had sniffed something foul in the new political air in Columbus. Certainly every incoming administration wanted to make appointments in order to control its own destiny, but Martin's request was so wide sweeping that even politicians well acquainted with patronage recognized that they were dealing with something unusual. Within a few weeks, the governor verified their suspicions. Operating through Margaret Allman, his director of public welfare, Martin sent out a questionnaire to all state employees, asking them to declare their political affiliation. With jobs so precious during the depression, many supervisors urged their workers to comply. One, however, did not. William F. Amrine, superintendent of the London, Ohio, prison farm, resigned in protest after twice refusing to obey the governor's order.[7] The public sided with Amrine and turned on Martin, whose reputation was already suffering after only a few weeks in office.

Martin would not back down. Oblivious to the fact that he may have pushed too fast and too far in undermining Ohio's civil service system, he turned on his critics. Myers Cooper had done the same thing when he was governor and did not suffer disapproval, he complained, and he offered $100 to anyone who could find a shred of criticism of his predecessor in the Harry P. Wolfe–owned *Columbus Dispatch* and *Ohio State Journal*. Martin was unapologetic about taking care of his own supporters, claiming that he was obligated to do so according to "all the rules of politics." On the heels of the governor's pronouncement, Highway Director John J. Jaster fired forty employees, including some under civil service protection. The move made financial sense, saving $85,000 annually, but its timing made the governor look bad by imparting the impression that the new regime was tearing down a perfectly good house just to build its own.[8]

Martin's brashness disturbed even some of his fellow Democrats, particularly in the state Senate. A month after swearing his oath of office, the Senate censured him. Martin's old Fourteenth Congressional District opponent in 1922, Frank Whittemore, introduced the motion to censure, which passed without debate. Most alarming and ominous for Martin was the realization that not a single Senate Democrat defended him. All the more disturbing was the fact that his fellow partisans held a three-man majority in the state Senate and could have defeated Whittemore's resolution had they supported their governor. But not a single Democrat voted, and Martin was censured by a unanimous "yes" vote from Senate Republicans alone. Majority floor leader Paul Yoder lamely defended his fellow partisans' inaction by declaring that they "didn't want to make an issue of the civil service fight." But there was no denying why the Democrats acted as they did—they recognized that their new governor was trouble, and they wanted no part of it. Martin was stung by it all but tried to explain the episode by declaring in a statewide radio address that Democratic and Republican leaders in the Senate had attacked him because of their "allegiance" to special interests and to advance their "personal ambitions."[9] Neither charge was elaborated, and the senators' "special interests" remained unnamed and their "personal ambitions" unexplained.

Martin believed that lashing out against his foes constituted a valid defense of his actions. That tactic became common for him; he used it throughout his gubernatorial term. He failed to realize that by constantly "getting back" at his foes he acquired the reputation of a mean-spirited, petty, and vindictive bully. Ohioans either appreciated him for his feistiness or disliked him for his prickliness. There was no middle ground where Martin L. Davey was concerned.

Even his closest friend, Francis Poulson, proved an embarrassment to the governor. Already known as "Pythias" to the governor's "Damon," the garrulous Poulson was a lightning rod for trouble, and when he got into it, Martin, at least indirectly, suffered too. One Sunday morning in 1935, Poulson was driving from Cleveland to Columbus when he jammed on his brakes at a red light at a Summit County crossroads. His car skidded and crashed into a tree. A dazed Poulson was taken to a nearby hospital and examined before returning to Cleveland.[10]

The wreck itself was scarcely noteworthy. Had Poulson not been so closely associated with Martin, it might not have even been reported in Cleveland newspapers. However, at the hospital $4,000 was discovered in Poulson's pockets, and he could not explain where it came from other than it "belonged to the Democratic Committee." Of course, no one believed him. He had for too long been linked to Martin's fund-raising schemes even though no one had any proof that the governor had a direct hand in Poulson's activities. Still, Poulson's revelations during the Harry Hopkins imbroglio led many to believe that where there was smoke, there was likely to be fire, a suspicion substantiated just two months after his auto accident when "Pythias" was accused of demanding a bribe from a Clevelander seeking a liquor license.[11]

Poulson denied the charge, but the state liquor department during Martin's administration was indeed troubled. Shortly after Prohibition ended in 1933, Ohio created a state monopoly over the liquor business. Under the White administration, enforcement was lax, and bootlegging continued to thrive while the department's chief enforcement officer, Edmund G.

"Damon" and "Pythias"—Governor Davey and his right-hand man, Frank Poulson, ca. 1936. Ohio Historical Society.

Mathews, looked the other way. When Martin took office, he ordered his liquor department head, James Miller, to fire Mathews, even though the enforcement chief was protected by civil service. In accordance with civil service regulations, Mathews was suspended pending a hearing before the state Civil Service Commission. The case never came up because a despondent Mathews liquored himself into oblivion before killing himself with a gunshot to the head. The story, already bizarre, took an even stranger turn when a friend of the enforcement chief later told Martin that Mathews intended to shoot the governor first. Luckily for Martin, Mathews never came after the governor.[12]

Martin regarded himself as the savior of the liquor department, but many suspected that he had merely turned it into his personal auxiliary. A disgusted WPA field agent (and confidante of Eleanor Roosevelt), Lorena Hickok, reported to her boss, Harry Hopkins, that the governor was forcing liquor dealers to buy licenses if they wanted to sell in Ohio, fees that then ended up in Martin's coffers. By 1936, it was rumored that Martin's manipulation of the state liquor department had generated a half-million-dollar slush fund.[13]

Martin was furious over the imputations and twice over the radio defended his supervision of the liquor department. The newspapers, particularly the *Cleveland Press, Youngstown Telegram, Toledo News-Bee, Columbus Citizen,* and the *Cincinnati Post,* he claimed, were out to get him by falsely charging that the liquor department was fraught with graft. He and he alone had rescued the department from the clutches of the "whisky trust" that had allowed all sorts of illegalities under George White. If there were "grafters" in the liquor department, he demanded that the newspapers name them. He was tired of their incessant innuendoes.[14]

To demonstrate that he had nothing to hide about any aspect of his administration, the governor in early 1935 called for an investigating committee to probe every department, bureau, and division of state government. Clarence O. Sherrill, the punctilious first city manager of Cincinnati, was asked to head the committee. Under Sherrill's lead, 130 business and civic leaders began a five-month-long investigation of the state's business practices. In October, the Sherrill Committee turned over to the governor a five-thousand-page report showing that the state could save $15 million annually by eliminating waste and inefficiency. The sum was nearly one-third of the state's yearly operating budget of $50 million.[15]

The Sherrill Committee had no particular axe to grind. Its members merely took the governor's charge seriously, investigated thoroughly, and then published their findings. Martin did not see it that way and interpreted the committee's recommendations as criticisms. The Sherrill Report, he claimed, was a thinly disguised attack on his administration surreptitiously conducted by still another unnamed political opponent. Through judicious planning and vetoes he had already shaved $9 million off the state budget, yet the Sherrill Committee gave him no credit for that. Years later Martin admitted that, given the many problems he faced during his first term, creating the Sherrill Committee was a big mistake because it did little more than demean his accomplishments and undermine his administration.[16]

Many of Martin's difficulties stemmed from the constant financial pressures generated by the Great Depression. There was never enough money to treat the myriad of problems the state faced, and the new governor was always torn between the need to provide necessary services to Ohioans and the recognition that an already-strained populace could not afford additional taxes. The reality of that had, at least in part, started the relief feud with Harry Hopkins. But providing relief funds to Ohio's needy was only one of Martin's pressing problems during his first term. Equally troubling was the state of Ohio's schools, hundreds of which had struggled to stay open since the 1933 passage of a ten-mill limitation amendment to the Ohio Constitution. The amendment cut property taxes by a third and in the process denied local governments and the schools a crucial source of revenue.[17]

Martin urged the legislature to pass a School Foundation Bill that would divert funds from the Ohio sales tax, gasoline, cigarette, and other state taxes to the schools by 1936. The measure was reasonable enough, especially given the schools' desperate straits. It passed the Democratic-controlled Senate, but encountered stiff opposition in the Republican-dominated House. There, conservatives worried that somehow the School Foundation Bill might aid parochial schools, assistance they inalterably opposed. Interestingly, Catholic legislators worried about the bill, too, because they feared that it might ultimately lead to state control of their schools, which shared the same financial plight as the public institutions.[18]

On this issue, Martin finally proved to be more statesman than politician. Ohio's dire school problems transcended partisan politics, and, although saying so was a banality, Ohio's future was very much at stake. On March 10, 1935, in another statewide radio address, he urged the legislature to act. The schools were, he stressed, "probably the most important public institutions we have." They were the very "citadel of our liberties" and "cannot be permitted to close."[19]

Despite Martin's plea, the school funding bill languished for months, delayed by fiscally and religiously conservative representatives. In the meantime, hundreds of schools closed their doors, many of them permanently. The grim reality, even among conservatives, was that Ohio's school system was in shambles. Martin's "massaging" of Catholic legislators in the lower house finally resulted in the passage of the School Foundation Bill in late May. Martin signed it, and on June 12, 1935, the bill became law. The measure consolidated many of Ohio's smaller schools, pumped lifesaving state money into the beleaguered system, and was one of the high points of Martin's governorship.[20]

The governor did not seem so noble later that summer when he got into what was little better than a dog fight with Ohio State University president George W. Rightmire. In Martin's defense, he was always scrambling to cut costs wherever he could to balance Ohio's books. One of his "victims" was Ohio State's biennial budget, from which the governor sliced $1,266,500 of the school's $7,155,600 appropriation, a drastic cut even when measured against the depression-ridden state's financial constraints. The governor reasoned that other state universities were faring well with per-student allocations far smaller than Ohio State's.[21]

President Rightmire countered the governor's charges of extravagance at Ohio State, claiming that the university had already tightened its belt by canceling 480 of its courses, fully 10 percent of its offerings. Moreover, Ohio State professors were among the lowest paid in the Western Conference, and other university employees, who had taken pay cuts when the depression began, had yet to see their salaries restored. The governor simply did not understand that the state's flagship university, with a vast educational mission, simply could not be compared to smaller public universities such as Kent State and Bowling Green.[22]

Rightmire may have been right, but Martin was not about to suffer a challenge from a mere university president. He himself was a college dropout and seemed threatened by academics, particularly professors. He claimed to "respect" them—but only "when they stay[ed] in the classroom." They were too much like Harry Hopkins's ego-driven social workers who foolishly thought they could apply useless classroom theories to cold and hungry citizens who wanted only to be rescued from their privation.[23] Rightmire was just one more of those "fuzzy" thinkers who had better learn to live in the real world, one of depression-generated financial constraints—the world Martin lived in every day.

The quarrel between governor and university president continued through the summer and into the fall of 1935 when it took a different turn. In October, university officials warned that Ohio State might have to cancel the rest of its football schedule. In Buckeye-crazed Columbus, that was incomprehensible—a sacrilege of the worst order. Should that happen, the governor certainly would feel the wrath of thousands of fans who placed their beloved football team above all else. Shutting down the majestic Horseshoe and, even worse, skipping the season-ending game with Michigan, their most bitter rival, were unthinkable to the legions of devoted fans.

If Ohio State administrators thought that so dire a threat would jolt Martin into reconsidering his budget cuts, they were badly mistaken. All they had done was give the clever and acerbic governor more ammunition. He was "glad" to know that the essential business of the Ohio State University was football and facetiously added, "We [state government] have done our part, because we have most of the football squad on the state payroll." The governor exaggerated when he said "most of the football squad," but had he claimed that "several" players were on the state payroll, he would not have been wrong. In fact, fourteen members of the team were employed as highway workers, legislative pages, guards in the Department of Public Works and the state auditor's office, and more.[24]

Angry alumni and football fans blasted the governor. "Petty stuff," complained one alumnus. It seems "as if Davey is . . . hunting for something to fight about." Another said he'd "like to see Governor Davey ousted from office" and yet another branded Martin's actions as "sort of childish."[25] And indeed they were. Martin could have remained silent until the budget flap was relegated to the back pages of the press, but he was too combative for that. Clearly, one of his major shortcomings was a quick temper, and that weakness seemed to be growing daily while he sat in the governor's chair. Many began to think that he was more a petulant child who had to "get every antagonist last" than he was the chief representative of the state. They had a right to expect better from their governor.

A shadowy figure had the last word in the now almost comical affair. One cold February night someone slung a dummy over his shoulder and sneaked from the Ohio State campus to a lamppost across the street. The next morning police found "Martin" dangling at the end of a rope with a sign around his neck, "the man for the back [out]house—Davey."[26] Buckeye fans in Columbus took their football very seriously.

Not all Martin's attention was devoted to budgets, legislative battles, or quarrels with Washington bureaucrats. Some things he did alone through the use of his executive powers. Although generally governors like uncontested power, the exercise of that power can be personally troubling. Martin learned that when for the first time in his life he literally held the power of life and death over a man.

Clevelander Peter D. Treadway was a thirty-eight-year-old career criminal accused of the brutal murder of Ruth Steese on December 30, 1932. At 1 P.M. that day, Steese had cashed a check for $191.25 at a Cleveland bank and then headed downtown. She never made it. Shortly before two, two children discovered her slumped in the back seat of her car, dead from a gunshot wound. The car had been driven to suburban Beachwood Village, a short distance from her downtown destination. Wound tightly around her neck was a rag, the kind commonly used by gas station attendants. A witness, William Hodgmann, told police that he had seen a man standing by the car, which had jumped the curb, and asked if he needed help. The man seemed agitated and waved off Hodgmann.[27]

Police took Hodgmann to the station to view several suspects who had already been rounded up, but none of them was the man standing alongside the victim's automobile. Two other witnesses, a bus driver and one of his passengers, told police that they had seen a man get on their bus shortly after the crime had been committed. Their descriptions matched Hodgmann's.[28]

That was as far as the case went. Absent any other clues, the murder remained unsolved until a series of seemingly unrelated events led police to Peter D. Treadway, who just happened to be a gas station attendant.

Six months after Steese's murder, Treadway, with a gunshot wound to his left leg, stumbled into a suburban Cleveland town hall, claiming that he had been robbed. Later, at the central police station, he studied mug shots and identified Benny Zock, a small-time Pittsburgh bootlegger, as his assailant. Zock was arrested, but when police interrogated him something seemed fishy about Treadway's story. One thing led to another until detectives wondered if Treadway might be connected to Steese's murder.

The original witness, William Hodgmann, failed to identify Treadway as the man he saw standing alongside Steese's car in Beachwood Village, but police nonetheless checked the filling station attendant's background. Treadway was never going to be nominated as anyone's citizen of the year. He had spent two years in prison for a robbery in Missouri and eleven in Pennsylvania for a murder committed during another robbery. Even after he was indicted for the Steese murder, he had escaped from the Cuyahoga County jail on February 23, 1934, and was caught two weeks later in Hannibal, Missouri, after robbing a local gas station.[29]

After questioning Treadway's coworkers, police believed they had their man. Treadway went on trial in Cleveland, was found guilty, and was sentenced to die in the Ohio State Penitentiary's electric chair. Throughout his ordeal he proclaimed his innocence, although three courts, including the Ohio Supreme Court, had denied his appeals. In addition, Governor George White had granted Treadway three death row reprieves as his lawyers desperately sought new evidence that would exculpate their client.

With only a day to go before his electrocution, Treadway petitioned Martin for one last stay of execution. The governor refused. Treadway, Martin explained to the press, had had numerous chances to prove his innocence. Thirteen different judges had reviewed the case, and each of them concluded that Treadway was guilty. There was nothing left to be done except carry out the sentence. Still, condemning even a convicted killer like Treadway bothered Martin. No matter his personal feelings, though, he could not overrule the courts.[30]

"I can't believe it," Treadway gasped when he learned that Martin had denied his eleventh-hour chance at life. On Saturday, June 1, 1935, at a little after 8 P.M., the condemned man, clad in a navy blue suit, with tie and socks to match, was strapped hand and foot into Ohio's electric chair. He stared at the crucifix held by the Catholic priest who accompanied him on the final walk from his cell to the death chamber, mumbled a quick prayer to the Virgin Mary, and awaited the 1,750 volts of electricity that would end his life. At 8:21 P.M. it was over.[31]

Interestingly, Martin never mentioned the first execution on his gubernatorial watch in his otherwise detailed autobiography. It was something he preferred to forget, even as he noted the other major events in his life. Years later, his trusted secretary, Myrna Smith, recounting her boss's governorship, barely noted the Treadway case: "The Governor refused to stop the execution after carefully reviewing the sentence" was all she wrote.[32]

Martin's anguish over Peter D. Treadway may have influenced his later actions in the case of still another criminal. In 1913, nineteen-year-old Carlton Buford Chilton had stolen money from an open vault in an untended bank in Calvin, Oklahoma. He and his accomplice then hopped a train to Arkansas, where he was given his share of the take, $400. The two split up, and Chilton moved to Pacific, Missouri, and wrote home to let family know his whereabouts. Shortly thereafter, a U.S. marshal arrested Chilton and returned him to Oklahoma for trial. Chilton's lawyer recommended that he plead guilty to burglary because he would probably be paroled in two years. Young and compliant, Chilton did as he was told and was sent to the Oklahoma Reformatory at Granite. He was a trusty, assigned to tend to a water pump at some distance from the prison grounds. For weeks at a time he never saw a prison guard, and in March 1914, overborne by the rash judgment of youth and with a railroad enticingly nearby, he took off, ending up in Texas where he worked for an oil company before enlisting in the military during the Great War. Honorably discharged in 1919, he returned to Texas for two years, then shipped out with another oil company to the British West Indies for a year. By 1923, he was back in the United States, held a succession of jobs, and even opened his own restaurant in Kilgore, Texas. The restaurant failed, however, and in 1930 Chilton moved to Cleveland, worked as an usher at Cleveland Stadium, an orderly at a military hospital, and a statistician in the U.S. Department of Labor, a job he got after writing President Roosevelt that he desperately needed work.[33]

At every stage since his escape from the Oklahoma Reformatory, he led an exemplary life, marrying and adopting a stepson. Friends, neighbors, co-workers, and everybody who knew him trusted him implicitly. A druggist-landlord testified that he let Chilton collect his rents for him and allowed the Oklahoman to guard the back of his drugstore while armed with a gun. No one had a bad thing to say about Carlton Buford Chilton.[34]

Unfortunately for him, Chilton's model life over the past twenty-two years did not negate the fact that he was a prison escapee. In 1936, authorities traced him to Ohio, and Oklahoma's governor authorized an assistant attorney general, Owen J. Watts, to go to Ohio to begin extradition proceedings through Governor Davey. After listening to Watts's arguments and consulting with his own lawyers, Martin held a hearing to determine if Chilton should be returned to Oklahoma. Watts, Chilton, his lawyers, and a hundred supporters jammed into Martin's office where each side presented its case. When witness after witness testified to Chilton's rectitude, kindness, and generosity, there was not a dry eye in the room. Tears trickled down Martin's cheeks as he absorbed the story of a young man who temporarily went bad and had spent the rest of his life atoning for it by being a patriotic citizen, good husband, father, and friend.[35]

At the end, Martin rose and sermonized, "If the intention of a penal institution is to reform, it is as clear as day that when a man reforms himself he has done an infinitely greater job." Pointing to Chilton, he continued, "This man is not a criminal by nature. A long time ago Christ said 'go and sin no more,' and so [Oklahoma's] request is denied."[36] Mrs. Chilton squeezed her husband's arm, one hundred people took their first full breath in nearly two hours, and Assistant Attorney General Owen J. Watts returned to Oklahoma alone.

The Treadway and Chilton cases represented the human face of the governorship. So much else of what Martin had to do every day was cold and automatic. Certainly there were personalities involved when he took on the legislature in a budget fight or stood on a platform hammering home a campaign speech to a cheering crowd. But all those things happened in the heat of battle when he rarely had a chance to look friend or foe in the eye. He was constantly rushing in order to finish a job because there was always another task at hand. Even the quarrel with Harry Hopkins, as personal as any could be, was nonetheless fought through the mails and Western Union, and on the front pages of the press. Busy men did things that way, in the process turning the personal into the impersonal. That certainly was not so in the cases of

Peter D. Treadway and Carlton Buford Chilton. What Martin did there was very personal indeed. In one case he helped take a life; in the other he restored one.

Fortunately for Martin, there were some problems he could avoid (but not ignore). The passage of the Wagner Act in 1935 gave workers the right to unionize America's larger industries and prevented management from using threats and intimidation to discourage unionization. Old animosities, however, died hard. Management felt threatened once its absolute powers over labor diminished. Workers now had the muscle to challenge ownership on wages and working conditions, and, emboldened by their new power, awaited the moment they could retaliate against their "oppressors."

Ohio's rubber industry was among the first to explode. In Akron, the industrial heart of Martin's old Fourteenth Congressional District, strikes over wages and working conditions broke out at Firestone, Goodyear, and Goodrich tire plants in 1936. Akron mayor Lee D. Schroy especially feared that the Goodyear strike might turn violent, and it nearly did. When five hundred Akron policemen marched to the tire plant on East Market Street to stop union picketing, they were blocked by thousands of rubber workers. Worried about what so many angry men might do, the police retreated. The conflict with Goodyear continued, with intermittent truces until 1941, when the company finally signed a contract with the United Rubber Workers, a Congress of Industrial Organizations affiliate.[37]

The Akron strikes were near enough to home to concern Martin, but one still closer worried him even more, not only because it was in his own backyard, but also because it was so violent. In Kent, a strike over wages and the installation of a company union broke out at the Black and Decker electric motor plant. Some 450 workers walked off their jobs in early May 1936, forcing the company to hire replacements. Tempers on both sides simmered until finally, on June 18, strikers and strike breakers went at each other with tear gas and guns. A little after 6 A.M., fifty strikers and sympathizers threw back the heavy chains barring the plant entrance. Simultaneously two vans, seemingly coming out of nowhere, raced onto company grounds. Twenty men armed with shotguns and tear gas leaped out, the lead man yelling, "Let 'em have it!" His cohorts swung open the factory gates and charged the plant. Company guards repelled them with shotgun blasts and tear gas. The strikers retreated across the street, and, from behind shrubbery, fired randomly into the factory. One striker suffered a gunshot wound to his leg, and another took a load of buckshot in the face. Ambulances rushed them and three tear-gassed strikers to Robinson Memorial Hospital in nearby

Ravenna. Within minutes, hundreds of workers from Kent's Twin Coach Company and Akron's rubber plants joined their union brethren on the Black and Decker site. The mayor and police chief debated whether they should ask the governor to send in the National Guard, but city and county law enforcement officers restored order. An uneasy truce of several weeks ensued until early July when the company agreed to a 5 percent wage increase and recognition of the workers' union. In return, the latter accepted a forty-hour, rather than a thirty-six-hour, workweek.[38]

In Columbus, Martin breathed a sigh of relief when he learned that local law enforcement had ended the violence in Kent. Had the fighting continued and had Kent officials asked for help from the National Guard, the governor would have faced a serious dilemma. Certainly he would have had to preserve the safety of Kentites but at the cost of alienating thousands of union members by appearing to take the side of their bosses. With union membership growing rapidly, that could have been political suicide. Fortunately for him, in 1936 he did not have to make that choice.[39]

Martin's days were so full that he almost forgot he had a family, but fortunately Berenice understood. By 1935 she had already been married to Martin for twenty-eight years and wedded to his political career almost as long. Evangeline was twenty-four and Martin Jr. seventeen. Martin Jr. was still in high school, but Evangeline had already graduated from Wellesley College in Massachusetts and fallen in love with a young engineer, Alexander Smith of Cleveland, a graduate of Yale University. In what was a brief but happy respite from his official duties, a proud Martin L. Davey gave away his daughter to Smith in a private October wedding ceremony in the governor's mansion.[40]

The governor adored his daughter. She had graduated from college with honors in 1933 and then worked as a stenographer at the Davey Tree Expert Company. She never capitalized on her name and was well liked by her coworkers. She was a sensitive young woman, acutely aware, for instance, that the stock market crash of 1929 likely affected her father's fortune. After some of her Wellesley classmates discussed how the market crash had devastated their fathers, she wrote hers and said she had carefully examined her expenses and believed it was her "duty" to "get along . . . on less money." Proud of his daughter's selflessness, Martin told her that everything was fine, and, although her eagerness to economize was appreciated, it was unnecessary.[41]

Evangeline and Berenice were not the only women important to Martin. A number of them had been crucial in his life, beginning with his mother, Bertha, who had held the family together while John Davey dreamed and philosophized the hours away until the public finally accepted the science of tree surgery. Berenice had become Martin's "rock" ever since their marriage in 1907. She, more than any other, understood her husband's obsession with politics and willingly shared him with his constituents.

Outside his family, no woman was more important to Martin than Myrna Smith, his longtime secretary, first at Davey Tree and then throughout his political life. He depended on her for virtually everything when he was governor, knowing that she could anticipate what he wanted and protect him from the unending hordes who simply "had to see the governor." She not only toiled daily for Martin, she also worked at least three or four nights a week to keep up with his schedule and correspondence. She was unswervingly loyal and committed to serving Martin and, through him, the citizens of Ohio. Martin was lucky to have her and knew it. Everyone recognized that she ran the governor's office, exposing Martin to the unfair charge that his was a "petticoat-government."[42]

Martin was equally protective of the women in his life and understandably upset when Berenice was subpoenaed to testify in a tax dispute involving the Davey Tree Expert Company. The Internal Revenue Bureau challenged Martin's 1930 tax return, claiming that he had underpaid the U.S. Treasury $4,500. Berenice was ordered to appear before the Board of Tax Appeals in Washington, D.C., because she was listed as "assistant to the president" (Martin) of the Davey Tree Expert Company and in that capacity had earned $9,000 for 1930 and 1931. The Internal Revenue Bureau claimed her salary was excessive and allowed Martin to deduct more from Davey Tree income than was legally allowable. The summons threatened Berenice with arrest if she did not comply.[43]

Martin's first instinct was to fight. How dare the government treat his wife as if she were some common scofflaw. He telephoned Washington and angrily but futilely demanded that the Internal Revenue Bureau rescind Berenice's summons. He intended to contest the tax charge to the end. However, as the December date for Berenice's appearance in Washington neared, he had second thoughts about having her testify before a hostile court. On December 11, 1935, one day before Berenice's scheduled appearance, he informed the Board of Appeals that he would pay his bill.[44]

Berenice's summons reminded Martin that he was not only a governor but a husband and father, too. Martin Jr. was generally well behaved but was rambunctious and sometimes driven by the derring-do of youth. He loved sports, especially football, and his Kent chums frequently assembled on the front lawn of the Davey residence for a good old-fashioned neighborhood game. The boys were so eager that in 1928 Martin hired a knowledgeable student from Kent State University to teach them the finer points of the sport. The boys learned quickly and soon joined a midget football league as the Kent Bearcats. Martin Jr., or Brub as he was called, suffered his share of bumps and bruises, but never gave Martin a scare until he was a teenager living in Columbus and jumped from the second story to escape a fire in a friend's house, breaking two toes in the process.[45]

Martin Jr's behavior may have had his father shaking his head, but events swirling about Evangeline generated more serious concern. In May 1936, Detroit police arrested nine members of a racist, nativist cult, the Black Legion, for murdering a WPA worker accused of beating his wife. It was vigilante justice at its worst and forced the black-robed and hooded cult into the daylight. Further investigation by Detroit police linked the Black Legion to the burning of Royal Oak, Michigan's original Shrine of the Little Flower, from which Father Charles E. Coughlin's radio broadcasts flayed Wall Street, capitalism in general, and politicians who did not see eye to eye with the vitriolic priest. The accusation was difficult to prove, but arson fit the Legion's vicious modus operandi. The cult was so violent that even the Ku Klux Klan had expelled two Michigan members because of their dual affiliation with the Black Legion.[46]

Shortly after the Detroit story broke, special investigators in Columbus revealed that Black Legionnaires in Ohio, incensed over Martin's 1934 stance on aid to parochial schools, planned to kidnap Evangeline in retaliation. The Ohio investigation led to two officers of the Legion who confessed that they heard their leader discuss the plot. The Davey family kept quiet about Evangeline's potential peril and tried to dismiss it as the "work of a crank," but nonetheless for months Martin's daughter was closely guarded by Columbus police and State Highway troopers.[47]

State and personal matters were not Martin's only concerns during his first gubernatorial term. By early 1936, with a second term in mind, he felt he had to curry favor with Franklin D. Roosevelt, who seemed headed toward even greater electoral success than he experienced in 1932. The quarrel with Hopkins hurt; it might have been over, but it had never truly been patched up and Martin remained persona non grata with the national administration. Months later, he was still inspiring the wrath of New Dealers. In November 1935, Raymond Moley, the former "Brain Truster" and one of the architects of the New Deal, denounced the Ohio administration and its leader, the "Joe Palooka" of governors, for their corruption. If Martin continued his errant ways, Ohio might well go Republican in 1936, Moley warned.[48]

Combative as ever, Martin struck back. Moley was nothing more than a "high-powered theorist in a gilded office," completely out of touch with the lives of ordinary Ohioans. Before criticizing the way Ohio was being run, he should examine his own failed role in the aborted London Economic Conference of 1933, which the United States suddenly rebuked when its program of tariff reduction and currency stabilization threatened Roosevelt's domestic program.[49] Without American support, the conference collapsed, leaving several nations to their own devices in coping with the worldwide depression.

Martin's angry retort to Moley was typical; once again his temper and sharp tongue overcame his common sense. Continuing his pattern of "I'll get you back" was counterproductive and juvenile. As a longtime political animal, he should have known better. Politicians put themselves before the public by choice. If they did not expect brickbats to fly their way, they should not seek public office. Martin, however, was not one to sit back and take his lumps.

Martin was perspicacious enough to know that the feud with Roosevelt and his surrogates could not continue without severe political consequences—likely defeat in the governor's race in 1936. He needed Franklin D. Roosevelt more than the president needed him, although Roosevelt, already counting electoral votes, worried over what Ohio might do in the 1936 presidential canvass. The breach between Columbus and Washington had to be healed.

An invitation to a White House reception provided Martin the perfect opportunity to salve old wounds. Arrangements were made for Martin, Poulson, and several Davey supporters to meet with the president and Democratic national chairman James Farley to discuss Ohio's role in the 1936 campaign. Poulson, as aware as anyone of the antagonism between the Ohio and national administrations, called the group the "harmony delegation." Getting the Daveyites in to see the president was especially crucial because only a few days earlier a crew of anti-Davey Democrats had visited the White House, and there could be little doubt that they left Roosevelt with an uncomplimentary impression of the Ohio governor. A testy Poulson informed reporters that it was about time to "tell official Washington the truth about the political situation in Ohio."[50]

At the last minute, Roosevelt canceled the White House reception. Martin did not take the cancellation personally because the president's decision left many other invited Democrats equally out in the cold. He traveled to Washington anyway, but his talks with the president were disappointing, largely a formality as part of Roosevelt's open-door policy toward any state governor.

Even more disheartening were the governor's discussions with James Farley. The national chairman politely, but firmly, suggested that Martin not be a delegate to the national convention later in the summer.[51] Martin offered no promises to Farley and returned to Ohio disappointed but undaunted.

The meeting with the president forced Martin to take stock of himself. He had come to the governorship under some of the most trying conditions in the state's history. The Great Depression had devastated Ohio's economy and demoralized its 6.5 million citizens. Throughout the state there was a crying need for services but precious little money to provide them. Those who were working wanted no new taxes, and it was remarkable that Martin had somehow balanced the state budget. Doing so was not easy, and every time he made hard choices he was bound to alienate someone. From the beginning, too, he believed that the state legislature was just waiting to see him stumble so it could pounce on him. He lamented that he had no reciprocal power over legislators.[52] They could go their merry ways, supporting the governor when they wanted to and attacking him if it seemed advantageous to do so.

Being governor was challenging, much more so than being a congressman. As a U.S. representative, Martin L. Davey was responsible for a single congressional district. As such, he was accountable to thousands of constituents and could operate on a more provincial scale. But the governorship was different. Now he was answerable to nearly seven million Ohioans. He rarely finished at the office before seven, then rushed home for dinner with Berenice and the rest of the family before working on more official business until midnight. Night after night he slipped wearily into bed, only to rise early and repeat the process the next day. He did not complain, however. He wanted the job and got it, but he did wish his fellow citizens knew how hard it was.[53] It was not so difficult, though, to stop him from seeking a second term.

Chapter Fourteen

Troubles

———————————— ❧ ————————————

OHIO REPUBLICANS HAD offered up a soft opponent against Martin in the 1934 gubernatorial race. Even though the vote was fairly close, Clarence Brown, with only the parochial school issue in his arsenal, was never a formidable foe. Republicans would not repeat their error in 1936. They turned to John W. Bricker from little Mount Sterling, Ohio, roughly midway between Columbus and Dayton. Bricker was already a proven commodity in Ohio politics, having won a number of local and state offices, including the state attorney generalship. Even more important, he had scaled the political ladder without controversy, making him an ideal opponent against Martin, who, after only two years in office, was already "tainted."

Martin Davey and John Bricker followed separate paths to their nominations in 1936. Bricker was so popular among Republicans that he was unopposed in the primary election. Martin, on the other hand, fought bitterly for his nomination with Stephen Young, an Ohio congressman who had attacked his fellow Democrat as "Ohio's . . . Public Liability No. 1." Young also derided the governor's boast of economy in office by claiming that government costs had risen by more than $19 million in Martin's first year of office alone.[1] Young promised to do better and give Ohioans the kind of government they deserved.

What angered Martin most were Young's attacks against the governor's integrity. On May 4, 1936, only eight days before the gubernatorial primary, the two Democrats clashed in Cleveland during a meeting of the Women's City Club and the League of Women Voters. Before that politically sophis-

ticated audience, Young charged his opponent with running a partisan machine fueled by forced contributions from state employees, such as those in
Toledo who were forced to buy at least four tickets at fifty cents each to a
Davey rally in their hometown. Ordinarily, such an accusation would have
precipitated an immediate verbal brawl, but, out of deference to the female
audience, Martin held his tongue.[2]

Martin seethed through the rest of the day and by evening could no longer
contain himself. In a speech broadcast over Cleveland radio station WHK,
he struck back by denigrating the diminutive Young's chances in the coming
election. "There is no contest of any consequence in the primaries; in fact
there is not the slightest reason or excuse for the existence of any opposition at
all." Young was nothing more than a ranting demagogue, and later that night
Martin predicted he would win the nomination by a five-to-one margin.[3]

Young's challenge in Cleveland could be sloughed off as typical campaign
rhetoric, but Martin faced others as well. On the same day that Young accused
Martin of extorting contributions from state workers, the Consumers League
of Ohio criticized Elaine Sheffler of the State Industrial Relations Department
for failing to apply Ohio's minimum wage law to women and minors. The
governor, the Consumers League claimed, had broken his promise to enforce
the law and had compounded the problem by firing an able minimum wage
superintendent to provide a political job for the unqualified Sheffler.[4]

Stinging though they were, none of the imputations mattered. Martin won
renomination, although by nowhere near the boastful five-to-one margin he
had predicted. The governor beat Young by little more than a hundred thousand votes, an easy win but a creditable showing for the Ohio congressman
who had waffled before deciding at the last moment to enter the primary. By
the time he did, most of the Democratic machinery had already lined up behind Martin.[5] Late on election night, with the outcome no longer in doubt, a
gracious Young urged Ohio Democrats to unite behind the governor, which
was exactly what Martin expected a defeated but loyal opponent to say.

Whatever the primary lacked in high drama was more than made up for
in the general election. Bricker opened the campaign with, "There's something wrong in Columbus." The Republican's declaration, more an accusation than a challenge, initiated a contest destined to become one of the
meanest in the history of Ohio. But the campaign did more than that; it
generated a bitter personal feud between two of the state's political giants, a
feud that lasted long after the election itself faded from memory.

From the beginning, Bricker hammered Martin with charges of corruption involving shakedowns and an ill-gotten million-dollar slush fund.

Celebrating Governor Davey's 52nd birthday with Miss Ohio at the Great Lakes Exposition, Cleveland, Ohio, July 25, 1936. Evangeline Davey Smith Collection, Martin L. Davey Papers, Kent State University Libraries, Special Collections and Archives.

Anyone who knew Martin L. Davey recognized that John W. Bricker was now in for the political fight of his life. When in good humor, Martin could be petulant and pugnacious; when in bad humor, he was mean, vengeful, and utterly unforgiving. Yet among friends he was absolutely charming. On one occasion, at a Columbus rally during the middle of the campaign, he delayed his speech until he had personally greeted several hometown supporters from Kent. After seeing to their comfort, Martin insisted that after his address they ride with him to a private dinner at Columbus's Neil House.[6]

His local newspaper, the *Ravenna-Kent Evening Record and Daily Courier-Tribune,* described him as a "master showman," acutely aware of the art of keeping his name on the public's lips. Even after he left the governorship, he mailed Christmas cards to nearly 180,000 people. Ever the cultivator of image, he dressed meticulously, drawing from an extensive wardrobe he carried even on trips. And, whenever traveling on official business, he squealed off in sleek automobiles, accompanied by two State Highway Patrol motorcycles, sirens screaming.[7]

Bricker paled next to his flamboyant opponent. While Martin strutted like a barnyard rooster, Bricker was subdued. Martin, with his slick pompadour and sartorial resplendency, had the look of a speakeasy owner; Bricker, with a shock of white hair and mild temperament, appeared courtly, even presidential. His friends, and some foes, called him "Honest John." No one ever called his opponent honest anything. And, while Martin enjoyed fast cars and motorcycle escorts, Bricker eschewed them. Once, during Bricker's second term as governor, his chauffeur followed a motorcycle policeman onto the grounds of the Ohio State Fair. When the escort hit his siren and flashed his lights, the crowds parted, leaving a path for the governor's car. Embarrassed by it all, Bricker ordered his driver to turn away from the throng. The police motorcycle continued ahead, clearing the way for no one.[8]

Bricker may have been less showy than Martin, but he too knew the art of politics. Capitalizing on Martin's widespread unpopularity in the press, he opened the campaign with a radio broadcast from Cincinnati, trumpeting how many newspapers, including several traditionally Democratic, were calling for Martin's defeat. That was true even for the *Cleveland Plain Dealer,* which Bricker pointed out had for the past ninety-one years endorsed Democrats for governor. The press's animosity toward Martin was understandable, Bricker claimed, because "they [the press] are the first to detect hypocrisy in public officials . . . [,] and they know that the hope for honest, efficient and good government in Ohio demands the present governor's defeat."[9]

Nothing energized Martin more than an attack on his integrity, and Bricker's broadcast had done exactly that. If his opponent chose to harp on Martin's unpopularity in the press, he would return the favor by claiming that Bricker was the lapdog of Harry P. Wolfe, the anti-Davey publisher of the *Columbus Dispatch* and the *Ohio State Journal.* Never one to mince words when affronted, Martin claimed that Wolfe owned Bricker "body and soul." "He controls my opponent," Martin said, "just as completely as though he had a ring in his nose." It was Wolfe, Martin claimed, who told Bricker he could not run for governor in 1934 but could do so in 1936. Wolfe's influence was so vast, Martin contended, that he and a few other Republican bosses had engineered Bricker's uncontested nomination as the party's standard bearer in 1936. Wolfe's "ownership" of Bricker, Martin asserted, was the "most important issue" in the race.[10]

Later in the campaign, Martin broadened his charges. Bricker was not simply in Wolfe's pocket but was also beholden to several political bosses who would collect their IOUs after they maneuvered their man into the governorship. Heading the list of those bosses were Martin's old Cuyahoga County nemesis, Maurice Maschke, and Edward Schorr of Cincinnati, the state Republican chairman. Such men, Martin contended, cared nothing about the public good, and Bricker would let them have their way because he was a "first-class yes-man."[11]

Martin's accusations rang hollow because he had one of the most questionable alliances in Ohio politics himself—with Francis Poulson, the Ohio Democratic Party chairman. Nothing involving Martin L. Davey passed unnoticed on Poulson's watch, particularly where fund-raising was concerned. Bricker claimed that Poulson was the power behind the governor's throne and extracted kickbacks for the Davey political machine from every contractor, supplier, and liquor dealer doing business with the state. In a series of addresses in Cleveland four days before the election, the Republican predicted that disgusted Ohioans would boot out of office the "two princes of public plunder."[12]

Certainly Bricker's charges were politically motivated, but Ohioans had only to examine the governor's record to recognize his instinct for politicizing any bureau, department, or commission. That instinct had mobilized Harry Hopkins in the Ohio relief crisis of 1935, which Bricker was only too happy to recall three weeks before the election. While Martin wanted to saturate Ohio's relief system with his own hacks, Bricker promised a network operated by employees protected by civil service. That would undo the patronage that sustained Martin's political machine and end his "miserable failure" in relief.[13]

Martin now recognized that John Bricker was no Clarence Brown. His Republican foe was intelligent, resourceful, and even cunning. The challenger had cleverly set several brushfires that Martin had to douse, keeping him constantly on the defensive. Not even Martin's School Foundation Bill was immune to Bricker's assault. He savaged that high point of Martin's first term because it fell $12 million short of funding Ohio's ailing schools and jeopardized the whole system.[14]

Martin was clever enough to anticipate Bricker's criticism, but he had to hedge to do so. The governor told a packed house in Lima's Allen County Memorial Hall that the school deficit could be easily covered by shifting some state monies to cover the shortage, and soon Ohio's economy would improve and allow extra revenues to be directed to the schools. Bricker's plans for Ohio schools, Martin averred, paralleled Kansas governor (and 1936 Republican presidential candidate) Alf Landon's. Kansas's school system under Landon was one of the nation's worst, Martin claimed, with schoolteachers earning a niggardly $25 a month. But what else could one expect from a state that provided eighty-four cents for each of its students? Even that eighty-four cents, Martin reminded his audience, came from a dog license tax![15]

Martin knew he had to take the offensive in the campaign and spared nothing in doing so. In mid-October, as Bricker campaigned in northwestern Ohio, he learned that Davey operatives had circulated letters charging that he wanted blacks driven out of the Republican Party. Fuming over the accusation, Bricker challenged the authors to "come out into the open." The letters were "lying and cowardly," and he immediately blamed Martin and Poulson for instigating them.[16]

Race-baiting, even in a heated campaign, was despicable, but Martin was in the political fight of his life against a man who had become more an enemy than a mere political rival. Consequently, he was willing to use every ploy to win in November, and his political ingenuity and capacity for scheming seemed boundless, particularly after he ordered Davey Tree Expert Company trucks to haul four tons of addressograph plates containing the names and addresses of sales tax vendors from the state sales tax office in Columbus to Davey Tree offices in Cleveland. He now had at the ready full lists of people who could be hit with a final-hour electioneering pitch. Upon hearing the news, Bricker, speaking in several Cleveland wards, said that the thieving governor had sunk to a new low.[17]

Martin's tactics indicated that he was in deep political trouble. However, he had another card to play. In his speeches, he had again been linking his political fortunes to Franklin D. Roosevelt's. Most Americans expected Roosevelt to sweep to victory in November, and no one could better benefit from his wide coattails than Martin L. Davey. This was especially true in 1936 because Ohio's presidential and state tickets were printed on a single ballot. Voters would have to make a special effort to split their tickets between president and governor, and many erroneously feared that doing so would negate their votes for Roosevelt, a concern that Martin capitalized on during the campaign.[18]

Martin's marriage to the president was no eleventh-hour strategy; he had plotted it long in advance. At the Democratic nominating convention in June, Martin delivered the Ohio speech seconding Roosevelt's nomination, and an impressive speech it was, bringing thousands to their feet in Philadelphia's Convention Hall.[19]

Martin did not stop there. When the fall campaign opened, he continued to tie himself to Roosevelt. His critics wondered how a governor who swore out an arrest warrant against the president's alter ego, Harry Hopkins, could now embrace the national administration. Martin responded: "It was not necessary to approve everything . . . to support a man for high public office." All one had to do was recall his "high percentage of good results."[20]

Martin Davey seconding Franklin D. Roosevelt's nomination in Philadelphia, June 1936. Evangeline Davey Smith Collection, Martin L. Davey Papers, Kent State University Libraries, Special Collections and Archives.

Although it took no special genius to recognize the wisdom of Martin's strategy, he had to be applauded for turning a huge liability, the bitter feud with Hopkins, into an asset, an apparent healing of the breach with Roosevelt. When the gubernatorial campaign began, Martin was a certain loser; now, with only a week to go, he and Bricker were neck and neck. The Republicans knew they were in trouble, and Martin made the best of it. Lamenting the president's immense popularity, one Republican commented that he would like to see Bricker run for governor when "Santa Claus" (Roosevelt) did not head the opposition ticket.[21]

The president was stronger than the governor everywhere in Ohio. The *Cleveland Plain Dealer* speculated that Roosevelt would have to carry the state by at least 150,000 votes for Martin to win; the president's margin in 1932 was less than 75,000. Martin was certain that Roosevelt's majority would be closer to 250,000, and he would "not be far behind."[22]

That prediction was largely preelection bluff. The Roosevelt edge might well be considerably less than Martin's deliberately inflated speculation. Consequently, Martin continued his chicanery to the end. On election day itself, November 3, Republican precinct workers in Cincinnati received tele-

grams from Columbus telling them to "forget Bricker and Landon and concentrate on county candidates." The telegrams were signed "Ed Shore," an
obvious misspelling of the name of Ed Schorr, the Republican state chairman. Despite understandable Republican suspicions, there was no provable
link between Martin and the spurious wires; they had been sent by a "mys-
terious stranger." Bricker and Schorr immediately denounced the telegrams
as forgeries. With the election still in doubt, Davey strategists were certainly
capable of such bold-faced trickery.[23]

Those last-minute machinations proved superfluous. Roosevelt swept
to a massive popular and electoral majority, carrying Ohio by more than
600,000 votes. Martin, riding on the president's broad coattails, beat
Bricker by 127,000. The governor's win was comfortable, but, considering
the enormity of the president's victory, it was disappointing. However, the
Democrats elected twenty-two of Ohio's twenty-four congressmen and captured huge majorities in both houses of the state legislature. The results were
similar at the national level. The House of Representatives went Democratic
334–89, and so did the Senate, 75–17. No party had ever before experienced
such an utter triumph. The Democrats so dominated the Capitol that some
of them had to sit on the Republican side of the aisle. But Bricker had run
three hundred thousand votes ahead of Alf Landon, meaning thousands of
Ohioans had split their tickets.[24] The implication was clear: Had Roosevelt
not roared through Ohio, Martin would have lost. The governor's success
was not really his own; it was the president's.

Strangely, Martin's victory was a defeat and Bricker's defeat was a victory.
The governor's was clearly a descending star while Bricker's stock was soaring. His remarkable showing against the Democratic landslide of 1936 promised every success for 1938, while Martin was essentially damaged goods with
an uncertain future. A subdued Martin L. Davey on January 11, 1937, swore
his second gubernatorial oath before Ohio chief justice Carl V. Weygandt,
this time in a quiet ceremony in the executive office at the statehouse.[25]

Martin had little time to brood. On the Thursday after his inauguration,
hard rains hit the southwestern part of the state. Cincinnatians and residents
of surrounding areas warily eyed the rising waters of the Ohio River and its
tributaries, the Miami, Little Miami, and Licking. W. C. Devereaux, a U.S. me-
teorologist, warned that Cincinnati would flood as waters from the engorged
tributaries rushed into the already-swollen Ohio. Concurrently, smaller rivers upstate, including Columbus's Scioto, overflowed their banks, flooding
lowlands all along the way. The prediction of temperatures in the teens, however, promised a cessation of the rain and an end to the flooding.[26]

The cold weather did not eventuate, temperatures remained in the forties, and the rains continued, although not so hard. Devereaux, his fears resurfacing, forecast that the Ohio would rise two feet at Cincinnati in the next few days. Other towns along the river began closing schools, boarding up stores, and moving factory machinery to higher ground as floodwaters rushed into their low-lying streets. All the way from Charleston, West Virginia, to St. Louis, Missouri, Greyhound busses started making detours as the flood moved into the Mississippi Valley. Crews from the Cincinnati Street Railway Company worked through most of Monday night, January 18, to lay 800 feet of emergency track above flooded railroad lines in the city.[27]

Pittsburgh, Pennsylvania, and Wheeling, West Virginia, which, along with cities in southern Ohio, had suffered $200 million in flood damage just the previous March, were hit again, along with Cincinnati's suburbs across the river in Kentucky. The Red Cross, American Legion, and numerous other groups began rescuing thousands of stranded families and moving them to higher ground. From Washington, D.C., Harry Hopkins promised WPA help to thousands of beleaguered families in Ohio, Kentucky, and Pennsylvania.[28]

The Ohio General Assembly responded, too, with $250,000 for immediate relief for the southern part of the state. In both houses, the vote was unanimous and needed only the governor's signature to go into effect. Martin, in the meantime, had already left Columbus for Cincinnati to survey the damage. What he saw and the reports he received were discouraging. One hundred thousand were already homeless, and eleven Ohioans had died in the flood. Pneumonia and scarlet fever epidemics had hit Indiana, and Louisville, Kentucky, was already under martial law when Martin reached Cincinnati at 8 A.M. on Monday, January 25. He settled in at the Parkview Hotel, ate a quick breakfast, met with local officials at City Hall, and began his inspection by crossing over a long suspension bridge linking Cincinnati with northern Kentucky. Rising waters on the Kentucky side nearly prevented him from returning to Cincinnati. At Red Cross headquarters, the governor promised National Guard help in getting fresh water to Cincinnatians who desperately needed it. Meanwhile, he ordered state sanitary engineers and health department nurses and doctors to flood-stricken areas, and the State Highway Department rushed two hundred trucks and a small army of workers to keep open the roads into Cincinnati. Tired but confident that he had done all he could in so short a time, the governor returned for a second meeting with Cincinnati's mayor and city manager, and ate dinner with national guardsmen at the local armory before returning to Columbus late that night to sign the emergency flood appropriation bill.[29]

Martin Davey inspects the Cincinnati flood, January 1937. Evangeline Davey Smith Collection, Martin L. Davey Papers, Kent State University Libraries, Special Collections and Archives.

By Tuesday, January 26, everything seemed well in hand. The floodwaters were beginning to recede, the threat of rain abated, and the worst was over. Martin knew, however, that more had to be done. Ohio had already endured two devastating floods prior to this one—one in 1913 and another in 1936. Adjacent Indiana and Pennsylvania and nearby Illinois had suffered similarly, so Martin telephoned their governors to determine their interest in advancing a plan for federal help in the flood-prone Ohio Valley. All three heartily approved, which Martin on February 1, 1937, reported to an equally enthusiastic Charles West, undersecretary of the interior, in Columbus. West left for Washington that night promising to take up the matter with President Roosevelt.[30]

West was not the only Washington official interested in helping. Martin's old bête noire, Harry Hopkins, promised WPA help in planning long-term solutions for southern Ohio's flooding problems. Setting aside their personal differences, Martin called Hopkins's gesture "the best news we have heard yet." The WPA director responded at least partially in kind: "The people of Ohio were doing a 'fine job' of meeting the emergency." The praise may not have been directed specifically at Martin, but not even the flinty Hopkins could ignore the governor's role in dealing with the disaster. Many southern Ohio communities responded by constructing massive floodwalls with gates that could be closed to hold off the Ohio River and its tributaries when they overflowed. The floodwalls were no absolute assurance against repetition of the 1937 flooding, but they minimized the devastation that swollen rivers could wreak.[31]

In some respects, the floods were one of Martin's easier problems. They were temporary, could be dealt with, and allowed him to exercise executive leadership, appearing almost heroic in the process. The more mundane task of providing relief monies for Ohio's unemployed, however, perpetually vexed Martin, particularly because the rural-dominated state legislature, largely insensitive to continuing unemployment in Ohio's cities, persisted in denying the governor sufficient funds to deal with the problem once and for all. Ohio's unemployment, thanks to a revivified economy and massive federal public works programs, was not so bad as it had been in the early thirties. But in 1937, about a half million Ohioans still depended on the state's dole.

Martin had contributed to Ohio's relief problem by adhering to his 1936 campaign promise of no new taxes. However, when it became obvious that the state could not provide for Ohio's needy, the governor urged legislators to increase relief appropriations. They refused.[32]

"Fine," said the governor, and then threatened to order the National Guard into struggling Cuyahoga, Lucas, and Summit counties to feed the poor. The prospect of uniformed troops setting up soup kitchens in Cleveland, Toledo, and Akron was too much for many Ohioans, who ridiculed the governor's preposterous plan. Preposterous or not, Martin's bluster worked. Angry but beaten legislators in November met in special session and appropriated $17 million to finance relief for 1938 and the remainder of 1937.[33]

Little did Martin know that 1937 would be a year of crises that not only challenged his ingenuity but also threatened his political future. Even though he was unaware at the time, some of his trouble began hundreds of miles away from Columbus in Flint, Michigan. Around Christmastime 1936, thousands of autoworkers at the General Motors plant in Flint, protesting wages, working conditions, and demanding collective bargaining between their United Auto Workers union and GM management, suddenly stopped working. They did not walk off the job; they simply sat alongside their machinery and refused to budge. Their bosses were dumbfounded. When they tried to bring in strikebreakers, the "sit-downers" repulsed them. Then, taking advantage of Michigan's brutal winter weather, the bosses turned off the heat; the strikers built bonfires. At management's urging, police stormed the factory; the protesters beat them back. From a safer distance, officers fired in tear gas; the strikers smashed windows to let in fresh air. When the police charged again, the autoworkers used the factory's own fire hoses to repel them.[34]

Confronted by a liberal Democrat, Frank Murphy, in the Michigan governorship, and a prolabor administration in Washington, D.C., GM surrendered in early 1937. Emboldened by its success, the UAW struck Chrysler Motors shortly after and triumphed there as well. When the Ford Motor Company, the last of the "Big Three," capitulated to the union in 1941, labor was three for three in the American automobile industry.[35]

The United Auto Workers union was an affiliate of the Committee of Industrial Organizations led by John L. Lewis, who had worked his way up through the ranks as a young turk in the United Mine Workers union.[36] By 1934, with the initial blessing (later recanted) of the American Federation of Labor, Lewis took unionization in a different direction by organizing separate industries instead of specific trades as the AFL had done since the days of Samuel Gompers.

The steel industry was next. In 1936, Lewis established the Steel Workers Organizing Committee, with Philip Murray as its chairman, and charged the group with unionizing America's half million steelworkers, a task made somewhat easier by the 1935 passage of the National Labor Relations Act, or, as it was better known, the Wagner Act.[37]

Lewis and the CIO struck gold on March 2, 1937. Through the delicate cultivation of a friendship with Myron Taylor, chairman of the board of U.S. Steel, Lewis negotiated a contract with the industrial giant. Taylor may have been susceptible to Lewis's blandishments, but he was still no fool. Lewis's cause was aided by not-so-subtle hints from Great Britain that war was looming in Europe, and the British wanted no interruption of their supplies of American steel. With the prospect of lucrative deals hanging in the balance, the last thing Taylor wanted was a strike. Independent steel manufacturers were stunned. Taylor was a turncoat who had made it worse for them. They knew what was coming—since "Big Steel" had rolled over for John L. Lewis and his CIO, "Little Steel" was next. Tom Girdler, chairman of the board of Republic Steel and rabidly antiunion, took the lead in denouncing the U.S. Steel contract and became the independent steel manufacturers' spokesman.[38]

The sixty-year-old Girdler was born in Silver Creek Township in rural Indiana, a place so "country" that everybody called it Silver "Crick." The nearest town was Sellersburg, with three hundred inhabitants, four stores, one of them a grocery, a flour mill, and two saloons. Girdler's family owned a cement plant, where teenaged Tom had a summer job moving heavy bags of cement on a handcart. The work was hard but not so arduous as that of the laborer filling the bags. This poor man had to bounce the bags once or twice to ensure they were full from top to bottom, stack them, two vertically and two horizontally, and then tilt them onto Tom's cart. Even with the easier job, the cement dust caked in Girdler's nostrils, coated his lips, and burned his skin.[39]

Girdler never escaped the memory of that summer in "cement hell" and believed that the toil had been good for his soul. If hard work had made him a better man, what was wrong in expecting the same from others? What he failed to recognize was that because of who he was he got to pull the cart after it was hand-loaded by the poor ox not fortunate enough to be a Girdler. Interestingly, too, even though Girdler believed that his was just a typical hardworking midwestern family, his parents had a servant, a German girl, who performed most of the Girdlers' mundane tasks.[40] Not too many typical hardworking midwestern families could afford hired help. Whether he recognized it or not, Tom Girdler grew up as a child of at least moderate privilege and consequently could not later in life empathize with the men who daily hoisted, stoked, and poured inside the noisy mills of Republic Steel until their backs finally gave out. Even more so, Tom Girdler in the spring of 1937 was not about to let John L. Lewis and the CIO tell him and the other Little Steel bosses how to run their companies. Together, Little Steel refused to negotiate anything.

The union had but a single weapon—a shutdown. On May 26, 1937, Philip Murray called a strike for 11 P.M. against Republic, Inland, and Youngstown Sheet and Tube. At Canton, Ohio, five hundred pickets, many armed with clubs, and 250 at nearby Massillon lined up to turn away the midnight shift. Eleven thousand workers in the two cities were officially off the job.[41]

Girdler referred to the strikers as a "mob" and suspected they were stirred up by outside agitators. He sent an eight-page message to his Republic workers, explaining the company's position. Wages and hours, he knew, were not the reasons for the strike. The CIO merely wanted to bring the independent steel operators to their knees by forcing them to sign a contract with the union. Once that happened, Girdler was certain that John L. Lewis and Philip Murray would then push for the closed shop and checkoff system. The former would prevent anybody who was not already a member of the union from getting a job with Little Steel, and the latter would compel the companies to collect union dues from each of Little Steel's fifty-nine thousand employees.[42] In essence, the companies would be doing the union's bookkeeping.

It was only a matter of time before tempers flared on both sides. In Canton, Franklin P. Manly, a Republic foreman, was shot in the legs and hand at the company's main gate. In Warren, Ohio, three workers said they were beaten by company police at midnight as they tried to leave their shifts, and three other men almost drowned when, to avoid pickets, they swam across the Mahoning River to get to their jobs.[43]

Two airplanes attempting to drop food to stranded workers in the Warren plant were fired on and circled away. Brick fights broke out between strikers and nonstrikers, and intermittent gunshots were heard everywhere. In Mentor, Ohio, near Cleveland, word circulated that armed men were guarding Girdler's home.[44] Just when it seemed as if things could not get much worse, terrible news came in from Chicago.

On Memorial Day, trouble erupted during a "peaceful" parade of strikers outside the city's Republic Steel plant. When the crowd failed to disperse upon police command, the pushing and shoving started. When it was over, ten marchers lay dead. Initially the public sided with the authorities against what local newspapers described as a "well-trained revolutionary cadre." Only later did a congressional investigation show that the police had instigated the deadly violence.[45]

Well-founded rumors spread that company foremen themselves were armed, and reporters began to hound Girdler, wanting to know when Republic officials had transformed their factories into mini-arsenals. The answer was, "for some time," but only for the "protection of property and employees." Almost all owners did it, he said, to prevent violence and theft.[46]

Alarmed by the escalating violence, Martin met with Girdler and three other steel officials in Columbus to talk. Afterward, he had nothing to say to reporters about their conversations. Pickets continued to circle Girdler's home and Republic headquarters in downtown Cleveland, and the Mahoning County sheriff wanted to outlaw the sale of beer and hard liquor in Youngstown.[47]

Violence in Youngstown did not need to be fueled by alcohol. Angry strikers beat two police officers, a striker was shot in the thigh, and fourteen pickets were jailed after taking a heavy dose of tear gas during a clash with police and sheriff's deputies.[48] Martin's meeting with company and union officials, scheduled for June 11 at the executive mansion, took on a new urgency.

Girdler declined Martin's invitation because the union had no legitimate cause. It demanded neither better pay nor improved working conditions; its sole purpose was to force Republic Steel and the other Independents to sign a CIO contract. There were no other issues; the dispute was nothing more than a contest of wills that John L. Lewis and his union were going to lose. As a concession to the governor, Girdler said J. A. Voss, Republic's director of industrial relations, with "full authority" to act on the chairman's behalf, would attend.[49] Girdler refused to sit at the same conference table with CIO representatives lest his mere presence give them an undeserved legitimacy.

The two sides met at the governor's mansion at 2:30 on Friday afternoon and worked until 12:40 Saturday morning with only an 8 P.M. break for a dinner of steak and sturgeon. Martin had drafted a seven-point formula that he believed gave something to both sides, including a union promise that it would not demand a closed shop or the hated checkoff system. Philip Murray of the Steel Workers Organizing Committee and his fellow unionists were ready to sign, but Voss (certainly acting under the strict orders of his boss) and the representatives of the other steel company at the meeting, Youngstown Sheet and Tube, refused to sign any agreement recognizing the union.[50] The meeting ended with the two sides as far apart as ever.

Exasperated by the stubbornness of Girdler and Frank Purnell, president of Youngstown Sheet and Tube, Martin tried again. He invited both men to another meeting in Columbus. No union officials would be there, he promised. He just wanted to hear directly why the two steel chiefs refused to sign any union contract. Both Girdler and Purnell wired the governor that "urgent engagements" elsewhere forced them to decline his invitation.[51]

Although hesitant to do so, Martin, recognizing that the steel dispute was beyond his power to resolve, sent a long telegram to President Roosevelt, asking for help. The president was well aware of events in Ohio but had refrained from intervening for the obvious reason that the strike was essentially the state's problem. But his political instincts also told him to stay out. The New Deal was clearly a friend to labor—everybody knew that. However, Roosevelt also recognized that his bitterest critics saw little difference between how New Dealers operated out of Washington, D.C., and how Soviet apparatchiks ran things from Moscow. The CIO had accepted Communists into its ranks, and now, during the heat of battle, it was too easy for the union's enemies to denounce it as a subversive "Red" auxiliary.[52] No matter his enormous electoral triumph the previous fall, the president did not even want to appear "pink," let alone red.

Still, the problems in Ohio could not be ignored. The president conferred with his secretary of labor, Frances Perkins, and then announced the creation of a three-man Federal Mediation Board, composed of Charles P. Taft, a Cincinnati lawyer; Lloyd K. Garrison, dean of the University of Wisconsin law school; and Edward F. McGrady, assistant secretary of labor. The board left immediately for Cleveland to hear both sides of the labor dispute and act as an arbitrator if asked.[53]

The Federal Mediation Board set up headquarters on the tenth floor of the Hollenden Hotel and scheduled separate meeting times on Monday, June 21, for the leading actors on both sides, John L. Lewis and Philip Murray at 9 A.M., and Tom Girdler, Frank Purnell, Eugene G. Grace, president of Bethlehem Steel, and Wilfred Sykes, assistant to the president of Inland Steel, at eleven.[54] The steel bosses may have refused to sit across from their union foes, but at least the federal mediation team had gotten them into the same hotel.

The union side appeared happier. Lewis, who could break an opponent with one of his fiery stares, joked with Murray and reporters even though he was bothered by a cold. He was ready to sign almost any agreement with the Independents. They, on the other hand, steadfastly refused to commit to anything. Their stubbornness was not surprising. Despite their cultivated graciousness, all the operators shared Girdler's opinion that the meetings were useless. To Girdler and the others, the mediation board had nothing to mediate because there was nothing to discuss. Girdler also felt that he and his cohorts were unfairly regarded as the "villains" in the strike. Moreover, Taft, Garrison, and McGrady, their pro-labor sympathies camouflaged but still evident, were, in Girdler's words, supporting "something [the labor movement] as vaporous and as deadly as poison gas."[55] He and the others had shown up in Cleveland just to mollify the president. They were closed to anything he or his mediation board would ever propose, and they would certainly never sit in the same room with John L. Lewis, Philip Murray, or any other union spokesman.

The steel men had something else in mind—strike or no strike, they were going to reopen their closed plants. That decision, combined with the failure of the Federal Mediation Board, was certain to precipitate violence, particularly in already overheated Mahoning and Trumbull counties. Martin could not let that happen. On June 22, 1937, the governor declared that he was sending the National Guard to Youngstown and Warren. To avoid even the appearance of partiality, Martin ordered the troops to keep open the steel plants that were still operating and keep closed those that were not. He followed that with a letter to state adjutant general Emil F. Marx explaining that the state could no longer shirk its "sovereign powers and its responsibility" and urging the National Guard commander to carry out his charge with "fidelity, calmness, impartiality, and firmness."[56]

Martin added Stark County to the list when he decided that the Republican mayor of Canton, James Seccombe, could not control violence there. The angry mayor snapped back that the governor was "playing politics" at Canton's expense. Everything was fine in the city; the strike-related violence that prompted Martin's order occurred outside Canton, beyond Seccombe's purview.[57] The troops went in anyway.

Martin's problems escalated after the Federal Mediation Board meetings collapsed. Girdler and the other bosses walked out, and, when asked by reporters whether he would return, the Republic Steel chairman, in a sneering reference to Roosevelt, responded, "The Great White Father hasn't asked me." Martin had tried to placate both sides in his original order to the National Guard, hoping that they might work out an agreement. With the discussions over, Martin could no longer play Solomon, and on June 24 he ordered the National Guard to allow willing workers ingress to the steel plants, closed or not. The "right to work is sacred," said the governor. "The right to strike is equally valid," he added, but those who wanted to return to work had every right to do so. Within days, thousands of steelworkers, under the watchful eyes of nervous national guardsmen, filed through factory gates to work twelve-hour shifts in Canton, Massillon, Youngstown, and Warren. There was no trouble. One month after it began, the strike was over. Little Steel had won; John L. Lewis and the CIO had lost. Public opinion, which, because of management's stubbornness had at first sided with labor, had, after the violence, swung in the opposite direction. Even many striking steelworkers were glad it was over and reluctantly agreed with anti-unionists that CIO really stood for "Collapsed in Ohio."[58]

The CIO asked the U.S. District Court in Columbus for an injunction against Martin's use of the National Guard, but that was an empty gesture that went nowhere. More troublesome were seven hundred angry CIO loyalists who descended on the statehouse to confront the governor. Martin invited representatives of the group inside to talk under less threatening conditions. His hands were tied, he explained. Frances Perkins had asked him to use his subpoena power to force Girdler and the other steel company executives into discussions with union officials, but that, he suggested, was tantamount to kidnapping. Girdler and the others were stubborn men, yet his subpoena powers could not be stretched that far.[59]

There was no political advantage in any of this for Martin. Rural Ohioans generally distrusted unions, and John L. Lewis, with his furry Neanderthal brow, reminded them of the scary European anarchists supposedly responsible for every American labor problem since Haymarket Square. So Martin scored some points there. At the same time, he lost support in big cities where unionism was on the rise. Either way, he made new enemies. In Washington, Roosevelt, disgusted both by the steel operators' intransigence and labor's new haughtiness, summarized the feelings of many Americans as he washed his own hands of the affair. "A plague on both your houses," he declared.[60]

Even as the steel strike wound down that summer, more trouble was brewing for the governor, this time in the Democratically controlled state Senate. Early in his first term, several Senate Democrats supported Martin, particularly during the relief dispute with Harry Hopkins. However, as the governor continued to politicize the state bureaucracy and retaliate against anyone who called him on it, that support evaporated. Six months into his second term, eighteen Senate Democrats allied with five Republicans to create a formidable anti-Davey bloc in Ohio's upper house.

Those twenty-three, ardently committed to a "no new tax" program, assailed what they believed was the governor's profligate spending and began chopping his budget. They did so with such relish that they became known as the "hatchet men."[61] By early 1938, they were no longer interested in merely hacking away at the governor's appropriations, they wanted his scalp, too.

A bitter floor fight over a majority leader for 1937–38 sparked a new wave of anti-Daveyism that threatened the governor as never before. Paul Yoder, one of the "no new taxers," had to vacate the leadership post because he had been elected lieutenant governor. Still, he wanted to pass his mantle to someone equally opposed to Martin's tax-and-spend philosophy. However, the senators settled on Keith Lawrence, a Clevelander less antipathetic to the governor's spending. Behind the scenes, Martin had helped Lawrence.[62]

Had Martin stopped there, he might have avoided trouble, but once again his uncontrollable fighting instincts got the better of him. When the antitax bloc attacked the governor's budget during the new legislative session, he struck back hard, publicly denouncing its members for disrupting the state government out of sheer spite.[63]

Unintimidated by Martin's latest tirade, the hatchet men proposed a seven-man investigating committee to probe every nook and cranny of the governor's scandal-scarred administration. Directing and organizing everything from behind the scenes in late September 1937 was the new lieutenant governor of Ohio, Paul Yoder, from his home in Eaton in Preble County, which he nicknamed Hatchet Heights. Yoder planned publicity, assigned tasks, and offered his home as a headquarters for what was already looming as a legislative witch hunt. "Never put off until tomorrow what you can do to Davey," he urged a correspondent before closing with, "Yours for bigger and sharper hatchets."[64] Two weeks later, former governor George White received a cryptic letter on Cleveland Trust Company stationery. Its opening paragraph was tantalizingly vague: "The man who wanted to see a representative of yours called on me this morning. He has a big grouch against Davey and Poulson and desires some moral and material support in his controversy and thought you might be sympathetic." Interestingly, either the writer or the recipient underscored the word "material," clearly hinting at the unnamed subject's possible motivation.

The letter writer's third paragraph teased as well: "He is now burning with resentment and anxious to expose the nefarious conduct of his co-conspirators."[65] Martin L. Davey did not know it at the time, but the mystery man mentioned in that letter believed he had enough on the governor to bring him down.

Meanwhile, the hatchet men promised to scrutinize the highway department, liquor department, and civil service bureau, three state agencies where corruption was supposedly rampant. Rumors of kickbacks, padded employment rolls, forced political assessments and, in the case of the civil service department, blatant circumvention of the rules had dogged the governor from the beginning of his first term in 1935. Martin denounced the "character assassins" behind the inquiry and vetoed a $50,000 appropriation to fund it.[66]

To prove that he had nothing to hide, the governor chose six engineering professors, two each from Ohio State, Purdue, and Cleveland's Case Institute, to investigate his conduct of the state highway department. The governor's move did not deter the senators, whose legislative inquiry was formally approved by the upper house on December 20. J. Ralph Seidner of Youngstown introduced the resolution and was chosen to lead the investigation. James Metzenbaum, a Cleveland lawyer and former state senator, volunteered to act as legal counsel.[67]

Nothing energized Martin more than the prospect of a mean, drag-out fight. If the senators wanted a piece of him, they had better be prepared to sacrifice parts of their bodies as well. He requested time to air his side before the Senate but was denied. Undeterred, he got approval from the lower house to deliver what the press was already calling a "bombshell" message that would be simultaneously broadcast across the state on fourteen radio stations on January 3, 1938. A few days before his scheduled address, in a defiant and sarcastic gesture, he wired each state senator, asking him to attend. If the senators would not let him go to them, he would "invite" them to come to him. "I can assure you," he wrote, "that the subject matter will be interesting."[68] The snide invitation represented Martin Davey at his facetious best.

Tensions heightened on both sides a few days before Martin's appearance in the House chamber. The Senate investigating committee subpoenaed Francis Poulson to testify about what the press was already oxymoronically describing as "legal graft" in the Davey administration. Martin's alter ego was ordered to bring with him "all bank books, books of deposit, records of safety deposit boxes and vaults, books of account, records of receipts of funds, cash or other payments, records of income, copies of intangible tax returns, copies of federal tax returns, books of accounts, records of accounts and income from January 2, 1935 to December 1, 1937."[69] The Senate's excessive thoroughness stemmed from Poulson's reputation for evasiveness. Committee members wanted to make sure that their elusive quarry would not escape this time.

Some committee members suspected that Poulson, an attorney himself, might challenge the legality of the inquiry by ignoring the subpoena. But that was too simple a way out for Francis W. Poulson. He appeared before the committee on Monday, January 3, 1938, was sworn in, gave his name and age, "I hope to be fifty-one on May 12," and then was excused, not because the senators were suddenly uninterested in what he had to say, but because his mother had the misfortune of suffering a heart attack the previous Friday and was seriously ill under an oxygen tent in a Cleveland hospital.[70] Poulson, for more reasons than one, wanted to be by her bedside.

While Poulson "testified" in Columbus, Martin was finishing the most carefully prepared speech of his life. That evening at 7:15, with dozens of friends and loyal employees salted into the audience, the governor, escorted by two uniformed state highway patrolmen, mounted the speaker's rostrum in the packed House chamber, and one by one exposed several of the Senate hatchet gang for their own peccadilloes, many of which suggested that they should be the last to cast stones. Martin's revelation, for instance, about Senator William Boyd, who pled guilty to embezzlement charges in 1933 under his real name, William Boich, stunned almost everyone. J. Ralph Seidner, chairman of the Senate investigating committee, was singled out, too, for inexplicably demanding the pardon of a notorious Youngstown convict serving time in the state penitentiary.[71]

A lot of skeletons rattled out of closets that night. Most of the governor's charges against the senators could be explained away, but there was no doubt that Martin Davey enjoyed punching back. Most of the "victims" held their tongues until interviewed after the address, but an apoplectic George Morris twice shouted "liar" when Martin accused him of demanding the firing of an Education Department employee in return for supporting the governor's program.[72]

Paul Yoder suffered a fair share of abuse in the governor's speech as did the CIO, lobbyists who "infested" Columbus, and the *Cleveland Plain Dealer, Akron Beacon Journal,* and other Ohio newspapers that out of sheer meanness had unfairly turned Martin L. Davey into their personal whipping boy. But of all those excoriated that night, the most intriguing was an unnamed, self-righteous lawyer from Cincinnati who desperately wanted to be Ohio's next governor. Dubbed "Mr. X" by the *Columbus Dispatch,* there was no doubt that Martin's anonymous Pecksniff was Charles Sawyer.[73]

When he finished, Martin, with a state trooper guarding either flank, stepped from the rostrum, a weary but triumphant smile on his face. He strode right past some of the men he had just moments earlier enraged and embarrassed, glancing neither right nor left, until he exited the House chamber. Once again he had shown up his enemies. How many times would they have to test him before they realized they had more than met their match? Martin loved the fleeting satisfaction that accompanied "getting even," but very little good came of it. The governor's petulance made good press but bad politics. He believed that his Monday night diatribe set the record straight and wounded his enemies, but all it did was sabotage his second term and allow Republicans to smile even more over their political prospects in 1938.

The Senate investigation continued, uncovering among the more than twenty thousand state employees a few minor transgressions here and there, some for fudging time sheets, a handful for minor padding of expense accounts, and one for temporarily transferring two stenographers from their regular jobs in Columbus's Bureau of Motor Vehicles to Democratic headquarters to handle party mailings during the 1937 campaign.[74]

Although the investigators acted as if each revelation was a new Teapot Dome, their discoveries were only minor tempests in a very tiny teapot. All in all, it was hardly spectacular stuff. More cheating probably occurred during one of Warren G. Harding's notorious all-night White House poker games.

That all changed, or so the hatchet men thought, in February 1938, when the Senate investigation shifted to Cleveland to hear the testimony of one Lee Bradley, who claimed to "have the goods" on Martin L. Davey and Francis W. Poulson. Bradley was the unnamed Davey insider with the "big grouch" against the evil twins of Ohio politics, and he was eager to deliver their long overdue coups de grâce.

Bradley, born near Xenia, Ohio, in 1880, was by 1938 a sickly man weighing only 104 pounds after losing sixty-eight in the past year or so. In addition, he suffered from angina pectoris and was under a doctor's care. After graduating from high school in Dayton, Bradley job-hopped for years in the Midwest and East before finally settling in for several years with the Continental Motor Company in Muskegon, Michigan, where he began to dabble in politics by supporting Republican Chase Osborne's gubernatorial campaign.[75]

By the late 1920s he was back in Ohio, first in Toledo with the Ohio Machine Company, and then in Dayton, where he founded the Bradley Road Manufacturing Company, which made rubber road markers. By 1931, the company succumbed to the Great Depression, and Bradley was out of work, casting about to see what he could do. By chance he read a magazine article in which Martin Davey, then just a private citizen, supported the nomination of Newton D. Baker for president in 1932. Bradley wrote to Martin, explaining that the two of them were of like mind on Baker. Impressed by Bradley's letter, Martin telephoned him in Cleveland, where he was living at the time, and asked Bradley to drive to Kent to discuss their mutual hero. After several meetings over a span of weeks, Bradley convinced Martin that through his former business contacts he could generate considerable southern support for Baker. Martin put him on the Davey Tree Expert Company payroll, frequently paying him in cash.[76]

So far, Bradley's recollection of events jibed fairly well with Martin's, although Martin recalled that very little came of Bradley's efforts on Baker's behalf and that his expense accounts were "unusually high." Nothing yet, however, led Martin to believe that Bradley was anything other than what he purported to be, an enthusiastic supporter of Newton D. Baker for president. However, while Martin contended that he was interested in a Baker candidacy only because he thought Woodrow Wilson's secretary of war would be the best candidate in 1932, Bradley believed that Martin was primarily interested in finding a prominent Democrat upon whom he could fasten his own hopes for the governorship in 1934.[77]

By 1938, Bradley had been out of work for two years and was living on a "little nest egg" he had accumulated. Martin had discharged him in 1936, giving him his last paycheck through Poulson on June 17. Their relationship, according to Martin, had been essentially business, while Bradley contended it was strictly political, thinly disguised as business. Their parting was not amicable. Bradley believed that Martin owed him commissions for deals he had struck with General Motors, the Chrysler Corporation, and several other companies. Those deals, however, were not business transactions; they were, despite the cover of politeness by all concerned, nothing more than "shakedowns." Bradley, acting on Martin's behalf in March 1934, promised General Motors executive L. L. Tremper that when Martin won the governorship that fall, 50 percent of the state's auto and truck business (about $500,000 a year) would be given to General Motors if the company made a $25,000 "contribution" to the Kentite's campaign. Bradley's reward would be a healthy 10 to 35 percent commission on all General Motors vehicles bought by the state.[78]

This was exactly the kind of "dirt" the Senate investigators hoped to find when they queried their star witness on February 17, 1938, at Cleveland's Public Auditorium. Bradley fidgeted as he revealed detail after detail of meetings in Cleveland and New York hotels between Davey, Poulson, himself, and executives who were only too happy to do business with the state of Ohio in return for their support. Bradley assured the senators that he had letters and other documents (tucked away in a safety deposit box in Pittsburgh) that substantiated everything he said about the machinations of Martin L. Davey and Francis W. Poulson and their corporate coconspirators. Careful and edgy, at one point in the inquiry, Bradley checked a little black book for some facts and at another snapped at a photographer who took his picture.[79]

Martin and Poulson were never going to be mistaken for saints, but Lee Bradley did them one better. The night that "Damon" and "Pythias" were to leave for their postelection trip to Florida, they ate dinner with Bradley in Cleveland's Hollenden Hotel where Martin had a suite. Afterward, while Poulson answered a telephone call in another room, Bradley suggested to Martin that they work out with Chrysler the same deal that they had with General Motors. "Well," Martin said, "go ahead and see what you can do, but now, Lee, here is the arrangement. I want you and Frank [Poulson] to work together from now on. You go ahead and work this out [in] any way that is satisfactory to you two."[80]

As Bradley testified about that conversation, his lingering resentment was obvious. Envious because Martin and Poulson would soon be basking in the Florida sun, he jabbed the two: "Well this is December the 8th. You birds are going down to where the sun is shining. It is going to be a cold Christmas . . . don't you think you better toss a few in my lap?" Neither Martin nor Poulson had to guess what "toss a few in my lap" meant. Martin reached into his pocket and handed $500 to Bradley.[81] Suddenly the sun shone warm and bright on a December night in a Cleveland hotel—at least for Lee Bradley.

Bradley started negotiating with Chrysler officials but never got very far. Even though nothing materialized, he managed to wangle the company out of a brand-new Dodge sedan for himself, "the best Dodge made that year," he boasted to the investigating senators in Cleveland. When asked if he paid for the car, he responded as if insulted by the question: "I absolutely did not."[82] Shortly afterward, the committee adjourned so Bradley could catch a train for Pittsburgh to gather his "evidence" against Martin L. Davey and Francis W. Poulson.

Bradley's evidence, in the form of letters and telegrams between the participants in this sordid affair, proved that he had had frequent contact with them, but none of the documentation was a smoking gun linking Martin and Poulson to any illegality. Both men eluded their would-be Senate "executioners"—Poulson, by answering "I can't remember" to almost every question put to him by the investigating committee when he testified on January 12, 1938, and Martin, by filing perjury charges against Bradley in Cleveland Municipal Court, two days after his accuser's Public Auditorium appearance. The case was assigned to Judge Stanton Addams, who Bradley believed was too cozy with Martin. Bradley, in an affidavit of his own a few days later, requested a different judge.[83] The game of cat and mouse had begun, and Martin L. Davey had finally met his slippery match in a wizened con man long accustomed to surviving by his wits.

Still, life was not easy for Martin's latest nemesis. Understandably concerned about his safety after testifying against the governor, he complained about being watched to his attorney, Marvin C. Harrison, and to one of the interrogating senators. He worried, too, that harm might come to his family and in early March exiled himself to the Hollenden Hotel where he could be reached only by those who knew his room number, 564.[84]

The Senate investigation ground on through the end of February 1938. Other witnesses swore that Poulson's cronies got lucrative coal-purchasing contracts, and one of Martin's friends, John Nolan of Steubenville, Ohio, who did not own a single truck, nonetheless as a middleman received $143,000 from the state for transporting liquor to state stores. Still another witness, a highway department engineer, testified that Martin and Poulson, through "sweetheart" deals with pet contractors, paid far too much for road-paving materials. During the Davey-Poulson regime, the state supposedly had overpaid those contractors by $2 million in what the press quickly dubbed the "Hot Mix" scandal.[85]

The state Senate wanted to extend the inquiry, but the legislative session was to end on February 28, and it would take a two-thirds vote in both houses to stretch it into March. The House of Representatives, where Martin had more friends, refused to go along, much to the chagrin of the governor's Senate foes who loved every juicy tidbit they dredged up and wanted more. Though they lamented the end of their inquiry, they delighted in the Cuyahoga County grand jury's refusal to indict Lee Bradley on the perjury charges and savored the Davey-sanctioned professors' report that verified numerous hiring and financial improprieties in the State Highway Department. Martin survived what he called his "Russian Inquisition" and the calumnies of "one of the worst scalawags" he had ever met, Lee Bradley. There was, however, a significant casualty of the ordeal, the relationship between Martin and Francis Poulson. By April, the newspapers reported a rift between the two when Myrna Smith took over the collection of political assessments from state employees. Martin later announced that his old friend would not participate in the governor's bid for renomination. Poulson, of course, was stung by it all, but, like a good soldier, stood by his commander to the end.[86]

The hatchet men's report was damning, citing episode after episode of misfeasance and malfeasance, particularly in the highway and liquor departments. However, it offered scant proof of criminal wrongdoing. Instead, it was replete with statements such as, "there appears to be a general feeling that if political service is rendered to the administration, that is all that is really required," and "these [wasted] dollars could have gone to help the blind [and] the mentally defective."[87] Never in the history of American jurisprudence had anyone been fairly indicted on the grounds of a "general feeling" or because he was calloused to the plight of the "blind and mentally defective." Simply put, the Senate's report was not a bill of legal particulars; it was a screed that allowed Martin Davey's frustrated enemies to do with paper and pen what they could not do physically, pummel their hated foe until he cried "uncle." Knowing Martin L. Davey, there was fat chance of that.

Chapter Fifteen

Last Hurrah

―――――――――――――― ❦ ――――――――――――――

MARTIN L. DAVEY NEVER in his life shrank from a good fight. As a teen-ager, he had stood up to his father when the elder Davey snapped an order that Martin refused to obey. If he had the courage to defy his autocratic, spare-the-rod-and-spoil-the-child father, he could certainly muster the pluck to take on some feckless state senators who wanted his scalp. In fact, he relished the prospect of fighting back and was energized by it. If he had not already by early 1938 decided to run for a third gubernatorial term, the hatchet men sealed the deal. Retirement would mean his enemies had won.

Martin was closemouthed enough to keep his intentions secret, although his latest nemesis, Charles Sawyer, nearly got him to reveal his hand prema-turely. In early January 1938, just five days after Martin's eruption against his political foes on the Ohio House floor, the two men shared the spotlight in Columbus at the Democrats' Andrew Jackson Day dinner, an annual fete honoring the party's nineteenth-century progenitor. Although nearly ev-ery prominent Ohio Democrat was among the eight hundred packed into the Neil House ballroom, only Martin and U.S. commerce secretary Daniel C. Roper were scheduled to speak. Charles Sawyer was the most surprised man in the room when state party chairman Francis W. Poulson, hosting the event and sensitive to Sawyer's presence, asked him to address the crowd.

Had he been given fair warning, Sawyer might have been more circum-spect. What should have been a Democratic love feast (even if contrived) turned into a bloodletting as the Cincinnatian, without mentioning Martin by name, denounced the state administration for its graft and corruption.

"Hatred and suspicion" abounded in Columbus, and relationships with the national administration were strained at best and openly hostile at worst, he charged. Sounding like a candidate for governor even though he had not yet declared, Sawyer warned that unless things changed, Ohio Democrats were doomed in November.[1]

The atmosphere could not have been more tense had Sawyer spit in Martin's eye that January night. To his credit, the governor held back, ignoring as best he could the gauntlet Sawyer had thrown. Instead, he reviewed the accomplishments of his administration, lauded Franklin D. Roosevelt as one of the "most forward-thinking men on social problems," condemned Republicans for being out of step with the times, and then yielded the rostrum to Roper, who uttered a few banalities before the still-buzzing diners.[2]

A few days later, Martin, in an open letter, castigated Sawyer for his "bad manners" at the Jackson Day dinner. Sawyer's accusations, the governor stated, were "grossly unfair" and were not rebutted that very night because Martin "chose to observe the proprieties of the occasion [and] remain a gentleman." Sawyer was a "cowardly self-seeker" whose calumnies would leave "nothing but a trail of bitterness." He was a "poor sport," still licking his wounds from his loss to Martin in the Democratic gubernatorial primary in 1934, and he had betrayed his party because he (at least Martin claimed) had voted for John W. Bricker in 1936.[3] The consummate master of hyperbole, Martin condemned Sawyer for "stabbing him in the back with a poisoned dagger" and declared that his foe's low blow might force Martin to run again just to thwart Sawyer's "sordid, scheming selfishness." If the Cincinnatian wanted a fight, Martin promised to oblige.[4]

On the surface, it appeared that Sawyer indeed had been ungracious and ill-mannered at the Jackson Day dinner. But Martin failed to recognize that the Cincinnatian's diatribe was not unprovoked. Sawyer had been seething ever since Martin had attacked him, along with the hatchet men, only a few evenings earlier. Even though the governor had not mentioned Sawyer by name that night, no one had to stretch his imagination to know that he blamed the ambitious Cincinnatian for instigating the senate probe of Martin's administration. The way Sawyer saw it, Martin was the one who had thrown the first punch in their latest go-round.

Not to be outdone by Martin, Sawyer wrote his own open letter to the governor. In it he recounted their earlier friendship going back to their Oberlin College days and his unstinting support of Martin's political ambitions in the 1930s, even after the Kentite's mean-spirited attack against Sawyer's Procter and Gamble–connected wife during the 1934 primary campaign. Despite that "low blow" and contrary to Martin's most recent "lie," Sawyer did vote for him in 1934 and in 1936.[5]

Sawyer continued by listing the important Ohio Democrats Martin had alienated because of his meanness and venality, among them former governors James Cox, George White, and Vic Donahey, and current U.S. senator Robert J. Bulkley. Not even President Roosevelt escaped Martin's vitriol, according to Sawyer, much to the chagrin of Ohio Democrats who lamented the alienation of their party brethren in Washington, D.C.[6]

Sawyer's anger dominated his open letter, but even more damning was the unconcealed contempt he felt toward Martin. He lectured the governor as if he were a naughty schoolboy: "You talk a lot of nonsense about fights and punches, blows, etc. . . . As a matter of fact[,] I don't think you know much about fighting [at all]. The burdens of the governorship are getting you down. You must take care of yourself, old man." Sawyer concluded with a sneering P.S.—"I almost forgot to tell you in confidence that I will be a candidate for governor in the coming Democratic primary."[7]

Martin's enemies were ecstatic. The usually reserved, sophisticated Sawyer had given the governor a taste of his own medicine. The gloves were off, and there was no pretense of a contrived civility; Sawyer and Martin hated each other, and their upcoming contest would be not only political but personal as well. Martin wanted it that way and evidently his antagonist did too.

Martin had not yet formally declared for a third term, but Sawyer's sarcastic challenge could not be answered in any other way. In Steubenville, in late January, the governor told four hundred members of the Federated Democratic Women of Ohio that he was still undecided about entering the race, "but it [was] human nature to fight for something when someone tries to take it away."[8] Charles Sawyer and the state senators who were trying to topple him had been given fair warning. Martin Davey was coming back.

After enduring the brunt of the senate investigation in February 1938, Martin put his extraordinary organizational skills to work in anticipation of a third-term campaign. On April 4, hundreds of cheering supporters presented him with an eight-foot-high stack of petitions containing the signatures of a half million Ohioans who wanted the governor to run again. Frederick Pickens, business administrator of the State Old Age Pension Division, gave the petitions to Martin, who supposedly knew nothing about the massive volunteer effort on his behalf. Of course, no one believed that for even a second. Martin's feigned surprise was as sincere as his remark that he had not yet decided to run but after the enormous outpouring of support would "consider [doing so] very seriously."[9]

A day later, Martin formally announced his candidacy in Youngstown. The choice of venue was no accident. In typical Martin L. Davey style, the governor threw down his own gauntlet in the city to which he dispatched national guardsmen to preserve order in the Little Steel strike only months earlier. It was a nose-thumbing gesture aimed at his union critics, especially a craggy-browed son of a Welsh coal miner who thought that he and the CIO were more powerful than the governor of Ohio and even the president of the United States. The Youngstown showing was political theater at its best. Almost forgotten was Charles Sawyer, who had formally declared his candidacy six weeks earlier. That was understandable, though—his supporters had gotten only a paltry 120,000 signatures urging their man to run.[10]

By 1938, Martin had already endured so much criticism for his venality that he cared little about what his enemies might say or do. During the Harry Hopkins imbroglio of March 1935, Francis Poulson freely admitted that firms doing business with the state had been asked for contributions. Poulson's rationalization was simple: "If you can't get money from your friends, who can you get it from?" For Poulson, "friends" included state employees as well. Martin agreed with Poulson that those friends did not have to be voluntary. In the spring of 1938, the governor assessed each state worker 5 percent of his annual salary to finance his primary campaign. Employees may not have liked it, but they knew better than to squeal too loudly, and, although groups such as the Ohio League of Women Voters protested, the state Civil Service Commission received not a single complaint.[11] Silence, however, did not necessarily indicate assent. When Poulson defended the political levy before a thousand members of the Federated Democratic Women of Ohio in May, he was lustily booed, as was Martin himself when he rose to speak moments later. In what was an augury of things to come, Charles Sawyer, the mere challenger to the sitting governor, was cheered after every utterance.[12]

Like all incumbents, Martin was running against himself, or at least against his record. Any officeholder, from dogcatcher to president, inevitably made enemies along the way, and Martin, because of his testiness and pugnacity, had made more than most. And, since the summer of 1937, he had a formidable new foe, John L. Lewis and his CIO. Lewis wanted nothing more than to make Martin pay politically for sending in the National Guard to break the Little Steel strike.[13]

Martin knew that he would have to counter CIO opposition at every turn during his primary campaign. As a Democrat, he had always tried to befriend labor, although sometimes his experience as a businessman philosophically got in the way of that. He had to write off CIO support in 1938 but hoped that could be offset by help from the older, less militant American Federation of Labor. In a Cleveland address to 2,500 in May, he deliberately courted the AFL and tried to isolate the CIO from mainstream unionism by indicting Lewis's group for welcoming Communists into its ranks. "I'll let John Lewis take his Communists and see what he can do in patriotic Ohio, and I'll take my chances with the tried and true American Federation of Labor," he told the Clevelanders. When the governor said he was a friend of labor, he was booed, and a woman in the throng yelled, "That's a flowery statement, but it doesn't mean anything." "She must be a Communist," the governor retorted, drawing cheers from many.[14]

That Cleveland address set the tone for much of the rest of Martin's campaign. Wherever he spoke, the CIO invariably sent a contingent to heckle and rebut. In Toledo, he was jeered for fifteen minutes before police and his own bodyguards removed the troublemakers. Even during his speech, mean remnants here and there interrupted with boos and catcalls. Through it all, Martin kept his cool, but Myrna Smith, watching from the wings, later admitted that she was scared to death that the crowd would turn violent.[15]

The campaign was charged like no other. Grown men, public figures all, who should have known better, sank to the level of barroom toughs as they confronted one another on the hustings. At a Democratic rally in Fremont, Ohio, Harry Halper, a candidate for lieutenant governor, pummeled James Metzenbaum, another candidate for the office and counsel to the Senate investigating committee. Several men had to pull Halper off Metzenbaum and then continue to restrain him after the Cleveland lawyer accused Martin of orchestrating shakedown after shakedown since 1935. Martin, who had watched all this with as much amazement as anyone, worsened the situation by calling Metzenbaum a "little whippersnapper" and "the worst hypocrite in Ohio." Later that night, Charles Sawyer told his own crowd that if he were elected, he would be "a different kind of governor than Martin Davey."[16] No one who witnessed the embarrassing Fremont slugfest doubted that for even a moment.

Martin tried to restore some dignity to his campaign by highlighting his accomplishments. He was proud that he had used sound business principles in managing the state's finances and reminded an audience in Steubenville that he had balanced the budget without raising taxes, no small feat considering the incessant demands for school funding, relief, and old-age pensions.[17]

Unfortunately for Martin, such speeches were rare during the primary season of 1938. Far too often, plagued by CIO booing and heckling, the governor's appearances degenerated into circus sideshows, with Martin as the main attraction. Harried and desperate, he began to make bad decisions, the worst of which was asking Gerald L. K. Smith, a notorious racist, Jew-baiter and Huey Long acolyte, to stump for him late in the campaign. Burr Gongwer, the longtime Democratic boss of Cuyahoga County, was appalled that Martin had "disgraced the party" by allying himself with a man who "operate[d] in the sewers of race and religious prejudice."[18] Even former governor James M. Cox, long retired from politics, warned Ohio Democrats that renominating Martin L. Davey was a blueprint for disaster. He was going to vote for Sawyer and urged his fellow partisans to do the same.[19]

Smith's radio address two days before the election was relatively benign. He urged voters to renominate Martin as an antidote to John L. Lewis and his "conspiracy of Communists" and professed his respect for Catholics, Jews, and "Negroes." America's real enemies were Joseph Stalin, Adolf Hitler, Francisco Franco, and the Communist lapdog, Lewis, who, Smith reminded his listeners, ardently supported Charles Sawyer for governor.[20] All in all, it was a safe speech, with Smith attacking obvious enemies, except for John L. Lewis, the darling of militant unionists everywhere.

Both candidates concluded their campaigning in Cuyahoga County. Sawyer fired a final shot at Martin, who had criticized Sawyer for not being a "good American," although the Cincinnatian had been an army captain and served eight months in Europe during the Great War. "The nearest [Davey] ever came to wearing a uniform," Sawyer responded, "was when someone slapped a cap on his head when he was singing 'Sweet Adeline' at [an American] Legion convention where he never belonged."[21] Twenty years after the fact, Martin still had to rue the day Berenice filed his draft exemption form. Martin, of course, had no acceptable rejoinder and simply declared at the end, "We are going to win this primary three to one."[22]

Martin's prediction was total bluff. All the signs, especially Ohioans' general disgust with the unending controversy associated with the Davey regime, pointed to a Sawyer victory. Even former governor and now U.S. senator Vic Donahey, casting an absentee ballot, openly stated that he voted for Sawyer and hoped other Democrats would too. It was close, but in the end, thirty thousand more Democrats preferred Sawyer. Martin was the first incumbent governor in the history of the state to be denied renomination by his own party. He took it well, however. After his loss, Martin sat in shirtsleeves on the steps of the executive mansion and told reporters that he had been beaten before and survived. It was the same old Martin—defeat was disappointing but far from crushing.[23]

Of course, loud cheering could be heard in Washington, D.C. Franklin D. Roosevelt and his New Dealers had long regarded Martin as a political liability and were happy to have him out of the way at last. The national administration had played no small role in jettisoning the controversial governor when, a few days before the election, it threatened to withhold more than $1 million a month from Ohio pensioners because during the campaign Martin had sent them letters politicizing federal pension monies.[24] The fear of losing retirement checks if Martin continued in office scared many older voters into the Sawyer camp. The tactic might not have been entirely fair, but politics was politics.

Sawyer's Republican opponent in the fall was John W. Bricker, who for the second time received his party's uncontested nomination. Both men were so accustomed to jousting with Martin that they spent more time attacking his ghost than they did each other. Sawyer, for example, accused Bricker of arranging a "70–30 deal" through which Martin would control 30 percent of the state's patronage if he helped the Republican win in November. Bricker denied the charge, but Myrna Smith later swore that it was true, although Bricker reneged on the deal.[25] Bricker, on the other hand, demanded to know what Sawyer intended to do about Francis Poulson, who was Martin's right-hand man, not Sawyer's.[26] In fact, Poulson had already faded into the background months earlier, although he remained the titular head of the Ohio Democratic Committee for a while after Martin dumped him. Without Martin L. Davey around, there was little for Poulson to do other than serve as a straw man for Bricker.

Martin himself did nothing to help Sawyer. He stayed away from the party convention in September and did no campaigning in the fall. Many suspected that he would vote for Bricker in November. Given the governor's spitefulness, that was quite possible.

The election itself was almost anticlimactic. Bricker won by nearly 120,000 votes, Republicans captured 27 of the 35 state Senate seats and outnumbered Democrats in the lower house, 100–36, as Ohio voters let it be known that the Democrats had pushed far enough with their "New Deal."[27] It was time to pull back a bit.

That was not true for Martin L. Davey. In his final address before a joint session of the Ohio legislature, he decried the massive expansion of the federal government under Franklin D. Roosevelt and his New Deal theorists. Sounding more like a modern-day Republican than a Democrat, the retiring governor warned that an "avaricious federal bureaucracy" threatened states' rights and imperiled private business. That was especially true, Martin emphasized, now that Harry Hopkins, a thinly disguised socialist, was the nation's secretary of commerce.[28] He had been waiting for years to say some of these things. Now, with nothing to lose, he could. His candor might return to haunt him in 1940, but, blinded by the glare from his sinking political sun, a future in politics seemed to be on the far side of never.

Those last days in office were hectic. His friends, and he had many, gave him a testimonial dinner at one of his favorite Columbus haunts, the Neil House, five days before he left the governorship. While two thousand listened, nineteen speakers offered their thanks for the four-year gubernatorial ride, but no one's remarks that night were more heartfelt than Myrna Smith's. She, far better than most, knew the governor's human side, his capacity for kindness and loyalty.[29] Martin's enemies naturally thought him one-dimensional, easy to stir, quick on the trigger and eager (perhaps too eager) to return blow for blow in the political arena. What they did not see, as Myrna did, was the other side of the Vesuvian Martin, the Martin Davey whose devotion to family and friends emanated from the same emotional wellspring that made him so fearsome an enemy.

Margaret Allman, Martin's director of public welfare from the onset in 1935, got a dose of the fearsome Martin Davey in the waning hours of the administration. Allman had the temerity to refuse Martin's eleventh-hour "request" to appoint his most faithful servant of all, Myrna Smith, to the State Parole Board. The governor immediately had a secretary type the following letter:

January 5, 1939

Dear Mrs. Allman:

Pursuant to the authority conveyed on me by law, I am hereby removing you from the office of Director of the Department of Public Welfare, effective today, Thursday, January 5, 1939.

You will at once surrender all property of the State of Ohio in your possession to the custody of the Assistant Director of Public Welfare.

Sincerely yours,
Martin L. Davey

Governor[30]

Martin could scarcely wait until the letter was finished before marching in to show it, unsigned, to Allman. Stunned, she immediately issued Smith's commission.[31] Allman, who had always been loyal to Martin, now knew how his "victims" felt. When pushed, the governor had no qualms about devouring his own.

Perhaps it was simply weariness at the end that was finally getting to Martin. He was like a resentful man nearing retirement who no longer had to tolerate the stupidity and boorishness of his coworkers and acted accordingly in his final days on the job. At long last, he could tell the unvarnished truth without committing vocational suicide. It was almost fun for the governor. During his last few days in office, a jury in Mount Vernon, Ohio, convicted Ivan Ault, Martin's new state highway director, on two counts of "shaking down" civil service employees for campaign funds. Ault faced a fine and possible jail time. Martin pardoned him in a symbolic nose thumbing to all the antagonists who had tried to make his life miserable.[32] The final hours in office were more gratifying than most of the previous four years. He enjoyed telling his critics to "go to hell," as he had at his testimonial dinner on January 4.[33]

By inauguration day, January 9, 1939, Martin had but one official duty left—to stand on the statehouse steps and hand John Bricker his commission as governor. By 12:30 his formal role was over, and he watched his successor swear the oath of office.[34] Now Bricker would have to suffer the onslaught of well-wishers and sycophants. Martin, at last, was free of that.

After a few quick good-byes in Columbus, Martin and Berenice drove to Kent, where their hometown friends had planned an evening gala for the city's most famous son. A huge banner welcoming "M.L." stretched across the town square so that Martin and Berenice could not miss it as they drove to their rambling white clapboard home on West Main Street. At eight that evening, brass bands from Kent Roosevelt High School and Kent State University and a troop of boy scouts holding red flares aloft escorted Martin and Berenice through town to the Kent Opera House, where one thousand guests had gathered to honor their hometown hero. Loudspeakers were set up outside so the overflow crowd could hear the genuinely touched ex-governor reminisce about the place he always called home.[35] As he spoke, Martin could not help but note that his life had come full circle. Nearly thirty-nine years earlier, he had stood on the same opera house stage to deliver "Matter, Mind, and Spirit," his address to the Kent High School class of 1900.

For the first time in several years, Martin could devote all his time and energy to the Davey Tree Expert Company. Other family members had maintained it quite successfully while Martin's political career took him from Kent to Washington and Columbus before ending in 1939. By the time

Martin returned to Davey Tree full time, the business had changed. Davey workers were still renowned for their expert service and attention to detail, but their skills and equipment were more refined. Especially important in treating tree wounds now was an asphalt-based compound known as "Daveyite," whose ingredients came only from Egypt, Trinidad, and the Wasatch Mountains of Utah.[36]

Where once Martin had to balance massive state budgets of millions of dollars, he now had to worry about maintaining equipment and supplies. It was all a matter of scale, of course, but for Davey Tree the destruction of nine hundred ladders and the breakdown of 2,600 chain saws was as much a disaster as a million-dollar shortfall in the state's monthly relief allotment.

For Martin, it was almost like being back at Tarrytown, New York, in 1907, when he had to do everything to get the company off and running. He was just as eagle-eyed about details now as he had been then. Even so, his fastidiousness about running the company did not alienate his employees. He still knew how to treat people "right" to get the most out of them. As a measure of their affection, in 1939 Davey Tree employees donated in Martin's honor two stately elms for planting at the entrance of the state capitol.[37]

Martin was certainly busy enough as the Davey Tree Expert Company broadened its services from spraying, feeding, cabling, and removing trees to installing lightning rods in them, brush cutting, and, especially as World War II neared, line clearing to ensure that the nation's communications channels remained open.[38] Yet there was still something missing in his life—the excitement of politics. He knew that in many respects he was yesterday's news in Ohio Democratic circles—the spotlight still shone, albeit dimly, on Charles Sawyer and his chastened supporters from 1938, but that did not prevent Martin from periodically sniping away at Governor Bricker and staying in touch with various county organizations throughout 1939.[39]

By the spring of 1940, he was ready to give it another go. "I want to be elected governor again," he proclaimed, "in order to put humanity back into the Governor's office."[40] The Davey Tree Expert Company, although significant in his life, failed to fulfill him. He needed politics. "It is life, action. Everything connected with it deals with human beings. I like politics because I like people," he declared in a rebuke to the anti-Davey Cleveland Plain Dealer shortly before beginning his fifth try for the governorship.[41]

If he won the Democratic primary, Martin would face the incumbent, John Bricker, who now stood unopposed three times as the Republican nominee for governor. Bricker's confidence, bordering on cockiness, was understandable. His party was well organized, and the Democrats were in disarray after Charles Sawyer's loss in 1938. The former lieutenant governor and Democratic national committeeman had no interest in another run at the governorship, so the Democratic side of the race was wide open.

Despite his tarnished record, Martin, better organized than any of his rivals, emerged as the front-runner in the early maneuvering for the nomination. In March, buoyed by petitions of support from Democrats across the state, he formally announced his candidacy and in virtually the same breath denounced Bricker as "weak, selfish, and inhuman." Even Republicans, Martin claimed, were eagerly awaiting the opportunity to "retire him to private life."[42]

Martin's gubernatorial hopes soared when he easily defeated six other Democrats to capture the nomination. Only former governor George White approached being a serious contender, but Martin beat him by nearly three to one, 311,932–122,601. The other five candidates did little more than embarrass themselves by cluttering the race.[43] In the campaign, Martin uttered scarcely a word against his fellow Democrats; his strategy from the beginning was directed against Bricker.

Jubilant but weary after his victory, Martin spent the day at home catching up on his sleep. He justifiably savored his triumph, but quickly the critics began to swarm. The *Cleveland Plain Dealer* chided Democrats for "throwing opportunity to the winds" by nominating the controversial former governor. Even more ominous were some Democratic predictions that Martin's nomination in May spelled defeat in November.[44] The harshest public condemnation came from James M. Cox again, who proclaimed that Martin did not deserve reelection.[45] In Columbus, John Bricker had to smile. With the Democrats already squabbling among themselves, he could almost ignore Martin and contemplate victory in November.

Martin faced a serious problem before battling Bricker in the fall. Ohio Democrats were badly divided after the bitter struggle over the Democratic gubernatorial nomination in 1938. Sawyer won by repudiating Martin, a strategy that was not the Cincinnatian's alone. His fellow Democrats, certain that a continuation of the scandals that stamped Martin's administration portended disaster for the party, wrote a reform plank into the Democratic state platform in 1938. Accordingly, the Democrats promised an end to graft, shakedowns, and chiseling. The plank was clearly a slap at Martin. Recognizing that a campaign promising an end to Democratic "business as usual" offered the only chance to beat Bricker, Sawyer assumed the role of virtuous reformer. Unfortunately for the Democrats, the Davey faithful never forgave Sawyer's "treason" and refused to support their party's nominee, giving

Bricker an easy victory in the general election.[46] Now in 1940, the embittered Sawyerites were ready to return the favor by allowing Martin to fend for himself against the popular Bricker.

Martin's hardest task consequently was to reunite Ohio's Democratic Party. His political instincts keener than ever, Martin in July shattered tradition by summoning every Democratic county chairman and major state candidate to Kent for two days to organize for the coming campaign. With Martin orchestrating everything, the Democrats met in both large groups and one on one with the gubernatorial candidate to plan for November. Infected by Martin's enthusiasm, the attendees seemed to forget the bitterness that divided them and rallied behind their host, applauding enthusiastically whenever he rose to speak. At this point, the Democrats appeared willing to reconcile. They were now united and had high hopes for victory in November.[47]

The groundbreaking Kent conference was only the beginning for Martin. He advanced the party unity theme in a rousing speech at the Democratic state convention in Columbus on September 7. After proclaiming that the Ohio Democratic Party was stronger than it had been in years, Martin exhorted his listeners to carry Ohio for the "entire Democratic ticket, from President Roosevelt to county coroner."[48] His audience loved it; the cheers and applause were deafening.

Martin stepped back to take it all in, enjoying what he had wrought. Through hard work and ingenuity, he had reascended the political ladder, seemingly healed the wounds of 1938, and, by carefully avoiding calumnies against his primary opponents in 1940, appeared to have reunited the party. His ability to rise from the ashes to new popular heights had to confound his detractors. Martin L. Davey was back.

Bricker, though, as Martin had learned in 1936, was a wily foe. The Republican knew that Martin, in many respects, was his own worst enemy. He was happy to contrast his scandal-free administration with his predecessor's and let Martin's fellow Democrats, not all of whom subscribed to the Kent unity theme, turn on their own. James Metzenbaum, for one, gave voice to many disaffected Democrats when he declared that the Davey administration was "born in the cradle of shakedown," a sentiment echoed by Burr Gongwer and others.[49]

Martin could not escape the scandals associated with his governorship. Rather than defend his record, he struck back where Bricker was most vulnerable. The Republican governor, deeply steeped in his party's tradition of self-reliance, was viewed as cold and heartless, particularly among relief recipients in Ohio's large cities. Bricker believed that those cities should bear greater responsibility for their own relief programs, a philosophy that precipitated a bitter quarrel with Cleveland's Republican mayor, Harold H. Burton. Burton had complained since November 1939 that Governor Bricker stubbornly refused to call the state legislature into special session to appropriate monies to help Cleveland meet its relief emergency. Because of the governor's intransigence, sixty thousand Clevelanders, Burton declared, were but days away from cold and hunger. Commiserating in a telephone call to his fellow big-city mayor, Fiorello LaGuardia, now mayor of New York and head of the U.S. Conference of Mayors, asked Burton what he might do to aid Cleveland. Shortly afterward, in a speech in New York, LaGuardia scored Bricker for his meanness in refusing to respond to the human misery in Ohio. The criticism spread. In Washington, even Roosevelt's secretary of the interior, Harold Ickes, called the Ohio governor "heartless."[50]

Bricker and Burton met in Columbus and worked out a compromise solution to Cleveland's problems, but outside Ohio's big cities the governor's position on relief appealed to many who liked his financial conservatism and shared his antipathy to urban troubles. They were pleased to see the governor stand firm against pressure from Cleveland, Washington, and (as one Bricker correspondent was certain) even from Moscow.[51] However, by choosing a balanced budget over the needs of beleaguered citizens and by supporting rural over urban Ohio, Bricker opened himself to attack during the campaign of 1940, and Martin was quick to detect his opponent's vulnerability. In a press release in June, he struck: "[Bricker] has no more heart in [relief] than the fellow who kicks a stray and hungry dog, and then throws him a bone from a safe distance to keep the dog from biting him."[52] The former governor never let up. With only a week to go before the election, Martin, known for his colorful speech, came up with some of his best. Contrasting Bricker's "heartlessness" in relief with the Republican administration's kindness in feeding thousands of ducks stranded during a Lake Erie blizzard, Martin proclaimed the moral is, "If you want to eat while Bricker is governor, you'd better be a duck."[53] Few could match Martin in transforming an opponent's kind deed into a monumental human failing.

Martin, too, was an easy target, and Bricker was only too happy to remind Ohioans of the former governor's 1935 quarrel with Harry Hopkins. That dispute had exposed damning irregularities in the solicitation of campaign funds and disbursement of relief monies during the Davey administration. The former governor, Bricker charged, had abused the public trust before and undoubtedly would do so again.[54]

Back and forth the campaigning went. Martin was an experienced and clever candidate, but so was Bricker. The Democrat, however, had a card to play that his opponent did not—sitting in the White House was the trump card of all trump cards—Franklin D. Roosevelt, who was seeking an unprecedented third term. Martin's best hope was to link his fortunes once again with the president's, a strategy that saved Martin in 1936. Roosevelt was scheduled to speak in Cleveland only days before the election, and every self-respecting Democratic candidate had to be part of the event. Martin was to introduce the state candidates to the cheering throng of 23,500 crammed into every seat and aisleway of Cleveland's vast public hall. He recognized that the crowd was really there for Roosevelt and not for the Ohio Democratic slate. Consequently, after fulfilling his obligation to the state candidates, Martin began to fire the Public Hall assembly:

> . . . Who fed hungry people by the millions when they had no place to turn?
> Who was it who gave jobs to [the] unemployed?
> Who was it who gave us the great social security program?
> Who put humanity into the government of the United States?

To every rhetorical question, the frenzied Democrats roared, "Roosevelt!"[55] Had the president been on the platform at the moment, he would have been impressed by how Martin L. Davey could work an audience. But Roosevelt was still outside, inching his way through the mass of well-wishers jamming Cleveland streets. Once Roosevelt made it inside, Martin knew that the hour would be the president's, but until then the moment was his.

The cheering continued for Roosevelt when he finally reached the rostrum. After he finished his speech, he was off to Hyde Park for rest and a final fireside chat from the comfort of his study on the last Monday before the election. Martin had no such luxury; he campaigned hard to the end, addressing a crowd in Canton on the same Monday night. Bricker, after a round of speeches in Cleveland on Sunday, retired to Columbus for one final radio broadcast on election eve.

Even before the first votes were tallied, Bricker forces sensed victory. Republican state chairman Ed Schorr anticipated that his man's margin would be "unbelievably large."[56] A *Cleveland Plain Dealer* poll predicted that Bricker would carry Cuyahoga County alone by more than 112,000 votes.[57] In the other camp, Democratic state chairman J. Freer Bittenger, more a wishful thinker than an accurate forecaster, claimed Ohioans would elect Martin by a margin of 320,000.[58] More realistic Democrats seemed content that they had done their best for Martin by maintaining a harmonious front during the president's Cleveland speech.[59]

From the earliest returns onward, the outcome was never in doubt. The votes rolled in for Roosevelt and Bricker. When it was over, the president had easily fended off Wendell Willkie, a businessman, former Democrat, and surprise Republican Party nominee. Roosevelt carried Ohio by 150,000 votes, an easy win but nothing like the triumph of 1936 when he won the state by 600,000. Martin, more than anyone else, benefited from Roosevelt's enormous coattails in that election. Portentously, though, in 1936 Bricker had run 300,000 ballots ahead of Alf Landon. That feat was all the more remarkable because Ohioans had to split their tickets to vote for Bricker. The same was not true in 1940. In a presidential election decided more by human than Olympian proportions, Martin could not expect to coast on a Roosevelt tide. This time Bricker won by more than 364,000 votes, a record-shattering margin for an Ohio gubernatorial election. Moreover, he was only the second Republican to be reelected governor of Ohio in the first forty years of the twentieth century.[60] Especially painful to Martin was the fact that he barely carried his own Portage County.[61]

At 11:35 the next morning, Martin wired tersely to Bricker: "Congratulations on your reelection and best wishes for a successful administration." Bricker waited more than two weeks before acknowledging Martin's wire with one equally brief: "Thank you for your telegram of congratulations."[62] It was no accident that neither man addressed the other as "governor," with Bricker making sure that the salutation in his telegram read, "Dear Mr. Davey." The election was over, but there was neither a good loser nor a gracious winner. After two fierce campaigns, neither man could stomach the other.

Martin tried to put the best face on the results, citing several reasons for his loss. First, Bricker enjoyed all the advantages of an incumbent. State employees, eager to keep their jobs, had worked hard to get their boss reelected, and voters, more willing to support a sitting administration, had swollen Bricker's campaign coffers. The split ticket separating Martin from Roosevelt on the ballot had also hurt, the former governor acknowledged. And the charges of corruption involving kickbacks from contractors doing business with the state and special deals with friends of the administration resurfaced to haunt him in the 1940 campaign. Looming large, too, was the inescapable reality that Ohio Democrats, weary of Martin's misbehavior in office and angry because he refused to help Sawyer in 1938, were willing to sacrifice their own man in 1940.[63] Unfortunately, by 1940 Martin had alienated, often viciously, so many

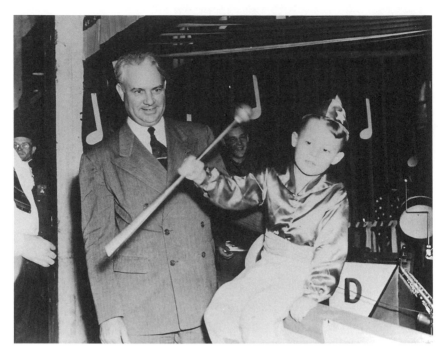

Governor John W. Bricker amazed by a young magician at the Ohio State Fair in 1941. Ohio Historical Society.

of his fellow Democrats that they were happy to see him go. Ironically, Burr Gongwer, one of those estranged Democrats, had penned a motto, somewhat tongue in cheek, in 1918 that seemed apropos of the chastened Martin Davey of 1940: "Never do any person—no matter how obscure—an unkindness, UNLESS HE HAS IT COMING." Many Democrats believed exactly that—Martin Davey had it coming.

No man likes to admit that his time has come and gone, especially one as competitive and combative as Martin L. Davey. He was like the aging slugger who could not understand why his aching knees no longer carried him from first to third at the crack of a bat or the graying movie star who wondered, despite his wrinkled brow and sagging paunch, why he was no longer asked to play the romantic lead against Hollywood's latest ingenue. One of state senator John Taylor's friends best summarized Martin's ebbing political life in 1940: "Things have to get worse before they get better. This year will wash up Martin L. Davey, and . . . a lot of other birds who have been cluttering up the landscape."[64] Cluttering up the landscape, indeed. Martin Davey would prefer a thousand deaths to that.

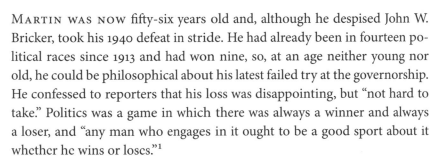

Chapter Sixteen

Finis

MARTIN WAS NOW fifty-six years old and, although he despised John W. Bricker, took his 1940 defeat in stride. He had already been in fourteen political races since 1913 and had won nine, so, at an age neither young nor old, he could be philosophical about his latest failed try at the governorship. He confessed to reporters that his loss was disappointing, but "not hard to take." Politics was a game in which there was always a winner and always a loser, and "any man who engages in it ought to be a good sport about it whether he wins or loses."[1]

Despite his postelection cheeriness, the former governor was weary. Myrna Smith had noticed how tired her boss looked after relentlessly traveling up and down the state in the campaign against Bricker. In addition to the physical demands of the contest, the constant worrying about thousands of details took a mental toll. Myrna sensed that Martin seemed almost glad to lose because now he would not have to return to the pressures of life in Columbus.[2]

Retirement from politics did not mean retirement from life. Martin still had the Davey Tree Expert Company to run. The firm now had over one thousand employees and offices in seventy cities. Martin stepped easily into the business because he operated it according to a timeless credo: "Do it right or not at all," his father's oft-repeated mantra of long ago.[3]

Martin brought to work the same organizational skills that had served him so well in politics. Concerned about the future, he enlarged the company's board of directors from nine to seventeen, thereby bringing in more executive talent. The company remained in Davey family hands, though, with Martin as president and brothers Paul and Jim as vice presidents. Under Martin's guidance, the firm did more than $2 million worth of business in 1940.[4]

Even though things were going well, Martin still worried about the future. Some of his concerns were alleviated when his son, Martin Jr., joined the company in 1940 after graduating from Yale University with a degree in botany and business administration. Hiring his son assured continuity of ownership, but Martin wanted to ensure that the company would always be family owned. In March 1945, he wrote the Bureau of Internal Revenue inquiring about federal tax implications for a family corporation that would provide stockholders (primarily family members) an annual income based on their company stockholdings. If individuals wanted to sell their stock, it would be to the corporation. Always thinking ahead, he did not want the Davey Tree Expert Company and its owners to be double taxed, once as a corporation and then again as individual taxpayers.[5]

Expansion, too, was always on Martin's mind. In 1940, the company tried to hire three hundred additional workers, but was hard-pressed to do so because the war in Europe had so stoked American industry that young men had any number of job opportunities besides Davey Tree. The shortage of available workers was compounded after December 7, 1941, when the Japanese attacked Pearl Harbor and America, too, was at war. More than five hundred Davey Tree men went into the service, including Evangeline's husband, Alexander Smith, and Martin Jr.[6]

The war drained tons of steel, millions of tires, and countless gallons of gasoline from domestic use. Davey Tree, heavily dependent on steel for saws and on tires and gasoline for its trucks, was especially hard hit. Martin was forced to curtail business and cut jobs. The sales force dropped from 65 to 20 and field workers were cut to 350. Forty sales territories were eliminated altogether.[7]

Several months earlier Martin had been reminded of his mortality. On Saturday, February 7, 1941, he went to bed early in preparation for a business trip to New York. In the middle of the night he was awakened with what he thought was severe indigestion. When household remedies failed to help, he called his family physician at four in the morning and was given opiates. They eased the pain, but Martin knew that something was seriously wrong. He called Myrna that Sunday and asked her to cancel his New York appointments.[8]

On Monday, feeling slightly better, Martin rose, bathed and got dressed. Downstairs was Martin Jr., waiting to drive his father to the world-renowned

Cleveland Clinic. An hour later, Martin Jr. left his father at the clinic entrance and went to park the car. When he returned, an impatient Martin was already inside filling out admission forms. Once he was admitted, doctors discovered that Martin had survived a severe heart attack; a thrombosis had clogged one of the main arteries leading from his heart. The only "cure" was months of bed rest. He did not leave the Cleveland Clinic until early May and had to remain inactive months longer at home.[9]

He spent time writing his autobiography and observing Davey Tree affairs from afar. By October 1941, he was well enough to address the Canton Forum, although he needed a cane to get around and confessed to feeling "a little tired." He looked dapper and, despite his brush with death in February, was as mentally sharp as ever. There was even some idle talk that in 1942 he might run again for governor.[10]

Later in the year, he returned to work at Davey Tree and, after the Pearl Harbor attack, was asked to lead the Kent war bond drive. Against his doctor's advice, he accepted the job and was so successful that he agreed to chair five more. The Davey Tree Expert Company purchased $50,000 worth of war bonds and individual employees bought nearly $40,000 more. Martin was especially proud of his certificate of appreciation from the United States Treasury awarded in December 1945.[11]

This should have been a good time in Martin's life. The business with its wartime cutbacks was somewhat troubling, but his personal life was going well, although he worried about Martin Jr., who had gone off to war in February 1943. Unfortunately, though, Martin could not forget his old foe, John W. Bricker. Bricker had won a third gubernatorial term in 1942 and in 1944 ran for vice president on the losing Republican ticket alongside Thomas E. Dewey, all stepping stones to two terms as a U.S. senator in 1946 and 1952.

Bricker's success galled Martin. Even before the 1940 election, Martin had sent several sneering, mean letters to Bricker, denouncing him for transgressions largely magnified if not entirely contrived.[12] A 1943 *Time* magazine article on Bricker in which the governor claimed that he had inherited a deficit of $40 million from Martin enraged the former governor. He asked one of his old secretaries, John Caren, and state auditor Joseph Ferguson to send him financial information rebutting Bricker's remark.[13] A similar piece in the May 1944 issue of *Cosmopolitan* magazine prompted an angry complaint to the editor and a slew of "Dear Friend" letters alerting longtime supporters to the "truth."[14]

Martin was relentless. On December 1, 1944, he challenged Bricker. He would put up $1,000 if the governor would do the same, and submit the facts and figures to an independent accounting firm to see who was right about the state's financial affairs when Martin turned over the governor's office to his Republican successor.[15] Bricker did not respond, intelligently refusing to be lured into a personal fight with a bitter loser. He was far better off standing above the fray and letting Martin appear childish as he tried to taunt a sitting governor into an undignified go-round that would never settle anything.

Bricker's silence pushed Martin over the brink. In May 1945, in a futile effort to "get" his old foe, Martin asked the Bureau of Internal Revenue to investigate Bricker's finances. Insisting on anonymity, Martin asked how, despite Bricker's meager annual salaries of $5,000 or $6,000 as a nearly perpetual public servant, the governor could purchase a house and farm worth $135,000 and own, as Martin had heard, 116 suits. Many of Bricker's suspected ill-gotten gains, according to Martin, came from shady real-estate and banking deals engineered by Columbus businessman John W. Galbreath, Bricker's close friend and political confidant. "There is enough in this memorandum to make a good start," he wrote. "I think there is plenty of pay dirt. The trail should lead into interesting places."[16]

Martin's behavior now bordered on the bizarre. He could not let bygones be bygones and had become increasingly sensitive to the slightest criticism. The previous November, he sued Cincinnati mayor James Garfield Stewart, who was campaigning for governor. In a Cleveland speech on October 31, 1944, Stewart, in stressing how honest he would be, compared himself to a corrupt Martin, who "left the state on the verge of bankruptcy." In his lawsuit, which was dropped, Martin claimed that Stewart had "personally humiliated" and "greatly injured" him and sought $1 million in damages. Contrary to Stewart's insinuations, Martin claimed that he had "never made one dollar in politics" and his many years of political service had "cost [him] a small fortune."[17]

While as combative as ever with some, Martin mended fences with others, including John Taylor, one of his old state Senate foes from 1938, and even President Franklin D. Roosevelt, with whom Martin had been sparring for years. He especially appreciated Taylor's refusal to dredge up the hatchet men episode during the gubernatorial primary of 1940 and ardently supported the president's all but open alliance with Great Britain in September 1941, despite a torrent of opposition from America's strident Isolationists and America Firsters.[18]

He was, above all else, a patriot. Besides leading Kent's war bond drives, at his urging Davey Tree Expert Company employees kept in touch with their coworkers in the military. Martin himself wrote many of the letters to pump up the spirits of company servicemen overseas and let them know they were not forgotten by their old boss. In addition, the company published and disseminated free of charge 25,000 copies of a booklet, *Vegetable Garden Guide,* as part of the government's Victory Garden program, whose purpose was to encourage Americans to grow their own food, thereby freeing up farm produce for soldiers at the front.[19]

Meanwhile, Martin, again looking to the future, in 1942 got Davey Tree to buy the Kent City Bank, which had been closed since the bank holiday of 1933. The price was right—$29,800—and shortly afterward the bank was open for business. Two years later, Davey Tree bought five thousand acres of valuable timberland in North Carolina, diversifying its assets all the more.[20]

Martin was also perspicacious enough to recognize that the war was not going to last forever and that the Davey Tree Expert Company had better be prepared to deal with a changing economy. To that end, he proposed the resumption of the company's training program, the reestablishment of the Davey Tree Institute, and a stepped-up advertising campaign. Also, servicemen returning to work would need a refresher course before taking to the trees again. And, last but by no means least, Martin intended to hire a cadre of salesmen to "retake" the forty sales territories that had been abandoned because of manpower shortages during the war.[21]

Beginning in May with the end of the war in Europe and continuing into August after the war in the Pacific, Davey workers trickled back to their old jobs. Included among them were Evangeline's husband, Alexander Smith, and Martin Jr., to whom Martin intended to turn over control of Davey Tree. On February 5, 1946, the board of the Davey Tree Expert Company voted on a succession plan that left Martin Jr., Smith, and J. Harlan Carson, a nephew, as members of an operating committee to run the company after Martin's death or incapacitation.[22]

Employees were apprised of all this through Martin's editorials in the Davey *Bulletin,* a company periodical. Although he and a handful of others were clearly in charge, he knew that no business thrived unless its workers in the field, the ones dealing directly with the public, were satisfied with the company and projected that satisfaction to customers. Martin was an enlightened boss, interested in the welfare of his employees. He encouraged them to purchase life insurance and had the company buy twenty-year endowment policies for longtime workers.[23]

At sixty-one Martin was finally at peace. He no longer had to worry about how a recalcitrant state legislature might savage his budget or suffer vicious

Governor Davey in the serenity of retirement, ca. 1945. Evangeline Davey Smith Collection, Martin L. Davey Papers, Kent State University Libraries, Special Collections and Archives.

attacks by political opponents and venomous newspaper editors. A succession plan naming twenty-eight-year-old Martin Jr. as his replacement was in place, and to most he seemed to have recovered from his 1941 heart attack.

By December 1945, though, he knew he was not the same man who campaigned day and night across the state to become governor. Almost as soon as Martin Jr. was discharged from the army that month, Martin Sr. met with his son nightly to discuss the company and its personnel. Martin knew everybody, and his knowledge of their strengths and weaknesses was uncanny.[24] It was this same attention to detail and people that launched and sustained his long political career.

On December 19, 1945, he wrote a long letter to his son, advising him what and what not to do. "Above everything," he wrote, "make your word good" and "treat your employees as human beings." He added, "never do anything while you are angry," advice he should have followed himself while governor. Martin continued with warnings about a selfish world (not necessarily all bad because selfishness can generate ambition and progress), and the dangers of succumbing to flattery.[25]

The letter, a passing of the torch really, was Martin Davey at his philosophical best. There was no self-pity in it, no expression of regret. It was the kind of letter that a man could write to his son only after he had lived most of his life and wanted to pass on what he had learned. It was also the kind of letter a man would write when he felt that perhaps his time was short.

Martin was still full of life on March 30, 1946, when he and several friends gathered at the big white house on West Main for a Saturday evening of bridge, Martin's postpolitical passion. Shortly after midnight, as the women were removing snack-laden dishes and the men were folding the card tables, Martin collapsed in the middle of the living room. Dr. A. Sellew Roberts, the history department chair at Kent State University, was closest to Martin and immediately bent down to loosen his necktie. Martin gasped for air and tried to sit up but fell back, groaned once, and then lay still. Family physician S. A. Brown was quickly summoned and pronounced Martin dead.[26]

Everyone in the house was stunned, and Berenice, a wife one moment and a widow the next, was devastated; in an instant, gone was her husband of nearly forty years. There was no warning, no hint that something was seriously wrong with Martin. He had recovered from his thrombosis five years earlier and was only sixty-one. Everyone believed that he still had years to go. Only he knew how tired he felt and in his December letter to Martin Jr. sensed that his time was drawing nigh.

The body was taken to Bissler's funeral home just a few blocks away on West Main, and services were set for 2 P.M. on Wednesday. By early Sunday morning all of Kent knew that the city's most famous son had died, and shortly after that so too did the rest of Ohio and the nation. Tributes, oral and floral, poured into the city, and flags flew at half-mast. Businesses planned to close their doors from 1:30 to 3:30 during the obsequies. From Columbus, Democratic governor Frank Lausche, Bricker's successor, praised Martin and said he and his cabinet would attend the funeral.[27]

Over the next two days, three thousand mourners filed by the open casket in Bissler's salon, inundated with flowers from Martin's many friends and associates. On Wednesday, at 2 P.M., Robert Guinther, Martin's friend and lawyer, began his eulogy, likening the former governor to a fallen Roman warrior mourned by his friends: *"De Mortibus Nihil Nisi Bonum."* Guinther intoned, "Of the dead, let nothing be said but good."[28]

After 450 mourners filed past for a final look at the man who had led Ohio politics for a generation, eight pallbearers lifted the casket onto a hearse for the short ride up Mantua Street to Standing Rock Cemetery, the very place transformed many years earlier by John Davey. The eight men carried the casket to a canopy over the grave. Governor Lausche walked to it and stood by himself, head bowed, for several minutes. A moment later, the Reverend Dana McDonald, pastor of Martin's First Christian Church, said a final prayer, and it was over. Martin L. Davey, once one of Ohio's most dynamic politicians, was lowered into the ground between his mother Bertha and his little daughter Mary Berenice, dead long ago.[29]

Condolences flowed into the Davey household for days. All were exceedingly solicitous and comforted the grieving family. Even the newspapers that flayed Martin while he was governor were kind and printed nothing foul about him. There was, however, one exception—the *Akron Beacon Journal*. Martin's longtime journalistic harpy praised the former governor for providing better roads, improving Ohio's banking system, and getting rid of an incompetent prison warden but devoted more space to a rehashing of Martin's "sins," large and small.[30]

The *Beacon Journal*'s meanness infuriated Myrna Smith, who dashed off a telegram of rebuke to the paper's editor. "You must have gotten great satisfaction from the fact that for the first time you were able to hurt [Martin Davey] and he was not able to fight back," she retorted. That was true, but loyal Myrna was still there to "fight back." Martin was finally at rest, but he had left behind an avenging angel who was not.[31]

Epilogue

THE BROAD SWEEP of the family plot in Standing Rock Cemetery reminds one of a battlefield with the names of the fallen forever preserved in marmoreal splendor. The whole cast of characters is here. Underfoot lie John Davey, his wife Bertha, and all their offspring. In their midst repose Martin and Berenice Davey and their children, Evangeline, Martin Jr. and Mary Berenice. Also there in the Davey plot is Harmon Carson, Martin Davey's brother-in-law, whose burly body warmed the winter beds of the Davey boys while they were growing up in a ramshackle farmhouse two miles outside of Kent.

Fittingly, next to the road and closest to passersby is Martin L. Davey who craved an audience in life and is nearest one in death. He was once compared to Huey Long, the flamboyant Louisiana governor of the 1930s, who made more friends than enemies but was gunned down by one of the latter when he was in the prime of his physical and political life.[1] Nobody ever took a shot at Martin, but along the way he accumulated enough enemies who probably wanted to.

As a "pure" politician, Martin Davey had few peers. He refined politics to an art form, much of it predicated on his ability to read people with unerring accuracy. He detected any opening that might allow him to win over a potential voter. And no one ever more carefully practiced stump oratory. He looked directly into the eyes of his listeners, watching every grin, grimace, and arched eyebrow to see if he was reaching them.[2]

He had honed his political philosophy to a few key points. Politics was no "pink tea party," he was fond of saying, and any man who failed to make enemies along the way probably was not doing anything. And, cynically but accurately, he believed people could be counted on to "vote their major prejudices," and he assiduously cultivated those prejudices.[3]

Martin made just enough mistakes to let his enemies think that "now they had him." Generally, those errors were rooted in bad judgment as he tried to wriggle off the hook when a political opponent backed him into a corner as Charles Dick had over the embarrassing draft exemption issue in 1918. Berenice had "saved" him then, but she was not around in 1926 when Al Smith nearly ran him out of the governor's mansion after Martin pressed too hard for Smith's participation in a tree-planting ceremony at the sesquicentennial celebration in Philadelphia. Martin was far less interested in Smith's presence than he was in promoting the Davey Tree Expert Company during the nation's well-publicized birthday party.

His gift for self-aggrandizement, rooted deeply in ego, left Martin with some blind spots. He failed to see, for example, how weak and whiny he appeared before his colleagues when he called for a question of personal privilege in 1926 to explain his frequent absences from the House of Representatives. In seven years, the congressman from Ohio's fabled Garfield district had missed more than five hundred roll calls out of a thousand. Although Martin was not the king of House absentees, his record was shameful, and the peppery Fiorello LaGuardia was only too happy to remind the Ohioan of that fact on the House floor.

Martin's ego was operating at maximum efficiency in 1932 when he tried to wangle a cabinet appointment out of Franklin D. Roosevelt. Without any practical experience apart from running the Davey Tree Expert Company and absent any personal ties to the president-elect, Martin nonetheless asked to be named secretary of agriculture and had no compunction about promoting his own candidacy, even to the point of getting thousands of Ohioans to recommend him to the president. His importuning was tactless, and exposed him to public criticism even before he moved into the highly visible governor's chair in 1935.

Not surprisingly, the press frequently called him a liar. Was he mendacious? Probably, but no more so than the average politician. He claimed that he was surprised when Harry Hopkins in 1935 initiated an investigation into Ohio relief and swore he did not learn about it until he and Francis Poulson read the newspapers while taking a leisurely drive to Wheeling, West Virginia. Supposedly, Martin and Poulson, weary of the political grind, decided to leave Columbus to "get a little rest." Martin conveniently stayed in a hotel on Saturday night (reporters would not know where he was) and, after rising on Sunday morning, met Poulson, who had bought several morning newspapers to read on the way to West Virginia. Martin's driver arrived at the hotel at 9 A.M.; the two pols got in the car and rode for an hour before glancing at the newspaper headlines announcing the Hopkins investigation.[4]

No one who knew "Damon" and "Pythias" would ever believe that story. These two men were addicted to the news. They could not ride blissfully along, enjoying the countryside, without at least checking the headlines in the Columbus papers. More realistically, the two knew that the Hopkins story was going to break and realized that they had better escape Columbus and prepare a response before reporters descended on them in droves.

Was Martin dishonest? No, but he certainly was shady. He had a knack for skirting the law that infuriated his enemies, but, despite their most strenuous investigations, neither he nor any of his inner circle was ever found guilty of a crime. The Senate investigators of 1938 desperately tried to prove that Martin was a crook, but they generated far more smoke than fire.

Still, Martin sometimes barely stayed honest. Loyal Myrna Smith provided evidence of that. During the 1938 gubernatorial primary, Charles Sawyer accused Martin of trying to buy the Democratic nomination with $250,000 from his legendary slush fund. According to Sawyer, Martin promised precinct workers a total of $125,000 if they supported him and another $125,000 in bonuses if Martin won. After the election, Smith wrote to Evangeline, saying that the story was essentially true. Myrna was alone in the governor's mansion, with only a penitentiary trusty present, when several Democratic county chairmen or their surrogates came to collect. Before the day was over, Smith handed out $88,000 in cash, money that she suspected would never end up in the hands of the precinct workers.[5]

Was the payoff illegal? Technically, no. Martin had a "right" to reward people who did a good job, but his payments certainly smelled like bribery, especially since they were made in cash. And, even if the payments were not illegal, where did the money come from? As a successful businessman, Martin had deep pockets, but they were not that deep. Likely his critics were right; somehow, by fair means or foul, Martin had amassed a private treasury that he could use at his discretion.

Most intriguing of all the curiosities about Martin L. Davey centers on his relationship with the Ku Klux Klan. Con Mulcahy, the Summit County pol, and others had accused him of Klan sympathies, and James A. Colescott, Ohio's grand dragon, frequently surfaced as Martin's bête noire in several elections, but no one could ever prove that Martin was a Klansman or ever solicited Klan support in any of his campaigns. However, in October 1939, Martin, already out of office, received an interesting letter, which, because of its meanness and puerility, had to be discounted. Nonetheless, its author described

Martin's kinship with the Klan in such detail that even a doubter would have wondered what was true and what was not. Specifically, the writer described a moonlit night in Medina County when Martin, under a fiery cross, was "taken into the 'honored order' and orated on liberty, freedom and Americanism." Martin, the letter writer claimed, "shook with emotion when [he] praised all the things that the Klan stood for." Some of the Klansmen there that night said it was the best speech on freedom that they had ever heard.[6]

If the poison pen author was right, Martin had performed political magic by ensuring that every other man there on that moonlit night remained forever silent. Given Martin's fame, that was highly unlikely. The writer further discredited himself by rehashing nearly all of Martin's gubernatorial transgressions and nicknaming him "Leggs" [sic] Davey, after the New York gangster Jack "Legs" Diamond, who gained the sobriquet by running out on his friends when the heat was on. Martin, according to the letter writer, had done the same to Al Smith, Vic Donahey, and even Franklin D. Roosevelt.[7]

Martin's alleged Klan associations in and of themselves were not necessarily damning. Many politicians in the 1920s were similarly "tainted." However, when one incorporates James A. Colescott's persistent "link" to Martin with Martin's ties to shifty Lee Bradley, and adds these two associations to Martin's relationship with the wheeling and dealing Francis Poulson, a disturbing question arises. Why would a rich, refined businessman/politician from Kent associate with such scoundrels?

The answer to that is Martin Davey himself was a bit of a scoundrel. He had certainly risen to a lofty station in life by the time he won his first mayoral race, but he never forgot the hard lessons of his youth. As a boy, he had to compete to survive, and he carried that experience with him into politics. If he had to court Klansmen in the 1920s to win, he could rationalize doing that. If it took colluding with the conniving Lee Bradley and the "I'll do anything" Francis Poulson to win in the 1930s, he was willing to do that, too.

Martin brought this psychological baggage with him to Columbus in 1935. The newspapers detected it first, and his opponents were quick to follow. Americans want their political leaders to be absolutely honest but expect otherwise. They can tolerate those who fall short as long as they are not too "slick." Unfortunately, Martin L. Davey, with his tailored suits, turkey gobbler strut, and no-holds-barred approach to politics, was more than many Ohioans could take. They disliked him, even hated him, but, still, not a single one could ever say that Martin L. Davey had not given friend and foe alike the political ride of their lives.

Notes

1. BEGINNINGS

1. MLD, "Autobiography," 6, box 7, folder 3, Martin L. Davey Papers, MSS 339, Ohio Historical Society, Columbus (hereafter OHS).

2. Ibid., 32.

3. Another sister, Rosella, died in infancy.

4. John Davey, "Writings," 2–4, unpublished and undated manuscript, Miscellaneous Papers, Davey Tree Expert Company, Kent, Ohio. Internal evidence indicates that this manuscript was written when Davey was in his seventies.

5. Ibid., 4; Sue Gorisek, "A Man Ahead of His Moment," *Ohio* 15 (Oct. 1992), 30.

6. MLD, "Autobiography," 2.

7. Robert E. Pfleger, *Green Leaves: A History of the Davey Tree Expert Company* (Chester, Conn.: Pequot Press, 1977), 5; radio speech by MLD, Feb. 16, 1930, WEAF New York, Kent State University Library Special Collections, Kent, Ohio (hereafter KSU Special Collections); John Davey, "Writings," 7.

8. Pfleger, *Green Leaves*, 5; John Davey, "Writings," 6.

9. Pfleger, *Green Leaves*, 6.

10. MLD, "Autobiography," 2; Pfleger, *Green Leaves*, 7; "The Seeing Eye," *Warren (Ohio) Tribune Chronicle*, Feb. 14, 1945, Miscellaneous Papers, Davey Tree Expert Company.

11. Even in death John Davey is not far from his beloved trees. A massive oak springs from atop his grave in Standing Rock Cemetery in Kent, Ohio.

12. Pfleger, *Green Leaves*, 8.

13. Ibid., 8, 10–12.

14. MLD, "Autobiography," 1.

15. Karl H. Grismer, *The History of Kent: Historical and Biographical* (Kent, Ohio: Courier-Tribune, 1932), 61, 63, 66, 65.

16. MLD, "Autobiography," 5; Grismer, *History of Kent,* 65.

17. MLD, "Autobiography," 6–9.

18. Davey's gubernatorial campaign literature in 1936 said the house had three rooms. See *They Love Him for the Enemies He Has Made,* 6, Portage County Historical Society, Ravenna, Ohio; MLD, "Autobiography," 10.

19. MLD, "Autobiography," 11–12.

20. Ibid. John Davey believed the old English ways were superior. America would be better off, he wrote, if parents exercised a "Master's Authority" over their children. See John Davey, "Writings," 2.

21. MLD, "Autobiography," 13–18.

22. Pfleger, *Green Leaves,* 14; MLD, "Autobiography," 17.

23. MLD, "Autobiography," 17–20.

24. George Alfred Henty (1832–1902) was widely read by a whole generation of boys. MLD, "Autobiography," 20.

25. MLD, "Autobiography," 21–25.

26. "The Davey Family, which gave America the Science of Tree Surgery, now gives Ohio a Great Governor," The Independent Voters Davey-For-Governor Club, 1934, 1, box 7, folder 1, MLD Papers, OHS; MLD, "Autobiography," 25.

27. MLD, "Autobiography," 25–27.

28. Ibid., 27; Grismer, *History of Kent,* 104–5.

29. MLD, "Autobiography," 28–29; Grismer, *History of Kent,* 85.

30. MLD, "Autobiography," 28–32.

31. Ibid., 33; scrapbook, Reed Memorial Library, Ravenna, Ohio.

32. MLD, "Autobiography," 33–35.

2. THE YOUNG SALESMAN

1. John Davey, *The Tree Doctor: A Book on Tree Culture* (Akron, Ohio: Commercial Printing Co., 1902), 4.

2. "The Ohio Story," typescript of radio show broadcast on Mar. 21, 1947, WTAM Cleveland, Miscellaneous Papers, Davey Tree Expert Company; Pfleger, *Green Leaves,* 19–22.

3. *Cleveland Plain Dealer,* Mar. 24, 1918.

4. John Davey, "Presenting a Book to the World," handwritten manuscript, 1910, Miscellaneous Papers, Davey Tree Expert Company.

5. MLD, "Autobiography," 35–36.

6. Ibid., 36; Pfleger, *Green Leaves,* 23–25.

7. MLD, "Autobiography," 38–42.

8. Ibid., 42; Jan Cigliano, *Showplace of America: Cleveland's Euclid Avenue, 1850–1910* (Kent, Ohio: Kent State Univ. Press, 1991), 2.

9. MLD, "Autobiography," 42–44.

10. Davey and others simply called it the World's Fair.

11. MLD, "Autobiography," 36–37.

12. Ibid., 44–49.

13. Ibid., 50–53.

14. Ibid., 23.

3. SCHOLAR AND ATHLETE AT OBERLIN

1. Mark L. Thomsen to Geo.[rge] M. Jones, Mar. 13, 1903; MLD to Jones, Mar. 18, 1903, both in Martin L. Davey Papers, Oberlin College Archives, Oberlin, Ohio; *Academy Legislation, Oberlin, 1905, 3–4*, Series 2, Printed Material, 1871, 1904–16, Oberlin College Archives.

2. George M. Jones to MLD, Apr. 1, 1903; MLD to Jones, Sept. 19, 1903, both in MLD Papers, Oberlin College Archives.

3. George M. Jones to MLD, Apr. 19, 1904; MLD to Jones, Aug. 19, 1904, both in MLD Papers, Oberlin College Archives.

4. George M. Jones to MLD, Aug. 22, 1904, MLD Papers, Oberlin College Archives.

5. MLD to George M. Jones, Sept. 2, 1904, MLD Papers, Oberlin College Archives; Oberlin College Certificate of Applicant for Admission, Series 1, Operating Records, 1901–16, Admissions Records, box 2, Oberlin College Archives.

6. Edward Henry Fairchild, *Historical Sketch of Oberlin College* (Springfield, Ohio: Republic Printing Co., 1868), 3, 5; James Harris Fairchild, *Oberlin: Its Origin, Progress and Results: An Address Prepared for the Alumni of Oberlin College, Assembled August 22, 1860* (Oberlin: R. Butler, 1871), 3.

7. E. H. Fairchild, *Historical Sketch,* 6.

8. Pamphlet, 2, Series 2, Printed Material, 1871, 1904–16, Oberlin College Archives.

9. John Barnard, *From Evangelicalism to Progressivism at Oberlin College, 1866–1917* (Columbus: Ohio State Univ. Press, 1969), 121.

10. Ibid., 109–10.

11. Pamphlet, Series 2, Printed Material, 1871, 1904–16; File 23, Oberlin Academy, both in Oberlin College Archives. Oberlin trustees abolished the Academy in June 1916.

12. *ETEAN* (Oberlin Academy yearbook), vol. 1, June 1914, 6–9, box 12, Miscellaneous Publications, 1914–15, Oberlin College Archives.

13. George M. Jones to MLD, Sept. 6, 1904, MLD Papers, Oberlin College Archives.

14. MLD, "Autobiography," 54–57.

15. *Academy Legislation, Oberlin, 1905, 7–8*. The same stringent hours did not apply to boys, although they were hardly free to do as they pleased. For instance, they were not even allowed to attend the meetings of the young ladies' literary society.

16. MLD, "Autobiography," 57–62.

17. MLD, *Why I Carry $1,000,000 Life Insurance* (Indianapolis: Rough Notes Co., 1926).

18. MLD, "Autobiography," 62; *Oberlin Review,* Oct. 12, 1905.

19. *Oberlin Review,* Oct. 19, 1905.

20. "Academy Yells," Miscellaneous Publications, 1871, 1904–16, Oberlin College Archives; MLD, "Autobiography," 62–63; *Cleveland Plain Dealer,* Oct. 22, 1905.

21. MLD, "Autobiography," 63–66.

22. Pfleger, *Green Leaves,* 26.

23. MLD, "Autobiography," 71–72.

24. Pfleger, *Green Leaves,* 26–27; MLD, "Autobiography," 71.

25. MLD, "Autobiography," 69–76.

26. Pfleger, *Green Leaves,* 28.

27. MLD, "Autobiography," 77.

28. Ibid., 67.

4. A BUSINESS IS BORN

1. John Davey, *John Davey's Primer on Trees and Birds* (Akron, Ohio: Werner Co., 1905), 7.

2. John Davey, "Presenting a Book to the World," Miscellaneous Papers, Davey Tree Expert Company.

3. Miscellaneous Papers, Davey Tree Expert Company.

4. Private secretary of King Edward VII to John Davey, Nov. 15, 1905, Miscellaneous Papers, Davey Tree Expert Company.

5. John Davey, *Davey's Floral and Landscape Educator,* Nov. 1878, 6, Miscellaneous Papers, Davey Tree Expert Company.

6. Berenice Davey to G[u]iles Davenport, June 25, 1953, Miscellaneous Papers, Davey Tree Expert Company; *The Davey Tree Surgeons' Bulletin* 1.7 (Apr. 2, 1910): 11, Miscellaneous Papers, Davey Tree Expert Company.

7. Goodrich had read *The Tree Doctor* and was so impressed that he hired Davey to treat some diseased trees on his Akron estate. See *Cleveland Plain Dealer,* Mar. 24, 1918.

8. MLD, "Autobiography," 77–78.

9. Pfleger, *Green Leaves,* 32.

10. MLD, "Autobiography," 78–80.

11. Ibid., 80–81. John Archbold became one of the Davey company's most ardent supporters, writing glowing testimonials that the Daveys used in their advertising. See John D. Archbold to John Davey, July 15, 1907, and Archbold to MLD, May 24, 1910, advertisements, Miscellaneous Papers, Davey Tree Expert Company.

12. MLD, "Autobiography," 81–89.

13. Ibid., 89–90; "The Ohio Story," 4, Miscellaneous Papers, Davey Tree Expert Company.

14. MLD, "The Story of the Davey Organization," 1–3 (n.d.), Miscellaneous Papers, Davey Tree Expert Company; Pfleger, *Green Leaves,* 48.

15. While in the Pittsburgh area with a tree crew, Jim Davey and a few fellow workers dated some young women who had never heard of tree surgery. One of them, a bit confused, asked Davey if he and his men "skinned trees" for a living. He jokingly said "yes," and from then on his tree men called themselves "tree skinners." See MLD, "Autobiography," 70; Pfleger, *Green Leaves,* 43, 48.

16. MLD, Editorial, *Davey Tree Surgeons' Bulletin* 1.2 (Feb. 26, 1910): 2; MLD to C. C. Weybrecht, Apr. 9, 1918, Miscellaneous Papers, Davey Tree Expert Company; MLD, "Story of the Davey Organization," 2.

17. *Davey Tree Surgeons' Bulletin* 1.6 (Mar. 26, 1910): 1, Miscellaneous Papers, Davey Tree Expert Company.

18. Scratchbook No. 4028, 1910, Miscellaneous Papers, Davey Tree Expert Company; *Davey Tree Surgeons' Bulletin* 1.6 (Mar. 26, 1910): 2; hand-penciled list of Davey company wages, 1909–33, Miscellaneous Papers, Davey Tree Expert Company.

19. Pfleger, *Green Leaves,* 49–50, 35–36.

20. *Davey Tree Surgeons' Bulletin* 1.1 (Feb. 19, 1910): 1, Miscellaneous Papers, Davey Tree Expert Company; Pfleger, *Green Leaves,* 40.

21. *Davey Tree Surgeons' Bulletin* 1.1 (Feb. 19, 1910): 3, 8; ibid., no. 7 (Apr. 2, 1910): 1, Miscellaneous Papers, Davey Tree Expert Company.

22. MLD, "Autobiography," 90–91.

23. *The Garden Magazine* 11.2 (Mar. 1910): 65; ibid., no. 3 (Apr. 1910): 152; ibid., no. 4 (May 1910): 224, Miscellaneous Papers, Davey Tree Expert Company. The company struck similar themes in subsequent advertising, trying to impress readers that trees, like humans, were priceless, living organisms deserving of the finest care. See *The New Country Life* (Aug. 1917), 4–5, Miscellaneous Papers, Davey Tree Expert Company.

24. Berenice Davey to G[u]iles Davenport, June 25, 1953, Miscellaneous Papers, Davey Tree Expert Company.

25. MLD, "Autobiography," 94–97.

26. Ibid., 97, 101–2; *Davey Tree Surgeons' Bulletin* 1.7 (Apr. 2, 1910): 5, Miscellaneous Papers, Davey Tree Expert Company.

27. MLD, "Autobiography," 95–102.

28. Landon Warner, "Judson Harmon," in *The Governors of Ohio,* Ohio Historical Society (Columbus, Ohio: Stoneman Press, 1954), 152–53; MLD, "Autobiography," 102–3.

29. MLD, "Autobiography," 103–5.

30. Frank Freidel, *America in the Twentieth Century,* 3d ed. (New York: Alfred A. Knopf, Inc., 1970), 86–94, 107.

31. MLD, "Autobiography," 105–6; Pfleger, *Green Leaves,* 38.

32. MLD, "Autobiography," 106.

5. "BOY WONDER" MAYOR

1. MLD, "Autobiography," 107.

2. Grismer, *History of Kent,* 97–98.

3. MLD, "Autobiography," 109–10.

4. *Kent Courier,* Sept. 5, 1913.

5. MLD, "Autobiography," 108–12.

6. *Akron Beacon Journal,* Nov. 5, 1913. Although dubbed "the boy wonder," the youthful Davey was no anomaly in Kent politics. The village had a history of choosing young officials. For example, in 1900 residents elected a twenty-two-year-old as mayor, and in the same year a twenty-three-year-old was appointed postmaster. See Grismer, *History of Kent,* 104.

7. Record of Ordinances, 1906–24, 79, 223, 122, Office of Clerk of Council, Kent, Ohio; *Ravenna Republican,* July 8, 1915.

8. *Ravenna Republican,* May 18, 1916.

9. Ibid., Mar. 9, 1916.

10. Ibid., Mar. 30, 1916.

11. Ibid., Sept. 7, 1916; Record of Meetings of Council, 1, Sept. 25, 1916, Office of Clerk of Council, Kent, Ohio.

12. *Ravenna Republican,* Apr. 9, May 7, 1914.

13. Record of Ordinances, 1906–24, 124, Office of Clerk of Council, Kent, Ohio; Grismer, *History of Kent,* 99–100.

14. Grismer, *History of Kent,* 100.

15. Ibid.; MLD, "Autobiography," 119.

16. Grismer, *History of Kent,* 102–3.

17. Ibid., 103, 206–7.

18. Ibid., 103–4; MLD, "Autobiography," 108.

19. Grismer, *History of Kent,* 110.

20. MLD, "Autobiography," 113.

21. Record of Ordinances, 1906–24, 77–78, Office of Clerk of Council, Kent, Ohio; *Ravenna Republican,* Apr. 3, May 4, 1916; MLD, "Autobiography," 114.

22. MLD, "Autobiography," 115–16.

23. *Ravenna Republican,* Aug. 6, 1914.

24. MLD, "Autobiography," 116–18.

25. Ibid., 118–19; Randolph C. Downes, *The Rise of Warren Gamaliel Harding, 1865–1920* (Columbus: Ohio State Univ. Press, 1970), 213–14. Harding also helped the publishers of the *Accuser,* another anti-Catholic newspaper, distribute anti-Hogan articles and supported the Junior Order of American Mechanics, a nativist, anti-Catholic organization, in its attempts to restrict the flow of Catholic immigrants from southern and eastern Europe to the United States.

26. MLD, "Autobiography," 119–20; *Ravenna Republican,* Nov. 4, 11, 1915.

27. MLD, "Autobiography," 119–20.

28. *Ravenna Republican,* Feb. 3, 28, 1916.

29. MLD, "Autobiography," 122–23.

30. Kendrick A. Clements, *The Presidency of Woodrow Wilson* (Lawrence: Univ. Press of Kansas, 1992), 134.

31. MLD, "Autobiography," 121.

32. George Donelson Moss, *America in the Twentieth Century,* 2d ed. (Englewood Cliffs, N.J.: Prentice Hall, 1993), 81–82.

33. MLD, "Autobiography," 124.

34. *Ravenna Republican,* Mar. 5, 1917.

35. Ibid., June 25, 1917; *Akron Beacon Journal,* Nov. 7, 1917.

36. MLD, "Autobiography," 125. Although Martin's confiscation of coal was extraordinary, his action was not unique. The bitter winter of 1916–17 compelled 200 other officials throughout the state to do the same in the name of humanity. *Akron Beacon Journal,* Nov. 7, 1917.

37. MLD, "Autobiography," 125–26, 128–30.

38. Ibid., 121; *Ravenna Republican,* Nov. 2, 1916.

39. MLD, "Autobiography," 130–32.

40. Landon Warner, "James M. Cox," in *Governors of Ohio,* 156–58.

41. MLD, "Autobiography," 131–34, 136.

42. *Akron Beacon Journal,* Oct. 21, 1918.

43. Ibid., Oct. 12, 1918.

44. Ibid.

45. Ibid.

46. Moss, *America in the Twentieth Century* (2d ed.), 81–82. By the end of the war, twenty-four million men had complied with the law, nearly five million had been drafted, and two million of those were shipped to France.

47. *Akron Beacon Journal,* Oct. 25, 1918.

48. Ibid., Nov. 2, 1918.

49. Ibid., Oct. 30, 1918.

50. Ibid., Oct. 25, 1918.

51. MLD, "Autobiography," 134; *Akron Beacon Journal,* Nov. 2, 1918.

52. *Akron Beacon Journal,* Nov. 4, 1918. Several pages of this issue of the *Beacon Journal* are misdated Oct. 4.

53. Ibid., Nov. 6, 7, 8, 1918; Carl Wittke, ed., *The History of the State of Ohio,* Vol. 6: *Ohio in the Twentieth Century, 1900–1938* (Columbus: Ohio State Archaeological and Historical Society, 1942), 33.

54. MLD, "Autobiography," 136–40.

55. MLD to Village Council, Kent, Ohio, Nov. 23, 1918, in Record of Meetings of Council, 287, Office of Clerk of Council, Kent, Ohio.

6. OFF TO CONGRESS

1. Constance McLaughlin Green, *Washington, Capital City: 1879–1950,* 2 vols. (Princeton, N.J.: Princeton Univ. Press, 1963), 2:250–51, photo. 18.

2. Ibid., 258, 252–53.

3. *Congressional Record,* 65th Cong., 3d sess., 1918–19, 11; MLD, "Autobiography," 140.

4. MLD, "Autobiography," 140–41.

5. *New York Times,* Dec. 3, 1918.

6. Ibid.

7. MLD, "Autobiography," 141.

8. Ibid., 143; Paul Davey to John and Bertha Davey, Jan. 16, 1919, in *Kent Courier,* Feb. 13, 1919.

9. MLD, "Autobiography," 143–44.

10. *Congressional Record,* 65th Cong., 3d sess., 1918–19, 2172; MLD, "Autobiography," 144–45.

11. MLD, "Autobiography," 145; *Kent Courier,* Feb. 6, 1919.

12. Martin Davey's feelings ran deep after Happy's death. Years later he confessed of "resenting" Happy's original physician. MLD, "Autobiography," 145.

13. Ibid., 145–47.

14. *Congressional Record,* 66th Cong., 1st sess., 1919, 2837; MLD, "Autobiography," 147.

15. MLD, "Autobiography," 148.

16. *New York Times,* Nov. 12, 1919.

17. Ralph de Toledano, *J. Edgar Hoover: The Man in His Time* (New Rochelle, N.Y.: Arlington House, 1973), 48–49.

18. Ibid., 50–51.

19. Ibid., 51; Hank Messick, *John Edgar Hoover: An Inquiry into the Life and Times of John Edgar Hoover and His Relationship to the Continuing Partnership of Crime, Business and Politics* (New York: David McKay Co., 1972), 11, 14.

20. *Akron Beacon Journal,* Nov. 20, 21, 18, 1919.

21. *Congressional Record,* 66th Cong., 1st sess., 1919, 6980; MLD, "Autobiography," 151.

22. *Congressional Record,* 66th Cong., 1st sess., 1919, 8697; *Akron Beacon Journal,* Oct. 19, 1920. Davey's measure was broader than the sedition law Congress passed in 1918 while the United States was still at war with the Central Powers. The 1918 act was intended primarily to protect the military from outside subversion and penalized anyone who openly supported Germany during World War I. See Alfred A. Kelly, Winifred A. Harbison and Herman Belz, *The American Constitution: Its Origins and Development,* 7th ed., 2 vols. (New York: W. W. Norton, 1991), 2:513.

23. *Congressional Record,* 66th Cong., 2d sess., 1920, 2574.

24. Ibid., 2579.

25. MLD, "Autobiography," 151–53.

26. Walter LaFeber, *The American Age: United States Foreign Policy at Home and Abroad since 1750* (New York: W. W. Norton, 1989), 307–8.

27. Clements, *Presidency of Woodrow Wilson,* 190.

28. Robert H. Ferrell, *American Diplomacy: A History,* 3d ed. (New York: W. W. Norton, 1975), 493–94.

29. MLD, "Autobiography," 153–55.

30. Clements, *Presidency of Woodrow Wilson,* 196–202.

31. MLD, "Autobiography," 154–56.

32. *Congressional Record,* 65th Cong., 3d sess., 1918–19, 169; 66th Cong., 2d sess., 1920, 6599–600; 66th Cong., 3d sess., 1921, 2031–32.

33. Ibid., 66th Cong., 2d sess., 1920, 5669–70. To fortify his remarks, Martin, an excellent storyteller going back to his days as a salesman, related the poignant tale of a young Bolshevik captured as a spy during the Russian civil war of 1918–21. An American who befriended the mortally wounded Russian asked him why he was a Bolshevik. He responded, "They hold my mother as a hostage, and if I fall she dies." He then drew some money from his pocket and asked his captors to get it to his poor mother, imploring them at the same time to let the Bolsheviks know that he "died for them so that [his] old mother may live." Ibid., 5670.

34. Ibid., 66th Cong., 3d sess., 1920, 239.

35. James M. Cox, *Journey Through My Years* (New York: Simon and Schuster, 1946), 241–42.

36. MLD, "Autobiography," 160.

37. *Akron Beacon Journal,* Nov. 3, 1920.

38. MLD, "Autobiography," 150.

39. *Akron Press,* Oct. 23, 1920; *Cleveland Plain Dealer,* Oct. 29, 1920.

40. *Cleveland Plain Dealer,* Oct. 30, 1920; *Akron Evening Times,* Oct. 30, 1920.

41. MLD, "Autobiography," 157–58; *Akron Beacon Journal,* Oct. 6, 1920; *Ravenna Republican,* Oct. 27, 1920.

42. J. R. McQuigg to Summit County American Legion Council, Oct. 23, 1920, *Akron Sunday Times,* Oct. 24, 1920.

43. *Akron Beacon Journal,* Oct. 25, 27, 1920.

44. Ibid., Oct. 26, 1920.

45. Ibid., Oct. 18, 26, 15, 1920.

46. Ibid., Oct. 30, 1920.

47. *Ravenna Republican,* Oct. 27, 1920; *Akron Sunday Times,* Oct. 31, 1920; *Akron Evening Times,* Nov. 1, 1920; *Akron Beacon Journal,* Nov. 1, 1920.

48. Martin's victories in Summit County and Akron were short-lived. The Summit County Board of Elections reported that a broken tabulating machine had mistakenly credited Martin with 500 votes that were supposed to go to Knight. Knight ended up with a 50-vote victory in Summit County and a 211-vote margin in Akron. See *Ravenna Republican,* Nov. 12, 1920. A Democratic member of the Board of Elections later told

Martin that the results were actually changed to spare Knight the embarrassment of losing both his hometown and county. Since the election result was unaffected, no true harm was done. See MLD, "Autobiography," 162; *Ravenna Republican*, Nov. 5, 1920.

49. *Akron Evening Times*, Nov. 4, 1920.

50. *Akron Beacon Journal*, Nov. 4, 1920.

51. MLD, "Autobiography," 159–60, 162.

52. *Congressional Record*, 66th Cong., 3d sess., 1921, 4488–89.

7. OUT OF OFFICE

1. Green, *Washington*, 2:275.

2. MLD, "Autobiography," 164.

3. Grismer, *History of Kent*, 111–16.

4. *Cleveland Plain Dealer*, pictorial, Apr. 7, 1918, John Davey file, Miscellaneous Papers, Davey Tree Expert Company.

5. Pfleger, *Green Leaves*, 85–88.

6. Ibid., 88–89.

7. MLD, "Autobiography," 164–72.

8. *Akron Beacon Journal*, Oct. 27, Nov. 1, 3, 1922.

9. MLD, "Autobiography," 174–76.

10. Wittke, *History of Ohio*, 6:40.

11. MLD, "Autobiography," 177–80.

12. Ibid., 179; Wittke, *History of Ohio*, 6:40.

13. MLD, "Autobiography," 179.

14. *Akron Beacon Journal*, Oct. 12, 1922.

15. *Ravenna Republican*, Oct. 27, 1922.

16. Ibid., Nov. 1, 1922; *Akron Beacon Journal*, Nov. 6, 1922.

17. *Akron Beacon Journal*, Oct. 20, 1922.

18. Ibid., Oct. 31, 1922.

19. *Akron Evening Times*, Nov. 6, 1922; *Akron Press*, Nov. 1, 1922.

20. *Akron Beacon Journal*, Nov. 7, 1922.

21. Ibid., Nov. 8, 1922; *Akron Evening Times*, Nov. 8, 1922; *Ravenna Republican*, Nov. 8, 13, 1922.

22. *Akron Beacon Journal*, Nov. 9, Oct. 21, 1922.

23. MLD, "Autobiography," 174; *Akron Beacon Journal*, Nov. 9, 1922.

8. BACK TO WASHINGTON

1. Calvin Coolidge, *The Autobiography of Calvin Coolidge* (New York: Cosmopolitan Book Corp., 1929), 173–74.

2. Ibid., 175–76.

3. Francis Russell, *The Shadow of Blooming Grove: Warren G. Harding in His Times* (New York: McGraw-Hill, 1968), 592–96.

4. Ibid., 596–600.

5. Ibid., 600–601.

6. Ibid., 601–3.

7. MLD, "Autobiography," 183. Martin may have caught the president in one of his rare talkative moments. Coolidge lamented that the unceasing demand for "public utterances" was one of the "most appalling trials" he was subjected to. He so despised addressing the public that he even counted the number of words in a typical year's worth of speeches (75,000). Public speaking, he complained, was exacting work requiring the most careful attention because each word would be "dissected at home and abroad to discover its outward meaning and possible hidden implications." Coolidge, *Autobiography*, 219–20.

8. MLD, "Autobiography," 199–200.

9. *Congressional Record,* 68th Cong., 1st sess., 1924, 4362, 4367.

10. MLD, "Autobiography," 184.

11. Grover Cleveland, during his first term as president, was so appalled by Congress' freewheeling where Civil War pensions were concerned that he vetoed more than 200 private pension bills. He also vetoed a Dependent Pension Bill that would have granted pensions to all disabled veterans even if their disabilities were not service related.

12. Claude M. Fuess, *Calvin Coolidge: The Man from Vermont* (Hamden, Conn.: Archon Books, 1965), 382–83.

13. MLD, "Autobiography," 184–85.

14. Cited in Freidel, *America in the Twentieth Century,* 257.

15. Ibid., 257–59.

16. Fuess, *Coolidge,* 383–84.

17. Freidel, *America in the Twentieth Century,* 259; Fuess, *Coolidge,* 384.

18. MLD, "Autobiography," 185. Davey was right. Between 1920 and 1929, farm income dropped from 15 to 9 percent of the national economy. See Freidel, *America in the Twentieth Century,* 259.

19. MLD, "Autobiography," 200; *Cleveland Plain Dealer,* Nov. 9, 1923.

20. MLD, "Autobiography," 200.

21. Ibid., 200–201; *Cleveland Plain Dealer,* Dec. 11, 1924.

22. MLD, "Autobiography," 201.

23. Ibid., 186–88.

24. Ibid., 189. Rockwell, who did engineer McAdoo's candidacy at the national convention, refused to let bygones be bygones. He turned down Martin's request for complimentary tickets to the convention. *New York Times,* June 13, 1924.

25. *New York Times,* June 13, 1924.

26. MLD, "Autobiography," 189.

27. *New York Times,* July 1, 1924.

28. Ibid.

29. Ibid., July 2, 4, 1924.

30. Ibid., July 5, 1924.

31. Ibid., July 2, 4, 1924.

32. Ibid., July 2, 1924.

33. William G. McAdoo to Thomas J. Walsh, July 9, 1924, *New York Times,* July 9, 1924.

34. *New York Times,* July 10, 1924.

35. Ibid.

36. MLD, "Autobiography," 192.

37. Arnold S. Rice, *The Ku Klux Klan in American Politics* (New York: Haskell House, 1972), 15, 17.

38. Ibid., 16–18.

39. Kenneth T. Jackson, *The Ku Klux Klan in the City, 1915–1930* (New York: Oxford Univ. Press, 1967), 164–66.

40. Rice, *The Klan in American Politics,* 13.

41. Jackson, *The Klan in the City,* 166.

42. MLD, "Autobiography," 193–97.

43. Clyde W. Osborne, Grand Dragon of Ohio, to "all CYCLOPS, KLIGRAPPS, AND LOYAL KLANSMEN IN THE REALM OF OHIO," Oct. 23, 1924, box 1, folder 1, Maurice Maschke Papers, MSS 20, Ohio Historical Society. Interestingly, although this letter was secret (its contents were to be passed on orally), it ended up in Maurice Maschke's hands, adding to the suspicion that the Ohio Republican Party boss was kept abreast of the Klan's plans. Rice, *The Klan in American Politics,* 74–75; Jackson, *The Klan in the City,* 169.

44. MLD, "Autobiography," 198.

45. *Akron Beacon Journal,* Oct. 20, 23, 1924.

46. Ibid., Oct. 28, 29, Nov. 1, 1924.

47. Ibid., Oct. 29, Nov. 5, 6, 1924.

48. Freidel, *America in the Twentieth Century,* 247; Moss, *America in the Twentieth Century* (2d ed.), 125–26.

49. *New York Times,* Aug. 12, 15, 1924; Freidel, *America in the Twentieth Century,* 247–48; MLD, "Autobiography," 201.

50. MLD, "Autobiography," 203–6.

51. Ibid., 207; *Ravenna Republican,* Mar. 8, 1926; *Akron Beacon Journal,* Mar. 8, 1926.

52. Pfleger, *Green Leaves,* 102.

53. Russell F. Weigley, ed., *Philadelphia: A 300-Year History* (New York: W. W. Norton, 1982), 571–72.

54. Ibid., 573.

55. Edwin Wolf II, *Philadelphia: Portrait of an American City* (Harrisburg, Pa.: Stackpole Books, 1975), 294; Weigley, *Philadelphia,* 573.

56. MLD, "Autobiography," 208–10.

57. Ibid., 210–11.

58. *Congressional Record,* 69th Cong., 1st sess., 1926, 12, 283–85.

59. Martin's idol, Thomas Jefferson, was himself a bundle of contradictions. He preached fiscal and military restraint yet spent $15 million for the Louisiana Territory and sent the U.S. Navy to war against the Barbary States. He stood for freedom of speech but tried to remove some of his most strident critics in the judiciary. He argued that government should play a minimal role in people's lives but constantly stretched his presidential powers to advance his program.

60. *Congressional Record,* 69th Cong., 1st sess., 1926, 684, 770–71.

61. MLD, "Autobiography," 212.

62. Newspaper accounts, Feb. and Mar. 1926, box 7, folder 26, MLD Papers, OHS.

63. *Congressional Record,* 69th Cong., 1st sess., 1926, 4341.

64. Ibid.

65. Ibid., 4347.

66. MLD, "Autobiography," 214–15; *Congressional Record,* 69th Cong., 1st sess., 1926, 4342.

67. *Congressional Record,* 69th Cong., 1st sess., 1926, 4342.

68. Ibid., 4343, 4346.

69. MLD, "Autobiography," 242.

70. Ibid., 211.

71. Ibid., 215–16.

72. *Akron Beacon Journal,* Nov. 1, 1926.

73. MLD, "Autobiography," 217–18; *Akron Beacon Journal,* Oct. 28, 1926.

74. *Akron Beacon Journal,* Oct. 26, 1926. Marting protested to Missouri senator James A. Reed, who had gained the sobriquet "The Missouri Cyclone" by investigating corrupt senatorial campaigns in Illinois and Indiana. Ibid., Oct. 27, 1926.

75. Ibid., Oct. 29, 30, Nov. 1, 1926.

76. MLD, "Autobiography," 217.

77. *Akron Beacon Journal,* Nov. 3, 4, 1926.

78. Counting his 1918 short term.

79. *Congressional Record,* 69th Cong., 2d sess., 1927, 3717–19, 4249–50.

80. Ibid., 3717; MLD, speech before the International [Life Insurance] Underwriters' Convention, Atlantic City, Sept. 16, 1926, cited in *Congressional Record,* 69th Cong., 2d sess., 1927, 5286.

9. GOVERNOR?

1. MLD, "Autobiography," 235–37, 241–43.

2. *Congressional Record,* 70th Cong., 1st sess., 1928, 5452; John Toland, *The Great Dirigibles: Their Triumphs and Disasters* (New York: Dover, 1972), 232.

3. *Cleveland Plain Dealer,* Mar. 28, 1928; *Congressional Record,* 70th Cong., 1st sess., 1928, 5452–55.

4. MLD, "Autobiography," 238–39.

5. *Congressional Record,* 70th Cong., 1st sess., 1928, 5452–55, 5458–59.

6. Henry Cord Meyer, *Airshipmen, Business and Politics, 1890–1940* (Washington, D.C.: Smithsonian Institution Press, 1991), 84–85; Robert Jackson, *Airships: A Popular History of Dirigibles, Zeppelins, Blimps and Other Lighter-Than-Air Craft* (Garden City, N.Y.: Doubleday, 1973), 183–84.

7. MLD, press release, Feb. 23, [1928], box 1, folder 1, MLD Papers, OHS.

8. J. K. Falls, pastor, First Church of Christ, Kent, to "Dear Brother Pastor," May 24, 1928; F. E. Haymaker (Lincoln Ford dealer), Kent, to "Dear Sir," n.d. [1928]; and various other mss, all in box 1, folder 1, MLD Papers, OHS.

9. MLD, "Autobiography," 226.

10. *Akron Beacon Journal,* Aug. 2, 1928; *Ravenna Evening Record,* Aug. 8, 1928; MLD, "Autobiography," 226.

11. MLD, "Autobiography," 219–20.

12. *Ravenna Evening Record,* Aug. 14, 15, 1928; MLD, "Autobiography," 226.

13. MLD to "Dear Friend," Apr. 7, 1928, box 1, folder 1, MLD Papers, OHS.

14. *Kent Courier,* Apr. 17, 1928.

15. David Burner, *Herbert Hoover: A Public Life* (New York: Alfred A. Knopf, 1979), 190.

16. Ibid.

17. Edward Eugene Robinson and Vaughn Davis Bornet, *Herbert Hoover: President of the United States* (Stanford, Calif.: Hoover Institution Press, 1975), 18.

18. Richard O'Connor, *The First Hurrah: A Biography of Alfred E. Smith* (New York: Putnam's, 1970), 211.

19. Herbert Hoover, *The Memoirs of Herbert Hoover,* Vol. 2: *The Cabinet and the Presidency, 1920–1933* (New York: Macmillan, 1952), 199.

20. O'Connor, *First Hurrah,* 206.

21. Ibid., 207–9.

22. Ibid., 209–10.

23. Charles C. Marshall, "An Open Letter to the Honorable Alfred E. Smith," *Atlantic Monthly* 139 (Jan.–June 1927): 540–49; Edmund A. Moore, *A Catholic Runs for President: The Campaign of 1928* (New York: Ronald Press, 1956), 66.

24. Moore, *A Catholic Runs for President,* 64–65.

25. Alfred E. Smith, *Up to Now: An Autobiography* (New York: Viking, 1929), 411–12.

26. Hoover, *Memoirs: Cabinet and Presidency,* 205–6.

27. Maurice Maschke Inventory, Maschke Papers, OHS; John D. Fackler to "Dear Sir," Aug. 10, 1928, Maurice Maschke Papers, box 1, folder 1, OHS.

28. *Akron Beacon Journal,* Oct. 23, 1928.

29. Ibid.; MLD, press release, Oct. 24, 1928, box 1, folder 2, MLD Papers, OHS.

30. *Akron Beacon Journal,* Nov. 1, 1928.

31. *Ravenna Evening Record,* Oct. 25, 1928.

32. *Cleveland Plain Dealer,* Nov. 1, 1928.

33. Ibid.; *Ravenna Evening Record,* Nov. 3, 1928.

34. *Cleveland Plain Dealer,* Nov. 5, 1928.

35. Ibid., Nov. 7, 1928.

36. Martin L. Fausold, *The Presidency of Herbert C. Hoover* (Lawrence: Univ. Press of Kansas, 1985), 30.

37. MLD, "Autobiography," 232, 227.

38. Ibid., 229–31.

39. Circular File sent out by Frank Bechtle, president, Davey Hometown Club, n.d. [probably Feb. 1929], box 11, folder "Davey," Myers Y. Cooper Papers, MSS 337, OHS.

40. For example, see Earl H. Wells to MLD, Nov. 19, 1928, box 7, folder 26, MLD Papers, OHS; MLD, "Autobiography," 232.

41. MLD, "Autobiography," 233; "Dear Friend" letters, Dec. 19, 1928, box 1, folder 2, MLD Papers, OHS; MLD to Earl H. Wells, Dec. 7, 1928, box 7, folder 26, MLD Papers, OHS.

42. *Kent Courier,* Nov. 20, 1928.

43. MLD, "Autobiography," 247–52; *The Davey Bulletin* 83.9 (Sept. 1994): 6, Miscellaneous Papers, Davey Tree Expert Company.

44. MLD, "Autobiography," 253–54.

45. Ibid., 255–56.

10. THE GREAT DEPRESSION HITS HOME

1. Radio address, Feb. 16, 1930, typescript, KSU Special Collections.

2. Ibid.

3. MLD, "Autobiography," 253.

4. *Ravenna Evening Record,* Sept. 22, 1929.

5. A third newspaper, the *Hudson Herald,* owned by the *Kent Courier,* was also part of the deal. See *Ravenna Evening Record,* Sept. 23, 1929.

6. MLD, "Autobiography," 272–73.

7. Ibid., 274.

8. Pfleger, *Green Leaves,* 122.

9. MLD, "Autobiography," 275–76; Pfleger, *Green Leaves,* 122.

10. MLD, "Autobiography," 288–89.

11. Pfleger, *Green Leaves,* 123.

12. MLD, "Autobiography," 289–92.

13. *Ravenna Evening Record,* Oct. 22, 1929.

14. George Donelson Moss, *America in the Twentieth Century,* 5th ed. (Upper Saddle River, N.J.: Pearson Prentice Hall, 2004), 153.

15. Ibid., 153–54.

16. Freidel, *America in the Twentieth Century,* 285.

17. Pfleger, *Green Leaves,* 124–25.

18. Ted Morgan, *FDR: A Biography* (New York: Simon and Schuster, 1985), 332.

19. MLD, "Autobiography," 277–79, 281.

20. Cited in Freidel, *America in the Twentieth Century*, 299.

21. MLD, "Autobiography," 296.

22. Ibid., 284–85.

23. Helen M. Burns, *The American Banking Community and New Deal Banking Reforms, 1933–1935* (Westport, Conn.: Greenwood Press, 1974), 34.

24. Ibid., 34–35.

25. Ibid., 40.

26. Ronnie J. Phillips, *The Chicago Plan and New Deal Banking Reform* (Armonk, N.Y.: M. E. Sharpe, 1995), 37.

27. Burns, *American Banking Community*, 41–42.

28. Phillips, *Chicago Plan*, 41–43; Freidel, *America in the Twentieth Century*, 306–7.

29. Freidel, *America in the Twentieth Century*, 307; Burns, *American Banking Community*, 49.

30. Wittke, *History of Ohio*, 6:202–3.

31. Grismer, *History of Kent*, 161; MLD, "Autobiography," 292–93.

32. MLD, "Autobiography," 294–95.

33. Ibid., 307–10.

11. GOVERNOR!

1. *Ravenna Evening Record*, Sept. 23, 1929.

2. Martin's reluctance to seek the governorship was sincere. He did not even want to do so in 1932. He responded churlishly to a correspondent who chided him for supporting the "wet" Al Smith in 1928 and therefore refused to sign a petition supporting Martin for governor in 1932. Usually diplomatic with all his correspondents, Martin lectured his critic that he had not authorized any nominating petitions in his name and had not asked "you or anyone else to circulate a petition for me. Holding public office is not necessary to my happiness, and I certainly do not need a job." J. E. Welday to MLD, Mar. 8, 1932, and MLD to Welday, Mar. 12, 1932, both in box 7, folder 26, MLD Papers, OHS.

3. Robert Leslie Jones, "George White," in *Governors of Ohio*, 174–76.

4. MLD, "Autobiography," 258–61.

5. Wittke, *History of Ohio*, 6:55.

6. MLD, "Autobiography," 265–66.

7. James A. Garfield, diary, Mar. 14, 1877, microfilm, Rutherford B. Hayes Presidential Center, Fremont, Ohio; Theodore Clarke Smith, *The Life and Letters of James Abram Garfield*, 2 vols. (New Haven, Conn.: Yale Univ. Press, 1925), 2:654.

8. MLD, "Autobiography," 267–68.

9. Wittke, *History of Ohio*, 6:59–62.

10. Pfleger, *Green Leaves*, 114.

11. MLD, "Autobiography," 299–301.

12. Ibid., 302. Davey's uncomplimentary assessment of Hopkins (his "wild

look"; seemed "unbalanced"; easily spent other people's money, etc.) was made years after a bitter personal clash with Roosevelt's relief factotum.

13. Ibid., 302–3.

14. No meeting was more significant for Martin as he moved ahead with his political career in the 1930s. He and Poulson forged one of the tightest bonds in Ohio politics, and together the two weathered numerous accusations of scandal and corruption that marred Davey's governorship. MLD, "Autobiography," 312–13.

15. Ibid., 314, 318–19.

16. *Canton Repository*, Aug. 14, 1934.

17. MLD, "Autobiography," 316.

18. Such charges were commonplace for Davey. In all his campaigns, particularly those against John Bricker in 1936 and 1940, his opponents were always in the grip of one iron-fisted political boss or another. *Cleveland Plain Dealer*, July 17, 1934; MLD, "Autobiography," 285.

19. *Akron Beacon Journal*, July 19, 1934; *Cleveland Plain Dealer*, July 19, 1934; *Canton Repository*, Aug. 5, 1934.

20. *Cleveland Plain Dealer*, July 24, 29, 1934; *Canton Repository*, Aug. 8, 1934.

21. *New York Tribune*, Oct. 10, 1880; *Cleveland Plain Dealer*, July 25, 1934; *Canton Repository*, Aug. 7, 1934.

22. *Cleveland Plain Dealer*, July 27, 1934.

23. *Ravenna Evening Record, Akron Beacon Journal, Cleveland Plain Dealer*, and *Canton Repository*, all Aug. 4, 1934; *Ravenna Evening Record*, Aug. 7, 1934; *Canton Repository*, Aug. 12, 1934.

24. There is a letter written in almost childish scrawl from a Summit County Klansman claiming that he had passed out campaign literature (from the Summit County Klan office) for Martin during the 1920s. In 1934 this correspondent inquired about a job for his brother, and Martin's response was as tepid as any could be. Eldon B. Anderson to MLD, Aug. 12, 1934 [Sept. 12, 1934?], and MLD to Anderson, Sept. 17, 1934, both in box 4, folder 4, MLD Papers, OHS.

25. MLD, "Autobiography," 316–18.

26. *Canton Repository*, Aug. 16, 1934.

27. *Cleveland Plain Dealer*, Aug. 16, 1934; MLD, "Autobiography," 331; *Canton Repository*, Aug. 16, 1934.

28. *Cleveland Plain Dealer*, July 22, 1934.

29. Brown speeches, July 27 and Aug. 3, 1934, typescripts, box 3, folder 3, Clarence J. Brown Papers, MSS 279, OHS; *Cleveland Plain Dealer*, July 29 and Aug. 16, 1934.

30. Clarence J. Brown, "A Pledge to All Who Ask Better Government," box 3, folder 3, Clarence J. Brown Papers, OHS; MLD, "Autobiography," 338.

31. MLD, "Autobiography," 338, 334.

32. Ibid., 335–38.

33. Campaign schedule for Tuesday, Oct. 9, 1934, box 3, folder 10, MLD Papers, OHS; MLD, "Autobiography," 342–43.

34. MLD, "Autobiography," 343.

35. Daniel S. Young to MLD, Sept. 1, 1934; Myrna Smith to Judge Dean F. May, Sept. 10, 1934; Smith to W. B. Gongwer, Sept. 10, 1934; Smith to Daniel S. Young, Sept. 11, 1934, all in box 4, folder 4, MLD Papers, OHS; Paul S. Hartell to MLD, Sept. 7, 1934, and MLD to Hartell, Sept. 14, 1934, box 2, folder 6, MLD Papers, OHS.

36. Antoinette Neiman to MLD, Sept. 11, 1934, and MLD to Neiman, Sept. 21, 1934, box 1, folder 3, MLD Papers, OHS.

37. Alfred A. Benesch (president, Cleveland Board of Education) to MLD, Aug. 20, 1934, and MLD to Benesch, Aug. 27, 1934, box 1, folder 3, MLD Papers, OHS. Martin later appointed Benesch as director of commerce. Try though he might, Davey could not shake the Colescott link. Late in the campaign, the grand dragon claimed that Martin had asked him to mail 80,000 Klansmen a message saying that the Ku Klux Klan supported the Davey candidacy. Colescott said he refused the request. *Akron Beacon Journal,* Nov. 2, 1934.

38. Clarence J. Brown, press release, Oct. 15, 1934, box 3, folder 3, Clarence J. Brown Papers, OHS.

39. Oct. 26 and 31, 1934. See also *Akron Beacon Journal,* Oct. 16, 1934, *Canton Repository,* Oct. 16 and Nov. 3, 1934, and *Ravenna Evening Record,* Nov. 3, 1934; Gardner H. Townsley to Clarence J. Brown, n.d., box 3, folder 3, Clarence J. Brown Papers, OHS. Townsley, whose return address said, "Return in Five Days to the *Akron Beacon Journal,* Akron, Ohio," told Brown that John Knight had ordered one of his reporters to "write something to skin Davey."

40. Report by George Eppley, Sept. 21, [1934]; Nellie Kelly to Carl Bauer, Oct. 17, 1934, both in box 1, folder 3, MLD Papers, OHS.

41. *Akron Beacon Journal,* Oct. 11, 1934.

42. Ibid., Oct. 12, 1934.

43. Ibid., Oct. 22, 1934.

44. *Canton Repository,* Oct. 21, 1934; *Akron Beacon Journal,* Oct. 30, 1934.

45. MLD, "Autobiography," 328–29.

46. Daniel P. Conway to MLD, Sept. 8, 1934; John F. Cantwell to MLD, Sept. 22, 1934; A. L. Burgstaller to MLD, Oct. 6, 1934, all in box 2, folder 3, MLD Papers, OHS.

47. *Youngstown Vindicator,* Sept. 22, 1934, and *Youngstown Telegram,* Sept. 22, 1934, clippings in box 2, folder 3, MLD Papers, OHS.

48. Alvin W. Craver to Francis Poulson, Sept. 19, 1934; Craver to MLD, Sept. 19, 1934; *Youngstown Vindicator,* Sept. 22, 1934, clipping; Alvin W. Craver to MLD, Sept. 29, 1934; MLD to Martin Dunn, Oct. 4, 1934, all in box 2, folder 3, MLD Papers, OHS.

49. Jeannette N. Craver to Myrna Young Smith, Nov. 18, 1934, box 2, folder 3, MLD Papers, OHS.

50. *Canton Repository,* Oct. 26, 1934. Had Martin not later turned out to be so troublesome to the national administration, this likely would have been true.

51. Robert A. Taft to Simeon D. Fess, Aug. 22, 1934, box 3, folder 3, Clarence J. Brown Papers, OHS; Wittke, *History of Ohio,* 6:77–78.

52. *Cleveland Plain Dealer,* Nov. 4, 6, 1934.

53. MLD, "Autobiography," 341.

54. Nov. 8, 1934. The president of the Ohio Valley Bank Company in Gallipolis tried to console Brown—"No one could have made a better showing as evidenced by the results from Maine to Oregon"—and predicted an "orgy of spending" if the Democrats retained power in 1936. S. H. Eagle to Clarence Brown, Nov. 7, 1934, box 3, folder 3, Clarence J. Brown Papers, OHS.

55. MLD, "Autobiography," 341–42; *Canton Repository,* Nov. 8, 1934.

56. MLD, "Autobiography," 351.

57. Ibid., 349–51; *Ravenna Evening Record,* Nov. 7, 1934; *Canton Repository,* Nov. 9, 1934; *Akron Beacon Journal,* Nov. 7, 1934.

12. BATTLING THE ROOSEVELT BUREAUCRACY

1. MLD, "Autobiography," 357; *Cleveland Plain Dealer,* Jan. 15, 1935.

2. MLD, "Autobiography," 357–59.

3. Ibid., 354–55.

4. Ralph J. Donaldson, "Martin L. Davey," in *Governors of Ohio,* 180.

5. Ibid.

6. The *Cleveland Plain Dealer* aptly described the governor: "When he contemplates some rank injustice his eyelids narrow. He looks like a fighter, lithe, supple, capable of turning some break to his advantage." Martin himself said, "I never went out looking for a fight, and I never ran away from one." Undated clipping in Harold Davey to MLD, Oct. 15, 1934, box 5, folder 14, MLD Papers, OHS; *New York Times,* Mar. 18, 1935.

7. David J. Maurer, "Relief Problems and Politics in Ohio," in John Braeman, Robert H. Bremner, and David Brody, eds., *The New Deal: The State and Local Levels,* 2 vols. (Columbus: Ohio State Univ. Press, 1975), 2:81–83; Wittke, *History of Ohio,* 6:70.

8. Democratic politicians flooded Hopkins with complaints that the best interests of the party were ill-served through nonpartisan relief administration. See Searle F. Charles, *Minister of Relief: Harry Hopkins and the Depression* (Syracuse, N.Y.: Syracuse Univ. Press, 1963), 74–76, and Edwin P. Hoyt, *The Tempering Years* (New York: Scribner, 1963), 88. Transcripts of telephone conversations with state relief directors and other officials, Ohio–South Dakota (hereafter telephone transcripts), Dec. 11, 1934, and Feb. 2, 1935, container 77, Harry Hopkins Papers, Franklin D. Roosevelt Library, Hyde Park, N.Y. Hopkins knew of Martin's intention in early Dec. 1934 through a telephone conversation with Ohio's U.S. senator Robert Bulkley and acquiesced in it during a call to the governor on Jan. 19, 1935. See telephone transcripts, Dec. 8, 1934 and Jan. 19, 1935.

9. *Cleveland Plain Dealer,* Mar. 2, 1935.

10. Ibid., Mar. 1, 1935. The *Cleveland Plain Dealer* ridiculed Martin for stating that the CCRA had 1,500 workers. The actual figure was 2,000. Moreover, the news-

paper pointed out that only three days before his election the governor had lauded the CCRA for its efficiency. See ibid., Mar. 2, 4, 1935.

11. Ibid., Mar. 3, 1935. The starting salary for a CCRA social worker was $80 a month. Grossman, a practicing attorney, donated his services. Hopkins press conference, Mar. 5, 1935, typescript, Federal Relief Agency Papers, Confidential Political File, 1933–38, box 36, Harry Hopkins Papers.

12. *Cleveland Plain Dealer,* Mar. 3, 6, 1935; *New York Times,* Mar. 17, 1935; Harry Hopkins to MLD, Mar. 8, 1935, Federal Relief Agency Papers, Confidential Political File, 1933–38, box 36, Harry Hopkins Papers.

13. Hopkins press conference, Mar. 5, 1935, typescript, Federal Relief Agency Papers, Confidential Political File, 1933–38, box 36, Harry Hopkins Papers.

14. [MLD] to [?], n.d., box 6, folder 6, Miscellaneous Material, MLD Papers, OHS; *Cleveland Plain Dealer,* Mar. 7, 1935.

15. Martin was, of course, already an effective radio broadcaster, using the medium in his own version of fireside chats broadcast throughout Ohio. See Maurer, "Relief Problems and Politics in Ohio," 91.

16. Martin revealed that he had received reports of beer parties being held in relief offices and that residents of Kentucky, Michigan, and Pennsylvania were coming to Ohio for relief handouts. In another attack on the CCRA, the governor, perhaps purposely forgetting that large cities are especially affected by unemployment, charged that Cleveland, with one-sixth of the state's population, absorbed one-fourth of Ohio's relief allotment. He also upbraided the FERA for filling relief positions with young social workers who neither needed the money nor were suited for the job. *Cleveland Plain Dealer,* Mar. 10, 1935.

17. Ibid., Mar. 12, 1935; Harry Hopkins to MLD, Mar. 8, 1935, Federal Relief Agency Papers, Confidential Political File, 1933–38, box 36, Harry Hopkins Papers; J. P. Harris to Harry Hopkins, Feb. 9, 1935, Federal Relief Agency Papers, FERA-WPA Legislative and Legal Proceedings, 1933–39, container 80, Harry Hopkins Papers.

18. *Cleveland Plain Dealer,* Mar. 12, 1935.

19. Ibid., Mar. 13, 1935.

20. Ibid., Mar. 16, 1935; telephone transcripts, Mar. 14, 1935, container 77, Harry Hopkins Papers.

21. Harry Hopkins to Franklin D. Roosevelt, Mar. 11, 1935, Federal Relief Agency Papers, Confidential Political File, 1933–38, box 36; Harry Hopkins, diary, Mar. 16, 1935, Personal and Financial Matters, 1933–45, box 6, all in Harry Hopkins Papers.

22. Harry Hopkins, diary, Mar. 16, 1935, Personal and Financial Matters, 1933–45, box 6, Harry Hopkins Papers; Franklin D. Roosevelt to Harry Hopkins, Mar. 16, 1935, in Samuel I. Rosenman, ed., *The Public Papers and Addresses of Franklin D. Roosevelt,* 5 vols. (New York: Random House, 1938), 4:108.

23. *Cleveland Plain Dealer,* Mar. 17, 1935; *New York Times,* Mar. 17, 1935.

24. *Cleveland Plain Dealer,* Mar. 17, 1935; telephone transcripts, Mar. 18, 1935, container 77, Harry Hopkins Papers.

25. *New York Times,* Mar. 17, 1935.

26. Ibid. Many doubted Martin's purported ignorance of financial matters because the governor and Poulson were "as close as Damon and Pythias." See ibid., Mar. 18, 1935.

27. *Cleveland Plain Dealer,* Mar. 17, 1935.

28. *Journal of the House of Representatives of the State of Ohio,* 91st General Assembly, 1935 (Columbus, 1935), 116:436; *Cleveland Plain Dealer,* Mar. 19, 1935. He had gone to Newark, Ohio, for the warrant because he believed no judge in Columbus would give him a fair shake.

29. Party support for Martin was evident when six Democrats, three each from the House and Senate, were chosen for the ten-member investigating committee. A Republican proposal for a committee of twelve, with an equal split between Democrats and Republicans, was rejected. *Journal of the Senate of the State of Ohio,* 91st General Assembly, 116:329–30, 373; *Cleveland Plain Dealer,* Mar. 19, 21, 1935.

30. Telephone transcripts, Mar. 18, 1935, container 77, Harry Hopkins Papers.

31. *Cleveland Plain Dealer,* Mar. 19, 20, 1935; telephone transcripts, Mar. 20, 1935, container 77, Harry Hopkins Papers; *New York Times,* Mar. 20, 1935.

32. *New York Times,* Mar. 23, 1935; *Cleveland Plain Dealer,* Mar. 28, 21, 1935 Stillman's investigation in Trumbull County, for instance, revealed that relief administration workers constantly ignored rules and regulations. A review showed that hours worked, and sometimes even the names of employees, were falsified on payroll sheets. Eight people were discharged. See ibid., Apr. 14, 1935.

33. *Cleveland Plain Dealer,* Mar. 19, 20, 1935.

34. Ibid., Mar. 20, 1935.

35. Ibid. A partial listing of businesses solicited included the National Terminal Warehouse Company ($1,000), Hanna Coal Company ($1,000), Fred Essex Coal Company ($250), and United Colleries ($500).

36. A Franklin County grand jury also failed to indict the Davey "conspirators."

37. Hopkins, diary, May 14, 1935, Harry Hopkins Papers; *Cleveland Plain Dealer,* May 14, 1935.

38. *Cleveland Plain Dealer,* May 23, 1935.

39. Hopkins's retort to the Davey charge was appended to his Citizens League address: "I'd be less than frank if I didn't admit that you all want to know about the libel action against me. . . . I have this to say, I took the administration of relief in Ohio away from the governor and I have no intention whatever of giving it back to him. Since coming here I've heard a number of rumors that the governor's action in lifting the libel action against me was the result of a political deal, but I want to say, in just as plain a language as I can, that there was no understanding of any kind with anyone in Washington regarding the lifting of that libel action. I was told not to come to Ohio. I am here." *Cleveland Plain Dealer,* May 25, 1935.

40. Hopkins, diary, May 13, 1935, Harry Hopkins Papers. Hopkins and Ickes fought over fund allotments to PWA and WPA, disagreed on other project allocations, and

constantly competed for the president's favor. See Charles, *Minister of Relief,* 106–27, and Harold L. Ickes, *The Secret Diary of Harold L. Ickes: The First Thousand Days, 1933–1936* (New York: Simon and Schuster, 1953), 1:337.

41. George McJimsey, *Harry Hopkins: Ally of the Poor and Defender of Democracy* (Cambridge, Mass.: Harvard Univ. Press, 1987), 54. A sampling of Hopkins's philosophical views on relief and New Deal reform can be found in the following articles and speeches: "Boondoggling: Boon or Bane?" *Christian Science Monitor Magazine* (Aug. 19, 1936): 4, 14; "Employment in America," *Vital Speeches* 3 (Dec. 1, 1936): 103–7; "The Future of Relief," *New Republic* 90 (Feb. 10, 1937): 7–10; "Should Relief Funds Be Administered by the States?" *Congressional Digest* 15 (June 1936): 189–90.

42. Robert E. Sherwood, *Roosevelt and Hopkins: An Intimate History* (New York: Harper, 1948), 77. The disputes were serious. For example, Governor Langer and some of his associates served prison terms after being found guilty of misusing public funds. See Charles, *Minister of Relief,* 76.

43. Lorena Hickok to Harry Hopkins, Oct. 10, 1935, Lorena Hickok Reports to Harry Hopkins, 1935, box 11, Lorena Hickok Papers, FDR Library. Roosevelt grumbled that a losing Democratic slate in Ohio hurt the national ticket in the off-year elections of 1938. Afterward, the president wrote Josephus Daniels: "In Ohio, Davey, the worst of our Governors, wrecked the whole ticket." Elliott Roosevelt, ed., *F.D.R.: His Personal Letters, 1928–1945* (New York: Duell, Sloan and Pearce, 1950), 4:827; see also James Farley, *Jim Farley's Story: The Roosevelt Years* (New York: Whittlesey, 1948), 149.

44. Wittke, *History of Ohio,* 6:80–82.

45. MLD, "Autobiography," 385; *Cleveland Plain Dealer,* Jan. 15, 1935.

13. RUNNING THE STATE

1. George W. Knepper, *Ohio and Its People* (Kent, Ohio: Kent State Univ. Press, 1989), 361; Walter Havighurst, *Ohio: A Bicentennial History* (New York: W. W. Norton, 1976), 139.

2. Havighurst, *Ohio,* 138–39.

3. Ibid., 139; Knepper, *Ohio and Its People,* 361.

4. *Columbus Citizen,* Nov. 7, 1934, MLD Papers, box 8, folder 15, OHS.

5. Charles B. Nuckolls Jr., "The Governorship of Martin L. Davey of Ohio" (master's thesis, Ohio State University, 1952), 19. The other cabinet members were Emil F. Marx, adjutant general; Earl H. Hanefeld, director of agriculture; Alfred A. Benesch, director of commerce; Dr. B. O. Skinner, director of education (Dr. E. L. Bowsher replaced Skinner in Aug. 1935); Judge Howard L. Bevis, director of finance; Dr. W. H. Hartung, director of health; John J. Jaster Jr., director of highways; Ora B. Chapman, director of industrial relations; T. S. Brindle, director of public works. MLD, "Autobiography," 375.

6. MLD, "Autobiography," 384–87.

7. *Cleveland Plain Dealer,* Feb. 6, 1935.

8. Ibid., Feb. 9, 1935.

9. Ibid., Feb. 14, 1935; MLD, radio address, Mar. 16, 1936, typescript, box 8, folder 4, MLD Papers, OHS.

10. *Cleveland Plain Dealer,* Sept. 9, 1935.

11. Myrna Smith, "Supplement to the Material Martin L. Davey Included in His Autobiography" (hereafter "Supplement—[year]"), 24, Davey Administration—First Year, 1935, box 7, folder 1, MLD Papers, OHS; *Cleveland Plain Dealer,* Nov. 13, 1935.

12. MLD, "Autobiography," 390–92.

13. Lorena Hickok to Harry Hopkins, Oct. 10, 1935, Lorena Hickok Reports to Harry Hopkins, 1935, box 11, Lorena Hickok Papers; *Cleveland Plain Dealer,* Oct. 29, 1936.

14. *Cleveland Plain Dealer,* Oct. 29, 1935; MLD, radio address, Apr. 20, 1936, typescript, box 8, folder 4, MLD Papers, OHS.

15. Wittke, *History of Ohio,* 6:79–80; Nuckolls, "Davey Governorship," 33–37.

16. *Ravenna Evening Record,* Oct. 18, 1935; MLD, "Autobiography," 387–88.

17. MLD, "Autobiography," 421.

18. Eugene H. Roseboom and Francis P. Weisenburger, *A History of Ohio* (Columbus: Ohio State Archaeological and Historical Society, 1961), 367; MLD, "Autobiography," 421.

19. Cited in Thomas H. Smith, ed., *An Ohio Reader: Reconstruction to the Present,* 2 vols. (Grand Rapids, Mich.: Eerdmans, 1975), 2:289.

20. Knepper, *Ohio and Its People,* 446; MLD, "Autobiography," 422–23; Smith, "Supplement—1935," 17, MLD Papers, OHS. Although it was self-aggrandizing for him to say so, Martin described the Foundation Bill as the "greatest public school bill in the history of this, or any other state." See *Ravenna Evening Record,* Oct. 1, 1935.

21. Nuckolls, "Davey Governorship," 40.

22. Ibid., 40–42.

23. MLD, "Autobiography," 395–96.

24. *Cleveland Plain Dealer,* Oct. 12, 1935.

25. Ibid.

26. Ibid., Feb. 7, 1936; Smith, "Supplement—1936," 7, MLD Papers, OHS. The Ohio State University budget dispute was embarrassing to Martin. He wanted no repeat of it and approved without challenge the school's full budget requests for 1937–1938. See Nuckolls, "Davey Governorship," 45.

27. *Cleveland Plain Dealer,* June 2, 1935.

28. Ibid.

29. Ibid.

30. Ibid., June 1, 1935.

31. Ibid., June 2, 1935.

32. Smith, "Supplement—1935," 16, MLD Papers, OHS.

33. *Cleveland Plain Dealer,* Sept. 1, 1936.

34. Ibid.

35. Ibid.

36. Ibid.

37. Andrew R. L. Cayton, *Ohio: The History of a People* (Columbus: Ohio State Univ. Press, 2002), 317–18; Knepper, *Ohio and Its People,* 379.

38. *Ravenna Evening Record,* June 18, 1936; *Cleveland Plain Dealer,* July 1, 1936.

39. In 1937 he would not be so lucky and had to send in the national guard to quell labor unrest in Youngstown, Warren, and Canton.

40. *Cleveland Plain Dealer,* Oct. 6, 1935.

41. MLD, "Autobiography," 351–52.

42. Ibid., 393–94. Not only was Smith the first woman to serve as personal secretary to an Ohio governor, Margaret Allman was Ohio's first female cabinet member, and Martin named the first woman, Edith M. Patterson, to a seat on the state's Liquor Control Board. *Cleveland Plain Dealer,* Feb. 12, 1935.

43. *Ravenna Evening Record,* Nov. 12, 1935; *Cleveland Plain Dealer,* Nov. 13, 1935.

44. *Ravenna Evening Record,* Dec. 12, 1935.

45. MLD, "Autobiography," 352–53; *Ravenna Evening Record,* Mar. 23, 1936.

46. *Ravenna Evening Record,* May 23, 26, 1936. In early June 1936, Martin received an anonymous letter full of anti-Catholic and anti-Italian prejudice, but which nonetheless indicated that the Black Legion was operating openly as far west as Kansas City, Missouri. See "A One Hundred Percent American" to MLD, May 31, 1936, box 7, folder 29, MLD Papers, OHS.

47. *Ravenna Evening Record,* May 28, 1936.

48. Smith, "Supplement—1935," 37, MLD Papers, OHS.

49. *Ravenna Evening Record,* Nov. 15, 1935.

50. *Columbus Dispatch,* Jan. 18, 19, 1936.

51. Ibid., Jan. 21, 26, 1936.

52. MLD to William D. Overman, Oct. 19, 1936, Vertical File Material 412, MLD Papers, OHS; MLD, radio addresses, typescripts, Dec. 23, 1935, box 7, folder 28, and Sept. 7, 1936, box 8, folder 4, MLD Papers, OHS.

53. MLD, "Autobiography," 367–68.

14. TROUBLES

1. *Cleveland Plain Dealer,* May 13, 1936.

2. Ibid., May 5, 1936.

3. Ibid.

4. Ibid.

5. Ibid., May 14, 13, 1936.

6. Karl B. Pauly, *Bricker of Ohio: The Man and His Record* (New York: Putnam's, 1944), 80; *Ravenna Evening Record,* Oct. 19, 1936.

7. *Ravenna-Kent Evening Record and Daily Courier-Tribune,* Apr. 1, 1946; *Cleveland Plain Dealer,* Apr. 1, 1946.

8. *Columbus Dispatch,* Mar. 26, 1986.

9. *Cleveland Plain Dealer,* Oct. 4, 1936.

10. Ibid., Oct. 7, 1936.

11. Ibid., Oct. 28, 1936; Maurice Maschke Inventory, Maurice Maschke Papers, OHS; *Ravenna Evening Record,* Oct. 16, 1936. Others on Davey's list were Rees H. Davis, a Cleveland lawyer; Nolan Boggs and Walter Brown of Toledo; Dan Brower from Dayton; and D. C. Pemberton of Columbus, whom Martin described as the "greatest lobbyist" in the state capital. *Cleveland Plain Dealer,* Oct. 27, 1936.

12. Ibid., Oct. 28, 29, and Nov. 4, 1936.

13. Ibid., Oct. 13, 1936.

14. Ibid., Oct. 23, 1936; *Ravenna Evening Record,* Oct. 29, 1936.

15. *Cleveland Plain Dealer,* Oct. 22, 1936.

16. *Ravenna Evening Record,* Oct. 16, 1936. Davey campaigners also claimed that Bricker was anti-Catholic and anti-Jewish. See also *Cleveland Plain Dealer,* Oct. 19, 1936.

17. *Cleveland Plain Dealer,* Oct. 30, 1936.

18. Wittke, *History of Ohio,* 6:48; Pauly, *Bricker of Ohio,* 80–81; Daniel E. Morgan to William A. Mason, Jan. 8, 1937, container 1, folder 2, Correspondence 1933–49, Daniel E. Morgan Papers, MSS 3069, Western Reserve Historical Society (WRHS), Cleveland, Ohio.

19. *Cleveland Plain Dealer,* June 27, 1936.

20. MLD, radio address, Oct. 8, 1936, typescript, President's Personal File (PPF 4348), Franklin D. Roosevelt Papers, FDR Library; *Cleveland Plain Dealer,* Oct. 9, 1936.

21. Claude C. Waltermire to Daniel E. Morgan, Nov. 19, 1936, container 1, folder 1, Correspondence 1933–49, Daniel E. Morgan Papers.

22. *Cleveland Plain Dealer,* Oct. 29, 1936.

23. Ibid., Nov. 4, 1936. MLD worried about Bricker's strength in Cincinnati's Hamilton County, which was also Charles Sawyer territory. As it turned out, only Cuyahoga County gave the attorney general a wider margin than Hamilton County's 10,000 votes. Ibid., Nov. 5, 1936.

24. Wittke, *History of Ohio,* 6:84–85. Davey had 1,540,093 votes to Bricker's 1,412,780. Morgan, *FDR,* 441; Pauly, *Bricker of Ohio,* 81.

25. Smith, "Supplement—1937," 6, MLD Papers, OHS.

26. *Cincinnati Enquirer,* Jan. 15, 16, 1937.

27. Ibid., Jan. 18, 19, 1937.

28. Ibid., Jan. 20, 22, 1937.

29. Smith, "Supplement—1937," 7, MLD Papers, OHS; *Cincinnati Enquirer,* Jan. 26, 1937.

30. *Cincinnati Enquirer,* Feb. 2, 1937.

31. Smith, "Supplement—1937," 9, MLD Papers, OHS; Wittke, *History of Ohio,* 6:190–91.

32. Nuckolls, "Davey Governorship," 59–61.

33. Ibid., 62–63.

34. Moss, *America in the Twentieth Century* (5th ed.), 204.

35. Ibid.

36. In November 1938 it became the Congress of Industrial Organizations.

37. Marcus A. Roberto, "Franklin D. Roosevelt, Martin L. Davey, and the 'Little Steel' Strike" (master's thesis, Kent State University, 1960), 12–15.

38. Saul Alinsky, *John L. Lewis: An Unauthorized Biography* (New York: Putnam's, 1949), 148–49; James A. Wechsler, *Labor Baron: A Portrait of John L. Lewis* (New York: W. W. Morrow, 1944), 68–69. Four main companies based primarily in Ohio and Pennsylvania comprised Little Steel: Republic Steel, Bethlehem Steel, Inland Steel, and Youngstown Sheet and Tube. Michael Speer, "The 'Little Steel' Strike: Conflict for Control," *Ohio History* 78 (Autumn 1969): 273, 275.

39. Tom M. Girdler, *Boot Straps: The Autobiography of Tom M. Girdler* (New York: Scribner's, 1943), 14, 56.

40. Ibid., 57. Also, Girdler's two sisters attended a private school in Louisville, Kentucky.

41. Roberto, "Little Steel Strike," 30; *Cleveland Plain Dealer,* May 26, 1937.

42. Girdler, *Boot Straps,* 329; *Cleveland Plain Dealer,* May 26, 1937.

43. *Cleveland Plain Dealer,* May 27, 1937.

44. Ibid., June 1, 1937.

45. Speer, "Little Steel Strike," 277.

46. *Cleveland Plain Dealer,* June 2, 1937.

47. Ibid., June 3, 1937.

48. Ibid., June 10, 1937.

49. Telegram, Tom M. Girdler to MLD, June 9, 1937, cited in *Cleveland Plain Dealer,* June 10, 1937.

50. *Cleveland Plain Dealer,* June 12, 1937.

51. Ibid., June 16, 17, 1937.

52. Roberto, "Little Steel Strike," 35, 42–43.

53. Ibid., 47.

54. *Cleveland Plain Dealer,* June 20, 1937.

55. Girdler, *Boot Straps,* 356–57.

56. MLD, proclamation, June 22, 1937, box 7, folder 8, MLD Papers, OHS; MLD to Gen. Emil F. Marx, June 25, 1937, box 7, folder 8, MLD Papers, OHS.

57. MLD to James Seccombe, mayor, June 20, 1937, File "John Davey—M. L. Davey," Davey Tree Expert Company; *Cleveland Plain Dealer,* June 20, 1937.

58. *Cleveland Plain Dealer,* June 22, 25, 26, 1937; James L. Baughman, "Classes and Company Towns: Legends of the 1937 Little Steel Strike," *Ohio History* 87 (Spring 1978): 176–78.

59. *Cleveland Plain Dealer,* June 27, 1937. Perkins denied asking Davey to "kidnap" anybody. She merely hoped that the governor would use the powers granted

him by the State Industrial Commission to get the two sides to meet face to face in hopes that they might reach an agreement.

60. Ibid., June 30, 1937. Labor, of course, unalterably opposed Martin, while business applauded him. The Ohio Chamber of Commerce was so pleased that the governor had helped beat the CIO that it printed and publicly disseminated his marching orders to Adjutant General Marx. See *Ohio: The State of Law and Order,* July 4, 1937, File "John Davey—M. L. Davey," Davey Tree Expert Company.

61. Nuckolls, "Davey Governorship," 73–74.

62. Ibid., 74–75.

63. Ibid., 75.

64. Five Democrats served: J. Ralph Seidner, chair; Emerson Campbell; Bernard R. Donovan; Thomas L. Gallagher; John Taylor. The two Republicans were A. D. Baumhart Jr. and Verner Metcalf. Paul Yoder, memorandum to Senators Seidner, Taylor, Baumhart, et al., Sept. 27, 1937; Yoder to Representative James Howsare, Sept. 27, 1937, both in box 1, folder 1, John Taylor Papers, MSS 205, OHS.

65. Edward B. Follett to George White, Oct. 11, 1937, box 54, folder F, George White Papers, MSS 338, OHS.

66. Nuckolls, "Davey Governorship," 76–77.

67. Ibid., 79–80. In his autobiography, Davey called Metzenbaum a "sanctimonious hypocrite" whose "slimy hand" could be seen virtually everywhere in the Senate's witch hunt. MLD, "Autobiography," 417–18.

68. For example, see MLD telegram to John Taylor, Dec. 30, 1937, box 1, folder 1, John Taylor Papers.

69. *Columbus Dispatch,* Dec. 31, 1937.

70. Ibid., Jan. 1, 2, 3, 1938. Nor did Poulson bring all the records called for in his subpoena.

71. Ibid., Jan. 4, 1938.

72. *Columbus Citizen,* Jan. 4, 1938, clipping in box 1, folder 15, John Taylor Papers.

73. *Columbus Dispatch,* Jan. 4, 5, 1937.

74. Ibid., Jan. 5, 1938.

75. "Statement of Lee Bradley," 1938, 1–2, container 22, folder 468, Marvin C. Harrison Papers, MSS 3799, WRHS.

76. "Statement of Lee Bradley," 3–5, Marvin C. Harrison Papers.

77. MLD, "Autobiography," 277–78; "Statement of Lee Bradley," 5, Marvin C. Harrison Papers.

78. Lee Bradley, sworn statement, Aug. 30, 1937, 16; "Transcripts of Proceedings Had on Thursday, February 17, 1938, Before the Subcommittee of the Senate Investigating Committee, Held in the Cleveland Public Auditorium, 1300 East Sixth Street, Convening at 11:30 o'clock, a.m.," 11, 19, 24, both in container 22, folder 468, Marvin C. Harrison Papers.

79. "Transcripts of Proceedings . . . February 17, 1938," 14ff, Marvin C. Harrison Papers.

80. Ibid., 36–38.

81. Ibid., 36–37.

82. Ibid., 54–55.

83. Lee Bradley, "Statement [and Testimony, 1938]," 5, 10–11, 13–23, container 22, folder 468, Marvin C. Harrison Papers; Smith, "Supplement—1938," 5, MLD Papers, OHS; MLD affidavit, Cuyahoga County, City of East Cleveland, Feb. 19, 1938, container 22, folder 468, Marvin C. Harrison Papers; Lee Bradley, affidavit, Cuyahoga County, City of East Cleveland, Feb. [25], 1938, Marvin C. Harrison Papers.

84. Lee Bradley to Marvin C. Harrison, Feb. 22, 1938; Verner E. Metcalf to Harrison, Mar. 2, 1938; Bradley to Harrison, Mar. 3, 1938, all in container 22, folder 468, Marvin C. Harrison Papers.

85. Smith, "Supplement—1938," 7, 19, 12, 16–17, MLD Papers, OHS. Martin, in a move that was purely spiteful, eliminated the engineer's position two weeks after he testified and promised to reinstate him with a big raise if he could prove his allegation.

86. Smith, "Supplement—1938," 14–15, 21, 11, 23, 27, MLD Papers, OHS; Nuckolls, "Davey Governorship," 86–87.

87. "Preliminary Report of Senate Investigating Committee," Feb. 28, 1938, 1–2, container 22, folder 468, Marvin C. Harrison Papers.

15. LAST HURRAH

1. *Cleveland Plain Dealer,* Jan. 9, 1938.

2. Ibid.

3. MLD to Charles Sawyer, Jan. 14, 1938, *Cleveland Plain Dealer,* Jan. 15, 1938.

4. Ibid.

5. Charles Sawyer to MLD, Jan. 18, 1938, *Cleveland Plain Dealer,* Jan. 19, 1938.

6. Ibid.; Walter Callahan and John H. James to Charles Sawyer, Feb. 6, 1939, container 22, folder 3, Robert J. Bulkley Papers, MSS 3310, WRHS.

7. Charles Sawyer to MLD, Jan. 18, 1938, *Cleveland Plain Dealer,* Jan. 19, 1938.

8. *Cleveland Plain Dealer,* Jan. 30, 1938.

9. Ibid., Apr. 5, 1938.

10. Ibid., Apr. 6, 5, 1938.

11. Smith, "Supplement—1938," 21, MLD Papers, OHS.

12. *Cleveland Plain Dealer,* May 22, 1938.

13. Charles K. McFarland, *Roosevelt, Lewis, and the New Deal, 1933–1940* (Fort Worth: Texas Christian Univ. Press, 1970), 81.

14. *Cleveland Plain Dealer,* May 25, 1938.

15. Smith, "Supplement—1938," 30, MLD Papers, OHS; *Cleveland Plain Dealer,* May 28, 1938.

16. *Cleveland Plain Dealer,* July 13, 1938. Martin had already become a bit of a joke among his fellow partisans. George White derisively referred to him as the "Duke of Kent"; others nicknamed him "white feather," the symbol of cowardice;

and Lee Bradley, obviously mocking Davey's constant protestations of innocence in every one of his nefarious affairs, called him "Snow White Davey." See Lee Bradley to George White, Sept. 15, 1938, box 54, folder B, George White Papers.

17. Primary campaign speech, 1938, typescript, box 7, folder 9, MLD Papers, OHS.

18. *Cleveland Plain Dealer,* Aug. 7, 1938.

19. James M. Cox to Hugh L. Nichols (former chief justice of the Ohio Supreme Court and Sawyer's campaign manager), Aug. 6, 1938, *Cleveland Plain Dealer,* Aug. 7, 1938.

20. Ibid., Aug. 8, 1938.

21. Ibid.

22. Ibid.

23. Wittke, *History of Ohio,* 6:88; *Cleveland Plain Dealer,* Aug. 11, 1938; Smith, "Supplement—1938," 49, MLD Papers, OHS. How much Davey was hurt by the animus of the CIO is difficult to ascertain. Sawyer won only 21 of Ohio's 88 counties, but almost all were in the state's populous industrial centers. Martin took 67 counties, almost all of them rural. Had he not opposed John L. Lewis and the CIO, he might have fared more poorly in the countryside and still lost the urban counties where he was already unpopular before the strike-ridden summer of 1937. See Smith, "Supplement—1938," 47, MLD Papers, OHS; and *Cleveland Plain Dealer,* Aug. 11, 1938.

24. Smith, "Supplement—1938," 54, MLD Papers, OHS. The cheering was no less loud in Ohio as many Democrats hoped they had seen the last of Governor Davey. See Charles La Croix to George White, Jan. 20, 1938, folder C; William Van Dyke Belden to White, Aug. 14, 1938, folder B; W. J. Cook to White, Oct. 21, 1938, folder C; White to Cook, Oct. 24, 1938, folder C, all in box 54, George White Papers.

25. Smith, "Supplement—1938," 55–56 insert, MLD Papers, OHS.

26. *Cleveland Plain Dealer,* Nov. 3, 1938.

27. Wittke, *History of Ohio,* 6:88.

28. *Cleveland Plain Dealer,* Jan. 4, 1939.

29. Testimonial dinner program and testimonial dinner speech typescript, Jan. 4, 1939, box 7, folder 16, MLD Papers, OHS.

30. MLD to Margaret M. Allman, Jan. 5, 1939, box 7, folder 16, MLD Papers, OHS.

31. Myrna Smith, undated handwritten note, box 7, folder 16, MLD Papers, OHS.

32. Smith, "Supplement—1939," 64, MLD Papers, OHS.

33. *Columbus Citizen,* Jan. 5, 1939, clipping in box 7, folder 16, MLD Papers, OHS.

34. *Cleveland Plain Dealer,* Jan. 10, 1939.

35. *Ravenna Evening Record,* Jan. 9, 10, 1939.

36. Pfleger, *Green Leaves,* 127–28.

37. Ibid., 128–29.

38. *The Davey Bulletin* 33.7 (July 1946): 6, Miscellaneous Papers, Davey Tree Expert Company.

39. For instance, see *Cleveland Plain Dealer,* Feb. 21, 1939, and MLD, "Speech Delivered to 2000 Allen County Democrats," June 19, 1939, box 7, folder 16, MLD Papers, OHS.

40. Transcribed shorthand notes, 1940, box 8, folder 1, MLD Papers, OHS.

41. Martin L. Davey, "Four Eventful Years as Governor," newspaper insert (1940), box 7, folder 17, MLD Papers, OHS.

42. Smith, "Supplement—1940," 2–3, MLD Papers, OHS.

43. *Cleveland Plain Dealer,* May 16, 1940; *Ravenna Evening Record,* May 18, 1940. The other Democratic candidates were William J. Kennedy, Herbert S. Duffy, Harold G. Mosier, James F. Flynn, and Frank A. Dye.

44. Parker La Moore to John Taylor, May 20, 1940; Taylor to La Moore, June 7, 1940; La Moore to Taylor, June 10, 1940, all in box 1, folder 1, John Taylor Papers.

45. Quoted in *Cleveland Plain Dealer,* Oct. 31, 1940.

46. Richard O. Davies, *Defender of the Old Guard: John Bricker and American Politics* (Columbus: Ohio State Univ. Press, 1993), 44–46.

47. *Ravenna Evening Record,* July 9, 1940.

48. MLD, "Speech at the Democratic State Convention," Sept. 7, 1940, box 7, folder 18, MLD Papers, OHS.

49. *Cleveland Plain Dealer,* Nov. 1, 1940.

50. Ibid., Dec. 6, 1939; *New York Times,* Dec. 6, 9, 1939.

51. Ceylon E. Hudson to John W. Bricker, Dec. 9, 1939; F. C. Huth, P. O. Huth, and E. W. Conner to Bricker, Nov. 9, 1939 [should be Dec. 9]; J. W. Huddle to Bricker, Dec. 13, 1939, and J. H. Johnson to Bricker, Dec. 30, 1939, all in box 134A, John W. Bricker Papers, MSS 340, OHS.

52. MLD, press release, June 17, 1940, box 8, folder 1, MLD Papers, OHS.

53. *Cleveland Plain Dealer,* Oct. 29, 1940.

54. Ibid., Oct. 8, 1940.

55. Ibid., Nov. 3, 1940.

56. *Akron Beacon Journal,* Nov. 3, 1940.

57. *Cleveland Plain Dealer,* Nov. 3, 1940.

58. *Akron Beacon Journal,* Nov. 3, 1940.

59. Robert J. Bulkley to James White Shocknessy, Nov. 4, 1940, container 23, folder 5, Robert J. Bulkley Papers.

60. Davies, *Bricker,* 70. George K. Nash (1900–1904) was the first. See Robert H. Bremner, "George K. Nash," in *Governors of Ohio,* 136–39.

61. *Ravenna Evening Record,* Nov. 6, 1940. Davey's margin was 734 votes.

62. MLD to John W. Bricker, Nov. 6, 1940; Bricker to MLD, Nov. 22, 1940, both in box 135, John W. Bricker Papers.

63. "Facts from a Study of Election Statistics [1940]," box 7, folder 18, MLD Papers, OHS; *Cleveland Plain Dealer,* Nov. 6, 1940; Donaldson, "Martin L. Davey," in *Governors of Ohio,* 182.

64. Smith, "Supplement—1940," 5–6, MLD Papers, OHS; W. B. Gongwer, *What*

Ought to Be Every Man's Creed, pamphlet, container 1, folder 3, Walter Burr Gongwer Papers, MSS 3397, WRHS; Parker La Moore to John Taylor, May 20, 1940, box 1, folder 1, John Taylor Papers.

16. FINIS

1. MLD, statement, Nov. 6, 1940, box 2, folder 12, Evangeline Davey Smith Collection, KSU Special Collections.

2. Myrna Young Smith, "A Letter to Martin L. Davey from His 'Man Friday,'" Mar. 31, 1946, in *The Davey Bulletin* 33.7 (July 1946): 8–9, Miscellaneous Papers, Davey Tree Expert Company. Smith wrote this as a eulogy to Davey on the day of his death.

3. *Cleveland Plain Dealer,* Apr. 1, 1946; *Davey Bulletin* 85.4 (July/Aug. 1996): 20, Miscellaneous Papers, Davey Tree Expert Company.

4. Pfleger, *Green Leaves,* 129–30.

5. Ibid., 129; MLD to Joseph D. Nunan Jr., commissioner, Bureau of Internal Revenue, Mar. 21, 1945, box 7, folder 22, MLD Papers, OHS.

6. Pfleger, *Green Leaves,* 133.

7. Smith, "A Letter to Martin L. Davey," 9; Pfleger, *Green Leaves,* 132–37.

8. "Some of the Correspondence During Davey's Term of Office," box 2, folder 54, Evangeline Davey Smith Collection.

9. Ibid., Smith, "Supplement—1941," n.p., MLD Papers, OHS; undated and unidentified newspaper clipping, box 2, folder 44, Evangeline Davey Smith Collection.

10. Smith, "Supplement—1941," n.p., MLD Papers, OHS.

11. "Some of the Correspondence During Davey's Term of Office," box 2, folder 54, Evangeline Davey Smith Collection; Pfleger, *Green Leaves,* 134–35; "Certificate of Appreciation," Dec. 31, 1945, box 2, folder 38, Evangeline Davey Smith Collection.

12. MLD to Gov. John W. Bricker, Aug. 2, 1940; MLD to Bricker, Aug. 10, 1940; MLD to Bricker, Aug. 24, 1940; MLD to Bricker, Aug. 31, 1940, all in Vertical File Material 1491, MLD Papers, OHS.

13. MLD to John M. Caren, Apr. 26, 1943, and MLD to Joseph T. Ferguson, Apr. 26, 1943, both in box 2, folder 34, Evangeline Davey Smith Collection.

14. MLD to the Editor, *Cosmopolitan,* June 2, 1944, Vertical File Material 1491, MLD Papers, OHS; MLD to "Dear Friend," June 2, 1944, box 2, folder 34, Evangeline Davey Smith Collection.

15. MLD to Gov. John W. Bricker, Dec. 1, 1944, box 2, folder 34, Evangeline Davey Smith Collection.

16. MLD to Joseph D. Nunan Jr., May 4, 1945, box 7, folder 22, MLD Papers, OHS.

17. MLD, Petition for Slander, Nov. [n.d.], 1944, Portage County Court of Common Pleas; Statement by MLD [n.d.], both in box 2, folder 37, Evangeline Davey Smith Collection.

18. Myrna Smith to John Taylor, Apr. 12, 1940, box 1, folder 1, John Taylor Papers; "Address by Martin L. Davey, Former Governor of Ohio[,] Before the Annual

Convention of the Federated Democratic Women of Ohio, Columbus," Sept. 20, 1941, box 7, folder 22, MLD Papers, OHS.

19. Pfleger, *Green Leaves,* 133–35.

20. Ibid., 135.

21. Ibid., 135–37.

22. Ibid., 138.

23. Robert L. Bowen, "Martin L. Davey and Life Insurance," *Field Notes: The Field Magazine of the Northwestern Mutual Life Insurance Company* 46.6 (Feb. 1947): 5.

24. Pfleger, *Green Leaves,* 141–42.

25. Ibid., 142–48.

26. *Ravenna-Kent Evening Record and Daily Courier-Tribune,* Apr. 1, 1946.

27. Ibid.

28. "A Memorial Address by Robert Guinther," Apr. 3, 1946, box 2, folder 47, Evangeline Davey Smith Collection.

29. *Cleveland Plain Dealer,* Apr. 4, 1946.

30. *Akron Beacon Journal,* Apr. 1, 1946.

31. Myrna Smith to the Editor, *Akron Beacon Journal,* Apr. 2, 1946, box 2, folder 52, Evangeline Davey Smith Collection. Rarely did anyone have so loyal and dedicated a secretary as did MLD. For thirty years after his death, Myrna went twice a week to the Cleveland Public Library and the Kent State University Library to read and transcribe microfilmed newspaper accounts of Martin's gubernatorial years in order to finish his autobiography. Only failing eyesight in her mid-seventies prevented her from completing the task. See Myrna Smith to Alexander M. Smith, Nov. 16, 1976, box 7, folder 19, MLD Papers, OHS.

EPILOGUE

1. Smith, "Supplement—1938," 32. Even Davey's hometown newspaper likened him to P. T. Barnum, always a master showman. See *Ravenna-Kent Evening Record and Courier-Tribune,* Apr. 1, 1946.

2. MLD, "Autobiography," 247.

3. Ibid., 325, 371; Donaldson, "Martin L. Davey," in *Governors of Ohio,* 180.

4. MLD, "Autobiography," 404–5.

5. Smith, "Supplement—1938," 45; Myrna Smith to "Vange" [Evangeline Davey Smith], n.d., in Smith, "Supplement—1938," 44–45, both in MLD Papers, OHS.

6. The anonymous letter, signed "Affectionately, Hot Mix," in obvious reference to the paving scandal that haunted Martin, was postmarked Oct. 14, 1939, and mailed from Akron. Box 7, folder 29, MLD Papers, OHS.

7. Ibid.

Bibliography

PRIMARY SOURCES

Manuscript Collections

Davey Tree Expert Company, Kent, Ohio
    John Davey
    Martin L. Davey
    Miscellaneous Papers
    Scratchbooks
Rutherford B. Hayes Presidential Center
    James A. Garfield Diary
Kent State University Library Special Collections, Kent, Ohio
    Evangeline Smith Davey
    Martin L. Davey
Oberlin College Archives, Oberlin, Ohio
    Academy Legislation
    ETEAN
    Martin L. Davey
    Miscellaneous Publications
Ohio Historical Society, Columbus, Ohio
    John W. Bricker
    Clarence J. Brown
    Myers Y. Cooper
    Martin L. Davey
    Martin L. Davey Autobiography
    Maurice Maschke
    John Taylor
    George White
Reed Memorial Library, Ravenna, Ohio
    Early Portage County Scrapbook

Franklin D. Roosevelt Presidential Library and Museum, Hyde Park, New York
  Lorena Hickok
  Harry Hopkins
  Harry Hopkins Diary
  Franklin D. Roosevelt
Western Reserve Historical Society, Cleveland, Ohio
  Robert J. Bulkley
  Walter Burr Gongwer
  Marvin C. Harrison
  Daniel E. Morgan

DIARIES AND MEMOIRS

Coolidge, Calvin. *The Autobiography of Calvin Coolidge.* New York: Cosmopolitan Book
    Corp., 1929.
Cox, James M. *Journey Through My Years.* New York: Simon and Schuster, 1946.
Farley, James. *Jim Farley's Story: The Roosevelt Years.* New York: Whittlesey House,
    1948.
Girdler, Tom M. *Boot Straps: The Autobiography of Tom M. Girdler.* New York: Scribner's,
    1943.
Hoover, Herbert. *The Memoirs of Herbert Hoover: The Cabinet and the Presidency, 1920–
    1933.* Vol. 2. New York: Macmillan, 1952.
Ickes, Harold L. *The Secret Diary of Harold L. Ickes: The First Thousand Days, 1933–1936.*
    Vol. 1. New York: Simon and Schuster, 1953.
Smith, Alfred E. *Up to Now: An Autobiography.* New York: Viking, 1929.

SECONDARY SOURCES

Books, Articles, Theses, and Pamphlets
Alinsky, Saul. *John L. Lewis: An Unauthorized Biography.* New York: Putnam's, 1949.
Barnard, John. *From Evangelicalism to Progressivism at Oberlin College, 1866–1917.* Co-
    lumbus: Ohio State Univ. Press, 1969.
Baughman, James L. "Classes and Company Towns: Legends of the 1937 Little Steel
    Strike." *Ohio History* 87 (Spring 1978): 175–92.
Bowen, Robert L. "Martin L. Davey and Life Insurance." *Field Notes: The Field Magazine of
    the Northwestern Mutual Life Insurance Company* 46.6 (Feb. 1947): 3–5.
Braeman, John, Robert H. Bremner, and David Brody, eds. *The New Deal: The State and
    Local Levels.* Vol. 2. Columbus: Ohio State Univ. Press, 1975.
Burner, David. *Herbert Hoover: A Public Life.* New York: Knopf, 1979.
Burns, Helen M. *The American Banking Community and New Deal Banking Reforms.*
    Westport, Conn.: Greenwood Press, 1974.
Cayton, Andrew R. L. *Ohio: The History of a People.* Columbus: Ohio State Univ. Press,
    2002.
Charles, Searle F. *Minister of Relief: Harry Hopkins and the Depression.* Syracuse, N.Y.:
    Syracuse Univ. Press, 1963.

Cigliano, Jan. *Showplace of America: Cleveland's Euclid Avenue, 1850–1910*. Kent, Ohio: Kent State Univ. Press, 1991.

Clements, Kendrick A. *The Presidency of Woodrow Wilson*. Lawrence: Univ. Press of Kansas, 1992.

"The Davey Family, Which Gave America the Science of Tree Surgery, Now Gives Ohio a Great Governor." The Independent Voters Davey-for-Governor Club, 1934.

Davey, John. *Davey's Floral and Landscape Educator*. November, 1878.

———. *John Davey's Primer on Trees and Birds*. Akron, Ohio: Werner Co., 1905.

———. *The Tree Doctor: A Book on Tree Culture*. Akron, Ohio: Commercial Printing Co., 1902.

Davey, Martin L. *The Story of the Davey Organization*. Undated publication. The Davey Tree Expert Company.

———. *Why I Carry $1,000,000 Life Insurance*. Indianapolis: Rough Notes Co., 1926.

Davies, Richard O. *Defender of the Old Guard: John Bricker and American Politics*. Columbus: Ohio State Univ. Press, 1993.

Downes, Randolph C. *The Rise of Warren Gamaliel Harding, 1865–1920*. Columbus: Ohio State Univ. Press, 1970.

Fairchild, Edward Henry. *Historical Sketch of Oberlin College*. Springfield, Ohio: Republic Printing Co., 1868.

Fairchild, James Harris. *Oberlin: Its Origin, Progress and Results: An Address Prepared for the Alumni of Oberlin College, Assembled August 22, 1860*. Oberlin, Ohio: R. Butler, 1871.

Fausold, Martin L. *The Presidency of Herbert C. Hoover*. Lawrence: Univ. Press of Kansas, 1985.

Ferrell, Robert H. *American Diplomacy: A History*. 3d ed. New York: W. W. Norton, 1975.

Freidel, Frank. *America in the Twentieth Century*. 3d ed. New York: Knopf, 1970.

Fuess, Claude M. *Calvin Coolidge: The Man from Vermont*. Hamden, Conn.: Archon Books, 1965.

Gorisek, Sue. "A Man Ahead of His Moment." *Ohio* 15 (Oct. 1992): 29–32.

The Governors of Ohio. Ohio Historical Society. Columbus: Stoneman Press, 1954.

Green, Constance McLaughlin. *Washington, Capital City: 1879–1950*. Vol. 2. Princeton, N.J.: Princeton Univ. Press, 1963.

Grismer, Karl H. *The History of Kent: Historical and Biographical*. Kent, Ohio: Courier-Tribune, 1932.

Havighurst, Walter. *Ohio: A Bicentennial History*. New York: W. W. Norton, 1976.

Hopkins, Harry. "Boondoggling: Boon or Bane?" *Christian Science Monitor* (Aug. 19, 1936): 4, 14.

———. "Employment in America." *Vital Speeches* 3 (Dec. 1, 1936): 103–7.

———. "The Future of Relief." *New Republic* 90 (Feb. 10, 1937): 7–10.

———. "Should Relief Funds Be Administered by the States?" *Congressional Digest* 15 (June 1936): 189–90.

Hoyt, Edwin P. *The Tempering Years*. New York: Scribner's, 1963.

Jackson, Kenneth T. *The Ku Klux Klan in the City, 1915–1930*. New York: Oxford Univ. Press, 1967.

Jackson, Robert. *Airships: A Popular History of Dirigibles, Zeppelins, Blimps and Other Lighter-than-Air Craft*. Garden City, N.Y.: Doubleday, 1973.

Kelly, Alfred A., Winifred A. Harbison, and Herman Belz. *The American Constitution: Its Origins and Development.* 7th ed. Vol. 2. New York: W. W. Norton, 1991.

Knepper, George W. *Ohio and Its People.* Kent, Ohio: Kent State Univ. Press, 1989.

LaFeber, Walter. *The American Age: United States Foreign Policy at Home and Abroad Since 1750.* New York: W. W. Norton, 1989.

Marshall, Charles C. "An Open Letter to the Honorable Alfred E. Smith." *Atlantic Monthly* 139 (Jan.–June 1927): 540–49.

McFarland, Charles K. *Roosevelt, Lewis, and the New Deal, 1933–1940.* Fort Worth: Texas Christian Univ. Press, 1970.

McJimsey, George. *Harry Hopkins: Ally of the Poor and Defender of Democracy.* Cambridge, Mass.: Harvard Univ. Press, 1987.

Messick, Hank. *John Edgar Hoover: An Inquiry into the Life and Times of John Edgar Hoover and His Relationship to the Continuing Partnership of Crime, Business and Politics.* New York: David McKay, 1972.

Meyer, Henry Cord. *Airshipmen, Business and Politics, 1890–1940.* Washington, D.C.: Smithsonian Institution Press, 1991.

Moore, Edmund A. *A Catholic Runs for President: The Campaign of 1928.* New York: Ronald Press, 1956.

Morgan, Ted. *FDR: A Biography.* New York: Simon and Schuster, 1985.

Moss, George Donelson. *America in the Twentieth Century.* 2d ed. Englewood Cliffs, N.J.: Prentice Hall, 1993.

———. *America in the Twentieth Century.* 5th ed. Upper Saddle River, N.J.: Pearson Prentice Hall, 2004.

Nuckolls, Charles B., Jr. "The Governorship of Martin L. Davey of Ohio." Master's thesis. Ohio State University, 1952.

O'Connor, Richard. *The First Hurrah: A Biography of Alfred E. Smith.* New York: Putnam's, 1970.

Ohio: The State of Law and Order. Columbus: Ohio Chamber of Commerce, 1937.

Pauly, Karl B. *Bricker of Ohio: The Man and His Record.* New York: Putnam's, 1944.

Pfleger, Robert E. *Green Leaves: A History of the Davey Tree Expert Company.* Chester, Conn.: Pequot Press, 1977.

Phillips, Ronnie J. *The Chicago Plan and New Deal Banking Reform.* Armonk, N.Y.: M. E. Sharpe, 1995.

Rice, Arnold S. *The Ku Klux Klan in American Politics.* New York: Haskell House, 1972.

Roberto, Marcus A. "Franklin D. Roosevelt, Martin L. Davey, and the 'Little Steel' Strike." Master's thesis. Kent State University, 1960.

Robinson, Edward Eugene and Vaughn Davis Bornet. *Herbert Hoover: President of the United States.* Stanford, Calif.: Hoover Institution Press, 1975.

Roosevelt, Elliott, ed., *F.D.R.: His Personal Letters, 1928–1945.* Vol. 4. New York: Duell, Sloan and Pearce, 1950.

Roseboom, Eugene H., and Francis P. Weisenburger. *A History of Ohio.* Columbus: Ohio State Archaeological and Historical Society, 1961.

Rosenman, Samuel I., ed. *The Public Papers and Addresses of Franklin D. Roosevelt.* Vol. 4. New York: Random House, 1938.

Russell, Francis. *The Shadow of Blooming Grove: Warren G. Harding in His Times.* New York: McGraw-Hill, 1968.

Sherwood, Robert E. *Roosevelt and Hopkins: An Intimate History.* New York: Harper, 1948.

Smith, Theodore Clarke. *The Life and Letters of James Abram Garfield.* Vol. 2. New Haven, Conn.: Yale Univ. Press, 1925.

Smith, Thomas H., ed. *An Ohio Reader: Reconstruction to the Present.* Vol. 2. Grand Rapids, Mich.: Eerdmans, 1975.

Speer, Michael. "The 'Little Steel' Strike: Conflict for Control." *Ohio History* 78 (Autumn 1969): 273–87.

They Love Him for the Enemies He Has Made. Ravenna, Ohio: Portage County Historical Society.

Toland, John. *The Great Dirigibles: Their Triumphs and Disasters.* New York: Dover, 1972.

de Toledano, Ralph. *J. Edgar Hoover: The Man in His Time.* New Rochelle, N.Y.: Arlington House, 1973.

Vazzano, Frank P. "The Feud Renewed: Martin Davey, John Bricker and the Ohio Campaign of 1940." *Ohio History* 105 (Winter/Spring 1996): 5–24.

———. "Harry Hopkins and Martin Davey: Federal Relief and Ohio Politics During the Great Depression." *Ohio History* 96 (Summer/Autumn 1987): 124–39.

———. "Martin Davey, John Bricker and the Ohio Election of 1936." *Ohio History* 104 (Winter/Spring 1995): 5–23.

Wechsler, James A. *Labor Baron: A Portrait of John L. Lewis.* New York: William Morrow, 1944.

Weigley, Russell F., ed. *Philadelphia: A 300-Year History.* New York: W. W. Norton, 1982.

Wittke, Carl, ed. *The History of the State of Ohio.* Vol. 6: *Ohio in the Twentieth Century, 1900–1938.* Columbus: Ohio State Archaeological and Historical Society, 1942.

Wolf, Edwin II. *Philadelphia: Portrait of an American City.* Harrisburg, Pa.: Stackpole Books, 1975.

Newspapers

Akron Beacon Journal
Akron Evening Times
Akron Press
Akron Sunday Times
Canton Repository
Cincinnati Enquirer
Cleveland Plain Dealer
Columbus Citizen
Columbus Dispatch
Kent Courier
New York Times
New York Tribune
Oberlin Review
Ravenna Evening Record
Ravenna-Kent Evening Record and Daily Courier-Tribune
Ravenna Republican
Warren Tribune Chronicle
Youngstown Telegram
Youngstown Vindicator

Index